A New
History of
Spanish
Literature

A NEW
HISTORY OF
SPANISH
LITERATURE revised edition

Richard E. Chandler
Kessel Schwartz

Louisiana State University Press
Baton Rouge and London

Designer: *Glynnis Phoebe*
Typeface: *Baskerville*
Typesetter: *G & S Typesetters, Inc.*
Printer and binder: *Thomson-Shore, Inc.*

Library of Congress Cataloging-in-Publication Data

Chandler, Richard E. (Richard Eugene), 1916–
    A new history of Spanish literature / Richard E. Chandler
and Kessel Schwartz. — Rev. ed.
        p.   cm.
    Includes index.
    ISBN 0-8071-1699-8 (alk. paper). ISBN 0-8071-1735-8 (pbk.:
alk. paper).
    1. Spanish literature—History and criticism.   I. Schwartz,
Kessel.   II. Title.
PQ6033.C45   1991
860.9—dc20   91-2667
                                                       CIP

To Tag and Barbara

CONTENTS

Contents

Contents

PREFACE TO THE REVISED EDITION

Since the first edition of *A New History of Spanish Literature* appeared in 1961, momentous events have taken place in Spain, especially after the end of the Franco era, and nearly thirty years of prolific literary production has appeared. Consequently, the authors sensed the urgent need to update the book to 1990.

The revised edition does this; but in order to accommodate the large amount of material that the last thirty years have brought forth in all literary genres, other changes had to be made. The authors decided to delete some material from almost all literary periods, especially the earlier centuries, while at the same time discussing fully and comprehensively the literary production of the last three decades.

Despite the shortening, however, no author, period, or work treated in the first edition has been omitted in the revision. The reader who seeks a fuller discussion may consult the original edition, which is still available in most libraries.

We have followed the same organizational plan as in the first edition, treating again the entire history of a literary genre from its beginnings to 1990. This arrangement by genres allows for a succinct coverage of a literary type, but does not preclude the study of Spanish literature by periods, centuries, or ages.

The revised text is almost unique in its comprehensive coverage of Spanish literature from its beginnings to the present day in a reasonable number of pages. Special mention must be made of the nonfiction prose section, which analyzes a type of work that is ordinarily not discussed in manuals of this type.

The new edition is the product of the authors' lifelong study of the literature of Spain, and although, like the first edition, the revised edition reflects their reading of hundreds of studies by a variety of commentators on Spanish literature, history, and literary criticism, it also contains many independent analyses and critical judgments. Since writing the first edition, the authors have, in the light of further reading and study, changed some critical opinions and judgments on a few authors and works, and these new views are reflected in the revision.

The authors wish to express their gratitude to our copy editor, Angela Ray, who expertly edited the manuscript and conscientiously checked details that other editors might have overlooked.

It is the fond hope of the authors that this revised edition will be as helpful to generations of students of the next several decades as the original version has been to those of preceding years.

PREFACE TO THE FIRST EDITION

The organizational plan of *A New History of Spanish Literature* deviates somewhat from that of the traditional books dealing with this subject. The latter treat completely all the literary genres within a given cultural period before passing on to the next. The present volume, however, carries the study of a single genre from its origins to the present day before taking up another. Thus, for example, the entire history of the Spanish drama from the *Auto de los reyes magos* to Antonio Buero Vallejo is discussed here without the intrusion of distracting chapters on nondramatic literature. Likewise, the history of the novel is given without pause from its earliest appearances to Camilo José Cela and Carmen Laforet. Only one literary type at a time is discussed.

The authors believe that the reader, particularly the inexperienced one, will gain a clearer understanding of the history and development of the Spanish drama and of how the theater of one age leads into that of another if he is permitted to study all the drama at one time. When Renaissance and Golden Age drama are separated in the histories of literature by chapters on Renaissance lyric poetry, fiction, and nonfiction prose, a student sometimes finds it difficult to grasp the relationship between them. The same holds true for the other literary genres. What many teachers have done and what most serious students seem to want to do in order to arrive at a satisfactory knowledge of the history of any literary genre, is to combine those sections of a history of literature dealing with it and study them together as though they constituted one large chapter. *A New History of Spanish Literature* does this for the reader, thereby providing him, we believe, with a very workable and logical treatment of the subject. This arrangement demonstrates how each principal literary type has experienced a steady growth through interconnected and interdependent cultural ages, and how each period leads into the next and is dependent on the previous one. This allows not only for the horizontal approach in terms of a survey course, but also for examination in depth of one area or author. In the genre approach, however, we have not lost sight of the interaction of a given genre with the rest of Spanish literature, and we show these relationships whenever it is necessary for an understanding of the whole.

Naturally, the traditional literary ages, such as the Middle Ages, the Renaissance, the Golden Age, the Eighteenth Century, and the Romantic Period, have been adhered to. Those who prefer to read by ages rather than genres may do so by consulting the Table of Contents.

When this book is used as a textbook in the two-semester survey course in Spanish literature, the traditional division of the material may be followed, *i.e.*, from the beginnings to the end of the Golden Age and from the eighteenth century to the present day. Obviously, some of the effectiveness of the genre approach will be lost if this method is used, but the book can be readily adapted to it. The authors also believe that this volume will prove especially useful in period courses in which a preliminary historical survey of the subject must be made before concentrating on a certain age. The genre arrangement, for example, is made to order for those who wish to survey quickly the history of novelistic prose before concentrating on the realistic novel of the nineteenth century.

In Part 1 the reader will find a discussion of the general characteristics of Spain and the Spanish people, a rapid survey of the main literary schools and cultural movements, and a section devoted to the impact of Spanish letters on the world—in essence, the general trends of Spanish literature from its origins.

The reader will note that more space has been allotted to the literature of the twentieth century and to Part 6, "Nonfiction Prose," than to other areas. So far as we know, the contemporary age in Spanish literature has not received adequate treatment in any book in English, and any lack of proportion in this volume between the moderns and the preceding generations seems, therefore, justified. Studies of nonfiction prose are especially difficult to find in collected form. Consequently, the authors have devoted more space than usual to this very important and often neglected facet of Spanish letters.

This book was written with the Spanish majors and minors in American universities in mind. We have tried to prepare a volume which will meet the needs of these students, whether they be juniors and seniors encountering the history of Spanish literature for the first time or more advanced students in graduate studies. We hope to give them with this volume a basic tool which they can use throughout their study of Spanish literature and for refreshing their memories in later years. We trust, however, that our book will be useful to a much wider circle of readers— to the literary historian, to the student of comparative literature, to the intelligent tourist, and to all those interested for whatever reason in one of the world's most fascinating cultures.

The authors wish to acknowledge with gratitude the advice, encouragement, and help given them by Professor Nicholson B. Adams of the University of North Carolina. Special acknowledgment must be made also to earlier studies of Spanish literature and culture on which the present volume has built. To all these studies the authors express their indebtedness and appreciation.

A New
History of
Spanish
Literature

Part 1 SPANISH HISTORY, CULTURE, AND LITERATURE

GEOGRAPHY AND TOPOGRAPHY OF SPAIN

A. Geography

Surrounded on three and one-half sides by water and connected to France by a relatively narrow strip of mountainous land, Spain has historically been isolated and inaccessible. This has contributed to the development of *españolismo,* a spirit of self-reliance and independence coupled with a resistance to things foreign and a self-satisfaction with things Spanish. Spain did not achieve national unity until the late fifteenth century, when, under Ferdinand and Isabel, the nation was able to develop its great empire in the New World. Despite its isolated position, Spain suffered foreign invasions into the nineteenth century.

B. Topography

Spain is topographically divided by mountains and rivers into a number of different regions. Nevertheless, the high central plateau is the peninsula's most salient feature. Spain's rivers are not significantly navigable, owing to their steep fall from the central promontory and severe periods of drought.

The topographical division and diversity of the land has led to the development of regional patriotisms, reflected in the customs, dress, language, politics, local sympathies, and literature of its various parts. The *patria chica* has tended to take precedence over the *patria grande,* a fact that retarded the emergence of a truly national spirit and has maintained the separatist tendency of certain regions.

1

CASTILE

Castile is the center of everything Spanish, both historically and culturally. Its language became the official tongue of the nation. Its leaders accomplished national unity for the first time and lifted Spain to a position of power and prominence in the world.

Yet Castile is a bleak, uncompromising, austere, and difficult region in which to live. Life there is a continual struggle against nature's adversities; but from the Castilian's sober resistance to his land's austerities have come the toughness, hardiness, resiliency, majesty, obstinacy, courage, self-reliance, ability to endure hardship, and quiet restraint that have molded the Spanish spirit.

RACIAL ELEMENTS

Many peoples have shared in creating the present-day Spaniard, among them the Iberians, Phoenicians, Greeks, Celts, Carthaginians, Romans, Visigoths, Jews, and Moslems. The Romans perhaps exerted the strongest influence upon the country.

FORMATION OF THE LANGUAGE

Except for Basque, the only tongues to survive in Spain descended from Latin. The Castilian dialect that eventually became the national tongue emerged from Vulgar Latin. The Arabs and less significantly the Visigoths left their linguistic imprint upon Spanish. Fermín E. Gutiérrez estimates that 75 percent of the Spanish language descended from Latin, and 25 percent from all other languages spoken at one time or another in the peninsula.

Latin became the official language of Spain in 206 B.C. with the end of the Second Punic War. Its mother, Vulgar Latin, was an unwritten language, and few genuine records of it remain. Experts have been able to reconstruct it, however, through comparative studies of various other languages.

The *jarchas* (*kharjas*), poetic fragments of the eleventh century attached to Hebrew and Arabic poems, are the earliest literary specimens in Spanish. The earliest preserved literary work is the *Cantar de Mio Cid,* an epic poem composed in the twelfth century.

When Spanish emerged as a tongue separate from Vulgar Latin has not been ascertained with complete accuracy, but it probably had become an independent language by the eighth century. Nevertheless, most writing was done in Latin until the tenth century. Fernando III recognized Spanish as an official language in the thirteenth century, and Alfonso *el Sabio* firmly established it later in the same century. Spanish has been relatively stable since its birth, and the oldest forms of Spanish can be read by modern speakers of the language with little help.

Other languages spoken today in Spain are Basque and Catalan, but Spanish remains the official national tongue. It is also spoken by over 160 million people in various parts of the world, especially in Central and South America. It is a second language of the United States, spoken now by over 30 million persons.

RACIAL CHARACTERISTICS

A national Spanish type is difficult to describe, although regional types can be accurately identified. Nevertheless, certain characteristics seem to apply in a general way to the Spanish people as a whole. Some of these characteristics are stoicism, a sense of dignity and personal worth, individualism, democracy, humor, mysticism, social equality, self-criticism, disdain for creature comfort and material possessions, a sense of the absurd and the ridiculous, an adventuresome spirit, courage, honor, gallantry, and a preoccupation with and a matter-of-fact attitude toward death. Spaniards have consistently shown an inability to compromise on questions of faith and conviction, and they demonstrate a desire to behave as Christians.

HISTORY OF SPAIN

A. Pre-Roman

Until 1492 Spain's history was one of invasion and war. The Phoenicians and Greeks established trading posts and warred with each other and the native inhabitants, the Iberians. The Celts arrived in the sixth century B.C. and formed the Celtiberian race by intermarrying with the Iberians. The Carthaginians conquered large chunks of Spain in the sixth century B.C. They remained there until the Romans defeated them in 206 B.C. and took possession of the land.

B. The Romans

Rome's contributions to Spain were truly important. They included language, administration, roads, general culture, law, religion, and architecture. On the other hand, Spain contributed to Rome not only the riches of her soil but also leading intellectuals of the empire such as the Senecas, Lucan, Martial, and Quintilian.

C. The Germanic Invaders

German tribes invaded Spain in the early fifth century. The Visigoths, by virtue of their greater numbers and superior culture, remained in Spain as the ruling aristocracy for three centuries. They gave little to the country, but traces of their influence can be found in law, language, and customs and perhaps to some extent in the Spaniards' hardiness, spirit of adventure, and stoicism. According to one theory, Spanish epic poetry descended from the war songs of these Gothic ancestors.

D. The Moors

The Moors invaded Spain in A.D. 711, defeating the Visigoths. Most Spaniards continued to live in their homelands under a tolerant Moorish rule, but Visigoths and others from the most mountainous regions of the north began the nearly seven-century-long Reconquest.

The Moors made important cultural contributions, and Córdoba became a leading European cultural center. The Moors were advanced in mathematics, medicine, agriculture, and architecture. They were tolerant rulers and permitted Christian Spaniards, known as Mozárabes, many freedoms. They brought Greek and Oriental civilizations to Europe, a significant fact in the cultural history of the West.

4

Ferdinand and Isabel defeated the Moors in 1492, but cultural evidence of their seven-century occupation of the land is still abundant. The depth of their influence cannot be accurately measured, but the remark that "Africa begins at the Pyrenees" testifies to the extent to which Moorish Oriental culture penetrated that of Spain.

E. The Reconquest

The Reconquest of the peninsula began about A.D. 718 and culminated in 1492. After the Moorish invasion, small Christian kingdoms arose in the north. As the Arabic kingdoms of Spain grew weaker over time through division and internal strife, the Christians gradually drove them farther south, eventually expelling them from their last stronghold, Granada. The consolidation of political and military power under Ferdinand and Isabel led to the final defeat of the Moors.

F. Expansion and Discovery

The defeat of the Moors in 1492 coincided with Columbus' first voyage to the New World. Ferdinand and Isabel used all the resources of a united Spain to dominate the homeland and to colonize their newly claimed lands. Spain rose to world prominence, the arts flourished under the enlightened patronage of the queen, printing was introduced in 1474, and new universities were founded, giving rise to a veritable rebirth of learning and culture.

Carlos I, a Hapsburg and grandson of Ferdinand and Isabel, ascended the throne of Spain in 1516 and later, winning the crown of his grandfather, Maximilian of Austria, became emperor of Germany with the title Carlos V. Under his leadership the empire expanded to include large parts of Europe, namely Germany, the Netherlands, Sicily, Sardinia, Milan, Naples, and Portugal, as well as parts of North Africa. Carlos championed the Catholic faith in the face of the rising Protestant movements, and this, coupled with his constant wars with Francis I of France, denied him the time to govern Spain or even to devote much attention to problems there owing to his military campaigns elsewhere. Yet during his reign the Spanish Empire reached its apogee, and its influence spread worldwide.

Carlos V abdicated in 1556, and under Felipe II, his son, who occupied the throne until 1598, Spain began a slow decline that worsened under Felipe III, Felipe IV, and Carlos II, who died without heirs. Degeneration and downfall marked the reigns of the last two of these Hapsburg rulers and left Spain prostrate at the end of the seventeenth century. Yet during the Hapsburg dynasty, Spanish literature matured and rose to its greatest heights in what is now called the Golden Age. The French Bourbon dynasty replaced the Hapsburgs on the Spanish throne at the beginning of the eighteenth century.

G. The Eighteenth Century

The Bourbon monarchs accomplished much good inside Spain both culturally and economically, but their foreign policy was disastrous. The decline of the nation continued, and most of its European empire was lost. The American colonies grew restless and sought independence. Although a number of academies were established and reforms attempted, Spanish culture and literature languished.

H. The Nineteenth Century

Politically, this period was a struggle between the liberals seeking constitutional government and the conservatives wishing to retain an absolute monarchy. From 1808 to 1814 the French occupied the throne under Joseph Bonaparte. In 1814 Fernando VII returned as monarch. An attempt at constitutional government was made without success in 1812 and again in 1820. The king was forced to reinstate the liberal Cadiz Constitution, but in 1823 France intervened to restore the absolutist reign. Spain's worst despot, Fernando exiled the liberals, reinvoked the Inquisition, and lost most of the American colonies to independence. The Carlist Wars in 1833–1840 and 1873–1876, the forced abdication of Queen Isabel II in 1868, and the short reign of Amadeo de Saboya (1871–1873) led to the proclamation of the short-lived First Republic in 1873.

Alfonso XII, who took the throne in 1874, ruled in relative peace and calm during the last twenty-five years of the century. The War of 1898 with the United States closed the period on a despairing note as Spain lost the last of her New World colonies and the Philippines.

Despite the political and economic chaos of the nineteenth century, the period produced brilliant literature and saw the successes of Romanticism and the regional novel and the genesis of the Generation of 1898.

I. The Twentieth Century

Political, economic, and social woes continued to plague Spain, and Alfonso XIII was unable to find solutions. In 1923 General Primo de Rivera took control as military dictator, but in the face of rising civil discontent, he renounced his position. Alfonso XIII abdicated in 1931, and the Second Republic, which lasted from 1931 to 1936, was proclaimed.

An army mutiny broke out in Morocco in 1936 under General Francisco Franco Bahamonde, and within forty-eight hours Spain was plunged into a tragic civil war that lasted three years and cost one million Spanish lives. Franco established a military dictatorship and ruled Spain until his death in 1975.

Although Spain remained a nonbelligerent in World War II, her official sympathies lay with Germany and Italy. Following the war, Spain had few friends left in the world, and Franco's regime was condemned by the UN Security Council and was refused membership in the UN.

In 1947 Franco announced that Spain was again a monarchy. Nevertheless, Spain was refused Marshall Plan aid, and the nation's economic recovery was slow. Gradually, however, the world began to make peace with Spain. It was admitted into the UN, other countries sent back their recalled ambassadors, and the United States built sea and air bases in Spain after re-establishing diplomatic relations.

Juan Carlos I, who was proclaimed king after Franco's death in 1975, established a constitutional monarchy. He loosened the political bonds on the Spanish people and restored many of their civil liberties, including the right to vote. In recent years, Spaniards elected a Socialist government that at the present writing is still in office. The nation has made enormous progress, and although there is still much to be done, it appears that Spain, now a member of the European Economic Community, has joined and caught up with the twentieth century.

Literarily speaking, the twentieth century has seen a veritable second golden age. Spanish literary artists have shown great vigor and an ability to keep pace with and even surpass artistic ideas everywhere.

7

GENERALIZATIONS ON SPANISH CULTURE AND LITERATURE

The literature of Spain spans ten centuries, features thousands of writers, and includes every type of writing. It is a vast and complex field of human endeavor whose essential nature is difficult to define. Nevertheless, some characteristics seem to be typical of the whole.

A. Dualism

The juxtaposition of the real and the ideal runs through much of Spanish literature and exists in individual works as well as in two contrasting styles of writing, the traditional and the new, exemplified by the ballads and cultured poetry. It is seen also in the coexistence of the rustic and the chivalric, the human and the divine, and in the Spaniard's special aptitude for fusing together elements that in other countries are incompatible or antithetical. The Spaniard tends to preserve much from a fading literary age and adapt it to new tastes, a process evident, for example, in Spain's growth from the Middle Ages into the Renaissance. The authors of the *Celestina,* the *Quijote,* and *El libro de buen amor* demonstrate this dualism by harmonizing the elements noted above and converting into a homogeneous whole what might have been irreconcilable in other hands.

The real and the ideal may be combined in a single work, or each may exist as the dominant trait of a certain type of writing. Realism predominates in epic poetry, the *romancero,* the picaresque novel, certain types of the *comedia, costumbrismo,* the regional novel of manners, and in *tremendismo.* Idealism, dating as far back as the Marqués de Santillana, moves through the poetry of Garcilaso de la Vega, the novel of chivalry, the pastoral novel, the sentimental novel, and much of the lyric poetry of all ages.

B. Popular Spirit

Popularismo is recognizable in the Spaniard's repeated use of traditional folk themes in all ages and in a preference for the simple, least artificial verse forms. The use of assonance and the easily written eight-syllable line of verse imparts a folk flavor to the truly national creations—the epic, the ballads, the popular lyric, and the theater. The popular spirit is evident in the anonymity of many works. It runs like a unifying thread through Spanish literature, giving it a unique flavor and contributing to the markedly national character of Spanish letters and culture in general.

C. Individuality

Spanish literature has been traditionally free and self-forming. Its masterpieces are products of an unrestrained spirit, free of rules, unfettered by dogmas, and scornful of imitation of foreigners. Examples of this are the picaresque novel, a purely Spanish development; the *comedia nueva* of Lope de Vega and his followers; Romanticism, which existed long in Spain before other countries discovered it; and the Generation of 1898. Paradoxically, the Spaniard, resisting new importations, often tries them out before others do, turning to foreign sources only in moments of literary sterility. The imported elements frequently are not entirely assimilated and are disgorged, when possible, as repugnant and incompatible with national spirit and taste.

In view of this individuality, it was enigmatic that the Golden Age drama usually de-emphasized character development in favor of plot. Critics have assailed Spanish literature on this point, decrying its lack of depth of meaning, condemning an entire literature for the shortcomings of one genre in one age. Blind to circumstances peculiar to the Spanish theater that caused this phenomenon, they overlooked the fact that there are, indeed, some memorable characters in the Golden Age theater. Such detractors are also strangers to two of the world's greatest fictional characters, Don Quijote and Sancho Panza, and to other notable Spanish contributions to the world of literary figures: don Juan, Celestina, Lazarillo, don Alvaro, and many others.

D. Improvisation

The Spanish genius is largely undisciplined, impetuous, uncalculating, and given to quick improvising and verbosity. It often scatters its energies over many pieces rather than concentrating heavily on one. This inclination to improvise rather than refine and polish may have reduced the number of Spanish masterpieces, but it has freed the Spanish writer for astonishing flights and great outbursts of passion and exuberance. Improvisation does not necessarily mean carelessness, and one is often

9

amazed that so much good work can come from the pen of a single author.

E. Intellectual Concern

A scarcity of ideas and speculative thought down to the twentieth century has caused some to label Spanish literature as shallow and lacking in substance. This so-called intellectual poverty is due in some measure to the repressive effect of the Church and the Inquisition, which stifled intellectual or philosophical inquiry, discouraged speculation, and directed thought to spiritual ends rather than to metaphysical pursuits. Twentieth-century Spaniards have shown that they are fully capable of philosophical thought, but as a whole, Spanish literature has tended to moralize rather than to philosophize. As a consequence it is one of the richest literatures of the world in proverbs and folklore.

F. Criticism and Discontent

Gerald Brenan has noted that the Spaniards' realistic view of life has given them a tool to expose the evils of society and deceits of the world. He also notes that when young, Spaniards are vitally alive, but the lack of opportunities available in Spain leaves them disillusioned and passive; at times this results in a state of discontent, hopelessness, and despair. The critical attitudes of the picaresque novel and the Generation of 1898 illustrate this.

G. Other Characteristics

1. *Democracy.* Spanish literature, democratic in nature, often reveals the genuine national spirit, closely related to the folk. The epic, the ballad, proverbs, folk legends, and the drama were created for the people. The survival of interest in these forms of art is further evidence of the true democratic spirit of Spanish literature.

2. *Stoicism* has marked Spanish character since the days of Seneca. The Spaniard maintains a stoic attitude toward life's joys and adversities and faces death serenely. Menéndez Pidal lists a certain moral austerity as one of the characteristics of Spanish literature, due in part to the Spaniard's renunciation of vanities. The Spaniard's grave, dry, sometimes harsh, bitter, and sententious manner accentuates this facet of national character.

3. *Humor* pervades Spanish life, even in the most adverse circumstances. Spanish masterpieces are filled with it. *El libro de buen amor,* the *costumbrista* articles of the often mordant critic Larra, and the twentieth-century plays of Jardiel Poncela are just a few examples of this.

4. *Dignity and honor* are strong, often exaggerated concepts in the Spaniard, and a sense of personal worth permeates Spanish literature. The Spaniards' inability to maintain it in the modern world has been portrayed by many writers. But if they insist on respect for their own persons, they are also quick to grant it to others. Politeness, generosity, courtesy, and a feeling of social equality are all outgrowths of this sense of personal dignity.

CULTURAL AGES AND LITERARY SCHOOLS

A. The Middle Ages

The early Middle Ages, extending from about A.D. 500 to A.D. 1000, are of scant interest to students of literature, since the first Spanish literary specimens did not appear until the eleventh century.

The later Middle Ages, dating roughly from 1000 to 1500, saw a remarkable cultural flowering under Alfonso X, *el Sabio,* and the appearance of Spain's first important literary works. Among these are the *Cantar de Mio Cid,* the prose writings of Alfonso *el Sabio* and Juan Manuel, and the poetry of Berceo, Juan Ruiz, Pero López de Ayala, the Marqués de Santillana, Juan de Mena, and Jorge Manrique.

B. The Renaissance and Humanism

The term *Renaissance* describes the revival of learning and intellectual ferment that characterized the fifteenth and sixteenth centuries. Italy was the original center of this movement, and Spain's contacts with Italy were many. Spaniards traveled there in large numbers and absorbed the joyous spirit of the new age at the fountainhead, later carrying it back to their homeland. Despite the dampening effect of the Inquisition and the Counter Reformation, the Renaissance triumphed partially in Spain, helped along by Queen Isabel herself. Printing, introduced into Spain in 1474, disseminated the new learning and facilitated the creation of libraries.

Nevertheless, the Renaissance did not triumph as completely in Spain as it did elsewhere for the following reasons: the Inquisition's depressing effect; the Spaniard's reluctance to abandon his native tradition in favor of something foreign; and the Spaniard's dislike of literary rules and inability to accept those of Classical literature *in toto*.

1. *Humanists* first rose to importance as philologists in Spain. Queen Isabel, desiring to spread Spanish culture throughout her empire, commissioned Antonio de Nebrija to write his *Gramática sobre la lengua castellana* (1492), the first scientific study of a modern tongue. Nebrija's work points up the Renaissance interest in humanity and the Spaniard's native democratic spirit as well as the use of the Spanish language as an instrument of conquest.

Cardinal Jiménez de Cisneros founded the University of Alcalá de Henares, which was devoted to the teaching of the humanities. He organized the publication of the *Biblia Poliglota Complutense,* the world's first critical edition. This work represents the culmination of philological studies in Spain and stands as a monument to the enthusiasm and energy of its humanists.

2. *Erasmism* became prominent during the first half of the sixteenth century and exercised great influence on the court of Carlos V. Erasmus' criticism of ecclesiastical corruption, his defense of inner religion, and his insistence upon a return to a simple life based on faith and a primitive Christianity have never left the mainstream of Spanish literature.

3. *The Counter Reformation,* in which traditional forces opposed the new Humanism, was set in motion by Spanish theologians in 1545 at the Council of Trent. Felipe II closed Spain off from the rest of Europe and exercised a strict and repressive censorship on the writings of the time. Yet he founded the Escorial library and aided many universities. He represented within himself the struggle between the Renaissance belief in the individual and the medieval belief in authority.

The Renaissance began the Modern Age. It produced a new feeling of individual liberty. Mankind was no longer dominated by institutions of a universal character. Some Spaniards felt that the rules of the Church, which Scholastic philosophy had considered the only universal truth, were open to question and that works of truth and beauty could be produced independently of them.

The Renaissance, everywhere a very complex movement, in Spain raised the cultural level of the country, gave a fresh and powerful impetus to learning and experimentation, and provided the necessary cultural background for the literary Golden Age.

C. Mysticism

Mysticism is the experience of the divine presence in which the human soul achieves contact with God. It reached Spain quite late but fortuitously after Spanish poets had prepared the symbols and metaphors to express its lofty sentiments.

Spanish Mystics of the late sixteenth century tried to reach God through ascetic lives and special preparations, which included purification of the soul; penitence; discipline; abandoning things of the senses to achieve grace; contemplation; meditation; concentration of the soul, will, and feelings upon God; and union or spiritual marriage with God. The Spanish Mystics, unlike others, usually combined their Mysticism with realism, or at least a very apparent materialistic knowledge of life.

D. The Golden Age

The period of Spain's greatest literary glory is variously referred to as the *Siglo de Oro,* the *Edad de Oro,* or the *Epoca Clásica.* It spanned roughly a century and was the age dominated by Lope de Vega (1562–1635) and Cervantes (1547–1616). It was the era of the Hapsburg monarchs—Felipe II, Felipe III, and Felipe IV—during whose reigns Spain gradually declined in every aspect of public and private life. The nation was almost continually at war, and the lot of the average Spaniard was hard, the standard of living was very low, and taxes and interest rates were exorbitant. Corruption and graft abounded; all the wealth pouring in from the gold and silver mines of the New World could not pay the nation's debts. During the early years of the reign of Ferdinand and Isabel, many Jews and Moors, representing two of Spain's most productive classes, left the country rather than convert to Christianity, a choice given to them by the Catholic Sovereigns. Despite the troubled political, social, and economic conditions, cultural life in Spain surprisingly developed into the greatest flowering of genius the nation has ever known, the Golden Age. All the arts flourished: painting, architecture, sculpture, goldsmithing, music, and letters. It was in literature,

13

however, that the Golden Age earned its reputation. The drama succumbed to the domination of Lope de Vega, and a host of dramatists imitated him. Cervantes produced Spain's foremost literary work, *Don Quijote*. The picaresque novel flourished, and lyric poetry found some of its all-time great voices in Fray Luis de León and Luis de Góngora. It was an era of amazing fertility, immense creative power, and brilliant intellects.

1. *The Baroque* prospered in the seventeenth century. The intricately ornamental style used in art and architecture was also employed in literature by authors such as Góngora, Calderón, Quevedo, and Gracián, who made use of *conceptismo* and *culteranismo*. In some instances, brutality and ugliness, especially in the picaresque novel, reached the point of caricature.

2. *Gongorism,* named after Luis de Góngora, was the principal literary Baroque style and employed complicated grammatical devices and distorted word order. It is also known as *culteranismo* or *cultismo* because it was directed to a cultured audience. A parallel movement was *conceptismo,* an attempt to disguise meaning through clever ideas, plays on words, and witty sallies.

There is lack of agreement on the origin of Gongorism, but it was actually nothing new, for the embellished and inflated style, the renovation of the poetic vocabulary, and other Gongoristic characteristics date far back into Spanish literature. Gongorism had its counterparts in other countries. In France it was called *préciosité,* in England, Euphuism, and in Italy, Marinism. In Spain, however, poets took from abroad what they deemed good and combined it always with the popular to produce in the synthesis a work profoundly Spanish in spirit.

E. Neoclassicism

In its adherence to the literary models, aesthetics, and form of ancient Greece and Rome, this movement exhibited principles of restraint and regularity, using the *Poetica* of Aristotle and Horace as literary guides. A principal spokesman in Spain, Luzán, supported the decorum, verisimilitude, authority, rules, and reason promulgated by Muratori in Italy and Boileau in France. Neoclassic authors stressed form, discipline, restraint, and the idea that literature should serve some instructive, utilitarian, or didactic purpose. One should, they thought, observe good taste, strictly defined. In the theater, authors attempted to follow the so-called three unities of time, place, and action. In Spain, Neoclassicism made a belated appearance around the third decade of the eighteenth century and continued in vogue into the early nineteenth; but Spanish writers, unable to control their imaginations, could not adjust to the sometimes artificial and self-imposed restrictions.

F. The Eighteenth Century

This "silent century," as some have labeled it, was not uniformly dull, uninspired, or unproductive. The masses opposed the innovations of the lovers of French culture, who attempted to graft the French Classical tradition onto a naturally Romantic Spanish base and demanded that Golden Age drama continue to be played.

The first third of the eighteenth century can be viewed as a prolongation of the seventeenth. The cultured few attempted to bring Spain into line with foreign ideas, while the traditionalists insisted that the native Spanish was best. This struggle between the *afrancesados* and the *castizos* continued into the nineteenth century.

The eighteenth century was a period of intellectual ferment. Many learned institutions, such as the National Library, the Royal Spanish Academy, and the Academy of History, were founded. A number of journals appeared, dedicated to various kinds of polemics and social reform. The Bourbon monarchs, especially Carlos III, attempted sweeping reforms to improve social and cultural conditions, and writers were more concerned with ideas than art. The Enlightenment, or Age of Reason, and the social, scientific, and practical viewpoints of the *philosophes* found a mixed reception in Spain, and ideas of peace, progress, and justice clashed with more traditional Spanish values.

G. Romanticism

Romanticism had always existed in Spanish literature but became the dominant literary force in the fourth decade of the nineteenth century, dating roughly from 1833 to 1848. Its characteristics included liberalism; individualism; subjectivism; a desire for personal glory; Orientalism; a revolt against Neoclassicism; Christianity in opposition to paganism; pessimism; doubt; passion; unrestrained emotionalism; contempt for authority; a special language of blood, thunder, lightning, chains, and cadavers; an emphasis on the Middle Ages; a renunciation of the unities of time, place, and action in the drama; exoticism; and an

15

insistence upon the distant in time and space. An intense movement, it was short-lived but produced some excellent literary works.

H. *Costumbrismo*

Costumbrismo, in vogue during the early decades of the nineteenth century, consisted of short sketches and scenes, faithfully observed and recorded. They may be divided into *artículos,* short prose pieces that satirized current aspects of reality, and *cuadros,* more picturesque pieces with abundant local color. Larra, Mesonero Romanos, and Estébanez Calderón were the principal *costumbristas. Costumbrismo* set the stage for the nineteenth-century regional novel of manners.

I. Realism

Realism attempted, primarily in the novel, to reproduce reality in all its aspects. In its objective reproduction of everyday language and ordinary people, Realism wanted to convey an image of life in a real time and place, to re-create the strengths and weaknesses of human beings, as well as their clothes, customs, and dwellings. Several novelists in the second half of the nineteenth century argued whether Realism was a moral statement or an aesthetic entity. Palacio Valdés tried to distinguish between *realismo de vida* and *realismo de arte.*

J. Transition

During the transition period that followed Romanticism, culture and good taste fell upon sorry days. The result was the adoption of mediocre standards and art forms with the façade of depth that nevertheless could be understood with little difficulty. Literature was too often ironic, sentimental, superficially philosophical, and prosaic. The period was characterized by eclectic literary groping; authors were seeking but could not find a productive new course.

K. Positivism and *Krausismo*

Two philosophical movements had a profound impact in Spain in the latter part of the nineteenth century. Positivism, founded by the Frenchman Auguste Comte (1798–1857), insisted that thought passes through three stages: theological, metaphysical, and positive. The positive is the one on which to base one's observations.

Krausismo, named after the German Karl Krause (1781–1832), attracted an impressive group of Spanish intellectuals headed by Sanz del Río. Some tenets of this philosophy included a belief in self-education; a belief that we are all part of the infinite body that is God; the maintenance of a balance among reason, science, and religion; and a spirit of tolerance. Out of this came the famous Institución Libre de Enseñanza and the Generation of 1898, no small contributions to Spanish intellectual life.

L. Naturalism

Comte's Positivism, Darwin's theory of the origin of species, Taine's deterministic philosophy, Bernard's work in experimental medicine, and the growth of scientific thought in general led Emile Zola to believe that the novel could be treated scientifically also. In his experimental novel, he attempted to examine human beings under laboratory conditions and sought to analyze the effects of alcohol, heredity, and other factors upon his literary characters. The new literary movement, Naturalism, preached a deterministic philosophy and made use of objective and scientific observation untinged by subjective feelings. Naturalists felt society should be reformed, since the individual could not help himself, for his actions, even when seemingly voluntary, were the result of ancestral causes. To prove their contentions, Naturalists described low social classes, sensuality, and ugly, bestial, and erotic qualities of life that at times bordered on the pathological and pornographic.

Although Naturalism had its day in Spain, it never fully succeeded, because Spanish authors always put some of their personal passion for life into their works and were unable to achieve the cold and impassive objectivity of the French Naturalists. Catholicism, antithetical to Naturalism, also played a role.

M. The Generation of 1898

In the last decade of the nineteenth century, a group of young men who would later be called the Generation of 1898 rebelled against the complacency and sterility of Spanish life in their time and the literature produced in the preceding half century. They

17

set out to give new directions to literature and to destroy the sacred institutions that tradition had built. The Generation of 1898 was not a school or a reaction to the war between Spain and the United States. Its members were united, however, in their desire to break with the recent past, to analyze their national culture and destiny, and to diagnose the sickness that had led Spain downward since the sixteenth century.

The Generation of 1898 declared that Spain was decadent and needed change. Some believed that by resurrecting the true spirit of Spain to be found in the works of El Greco, in *Don Quijote,* and elsewhere, Spain might rediscover its glorious past and go on to greater glories. Others felt that the solution was the Europeanization of Spain. They spoke of living for life, of a new culture, and of synthesis of life. They had no answers but asked the right questions. The Existential overtones of much of their philosophy are obvious.

N. Modernism

Born as a negative reaction against preceding literature, Modernism's early phase was marked by attempts at stylistic renovation and a new sensibility. In their search for refinement, the poets sought symbols, such as the swan, which for them signified plastic elegance. Modernists used painting, music, and sculpture; emphasized the phonic and chromatic values of words; employed synesthesia; and sought the exotic.

In a later phase, Modernism concentrated on more meaningful themes. Influenced somewhat by French Symbolism, it nevertheless sought inspiration in Berceo and other Spanish poets. Modernism existed independently in Spain, but when the Nicaraguan poet Rubén Darío arrived there, he became its acknowledged leader. No universal agreement exists on the parameters of Modernism or on its definition.

O. Vanguardism

There were many avant-garde tendencies in Spain after World War I, and authors sought new forms of artistic expression. The poets strove to maintain their personal integrity and to express the inexpressible in a world of disappearing values. Innovative, they attacked the status quo and rejected conventional aesthetics and social and moral judgments.

18
    1. *Creacionismo* was a poetic doctrine elaborated by Vicente

Huidobro, a Chilean, who stressed that the poet should create as nature does rather than imitate nature's works. The creative act was all important. Gerardo Diego was *creacionismo*'s chief exponent in Spain.

2. *Ultraísmo* appeared in 1919. Guillermo de Torre coined the term. The movement stressed the urgency of an art without ties to the past and tried to avoid nonpoetic elements. It used peculiar spellings and mechanical terms in keeping with contemporary thought. Many of the poets of the Generation of 1927 were associated briefly with *ultraísmo*.

3. *Surrealism* sought to discredit rationalism and stress imagination. André Breton's manifesto (1924) stressed the suspension of the conscious mind to give free rein to subconscious manifestations. Surrealist poets identified with Freud's world of dreams and the use of psychoanalytic symbols and concepts. Azorín, Benjamín Jarnés, Gómez de la Serna, and Luis Cernuda were among Spanish writers who incorporated Surrealistic tenets into their works.

4. *Existentialism*, though better known in Germany and France, had Spanish exponents at a much earlier date. Holding that existence precedes essence and that one creates that essence by will power and action, Existentialism shows man hemmed in by boundary situations in his relationships to others and by the final barrier of death. Miguel de Unamuno, José Ortega y Gasset, Jacinto Grau, and Ramón Sender, among others, are Spaniards who exhibited Existential traits.

5. *Poesía pura*, first used by Paul Valéry, elicited much debate. Valéry stressed the intellect, while Brémond stressed emotion. Fernando Vela headed a conference on the subject in 1926 in Spain, but no agreement was reached. For Vela a pure poem was one that sensitized a poetic idea in its abstract form. Jorge Guillén, Spain's leading proponent of pure poetry, defined it as chemically pure and as what was left after the elimination of everything that was not poetry.

P. The Generation of 1927

In their first manifestation, the poets of this generation showed the influence of Surrealism, Freudian symbolism, and associative imagery of an intellectual or irrational nature. They also experimented with pure poetry and rebelled against anecdotal/conceptual imagery. This dehumanization gave way later to a poetry of implied human and Existential concern. Lorca substituted

19

the poor black of New York for the colorful Andalusian gypsy; Guillén, human preoccupations for his songs to the joy of life; and Salinas, a political and social conscience for a refined intellectualism. Many of these poets worked toward the revitalization of the style of Luis de Góngora on the three hundredth anniversary of his death. The purest Surrealist of all was Luis Cernuda, though Lorca, Alberti, and Aleixandre flirted with Breton's manifesto. Marked at times by unusual imagery and metaphorical ambiguities, the poetry of this generation may well be Spain's greatest.

Q. The Generation of 1936

This group of writers suffered two traumatic events, the proclamation of the Second Spanish Republic and the Spanish Civil War. At first disciples of the Generation of 1927, they soon imitated the stylized and graceful poetry of Garcilaso de la Vega (d. 1536) and rejected intellectual emphasis for a more intimate and human poetry. Their early poetry was light and joyful, but they also were interested in social and Existential problems. In their poetry one finds formal beauty, contemplation of nature, harmony, patriotism, and religious faith. Highly personal, their poetry contains nostalgic memories of infancy and friends and acknowledges their own mortality.

R. *Tremendismo*

Tremendismo, a new kind of Naturalism that accented environment instead of heredity as life's major deterministic factor, began after the Spanish Civil War. It deals with situations and events that are truly terrible or tremendous, from which its name derives. Feelings of abandonment and hopelessness, constant conflicts and clashes of personalities, and incessant frustrations and anguish contribute to the Existential and *tremendista* aspects of these writings. Witnesses of the horrors of the Civil War could not expunge their grim memories, and they continued to write about them.

S. Objectivism

Objectivism, which owed much to the *nouveau roman,* was a fictional technique used in Spain in the 1950s and 1960s. Attempting passivity in the depiction of problems, this technique may have been developed to avoid censorship. Striving to depersonalize, the authors avoided the psychological and any hint of subjectivity or personality. They sought to achieve photographic reality without any emotional input.

T. Other Literary Generations

There is little agreement on the nebulous generational divisions after the Generation of 1936. In fiction, some critics refer to the Generación de Medio Siglo, headed by Juan Goytisolo, who began writing in the 1950s. Another division is the Generation of 1968, represented by José María Guelbenzu. The second generation of postwar poets is sometimes called the Group of the 1960s or the Generation of 1968.

U. Spanish Influence on World Literature and Culture

Few Western nations have not felt the vigor and the originality of Spanish writers. English authors such as Fielding, Smollett, Foote, Steele, Keats, Southey, Shelley, and Byron and the entire genre of Restoration Comedy owe much to Spanish literature. *La Celestina* was translated into English, French, and Italian, and the picaresque and pastoral novels influenced writers in the British Isles. Cervantes was imitated by John Fletcher, Thomas Middleton, and William Rowley. Shakespeare may have known *La Celestina* and drawn from it in writing *Romeo and Juliet*. Some believe he drew from Juan Manuel in writing *The Taming of the Shrew* and from Jorge de Montemayor in composing *Twelfth Night* and *Two Gentlemen of Verona*. Ben Jonson knew the *Quijote*, Dryden knew Calderón, Walter Scott knew Cervantes, and Bernard Shaw adapted Tirso de Molina's don Juan in *Man and Superman*. Shelley praised Calderón and Cervantes' *Numancia*.

Many Spanish words have infiltrated the English of the United States of America, and there are hundreds of Spanish place-names scattered throughout the country. American writers owe a great debt to Spain, among them Cotton Mather, Henry Wadsworth Longfellow, William Cullen Bryant, James Russell Lowell, Washington Irving, W. D. Howells, Herman Melville, Mark Twain, Ezra Pound, John Steinbeck, and Ernest Hemingway. Alexander Hamilton held soirées to discuss Spanish literature with Thomas Jefferson, who knew Spanish well

21

enough to read the *Quijote* and write letters in Spanish. Benjamin Franklin wrote a Spanish textbook.

Spanish influence has been strong in France. The picaresque caused a stir there, as did Cervantes' *Novelas ejemplares,* from one of which sprang Victor Hugo's Esmeralda. Corneille adapted Guillén de Castro's *Las mocedades del Cid* in writing his *Le Cid,* Ruiz de Alarcón's *La verdad sospechosa* to produce *Le menteur,* and Lope de Vega's *Amar sin saber a quien* for his *La suite du menteur.* Similar examples can be cited in the novel and in the literature of Romanticism. Albert Camus adapted plays by Lope and Calderón, and Montherlant also used Spanish themes.

The cultural ties between Spain and Italy have been close since the days when Spain was a Roman colony, and influences have been felt on both sides. Torquato Tasso probably knew the *Amadís,* and Tirso's don Juan found his first foreign imitators in Italy. Verdi adapted the Duque de Rivas' *Don Alvaro* in his opera *La forza del destino* and García Gutiérrez's *El trovador* in *Il trovatore. Simón Bocanegra* was the source of Verdi's *Simone Boccanegra.*

Musicians of all ages and countries have found in Spanish music a charm and exoticism with which they invest their own compositions, and Spanish painting has had enormous influence in all Western nations. Velázquez, Murillo, Goya, Picasso, and Dalí are but a few of many world-renowned Spanish artists.

In Germany, Spanish letters have exerted an influence since the picaresque novel of the sixteenth and seventeenth centuries. German critics played an important role in the revival of worldwide interest in the Spanish epic, ballads, and especially the seventeenth-century drama. Such writers as the Schlegels, the Grimms, Goethe, Fichte, and Heine fell under the spell of medieval and Golden Age Spanish literature, and German critics ranked Calderón as the equal of Shakespeare.

In the sixteenth and seventeenth centuries, Spain was the only country of which it could be said that the sun never set on its soil. Spanish was the universal language. Spain possessed the world's largest and most powerful empire. Because of the unpopularity of the Counter Reformation, and the enmity and resentment of Spain's competitors in building colonial empires—notably England, France, and Holland—Spain was made an international scapegoat and the victim of a vicious propaganda campaign that portrayed all Spaniards as evil, greedy, cruel, fanatical, arrogant, and uncompromisingly Catholic. Distortions of truth, misrepresentations, outright lies, and exaggerations came to be and still are accepted as verified fact. This Black Legend has denigrated the Spanish people through the ages and is still alive today. One of the worldwide consequences of this is that the literature of Spain is the least studied and appreciated of all the great European literatures.

Part 2 EPIC AND NARRATIVE POETRY

FECUNDITY, PERIODS OF COMPOSITION, AND SUBJECT MATTER OF THE EPIC

A. Fecundity

Whether Spanish literature began with epic or lyric poetry is a moot question. The *jarchas* of the eleventh century are the earliest examples of Spanish literature yet discovered. The *Cantar de Mio Cid*, an epic poem, dates from the middle of the twelfth century, but its relatively advanced style and language imply that it echoes earlier epics. Furthermore, the *jarchas* are but poetic fragments attached to Hebrew and Arabic poems, while the *Cantar de Mio Cid* is a complete literary work. In other nascent European literatures, epic songs preceded lyric poetry. The analogy may be meaningful.

The *Cantar de Mio Cid* is Spain's oldest preserved complete literary work. Portions of other epics have been found, such as the *Roncesvalles* fragment, one hundred lines dealing with Charlemagne's defeat in the Pyrenees, and the *Rodrigo*, which recounts youthful exploits of the Cid.

It was natural that Spain's turbulent history, with nearly eight centuries of intermittent warfare against the Moors, should produce an abundant heroic literature. Despite the paucity of preserved epic poems, evidence of a rich epic literature is found in early histories. Lost poems have been reconstructed from allusions to them by writers of the thirteenth and fourteenth centuries, from later recastings of them in erudite verse forms, and from the ballads, detached fragments of epic poems.

B. Periods of Composition

Menéndez Pidal divides the period of the composition of Spanish epic poetry as follows: from the beginnings up to 1140, the

25

date of the *Cantar de Mio Cid;* from 1140 to the middle of the thirteenth century; and the late thirteenth and the fourteenth centuries, when primitive epic poetry degenerated, broke into fragments, was recast by learned poets, and finally ceased to be cultivated.

C. Subject Matter

Epic poems were composed about many heroes in addition to the Cid, including Bernardo del Carpio, the only fictitious warrior in the Spanish epic; Rodrigo, *el último godo,* who supposedly lost Spain to the Moors; Los Infantes de Lara, seven brothers treacherously betrayed by their uncle; Fernán González, who gained the independence of Castile from León; and Rey don Sancho II, murdered by the infamous Bellido Dolfos. *El Infante don García* tells of the count of Castile who was murdered en route to his wedding; *La condesa traidora y el conde Sancho García* is the tale of a wife's infidelity; and *Gesta del abad Juan de Montemayor* tells the story of a miraculous victory over the Moors.

ORIGIN

A. The Theory of French Influence

Gaston Paris holds that Spanish epic poetry descended from French poems, which, he contends, were composed earlier and were greater in number. Arguments supporting Paris' theory are based on the fact that *cantar de gesta* seems to have been derived from *chanson de geste;* similarities of meter and versification; the presence of French troubadours and many other Frenchmen in Spain in the eleventh century, called there to aid in the Reconquest; and the influence of the Benedictine order of Cluny, which organized pilgrimages to Compostela and sent soldiers to Spain. In later periods French influence was no doubt vigorous, but scarcity of proof precludes the certainty of the French theory of origin or of any other.

B. The Theory of Germanic Imitation

Menéndez Pidal maintains that the Spanish epic originated in imitation of the heroic songs of the Goths, a Germanic tribe that invaded Spain in the early fifth century. He also denies that the French epic was earlier and richer in material, shows why Spain's epic poetry was destroyed, and proves the existence of an abundant Spanish epic literature. He reconstructed the poem *Los siete infantes de Lara* from early histories and propounded the theory of irregular versification to disprove the similarity of French and Spanish epic meter. The appearance of Gothic law, names, and customs in Spanish poems adds strength to the Germanic theory of origin.

C. The Theory of Monasterial Origin

Joseph Bédier maintains that French and Spanish epic poetry was written by monks in religious establishments along pilgrimage routes to entertain pilgrims. This provided the monks with a source of income, for travelers were naturally attracted to institutions offering some type of entertainment. If true, this theory suggests that the dominant influence on epic poetry was clerical. Priestly poets, like Berceo, only a step away from the popular *juglares,* injected epic clichés into their learned poetry.

D. The Theory of Andalusian Origin

Julián Ribera postulated the existence of an Andalusian epic, references to which are found in Arabic histories. The close relationship between the Oriental peoples and the Roman Empire, the intimate association between Spaniards and Moors, and Arabic allusions in the Spanish epic songs led Ribera to assume that an early Arabic poetry of heroic nature existed and influenced the origin of the Spanish poetry. Convincing proof, however, is lacking, and the case for an Arabic origin remains largely hypothetical.

E. Conclusions

Menéndez Pidal's arguments for Germanic origin are the most widely accepted and are rarely challenged. Modern criticism has adopted a moderate attitude, acknowledging that no theory should be excluded *in toto.* Thus, the Spanish epic could have originated in imitation of the Goths and fallen under Arabic influence shortly thereafter. Later, it could have assimilated many elements from the French; and the monks, the only copyists of the time, could have influenced these poems slightly.

METER AND VERSIFICATION

Spanish epic poetry shows a chaotic irregularity of meter and contains verses of from ten to twenty syllables. Menéndez Pidal asserts that the Spanish epic meter was a sixteen-syllable line of two hemistichs. This theory is widely credited and is supported by the fact that the meter of the ballads, detached fragments of epic poems, is the same.

RECONSTRUCTION OF LOST EPICS

Early Spanish historians accepted epic poems as bona fide historical sources and sometimes incorporated all or parts of them in their histories, occasionally not bothering to change the poetry to prose. From these sources complete epic poems have been reconstructed, the best known of which is Menéndez Pidal's *Los siete infantes de Lara.* The wealth of epic material in the histories like *La primera crónica general* and *La crónica de 1344* is weighty evidence of a rich Spanish epic poetry.

HISTORICITY AND REALISM

Of all primitive epic poetry, the Spanish is the most realistic. Except for Bernardo del Carpio, Spanish epic heroes were living human beings, an assertion proved by historical documentation, and the tales of their adventures are based largely on historical fact. Geography, place-names, laws, and customs have been verified. The supernatural, marvelous, and fantastic are almost totally absent, and the poetry is objective, sober, and terse. The realism and historicity of the Spanish epic are found nowhere else in primitive heroic poetry.

THE HEROIC TRADITION IN SPANISH LITERATURE

The virility, sobriety, generosity, dignity, honor, adventure, romance, nobility, hospitality, independence, faith, and all the other qualities that together represent the genuine Spanish spirit are found in Spain's epic poetry in pure form. Spaniards are fascinated by the heroic legends of their past, and writers in all ages have repeatedly turned to the glorious stories for inspiration and subject matter. This process of return is most clearly visible, however, in the Golden Age and the Romantic period.

THE *CANTAR DE MIO CID*

A. Date of Composition

Menéndez Pidal has set the date of the composition of the *Cantar de Mio Cid* in 1140. The Cid died in 1099. The original author of the poem is unknown. The only remaining manuscript was copied in 1307 by Per Abbat (Pedro Abad) from a much earlier original. The poem was first published in 1779 by Tomás Antonio Sánchez.

B. Construction

The preserved portion of the poem contains 3,735 lines of verse. Approximately fifty lines lost at the beginning have been reconstructed from the *Crónica de veinte reyes*. The poem has been arranged into three natural divisions by modern scholars: *Cantar del destierro, Cantar de las bodas,* and *Cantar de Corpes.*

C. Plot

The poem traces the story of the Cid's life from the moment of his exile from Castille to his return to grace at the king's court. The principal episodes are the following: the exile; the Cid's campaigns against the Moors; the conquest of Valencia, which marks the peak of the Cid's power and fame; the marriage of the Cid's daughters to the Infantes de Carrión; the beating of the Cid's daughters, who are left to die in the Robledo de Corpes; and the revenge of the Cid and the punishment of his enemies.

D. Artistic Qualities

Stylistically the poem is dry and sober, yet it has a stark, laconic quality that describes little but suggests much. The long descriptions of battle are exciting, but there are also naïvetés and understatements. Patches of dialogue add genuine dramatic qualities. The noble, serious poetry, as well as the sobriety, virile energy, realism, accurate detail, and terseness, makes the poem classic in style, restrained and dignified.

A social consciousness pervades the poem. The Cid, a nobleman but not of royal connection, conquered first the adversities of circumstance and then his enemies, the higher nobility. He triumphed by his own ability and courage and emerged a hero, while the hereditary noblemen were made to appear cowardly and ridiculous. An antifeudal, antiaristocratic spirit emanates from the poem, in keeping with the Spaniard's individualism and democracy, but national loyalties and love of king remain strong.

The poem is objective and realistic without the exaggerations of the French and German epics. The geography and the Cid's trips across Spain have been verified. A couple of incidents have a legendary ring to them, but the note of authenticity, the historical accuracy, and the directness of the style give the poem a realistic air found in no other primitive epic poetry.

E. The Life, Character, and Personality of the Cid

The Cid, Rodrigo Díaz de Vivar, was a man of flesh and blood, endowed with great strength of character and all the virtues. He was born around 1043 in Vivar, near Burgos. He was descended from Laín Calvo, one of Castile's first judges after it gained its independence, and from noble stock on his mother's side.

Rodrigo served King Sancho of Castile, who was treacherously murdered while attempting to conquer the city of Zamora, the stronghold of his sister, Urraca. Alfonso, Sancho's brother and king of León, was then declared king of Castile, but the Cid and others recognized him only after forcing him to swear three times that he had not conspired in Sancho's death, a humiliating experience for Alfonso. A lingering desire for revenge may have influenced Alfonso's decision to exile Rodrigo.

After being exiled, Rodrigo served the king of Zaragoza. He fought against both Moors and Christians, and his prowess as a soldier and leader earned him the title of the Cid, an Arabic word meaning "lord." No instance has been recorded of his failure in battle, and in the end he established himself as a virtual king after conquering the city of Valencia, where he died in 1099.

The Cid Campeador has become the national hero of Spain. According to the *Cantar de Mio Cid* and the ballads, he was full-bearded—a mark of virility and dignity—vigorous, brave, and a natural leader. Yet he was tender and wept unashamedly when moved. He was a faithful and loving husband and a devoted father. He was an ideal vassal and was always loyal to his king despite the latter's hostility. He continually sought to reconcile himself with Alfonso, sending him valuable booty and acceding to his wish that the Infantes de Carrión marry his daughters, a union the Cid thought unwise. He never sought revenge on the unjust king, though he had the power to conquer him.

The Cid of literature believed in justice, fairness, and equality and always shared his booty with his men. He had an abiding religious faith and consistently commended himself to God before a battle and took time to thank Him after a victory. He was generous to his captives but unrelenting in battle.

In short, the mature Cid of the poem embodies the spirit of Castile and possesses those admirable and enduring qualities that have been Spain's in her greatest moments.

The *Crónica de 1344*, the *Rodrigo*, and some ballads portray the man as a rash, impudent, insolent, petulant young nobleman quite different from the Cid of the *Cantar*. In a duel, he kills the father of doña Jimena, who then demands his hand in marriage as compensation. This episode, together with the meeting with a leper and a few other youthful exploits, are called the *mocedades*. The historical Cid is the mature, grave, and noble national hero of Spain.

The story of the Cid inspired later literary works, among them Guillén de Castro's *Las mocedades del Cid,* José Zorrilla's *La leyenda del Cid,* Eduardo Marquina's *Las hijas del Cid,* and Corneille's *Le Cid.* The foreigners Southey, Hugo, Herder, and Lecomte de Lisle also borrowed from the theme.

THE DEGENERATION OF THE EPIC

The primitive epic, written in an uncultured, unrefined age, reflected the attitudes and sentiments of the time. In the late Middle Ages, primitive art forms fell into disfavor. Popular minstrels were supplanted by erudite poets, and epic poetry passed out of the realm of true folk art and into that of the artificial and refined. Unable to identify with the poetry of the preceding age,

31

the learned poets lost their spontaneity and folk flavor. The thirteenth and fourteenth centuries witnessed the degeneration and disappearance of true popular epic poetry. The old poems passed into the histories, were rewritten in learned form, and broke down into ballads.

MEDIEVAL NARRATIVE POETRY

Nonepic poetry of the twelfth and thirteenth centuries was not clearly narrative or lyric but a combination of the two. Poets generally used Galician for their lyrical efforts; but as themes came in from outside national tradition, as moral intent grew, and as Castilian increased in prestige, lyric patches in that tongue began to appear in narrative poetry.

Angel Valbuena classified this narrative-lyric poetry into poetry in short verses of seven to nine syllables and long verse poetry written chiefly in the fourteen-syllable line of the *cuaderna vía*. Themes included lives of saints, Biblical tales, lives of heroes, and borrowed foreign themes. The authors thought of themselves as erudite poets who counted syllables, were conscious of their didactic responsibilities, and prided themselves on their artistry, characteristics that continued throughout the Middle Ages. Yet they were but a step away from the folk minstrels whose popular spirit they imbibed, directing their art to the masses.

A. Short Verse Narrative-Lyric Poetry

Religious themes dominated this type of poetry, and the debate or dispute was a popular device. Closely akin to the drama, the debate lent itself to satire and moralizing. The dominant foreign influence was French, and gallicisms appear in the language. At a time when Galician was used for lyric expression, these poems, along with those of Gonzalo de Berceo, represent the first stirrings of lyrical expression in Castilian. Important poems, all from the thirteenth century, include the following:

1. *Libre dels tres reys d'Orient* deals with the flight of the Holy Family into Egypt and the slaughter of the Innocents. It is anonymous.

2. *Vida de Santa María Egipcíaca,* author unknown, narrates in 1,451 lines the life of one of history's most interesting saints.

3. *Disputa del alma y el cuerpo*, anonymous, is a thirty-seven-line fragment of a debate between the body and the soul of a deceased man.

4. *Denuestos del agua y el vino* is an anonymous poem in which water and wine debate their virtues. Joined to it is the first preserved lyric poem in Castilian, *Razón de amor*. Though probably composed separately, the two poems are always mentioned together and are not entirely incompatible.

5. *Elena y María*, anonymous, is a forty-line fragment of a poem in which two girls debate the qualities of their lovers.

B. Narrative-Lyric Poetry in *Cuaderna Vía*

Learned poets and clerics created a verse form called *mester de clerecía*, based upon strict syllable count and arranged in quatrains of fourteen-syllable monorhymed verses. Used throughout the Middle Ages, this fixed form was known as *cuaderna vía*, a term first used in the *Libro de Aleixandre*.

The first Spanish poet whose name is known, Gonzalo de Berceo (1195?–1265?), wrote narrative poems in *cuaderna vía*, recounting principally the lives of saints and miracles of the Virgin. He is appreciated for the simple grace, humor, ingenuousness, candor, naïveté, sincerity, and occasional lyrical and dramatic qualities of his verse. The following are significant examples of medieval narrative poetry in *cuaderna vía: Vida de Santo Domingo*, by Berceo; *Vida de Santa Oria*, by Berceo; *Libro de Apolonio*, anonymous; *Poema de Fernán González*, anonymous; *Libro de Aleixandre*, anonymous; and *Poema de Yusuf*, anonymous.

C. Satiric and Moral Poetry

Moralizing was incidental in some medieval poems, but in others it was intentional as poets exalted some virtue or higher value, conveyed some moral truth, or attacked some abuse or vice.

Rabbi Sem Tob (1290?–1369?) was the first Jew to write in Spanish whose name has been recorded and also the first to write gnomic literature in Spanish. In his *Proverbios morales* he drew his maxims from the Bible, the Talmud, Oriental and Jewish sources, and the wisdom of the ages. He wrote his 686 quatrains with great concision and often compressed a great moral lesson in a few lines. He influenced later poets, including the Marqués de Santillana and Gómez Manrique.

The *Danza de la muerte* is the fifteenth-century Spanish treatment of a favorite medieval theme and is reputed to be the best extant specimen of its type. Death summons to his court all those who must pay him tribute, and thirty-three victims pass before him, ranging from an emperor and a pope down to representatives of the lowest classes. Each victim defends himself, but in the end the inevitable sentence is pronounced. All must die.

Coplas, political satires, appeared for the first time in the fifteenth century. The first was *Coplas de ¡Ay, panadera!,* an anonymous poem that satirized cowardly nobles in the battle of Olmedo.

In the vitriolic *Coplas del Provincial,* the nobility is pummeled with the grossest invectives, and ladies and lords, represented as nuns and monks, have their names recited as they parade before the Superior (Provincial) of a convent to hear accusations against them and to be assigned penances. In *Coplas de Mingo Revulgo* a shepherd named Mingo complains that the head shepherd (Enrique IV) has deserted his responsibilities, that the four dogs, symbolizing Justice, Fortitude, Prudence, and Temperance, have abandoned the flock, and that the wolves (the nobility) are devouring the poor sheep (the people). Gil Arribato listens to Mingo, who symbolizes the Spanish people, and reminds him that despite his lament he is not without guilt and that part of his misery is caused by his own sins. These *Coplas* far surpass the *Provincial.* While not insolent, they shoot pointed barbs of satire at the leading personalities of the day. The fact that all the *Coplas* are anonymous points up the danger of criticizing authority.

THE EPIC IN THE GOLDEN AGE

Golden Age poets, influenced by the Italians Ariosto and Tasso and desiring to create a heroic literature worthy of their great nation, composed many long, erudite epic poems that had nothing in common with the primitive type and are of scant interest today. They addressed a variety of themes, as seen in the following list.

Historical epics include *La dragontea* (1598), by Lope de Vega, and *Bernardo, o victoria de Roncesvalles* (1624), by Bernardo Balbuena.

Romantic epics include *Las lágrimas de Angélica* (1586), by Luis

Barahona de Soto, and *La hermosura de Angélica* (1588), by Lope de Vega.

Epics on American themes include *La Araucana*, in three parts (1569, 1578, 1589), by Alonso de Ercilla y Zúñiga (1533– 1594), judged by most to be the best epic of the Golden Age.

Epics were also written on Classical, burlesque, satiric, and religious themes.

THE EPIC IN THE ROMANTIC PERIOD

Romanticism reawakened an interest in the Middle Ages. Surfeited by the ancient topics of eighteenth-century Neoclassicism, nineteenth-century Romantic poets eagerly returned to national, heroic, exotic themes of the past, especially those dealing with the Moors, and invented a new poetic form, the *leyenda,* with which to express them. The *leyenda* was a form of narrative, semiepic poetry in which traditional themes were developed with a vague realism and little historical accuracy, overlaid with an imaginative and colorful lyricism. The Romantic poets had a special evocative power with which to revive legendary figures of the past and to re-create the atmosphere of chivalry.

A. Angel de Saavedra, Duque de Rivas (1791–1865)

The Duque de Rivas' best poetry was narrative rather than lyric. After attempting two narrative poems, *El paso honroso* (1812) and *Florinda* (1826), concerning Florinda's relationship with Rodrigo, the last Visigothic king, Rivas wrote a Romantic legend, *El moro expósito o Córdoba y Burgos en el siglo décimo* (1834). The poem, in twelve cantos, relates the medieval legend of the Infantes de Lara. Although it has been called a *romance histórico,* it is more a *leyenda* or *fantasía novelesca.* Pastor Díaz considered it to be "la más bella poesía romántica de la época," and Valera felt that it had no precedent. It was greeted as something fresh and new in its revival of the national past. Rivas added characters to the legend and changed Mudarra into a Romantic hero.

Romances históricos (1841) was inspired by the *romancero* and the ancient *crónicas* and exhibits a genuine patriotic note. Rivas attempted to revive some of the great moments and heroes of a bygone age. In addition to themes from the Middle Ages, he included as subject matter the discovery and conquest of the

New World, the court of the Hapsburgs, and independence. In these *romances,* as in his less successful longer *leyendas,* published in 1854, Rivas at times included a note of mystery and occasional horror, and his descriptive power overshadows his storytelling ability.

B. José de Espronceda y Delgado (1808–1842)

Primarily a lyric poet, Espronceda also wrote *leyendas,* the best of which is *El estudiante de Salamanca* (1840), a Romantic revival of the don Juan theme. He recounts the libertinage of Félix de Montemar, who in a vision witnesses his own funeral and is given the kiss of death by a skeleton. This poem and Espronceda's philosophical masterpiece, *El diablo mundo* (1841), which also contains narrative patches, are essentially compelling lyric poetry.

C. José Zorrilla y Moral (1817–1893)

Zorrilla had a true descriptive and narrative poetic talent, and this, combined with his facile skill as a versifier and genius for evoking Spain's chivalrous and romantic past, made him the best of the *leyenda* writers. He wrote many poems, frequently retelling in his own colorful manner an oft-used tale from legend and tradition.

One looks in vain for ideas in his works, but despite irregularities the reader is carried along by sheer descriptive charm, overlooking the poet's improvised manner and sometimes careless craftsmanship. His best-known *leyendas* are *A buen juez, mejor testigo,* which recounts the story of the *Cristo de la Vega* in which a statue miraculously serves as a witness; and *Margarita la tornera,* the tender story of the Virgin's intercession in a nun's troubles. *Granada* (1852), in nine books, though never finished, is probably Zorrilla's best combination of history and legend and is remarkable for its color and musicality.

THE *ROMANCERO*

A. General Characteristics

One of the most original and enduring monuments of Spanish literature and the richest collection of popular poetry anywhere is the Spanish *romancero*. The word means three things: the immense Spanish ballad literature dating from the Middle Ages; a collection of ballads; and a series of ballads dealing with one theme.

The ballad, called *romance* in Spanish, is a short epico-lyric poem written in sixteen-syllable lines divided into two equal hemistichs by a caesura, with the final word of each line assonating. Some collections print the ballad in eight-syllable lines with the even lines assonating.

The ballads reflect the traditional national spirit and mentality better than any other form of literature. Episodic in nature and related in origin to the primitive epic, they begin and end abruptly without exposition, implying an entire situation or identifying some hero with a few deft strokes. As the repository of genuine national spirit they have had a profound effect on Spanish literature and have consistently inspired writers of all ages.

B. The *Juglar* and the *Mester de Juglaría*

The *juglar,* the public entertainer of the Middle Ages, amused his audiences with recitations, music, acrobatics, and sleight of hand. More important, he was the reciter of *cantares de gesta,* a professional who earned his living acting and singing before the public whether in a palace or a marketplace. *Mester de juglaría* means the type of poetry recited, sung, and composed by the *juglares,* principally ballads and epics.

C. The Fragmentation Theory of Ballad Origin

Some nineteenth-century critics believed in the *cantilena* theory to the effect that ballads strung together formed epic poetry, but Menéndez Pidal rightly asserted that the ballads descended originally from the epics, representing the fragments of these poems preserved by the *juglares* when the epic was in its degenerative stages. The minstrels selected short portions from an epic to sing to a street-corner audience or were asked to repeat a particularly popular passage. These brief excerpts, remembered by the listeners and recited later at home, were passed on orally from generation to generation down to the twentieth century. Written collections began to appear, however, in the sixteenth century, and new ones are still being collected from the people of Spain and the New World.

The phenomenal oral existence of Spain's ballad literature over a period of some eight centuries is unique in the world of art. Through the communal transmission and development, several versions of the same ballad have been found, and they have all absorbed through this process the true spirit of the people. The ballad thus mirrors the Spanish soul more faithfully than all other genres.

The original ballads were fragments of epic poems. Later, known poets wrote ballads and used the ballad meter in the drama and in poems on varied themes. Even twentieth-century poets have used the ballad meter.

D. Classification

There are several thousand ballads of such variety that classification is difficult. We can, however, note a few important types: *Romances históricos* or *viejos tradicionales* are derived from the medieval epics and histories. *Romances juglarescos* are longer and treat subjects from the degenerate period. *Romances fronterizos* relate the heroics and amours of Christian and Moorish knights of the fifteenth century. *Romances novelescos sueltos* are tales of adventure but are not necessarily epic. *Romances eruditos* were written on old themes by erudite poets. *Romances líricos* or *artísticos* treat any theme and were written by recognized artists. *Romances vulgares* treat a great variety of themes and were written by street-corner poets.

E. Collections

Two important early ballad collections are *Cancionero sin año,* published in the middle of the sixteenth century by Martín Nuncio, and *Silva de varios romances,* published by Esteban G. de Nágera in 1550 and 1551.

Modern collections include *Romancero general* (1828–1832, 1849), by Agustín Durán; *Primavera y flor de romances* (1856), by Ferdinand Joseph Wolf and Konrad Hofmann; *Antología de poetas líricos castellanos* (1944–1945), by Marcelino Menéndez y Pelayo; and *Flor nueva de romances viejos* (1933), by Ramón Menéndez Pidal.

Part 3 THE DRAMA

ORIGIN: THE MEDIEVAL PERIOD

A. The Liturgical Drama

The drama in Spain, as elsewhere in Europe, probably sprang from the dramatic elements in the Church liturgy. These were gradually elaborated, and simple acting was introduced. The language used was Latin, and the themes were strictly religious, the first being the Christmas and Easter stories. Later those of Palm Sunday, the Epiphany, Good Friday, the Day of the Innocents, and the Corpus Christi festival were added. The first actors were clerics, and the first theaters were churches.

The shepherds in the Christmas story provided for an occasional comic element as well as the use of popular dialect. As secular elements increased and laymen replaced clerics as actors, the plays grew unseemly and were banished from the churches to the courtyards and the marketplaces. Here the authors and actors could take liberties of which the Church did not approve. Spanish replaced Latin, the liturgical influence diminished, and the popular drama began to flourish independently. Though the secular was thus divorced from the sacred, religious themes dominated throughout the Middle Ages.

B. The Popular Drama

Another drama, possibly a continuation of the Latin theater, flourished alongside the liturgical. No examples of this *teatro profano* exist today, and it is doubtful that any were ever written down. Proof of their existence is found, however, in references to them in other writings of the time, such as the *Siete partidas* of Alfonso *el Sabio*, which condemned them and referred to them as *juegos de escarnio*. Popular with the people but frowned upon by the Church for their sacrilegious satire and parodying of sacred matters, as well as for their obscenities and immoralities, these little dramas, mostly improvised, mark the genesis of a type of short one-act drama that has continued to modern times under a variety of names such as *paso, entremés, sainete,* and *género chico.*

C. Cycles of the Liturgical Drama

Numerous plays were written on the great themes of the Church, Christmas and Easter, forming what are called "cycles." Other cycles evolved also, commemorating additional Church festivals. Many moving episodes from the Scriptures also had their dramatic versions.

D. *El Auto de los reyes magos*

This play is the sole remaining example of Spain's liturgical drama, and part of it has been lost. It belonged to the Epiphany cycle and tells the story of the Magi's search for the Savior and Herod's wrathful opposition. Probably an offshoot of the Benedictine liturgy, it was based on a Latin play written in Orléans in the twelfth century. It surpasses its model, however, in its complicated versification, superior dramatic qualities, and inventiveness. It was probably composed about the middle of the twelfth century.

This, the second oldest work of Spanish literature, contains some elements of future Spanish drama: realism in depicting characters, tension in the doubts of the Magi and the reluctance of Herod's advisers to give him a straightforward answer, an attempt to suit the verse to the situation, the polymetric tendency, and the first soliloquy.

E. The Interlude

The liturgical drama flourished roughly from 900 to 1200. An interlude of three centuries followed from which no plays have been preserved, though they undoubtedly continued to be written, a fact attested to by Church documents of the thirteenth and fourteenth centuries. The technical and artistic improvements of the first preserved plays of the fifteenth century over the *Auto de los reyes magos* afford additional evidence.

THE EARLY RENAISSANCE

A. General Considerations

The early Renaissance contains but one important dramatist, Juan del Encina. Many others wrote drama, some with moderate success, considering the retarded state of the genre and the general cultural level. Toward the end of the period, however, plays appeared that gave evidence of real dramatic qualities, the Renaissance spirit, and signs of future potential.

B. Gómez Manrique (1412?–1490)

With his play *Representación del nacimiento de nuestro Señor*, Gómez Manrique broke the silence of the three empty centuries following the *Auto de los reyes magos*. The genuine dramatic qualities of this play show great refinement compared with the *Auto*, testimony of growth in the drama during the silent centuries. Gómez Manrique also wrote *Lamentaciones fechas para semana santa* and a considerable number of other works of various kinds.

C. Rodrigo de Cota (1405?–1470)

To this author have been attributed a variety of works, including the *Coplas del Provincial, Coplas de Mingo Revulgo,* and the first act of *La Celestina,* but the only work undoubtedly known to be his is a poem in debate style entitled *Diálogo entre el amor y un viejo.* Though it is a poem, Menéndez y Pelayo considers it a milestone in the history of the Spanish theater because of the artistry of its plot, dialogue, emotions, contrast, and dramatic techniques.

D. Juan del Encina (1468?–1529?)

Juan del Encina, who studied under Nebrija at the University of Salamanca and took religious orders early, is considered to be the father of the Spanish drama, for it is with him that the true Spanish drama begins.

Encina took the drama into the castles and palaces of the nobility and composed nearly all his 170 works before the age of thirty. In him are combined three literary currents: Latin poetry, the Classical theater, and the liturgical drama. One also finds in his works a realistic and popular element, inherited perhaps from the *teatro profano.*

In his early works, *Eglogas* written in imitation of Virgil's *Eclogues,* he achieved a comic effect through shepherds who speak an amusing gibberish called *sayagués,* a dialect that became a conventional comic device. His early themes were religious, and he combined elements of Classical poetry with the liturgical.

The increasing refinement and sophistication of his later manner are the result of his trips to Rome. A musician and composer of music, he anticipated the *zarzuela* of later centuries and injected music and dance liberally into his theater, a pattern followed in the Golden Age.

His chief works are *Egloga de Plácida y Vitoriano,* in which Plácida commits suicide because of her lover's scorn; *Egloga de Cristino y Febea,* a clear statement of the Renaissance spirit, which relates how Cristino is drawn from his hermit's retirement by Cupid to enjoy falling in love with Febea; and *Aucto del repelón,* a farce dramatizing a scuffle between Salamancan students and shepherds.

Encina's reputation as a dramatist has obscured his contributions in the fields of poetry and music. His most interesting poems are those on profane themes, though he wrote religious poems as well. Sixty-eight of his many musical compositions have been preserved in Francisco Asenjo Barbieri's *Cancionero musical* and have been recorded in modern times.

E. *La Celestina*

This famous work was never intended to be acted. It will therefore be treated in Part 4.

THE RENAISSANCE: PRECURSORS OF LOPE DE VEGA

A. General Considerations

In Spain, the Renaissance, in evidence from the last part of the fifteenth century, in the drama may be said to cover the period from 1517, the date of Torres Naharro's *Propaladia,* to 1616, the date of Cervantes' death. There is an obvious overlapping between this period and the Golden Age, as there is between the early Renaissance and the High Renaissance. Nevertheless, dramatists of the sixteenth century may conveniently be designated as precursors of Lope de Vega and the drama of the Golden Age.

Renaissance drama was characterized by experimentation and growth. Spaniards knew foreign drama but changed, adapted, refused, and in some cases accepted it according to their own tastes, clear evidence of *españolismo* and the Spaniard's individuality and love of freedom.

Not an age of dramatic triumphs, the sixteenth century refined the drama, enriched versification, broadened subject matter, invented new techniques, improved characterization and plot handling, and made the drama respectable. It remained for Lope to crystallize it into a system.

B. Bartolomé de Torres Naharro (1476?–1531?)

Torres, like Encina, has also been called the father of the Spanish drama, since he was the first to create truly Spanish characters and the first to establish rules for dramatic composition. He was the most important dramatist of his time.

Little is known of his life. He was a good student and a soldier in his youth and became a priest and later a favorite at the papal court of Leo X in Rome. We do not know whether he ever returned to Spain.

His principal publication, *Propaladia* (meaning "First Fruits"), was published in Rome in 1517 and contains a prologue and six plays. Two more were added later. Though performed in Rome, these plays were banned in Spain until 1545, when they appeared in mutilated form. In the prologue Torres set forth his rules for writing dramas, as follows: Plays should consist of five acts; comedy and tragedy should be separated; the number of characters should be limited to between six and twelve; plays are divided into two types—*comedias a fantasía,* based on fictional incidents that have the air of reality, and *comedias a noticia,* based on observed events (this points up once again two recurrent trends in Spanish literature, the idealistic and the realistic); and decorum, verisimilitude, and appropriateness of dialogue to the character should be observed.

Torres imitated Juan del Encina but soon surpassed him. With his sure dramatic instinct, Torres fixed the drama in the direction of the Golden Age. He was the first Spaniard to write comedy of intrigue and even hinted at the comedy of manners. He was the first dramatic satirist. He anticipated the *loa* by insisting upon an *introito,* a comic and burlesque poem recited by a rustic as a prologue, and upon an *argumento,* a versified plot summary spoken by an actor before the play began.

Torres emphasized plot more than character, an emphasis that was later a weakness of the Golden Age theater, and used the honor theme, writing the first "cape and sword" play. He wrote for educated audiences and scorned the *vulgo.* His continued residence in Rome and the banning of his plays in Spain cast doubt on his influence among Spaniards. His important plays are as follows:

1. *Comedias a noticia. Comedia soldadesca* portrays army life based on Torres' own experiences. *Comedia tinelaria,* the first play of satire, reveals the intrigue, thievery, and corruption in a cardinal's palace. Shocked by what he saw in Rome, Torres revealed in this play his Erasmian attitude toward the Church and the *curia.*

2. *Comedias a fantasía. Comedia himenea,* considered to be Torres' masterpiece, is the first "cape and sword" play and recounts a love affair, a point of honor, and an escape from tragedy. *Comedia Seraphina* relates a triangle love affair that ends happily.

C. Gil Vicente (1469?–1536?)

Gil Vicente was the first of the bilingual dramatists and one of the outstanding European writers of his era. He wrote forty-four dramatic pieces in all, eleven in Spanish, sixteen in Portuguese, and seventeen in mixed Portuguese and Spanish. Like his predecessors, he shunned the general public and wrote for the court.

Though he imitated Encina at first, he soon surpassed his model, and his later works show marked originality and breadth. Though he borrowed from many, he imitated nobody, assimilating his borrowings completely. The most original portion of his work is his farces, *Farsa dos físicos* and *O velho da horta,* which reflected the ancient *juegos de escarnio.* In his complex artistic personality he represented a union of the sacred traditions of the Middle Ages with the new freedoms of the Renaissance. As an Erasmist, he was critical of the Church. His sources and themes were varied: the Bible, the Church fathers and saints, eclogues, Torres Naharro's drama, French *mystères,* Spanish ballads, novels of chivalry, dances of death, fairy tales, and hymns and liturgies of the Church.

He was a musician and usually inserted a song in every drama. His rich and colorful lyricism, always musical and graceful, is of fundamental importance. He eclipsed Encina and overshadowed Torres Naharro, exceeding all in spirituality and inspiration. Dramatists of the Golden Age took lessons from him. His *Amadís de Gaula* (1533) and *Don Duardos* (1525) are the first plays based on novels of chivalry. *Barca de la gloria* (1519), the third of an allegorical trilogy, combines the Dance of Death theme with Erasmian comments and criticisms on social vices and customs. The first two parts of the trilogy are in Portuguese. *Comedia del viudo* (1514), one of Vicente's best works, tells with strong comic force, irony, and charming lyricism the story of the marriage of two brothers to a widower's daughters. *La comedia de Rubena* (1521), the first play of magic, presents the *bobo,* a descendant of the *pastor* and predecessor of the *gracioso,* along with fairies, witches, and much folklore.

D. Lope de Rueda (1510?–1565)

Lope de Rueda's uncommon talents in things dramatic led him to become a professional actor-manager-playwright who toured Spain with his troupe, performing in theaters and palaces and on street corners. One of his greatest contributions was that he democratized the drama, making it a popular institution, no longer the exclusive property of the aristocracy.

Though he composed longer dramas in imitation of the Italian theater and what he termed *coloquios pastoriles* modeled after Encina, Rueda found his true forte in the farce. To his some forty short, farcical compositions he gave the name *pasos.* These were very brief, one-act skits with a negligible plot, depicting everyday scenes in a realistic and comical manner with the sole intention to entertain. Perhaps they were intended to be used as prologues or between acts of longer plays, but a series of them could easily have been presented as an afternoon's entertainment. The *pasos* reflect real life and exhibit acute insights, gay wit, inventiveness, resourcefulness, and an always strong comic force. The language is realistic, picturesque, spicy, and sprinkled with the proverbs, phrases, and superstitions of the people. The characters, almost all taken from the lower classes, are stereotypes: the gypsy, the Negress, the matchmaker, the Biscayan, and the *bobo.* Rueda was the first to use prose in the drama, but few followed his lead. He was influenced by Boccaccio, Juan Manuel, and very likely the Italian *commedia dell'arte,* a totally improvised skit known in Spain at the time. He created the realistic comedy of manners, popularized the drama, and gave a strong impetus to the short dramatic skit.

Paso de las aceitunas, judged by some to be the best one-act play of the sixteenth century, is an adaptation of the "dreaming milk-maid" story relating a quarrel of a wife and husband over the price of olives that they will not reap until years later. Other titles of Rueda's plays are *Cornudo y contento, El convidado, El rufián cobarde,* and *Los criados.* Among his longer plays, influenced by the Italian theater, *Eufemia* is the best.

E. Juan de la Cueva (1550?–1610?)

At first, Juan de la Cueva took his dramatic themes from Classical antiquity. As his concept of the drama matured, he urged his countrymen to abjure Classical sources and write on national themes, though some of his own plays are based on Ovid and Virgil. He was the first to write drama based upon the epic traditions and legends of the *crónicas* and *romances.* In his *Exemplar poético* (1606), he set forth his dramatic doctrines, improving over Torres Naharro and filling the gap between Torres Naharro and Lope de Vega. His rules include the following: disregard of the unities; reduction of the number of acts to four; use of varied verse forms; use of national themes; introduction of royalty to the stage; use of the fantastic and supernatural; and mingling of comedy and tragedy.

He was not a skillful dramatist, for he was careless and an improviser, sometimes allowing his plots to back him into a corner from which he could extricate himself only by recourse to the supernatural, murder, and the like. Since he was neither highly cultured nor artistic, his merit lies largely in his role as an innovator. Despite his faults, he was one of the outstanding predecessors of Lope de Vega, lacking dignity and common sense, perhaps, but showing good dramatic instinct. Fourteen of his plays remain extant.

Los siete infantes de Lara (1579), *Bernardo del Carpio* (1579), and *La muerte del rey don Sancho y reto de Zamora por don Diego Ordoñez* are obvious dramatic reworkings of epic narrations preserved in the histories. *El infamador* (1581) was formerly considered a forerunner of Tirso's *El burlador de Sevilla,* but the hero, Leucino, is not a true don Juan type.

F. Miguel de Cervantes Saavedra (1547–1616)

Cervantes yearned to be a dramatist but could not compete with Lope de Vega. Though the two men were contemporaries,

Cervantes inclined toward the Classical conception of the drama and is best listed among Lope's predecessors. In this light, he had nothing of which to be ashamed as a dramatist and was in most respects the equal and perhaps the superior of others who preceded Lope. He fell short in the long drama, with the one exception of *Comedia del cerco de Numancia*, hailed by some as the most inspired play in the Classical tradition ever produced in Europe. It was revived in the Romantic period, played in 1809 during the siege of Zaragoza, and played again during the Civil War of the twentieth century to instill courage and patriotism in the hearts of the people. After Lope's advent, Cervantes ceased writing for the stage and in 1615 published *Ocho comedias y ocho entremeses nunca representados*. He noted in his work *Viaje al Parnaso* that he had written twenty or thirty *comedias*, but only ten of them survive.

His dramatic forte was the *entremés*, with which he succeeded admirably. The word *entremés* has several meanings, but in the theater it refers to a one-act piece, generally realistic and often satirical, played between the acts of a long drama. Cervantes' *entremeses* constitute the truly great part of his theater, and among them are the best of their kind ever written. In Cervantes' *entremeses* one finds a procession of lower-class types painted in master strokes. The dialogue is racy, spirited, and juicy. Here Cervantes reveals his kindness and love of humanity, his indulgent and never-bitter satire, and the same double vision of life, the conflict between idealism and realism, found in his masterpiece, *Don Quijote*. Plots are unimportant, but character delineation is masterful, and customs are faithfully reflected. In this style, Cervantes is not surpassed and has few equals. A few of his popular *entremeses* are *El retablo de las maravillas*, *La cueva de Salamanca*, *El viejo celoso*, and *La guarda cuidadosa*.

THE GOLDEN AGE

A. General Considerations

The progress achieved by Spain's sixteenth-century dramatists paved the way for the advent of the *comedia nueva* of Lope de Vega. Lope de Rueda's crude stages gave way to two great theaters in Madrid, the Teatro del Príncipe and the Corral de la

47

Cruz, and to others elsewhere. There was a public demand for theater, actors had gained respectability, and the time was right for a strong hand to synthesize all preceding elements into a cogent whole. That strong hand belonged to Lope de Vega, the prolific author and undisputed master of the theater who created the national drama that remained virtually unchanged for a century. He called his type of drama the *comedia nueva*.

The Golden Age of the drama, which stretched from 1592 with the advent of Lope as a dramatist to 1681, the date of Calderón's death, saw Spanish drama reach its peak. Thousands of plays were composed. The public consumed dramas at an amazing rate, and many an author's work went before an audience unrehearsed. A play was intended to be viewed once, and frenzied actors did not have time to learn their lines. It was a time of excitement, of incessant and urgent theatrical production, of keen rivalries among authors, of prodigies of wit and ingenuity and near miracles of energy and enthusiasm. An author who wrote fewer than one hundred plays was thought to be either lazy or lacking in inventiveness. It was a time when genius was common, a fact attested by the four great stars of the theater—Lope, Tirso, Alarcón, and Calderón—and a host of writers in other genres.

B. Lope Félix de Vega Carpio (1562–1635)

Lope de Vega, called the Phoenix of the Spanish stage, was an amazing genius whose accomplishments have become legendary. His unique fame rests not only upon the fact that he created a national drama for Spain, as Shakespeare did for England, but also upon the incredible bulk of his writing. Though no exact count can be made, his disciple, Juan Pérez de Montalbán, summed up the staggering total of 1,800 three-act plays and 400 *autos*. In addition, Lope wrote novels, short stories, lyric poetry, eclogues, epistles, and epic poems. Five hundred of his plays remain extant. He wrote three times more than the most prolific writers, such as Galdós, Balzac, Dickens, and Tolstoy.

Lope also found time for an adventurous life. He sailed with the Invincible Armada and during idle hours composed eleven thousand lines of verse, which he published in 1602 as an erudite epic under the title *La hermosura de Angélica*. His talent for amorous adventure is almost as astonishing as his literary fecundity, for his life was a series of love affairs and scandals. He married twice, had a number of mistresses, and fathered some fourteen children. In 1614, however, he took religious vows and pursued his priestly profession seriously. Yet he devoted one final great love affair to a married woman thirty years his junior, doña Marta de Nevares. Her blindness, the death of his son, the elopement of his only remaining daughter, and the poor reception accorded his last plays embittered his final days. He died in 1635 at the age of seventy-three. Four words sum up his life: writing, adventure, love, and religion.

Lope, taking the elements he needed from the inchoate drama of his time, substituted for it the child of his own cunning mind, the quick-moving, romantic, popular *comedia nueva*. His best themes came from national history and contemporary life, and with them he established a national drama with Spanish subject matter, independent of all rules and theories but his own. His personal doctrines, more defense than theory, appeared in a poem, *Arte nuevo de hacer comedias en este tiempo* (1609). There he established the need for artistic freedom and confessed that he wrote his plays not according to any precepts or canons but as the public liked them. The following are the formal aspects of Lope's theater taken from the *Arte nuevo:*

1. The play should have three acts. In the first act, it should have exposition, in the second, plot complication, and in the third, a sudden climax.

2. The unities are abandoned. Some pretense of unity of action is proposed even though Lope regularly violated it.

3. Comedy and tragedy could be mingled.

4. Noble and base characters could be mixed.

5. Lope recommended varied and appropriate verse forms, such as *redondillas* for love scenes, sonnets for soliloquies, *liras* for heroic declamations, romance for exposition, etc.

6. Puns, disguises, mistaken identities, etc., are used as devices to facilitate plot handling.

7. All themes—national, foreign, religious, heroic, pastoral, historical, and contemporary—could be used.

8. Fixed types are used, such as the *galán,* the *viejo,* and the *gracioso,* Lope's invention inherited in part from the *pastor, bobo,* and *parvo* of former dramatists. The *gracioso* was a nobleman's servant and in Lope's drama served as the antithesis of his master for comic relief, parodying his master on a lower level. In Alarcón he is the confidant and adviser; in Tirso he combines comedy and advice; in Calderón he spouts philosophy and puns.

Lope did not change the drama greatly in form, borrowed heavily from his predecessors, and disobeyed even his own rules. His eminence derived from the fact that he breathed the essence of national life into his drama, identified totally with the popular mind, adapted folk poetry to the stage, dramatized ballads, and wrote what the audience wanted. He was the voice of the people and the echo of a dynamic, proud, vigorous, active nation.

He had an immense range and variety, unequaled eloquence, and an astonishing facility for versification. Aiming at creating emotion, he contrived plot with ingenuity and amazing freshness, always persuasive and in good taste. He banished the ugly, base, and sordid from his work. His favorite themes were honor, monarchy, faith, and love. When he used other themes he gave them a Spanish flavor, identifying them with the national soul. He had charm, grace, eloquence, lightness of touch, and infallible tact, and his plays are brisk, clever, full of action and intrigue, animated, and above all entertaining. He had an uncanny instinct for the drama, unlimited energy, and a boundless imagination.

His success with the historical play, in which he was the protector of the people, the scourge of the oppressive nobleman, and the defender of the king, endeared him to the common folk. He handled the "cape and sword" play with ease and made it the truly national drama to remain unchanged forever.

Yet Lope was an improviser, perhaps by nature or in answer to the demands of an adulatory public. Since he wrote rapidly, he was never able to condense all his talents into one play. His plots are ingenious, and one marvels at their freshness and variety. But plot is not enough. His characters are sometimes shallow, and none competes with don Quijote or Hamlet. Yet on occasion he created great characters, especially female types. He dazzled with his versatility and cleverness, but one looks in vain for philosophical import or moral intent. He viewed his dramas as "pot boilers," regulated by his own infallible instinct and by audience reaction.

Despite these faults, which seem minor compared with his merits, Lope has inspired writers of all succeeding generations at home and sometimes abroad. His undeveloped ideas have often found fuller expression in the drama of others. A few deny him any lasting values; others enthrone him as a demigod. He was a unique figure, surpassed in ways by some of his followers but bowing to none in sheer spontaneity, brilliance, and creative power. Two of his better-known works are *El mejor alcalde, el rey,* a historical play in which a man of the lower class, oppressed by a nobleman, is avenged by the king himself; and *Peribáñez y el comendador de Ocaña,* another historical drama, stressing the Spaniard's inherent dignity and resistance to oppression. The nobleman is again the villain, and the king, the commoner's defender. Other famous plays are *Fuenteovejuna* and *El caballero de Olmedo.*

After his death, Lope was obscured by the brilliance of Pedro Calderón de la Barca, and he did not emerge from the shadows until German Romanticists of the nineteenth century rediscovered him. Yet he was still ranked the inferior of Calderón. In the twentieth century he has been generally regarded as Spain's foremost dramatic genius.

C. Tirso de Molina (1583–1648)

Tirso de Molina is the pseudonym of a Mercenarian friar, Gabriel Téllez, who devoted much time and energy to his order and finished his life as prelate of the monastery at Soria. He may have been the illegitimate son of the Duque de Osuna, a fact that, if true, would explain his complaints about his lack of social position and the injustices of certain social conventions. Tirso was a disciple of Lope de Vega's and agreed with him on the principles of dramatic composition, which he expressed in *Los cigarrales de Toledo* (1624). Had he devoted his entire life to the theater, he might have outshone Lope, for he had all the assets to become the greatest of playwrights. He was a master of the language, had a resourceful imagination, was ironic at times and sly at others, and had a clever way of introducing risqué situations. He was skillful in plot technique and unsurpassed in comic force, but he fell short of Lope's grace, facility, and lightness of touch. He surpassed Lope in character creation and showed a predilection for strange, extreme, or unusual types. His don Juan is the only Spanish dramatic personality to attain the worldwide renown of Hamlet, Othello, Romeo, and Faust. He was particularly skilled in creating spirited, bold female characters, who are particularly adept at compromising themselves and intrepid in pursuit of their lovers. He directed sharp satire at the hypocrisy of women, as in *Marta la piadosa,* but at the same time painted virtuous, noble women who relentlessly pursued their goals, generally the restoration of their honor. His men, on the contrary, are often weak, timid, and irresolute, lukewarm in love, and in the end

51

cornered by frank, daring women. His plots frequently are battles of wits between women, one of whom conquers in the end by being cleverer, more daring, and more ardent than her rivals.

Tirso's comic sense, always strong, is particularly evident in his *graciosos* and is irrepressible even in the most solemn moments, such as the final terrifying scenes of *El burlador de Sevilla.* His language is incisive, his satire frequent. He had a salacious spirit, at times a little streak of malice, and a fondness for daring themes, treating, for example, the question of incest in *La venganza de Tamar.* Consequently, as in the case of Juan Ruiz, the question has been asked whether he was a stern moralist in a seemingly quite permissive age or an indulgent monk. Whatever the case may have been, he was rebuked in 1625 by the Council of Castile for alleged obscenities and the portrayal of vices in his plays. This forced him to cease writing for the theater; some believe he never wrote again, others that he stopped for about ten years. He probably returned to his pastime sooner than suspected, however, for it seems improbable that he produced the four hundred plays ascribed to him between 1606 and 1625, given the demands of his vocation; and he wrote no plays in the last ten years of his life. He was the second most prolific dramatist of the Golden Age, but only about eighty-five of his four hundred works are known today.

Tirso's background as a priest enabled him to write the best religious plays of his time, but also because of his vocation, his genius never found its fullest expression. Yet nothing can obscure his admirable talents and the beauties of his works. After his death he was forgotten for nearly two hundred years until Dionisio Solís rediscovered him.

1. *El burlador de Sevilla y convidado de piedra* (1630), rated by some as the best Spanish play ever written, introduced the famed don Juan Tenorio to the world. The theme already existed in folklore before Tirso's day, but it was Tirso's distinction to treat don Juan artistically for the first time. Tirso's version of the don Juan legend is basically religious, showing that divine mercy is not infinite and that the unrepentant libertine is punished. Don Juan has fascinated the Spanish mind since his first appearance in this drama, in which bravery is his outstanding virtue, and he has become a world-renowned personality. This famous character has made the rounds of world literature, and his name has become a household word. Unfortunately, Tirso's name has been forgotten in don Juan literature,

and don Juan has been curiously distorted in the hands of others.

2. *El condenado por desconfiado* (1635) is hailed as Spain's best religious drama. A sinner is saved by repentance, and a religious man is condemned for too little faith.

Other well-known plays by Tirso are *El vergonzoso en palacio* (1621) and *La prudencia en la mujer* (1633).

D. Juan Ruiz de Alarcón (1581?–1639)

Born in Mexico, Juan Ruiz de Alarcón y Mendoza returned to Spain at about the age of twenty to attend the University of Salamanca. Five years later he went back to Mexico and was graduated from the National University. He then returned to Spain, where he remained, and began to compose for the theater.

His twenty-four plays, most of which were published in 1628 and 1634, make him the least productive of the four leading dramatists of the Golden Age. He followed Lope's tradition but deviated from it perhaps more than any writer of his time. Not an improviser, he carefully planned and wrote his plays. By insisting upon nearly Classical perfection of form, ethical significance, logic and reason, and the didactic function of the drama, he anticipated eighteenth-century Neoclassicism. He was concerned with human values and relationships and extolled courtesy, sincerity, honesty, chivalry, loyalty, discretion, and truthfulness as virtues to be admired, condemning odious types such as liars and slanderers. Alarcón's verse is not the equal of Lope's, but it has a dry, sober dignity that reflects the author's personality and his careful craftsmanship, which avoided the Gongoristic excesses of his day.

Alarcón was a hunchback, and his contemporaries cruelly taunted him about his deformity. He also had a knack for alienating people and had few friends. Embittered by all this, he turned to composing comedies of manners in which he defended virtuous conduct, partly to defend himself and partly to humiliate his detractors. By depicting human vices through character portrayal, he developed a technique of characterization that, along with his formula for writing comedies of manners, was copied by Corneille in *Le menteur,* adapted from *La verdad sospechosa,* and also by Molière.

Despite his personal suffering, little bitterness or cynicism carried over into his plays, and Alarcón exhibited a reflective, reasoned attitude toward life, a longing for the triumph of virtue, and a hope for cordiality in human relations. Unlike Lope, Alarcón did not write to please the public. He wrote for gain and fame and also because he had a message for the world. *La verdad sospechosa,* Alarcón's best drama, attacks the vice of lying. *Las paredes oyen,* another comedy of manners, shows the odiousness of slander. Other plays are *La prueba de las promesas* and *Mudarse por mejorarse.*

E. Pedro Calderón de la Barca (1600–1681)

Like Lope, Calderón wrote his first play as a boy and served in the military, but there the similarities of the two men cease. Calderón studied at Alcalá and Salamanca, won prizes for his poetry, and, adventurously youthful, engaged in several duels. His military service was more extensive than Lope's, and he was reputedly wounded in the hand.

Upon Lope's death, the nation recognized Calderón as the poet best fitted to carry on the master's work, and Felipe IV appointed him court poet. He never married but had at least one love affair. His son passed as his nephew until Calderón took orders, at which time he recognized him as his son. In 1651 Calderón was ordained a priest and withdrew from the world, although he continued to write one or two religious *autos* each year and mythological *comedias* for the entertainment of the court. His life, compared with Lope's tempestuous one, was quiet and assured. His last thirty years were spent in solitude, reading, and reflection.

He wrote much less than Lope, some 200 lyric poems, 120 *comedias,* 80 *autos,* and 20 shorter dramatic pieces. His plays can be roughly divided into two groups: the secular, and the religious and philosophical. He followed Lope's models and, in fact, recast some of Lope's plays and improved them.

His honor tragedies and his "cape and sword" plays are of greatest interest among his secular production. Though Lope had used the theme of the conflict between love and honor, Calderón showed the honor theme in its most abhorrent aspects. One must understand the Spanish point of honor (*pundonor*) and resulting social complications to comprehend Calderón's theater as well as the Golden Age drama in general. As a court poet Calderón understood the intricacies of the honor code and apparently condoned it despite its extremes.

Calderón's "cape and sword" plays represent the perfection of this type of drama, which was introduced by Torres Naharro and improved by Lope. Incredibly complicated plots, lovers' intrigues, honor dilemmas, sudden appearances, and many other tricks and devices to complicate and then disentangle the plot typify these plays. Calderón, the most profoundly Spanish poet of his era, speaks intimately to the Spaniard.

Calderón was king of the stage from Lope's death until his own in 1681. He lacked the spontaneity and variety of the Phoenix, but he frequently equaled and at times surpassed him in the sheer beauty and rapturous heights of his poetry. He was an aristocratic poet, did not cater to the public, and was more profound and philosophical than Lope. Lope was the improviser, Calderón was the planner. He was a formal and Baroque writer, susceptible to the exaggerations, distortions, and rotund style of *cultismo,* and he was the chief exponent of *conceptismo* in the theater. He brought to his work a fine power of reasoning, an intellectual outlook, a keen dramatic instinct, a delicate imagination, and a lyrical power unsurpassed in his day. His theater was more calculated, more elegant, and more refined than that of any other. Both his life and his drama show a steadily growing predilection for the allegorical, mythological, and metaphysical, and he finally withdrew from the human scene, preoccupied, perhaps, with the deeper concerns of life and dissatisfied with what the world had to offer, succumbing finally to the illusion that life is a dream.

As a writer of *autos sacramentales,* Calderón is supreme. The *auto,* cultivated in Spain since the time of Gil Vicente, is a one-act play, generally allegorical, that at some point or other treats the miracle of transubstantiation. Some believe that these short pieces represent the best of the Calderonian theater, for in them his fertile imagination had free rein and his sincere religious motives and faith found their purest expression.

Both Calderón and Lope fell into disfavor with the Neoclassicists of the eighteenth century, but Calderón was rediscovered by the German Romanticists of the nineteenth century, who worshiped him and pronounced him the equal of Shakespeare. This recognition of Calderón and lack of it for Lope has been ascribed to the easy accessibility of Calderón's works and the relative rarity of Lope's editions. Whatever his rating may be, all acknowledge Calderón's rare gifts. With him the drama gained in precision and power, grandeur and profundity of conception.

1. *La vida es sueño* (1635), Calderón's masterpiece, symbolizes

the struggle between free will and fate. It is deservedly famous and ranks among the foremost Spanish dramas of all time.

2. *El alcalde de Zalamea,* his best historical play and second only to *La vida es sueño,* was inspired by a drama of the same theme by Lope de Vega. It recounts the story of Pedro Crespo, a commoner with a high sense of personal honor and justice, who, elected mayor of Zalamea, orders the execution of an army captain who had kidnapped and raped his daughter. The mayor's action was later upheld by the king.

3. *El mágico prodigioso,* Calderón's best religious play, tells the story of a man who makes a pact with the devil to gain a woman's love.

4. *El médico de su honra,* his most horrifying honor tragedy, recounts how a husband, suspicious of his wife's infidelity, forces a physician to bleed her to death, washing away his dishonor in her blood.

Other plays include *La cena de Baltasar,* his best *auto; El príncipe constante;* and *La devoción de la cruz,* all examples of his religiophilosophical bent.

F. Guillén de Castro (1569–1630)

The fact that Guillén de Castro claimed to be a descendant of the Cid's ancestor, Laín Calvo, may have prompted him to write his great popular success, *Las mocedades del Cid* (1618), the first drama to deal with the Cid's exploits. Castro's Cid is the impetuous young man found in the *Rodrigo,* far removed from the sober, dignified national hero of the *Cantar de Mio Cid.* This play depicts the struggle in Jimena's heart between love and honor, the theme used by Corneille in *Le Cid.*

Castro was an admirer and imitator of Lope and composed a total of fifty plays. He was praised by Lope and other major writers of the *Siglo de Oro.* His success was due to his skillful use of themes from the ballads and folk legends of Spain and to his ability to transfer much of their heroic spirit to the stage.

G. Antonio Mira de Amescua (1577–1644)

Mira de Amescua was the illegitimate son of Melchor de Amescua y Mira, a fact that rankled him somewhat and may have accounted for his irascibility. He became a priest but did not take his profession seriously until his later years and spent most of his time writing for the stage. He followed Lope's lead but avoided Gongoristic tendencies.

His sixty dramas show a variety of types, and he is best remembered for *El esclavo del demonio* (1612), the story of a man's pact with the devil. This play may have influenced Tirso's *El burlador de Sevilla,* Calderón's *El mágico prodigioso,* and Moreto's *Caer para levantar* (1662).

H. Francisco de Rojas Zorrilla (1607–1648)

Rojas Zorrilla's success as a playwright began in 1636, when a number of his plays were presented. In 1637 Felipe IV called on him to write for the lavish entertainments held in honor of the visit to Madrid of María de Borbón, princess of Carignan.

Plagued by financial difficulties, Rojas ceased writing *comedias* in 1641 for the more lucrative work of composing *autos sacramentales.* Before his untimely death at the age of forty-one, Rojas had completed approximately one hundred plays, seventy of which were *comedias,* a large output considering the few years he lived.

Rojas is best remembered for *Del rey abajo, ninguno* (1650), known also as *García del Castañar,* a play that still has a great appeal for Spaniards, probably because it expresses so well their inherent love of freedom, equality, and dignity. Highly respected among his peers, Rojas collaborated in writing plays with Mira de Amescua and Calderón. He mitigated the excesses of the latter's treatment of honor, objecting to the king's omnipotence and championing women's rights. The immense popularity of *Del rey abajo, ninguno* overshadowed the obvious merits of Rojas' other works; his *comedias de graciosos* are especially good. French imitators, among them Corneille and Scarron, borrowed from him abundantly. Other titles are *Donde hay agravios no hay celos* (1637); *Entre bobos anda el juego* (1638); and *Cada cual lo que le toca,* which presents an unusual approach to feminine honor.

I. Agustín Moreto (1618–1669)

Moreto took minor orders in 1639 but had already gained a measure of success in Madrid's literary circles. He too wrote for the gala entertainments of Felipe IV's court. From 1657 until his death, however, Moreto was busy with religious affairs and withdrew from Madrid, although he continued writing for the stage up to his death. His correct, quiet, calm personality and his ordered and peaceful life account for the tranquillity in his writing.

Moreto was not resourceful or inventive, but he was skilled in borrowing from his fellow dramatists, often improving on their work and exceeding them all in stagecraft and in delicacy of touch, humor, and tact. This plagiarizing technique was practiced by all dramatists of the time and was not considered in any way dishonorable or criminal. In all, Moreto wrote over a hundred plays.

El desdén con el desdén (1654) improves in almost every detail on its model, Lope's *Milagros del desprecio,* and was imitated by Molière with little success in *Princesse d'Elide. El lindo don Diego* (1662) displays Moreto's skill at characterization. *El valiente justiciero* (1657) is based on the legend of Pedro *el Cruel.*

J. Lesser Dramatists of the Golden Age

1. *Juan Pérez de Montalbán* (1602–1638) is better known as Lope's biographer than as a writer, although there is some injustice in this. In the fifteen years of his literary activity, he wrote fifty-eight dramas, mostly on historical themes. Criticized for his slavish imitation of Lope, Montalbán was acknowledged even by his most vociferous critics to be popular with the public, a distinction that lasted well into the nineteenth century. Representative of his plays is *Despreciar lo que se quiere.*

2. *Luis Vélez de Guevara* (1579–1644), also a novelist, preferred historical themes and regal personages for his theater. Two of his plays are *Más pesa el rey que la sangre,* based on an episode from the life of Guzmán *el Bueno,* and *Reinar después de morir,* a dramatization of the tragic life of doña Inés de Castro.

3. *Luis Quiñones de Benavente* (1589?–1651) made his reputation with short dramatic pieces. He wrote hundreds of *entremeses, loas,* and *jácaras.* Next to Cervantes, he is Spain's best writer of *entremeses.*

THE EIGHTEENTH CENTURY

A. General Considerations

Following Calderón's death in 1681, Spanish intellectual life deteriorated. The last Hapsburg kings were inept, and political and economic stagnation and hopelessness were reflected in intellectual and literary life. The nation was exhausted from its immense efforts of the sixteenth and seventeenth centuries, and its spiritual and physical resources were drained.

Dramatists continued the Golden Age tradition of Lope and Calderón but produced nothing significant. More progressive writers tried to refashion the drama in imitation of the Classical qualities of the French literature of the age, but the attempt failed. The result was that, except for the work of Leandro Fernández de Moratín and Ramón de la Cruz, no successful drama was produced in Spain for 150 years.

The Neoclassic system failed in Spain, where art has always been free and national. Fettered and inhibited by foreign rules and regulations, Spanish writers could not create. They tried to write in the French manner, but the results were cold, graceless, and tasteless, correct imitations that failed to please the public or the critics. Neoclassic doctrinaires and critics could legislate art but could not create it. Neoclassicism did have the positive effect, however, of restoring some order, common sense, and decorum to the degenerate national drama.

B. Ignacio Luzán (1702–1754)

Luzán's sojourns in Italy and France gave him a cosmopolitan point of view that is reflected in his writings and doctrines. His *Poética o reglas de la poesía en general y de sus principales especies* (1737), corrected and modified in 1789, is based largely on the theories of Aristotle and Horace as reflected in the critical works of Boileau and Muratori and is the Spanish manifesto of Neoclassicism. Together with the efforts of the Academia del Buen Gusto, founded in 1749, it furthered the introduction of Neoclassicism in Spain. Luzán condemned Spain's Golden Age drama and proposed to transform literary taste and production by imposing upon them rules imported from abroad. His efforts failed in the end, but they set off a half century of polemics between the Classical devotees and the traditionalists.

Luzán did find something good in the drama of Lope and Calderón, but he rightly concluded that something went awry toward the turn of the seventeenth century, when language became obscured and turgid through the excesses of Gongorism, and good taste, common sense, and decorum disappeared. Blas Antonio Nasarre and Agustín Montiano, Luzán's disciples, carried his critical attitude toward the Golden Age to the extreme.

59

In drama, Luzán insisted that some virtue be exalted or some vice condemned and pleaded for a return to common sense, reason, morality, and simplicity. His work aroused Spaniards and stimulated an intellectual activity where little had existed before. Though unable to produce the literature they desired, Luzán and his disciples possessed a solid erudition and helped Spain emerge from one of her least productive eras.

Luzán's reforms in the drama include the following: observance of the three unities; limitation of the number of characters; variation of Golden Age stereotypes; strict observance of decorum, verisimilitude, and good taste; condemnation of loose imagination; use of blank verse instead of rhyme; insistence upon utilitarian justification; attention to costume; simplicity and clarity of style and avoidance of the excesses of Gongorism; and humor not found solely in the *gracioso*.

C. Ramón de la Cruz Cano y Olmedilla (1731–1794)

Ramón de la Cruz, the only dramatic author to run contrary to the Neoclassic current during the eighteenth century, wrote his first *décima* at the age of thirteen and at fifteen produced a *diálogo cómico*. He attempted unsuccessfully to write some tragedies in the Neoclassic fashion. The first Spaniard to translate *Hamlet*, he also reworked some dramas by Calderón. Finally deserting the sterile forms of Neoclassicism, he turned to realism and naturalness, with gratifying success.

With the failure of Neoclassicism, the public was ready for something new by the middle of the century. Much-needed social reforms instituted by the Bourbon monarchs made life more tolerable for Spaniards, who, more satisfied and relaxed, wanted to enjoy themselves. In response to the public resistance to Neoclassic theater and the resurgence of popular national spirit, Ramón de la Cruz almost singlehandedly brought national feeling and realism back to the stage. Through his *sainetes*, he gave the public what it wanted—a realistic theater based on observed customs, permeated with the spirit of Spain. He was scorned by the *afrancesados* but idolized by the public.

The *sainete* is a descendant of dramatic forms dating back to the mimes of Roman times. In Spain, the one-act farce began with the medieval *juegos de escarnio*. It was later cultivated by Juan del Encina (*Aucto del repelón*), Lope de Rueda (*pasos*), and Cervantes and Quiñones de Benavente (*entremeses*). In the

Golden Age, the *entremés* was played between the first and second acts of a longer play, and the *sainete* between the second and third. These types declined like everything else, but Ramón de la Cruz revived, renovated, and popularized the *sainete*. In his hands it became a one-act play in verse, about twenty minutes in length, with a negligible plot in which the comic element dominated.

The *sainete*, still used in the eighteenth century between acts, became a realistic portrayal of picturesque lower- and middle-class types of Madrid society and of Madrid life. The merit of Ramón de la Cruz's *sainetes* lies not in their short verse poetry, which was ordinary in quality, but in their documentary accuracy and portrayal of popular classes and interesting types of the day, such as *castañeras, majos, majas, manolos, petimetres,* and many others. Typical scenes that he re-created were dances, picnics, the marketplace, *tertulias,* and street quarrels. He satirized his contemporaries and ridiculed the *afrancesados* and their Neoclassic theater. He humorously mocked social abuses and vices in his trifling plots but always with vivid, accurate descriptions of Madrid life. He transferred to the stage without change what his eyes saw and his ears heard, for his creed was "Yo escribo y la verdad me dicta."

He inserted song and dance in his plays; used natural, colorful, idiomatic language; strove always to entertain; helped in the triumph of popular speech over the stilted, artificial language of Neoclassicism; and achieved lasting renown with a dramatic form that at best is a minor one. Some of his better-known *sainetes* are *La pradera de San Isidro, La casa de Tócame Roque, El Rastro por la mañana, Manolo,* and *El Prado por la noche.*

D. Leandro Fernández de Moratín (1760–1828)

After the death of his father, Moratín turned to writing and won two prizes from the Spanish Academy. Gaspar Melchor de Jovellanos secured him the position of secretary in the Spanish embassy in Paris. While there, Moratín frequented the salons and libraries, met Goldoni, translated two plays of his idol, Molière, and studied the French theater firsthand. Upon his return to Spain, he was patronized by Godoy and produced his first play in 1790, *El viejo y la niña. La comedia nueva o el café* in 1792 attacked the inanities in the theater at the turn of the century and ridiculed the hack writer Comella.

Though Moratín was timid and reserved, his sober and noble concept of the drama permitted him to satirize weaknesses and foibles. He believed that the drama should be a portrayal in dialogue of an event with realistic development of characters and speech and that it should exalt some virtue or truth or condemn some social evil. His masterpiece, *El sí de las niñas* (1806), reveals these principles and, as the first modern thesis play, condemns parental meddling in children's marriages. He followed Neoclassic principles in this play, although he used prose instead of verse and reduced the number of acts from five to three. Here, as in his plays in verse, *El viejo y la niña* (1790), *El barón* (1803), and *La mojigata* (1804), Moratín showed a special interest in the relations of youth and old age.

Having accepted from Joseph Bonaparte the position of director of the Royal Library, he felt his fellow Spaniards looked upon him as an *afrancesado,* and after withdrawing with the French when they fell from power, he eventually escaped to France, where he died in 1828.

Moratín's literary production is scant. His letters written during his extended travels in Europe are classed as the best in Spain, excepting those of Santa Teresa. He wrote only five original dramas. One regrets that his fears dried up his creative talents and splendid literary gifts, for he was the only Spaniard to combine successfully Neoclassicism and the Spanish spirit. Unlike Golden Age drama, Moratín's plays had simple plots, observed the unities, and were restrained.

Other works include a prose satire against literary affectation, quite humorous at times, *La derrota de los pedantes* (1789). In 1830 his *Orígenes del teatro español,* a study of the early Spanish drama, was published.

E. Minor Dramatists of the Eighteenth Century

1. *Nicolás Fernández de Moratín* (1737–1780), father of the more famous Leandro, was a vociferous critic of Calderón and Lope and a frequenter of all the literary academies and *tertulias.* He became the discussion leader at the Fonda de San Sebastián, a leading Neoclassic center in Madrid. Among his works are *La petimetra* (1762), which was the first Spanish Neoclassic attempt at comedy, though it was never performed; and three tragedies: *Lucrecia* (1763), *Guzmán el Bueno* (1777), and his best-known though equally unimpressive play *Hormesinda* (1770). Although

highly rated by the intellectuals, *Hormesinda* was a failure in the eyes of the public. Despite his efforts to imitate Neoclassic models, his best literary effort was a panegyric poem on bullfighting, *Fiesta de Toros en Madrid,* which succeeded because of its true national spirit.

2. *Agustín Montiano y Luyando* (1697–1765), one of the founders of the Academia del Buen Gusto, attempted unsuccessfully to put into practice his Neoclassic theories in two tragedies, *Virginia* (1750), which he hoped would serve as a Neoclassic model, and *Ataulfo* (1753). Lacking originality and creative ability, he insisted not only upon the three traditional unities of time, place, and action but also on a fourth that he called "unity of character."

3. *Vicente García de la Huerta* (1734–1787), though a Neoclassicist, somehow was able to surmount the coldness of the Neoclassic form and breathe a genuine Spanish flavor into his play *Raquel* (1778). This drama, written in strict conformity with Neoclassic rules, adhered to the three unities and the moral ending, though the author used three instead of five acts. According to Menéndez y Pelayo, it was "the great theatrical event in the reign of Carlos III." Although its exterior was Neoclassic, basically it was national in spirit, for it exemplified honor, bravery, gallantry, and an ardent Spanish nationalism, related in spirit to the Golden Age tradition. Its theme, which Juan Diamante, Lope de Vega, and Mira de Amescua had used before, concerns the love of Alfonso VIII for the Jewess of Toledo, Raquel.

4. *Tomás de Iriarte* (1750–1791), better known as a fabulist, is important in the Neoclassic theater for his two comedies, *El señorito mimado* and *La señorita malcriada,* the first about a dissipated youth and the second about a spoiled daughter and an indulgent father. Both appeared in 1788. His *Hacer que hacemos* (1770) was a failure, and his *El don de gentes* appeared posthumously.

A number of eighteenth-century authors, not primarily known as dramatists, tried their hand at this literary form. Their dramas include *El delincuente honrado* (1774), by Gaspar Melchor de Jovellanos (1744–1811); *Sancho García* (1771), by José Cadalso (1741–1782); *Las bodas de Camacho* (1784), by Juan Meléndez Valdés (1754–1817); *El duque de Viseo* (1801) and *Pelayo* (1805), by Manuel José Quintana (1772–1857); and *Zoraida* (1798), by Nicasio Alvarez Cienfuegos (1764–1809). Some authors,

63

among them Cándido María Trigueros (1736–1801) and Dionisio Solís (1774–1834), made revisions (*refundiciones*) of Golden Age plays.

ROMANTICISM

A. General Considerations

With the explosion of Romanticism in Spain in 1833, the unproductive formulas of Neoclassicism died, and Spain succumbed to the new literary fashion sweeping Europe. Romanticism was more a revolt against the precepts and moderation of Neoclassicism than it was a concrete literary movement. Consequently, Spain's dramatists abandoned all restraint, discarded the unities, mingled prose and verse, and mixed comedy with tragedy. Emotionalism, sensationalism, a sinister atmosphere, and the melodramatic replaced reason and moderation. Subjectivity replaced objectivity. Spaniards discovered Romanticism in Lope and Calderón and learned that the new movement was as much a revival as a revolt. There was a new interest in the national past, especially the Middle Ages, prompted in part by the studies of Johann Nicholas Böhl von Faber and the Schlegel brothers' enthusiasm for the *romancero* and Calderón. Violence, inexorable fate, and characters distinguished by their passions appeared on the Spanish stage. Musical and flexible poetry served as the vehicle for the mysterious and passionate.

Agustín Durán's influential document *Discurso sobre el influjo que ha tenido la crítica moderna en la decadencia del teatro antiguo español* (1828), in which he based his idea of Romanticism on the *Siglo de Oro,* Böhl von Faber's idea, defends the national theater; insists that each country must follow its own genius; declares that Spain's genius rests in the *Siglo de Oro* and in the popular element found in the epic, the *romancero,* and the theater; and maintains that Spanish literature declined because it left its natural bent.

B. Francisco Martínez de la Rosa (1787–1862)

Martínez de la Rosa, a compulsive neurotic about cleanliness, was in and out of politics all his life. Imprisoned and exiled for six years, he was freed by the *levantamiento de Riego* in 1820. Hated by the reactionaries and cruelly labeled "Rosita la pastelera," he attempted always to choose *el justo medio.*

Although he wrote one Romantic novel, *Doña Isabel de Solís* (1837), and other Romantic plays, Martínez de la Rosa is known primarily for two Romantic dramas: *Abén Humeya,* written in French in 1830, translated into Spanish in 1834, but not performed in Madrid until 1836; and *La conjuración de Venecia* (1834), in which some critics see the profound influence of Victor Hugo's *Hernani.* In *Abén Humeya* he stated that he wished to present a Spanish historical theme as something new and original but in keeping with good taste. *La conjuración de Venecia* presented for the first time the essential traits of Romantic tragedy: ubiquitous and inexorable fate, the pantheon, and unrestrained emotionalism. Yet the lovers are well drawn. In both plays, the author makes use of local color, disregards the unities, and cultivates the sensational and exotic, mystery, extravagance, and suspense.

C. Angel de Saavedra, Duque de Rivas (1791–1865)

The Duque de Rivas, born into a family of grandees, fought valiantly for the Republic and was wounded several times. For his political activities he was twice exiled, first as a liberal and later as a conservative. In after years he served his country in important posts at home and abroad.

While living on the island of Malta, he was urged by the Englishman John H. Frere, a Romanticist, to seek poetic themes in the history of his own country. This Rivas accomplished with the writing of *El moro expósito,* his first Romantic work.

Rivas wrote several Neoclassic dramas, such as *Aliatar* (1816), but he is most famous for the Romantic drama *Don Alvaro o la fuerza del sino* (1835), which confirmed the triumph of Romanticism in Spain. Here Rivas condensed all the aesthetic ideas of Romanticism and created a Romantic hero to compete with Werther or Manfred. Its premiere in Madrid was sensational, as Rivas ran the gamut of the elements of the Romantic theater: duels, nocturnal meetings, tempests, thunder, fate, and suicide.

Don Alvaro, the typical Romantic hero, is of mysterious origin, yet clearly a gentleman. Denied even a moment's happiness by an unrelenting fate, he is driven to commit crimes against his

65

will and even denied the solace of an honorable death. The drama is full of wild, emotional elements, and its verse is sonorous and passionate.

Despite the intense Romanticism of the play, Rivas, an excellent painter, made use of realistic local color at the beginning of each act through *cuadros de costumbres,* which portray situations true to life. This, along with a few comic elements, afforded relief from the tenseness of the plot. With his excellent plastic sense and power of observation, Rivas was able to give detailed instructions for stage settings, scenery, and machines. The implicit social commentary and Alvaro's final despair, defiance, and suicide add to this drama's unique impact. *Don Alvaro* was immensely popular in its day and is still readable. Its fame soon spread abroad, where it influenced Verdi's opera *La forza del destino.*

El desengaño en un sueño (1844), considered by many to be as important as *Don Alvaro,* is reminiscent of Gracián's *Criticón,* Shakespeare's *The Tempest,* and especially Calderón's *La vida es sueño.* On the basis of this work, Valbuena ranks Rivas second only to Calderón in symbolic drama. Readers have praised Rivas's poetry, dramatic interest, and especially his profound philosophical thought in this version of the theme of the awakened sleeper. Filled with the standard Romantic intrigue, mystery, apparitions, and murder, the play emphasizes disillusion with the world.

D. Juan Eugenio Hartzenbusch (1806–1880)

Hartzenbusch, son of a German father and Spanish mother, had to practice his father's vocation, cabinetmaking, when the absolutist reaction of 1823 deprived his family of all its wealth. Later his acknowledged erudition gained him good positions, and he was happily employed all his life.

In addition to solid works of literary criticism, Hartzenbusch wrote *costumbrista* sketches and poetry that was mostly erudite, moral, philosophical, and political. His fables reveal a good sense of humor. He translated French and Italian plays and later turned to reworking *comedias* of Lope, Tirso, and Calderón and producing editions for the *Biblioteca de Autores Españoles.* He wrote twenty-nine dramas, most of them carefully constructed and polished, in which he used historical, Biblical, and magical themes. He also wrote some thesis plays.

His place in Spanish literary history stems, however, from

his best play, *Los amantes de Teruel,* written in 1835 but not produced until 1837. Actually, he wrote two versions of this drama, based on an old Spanish legend used previously by other dramatists. The 1837 version contains five acts. The 1849 revision has four acts and changes especially the role of Margarita, Isabel's mother. Hartzenbusch may not have succeeded in producing the great love drama of the Spanish theater, but personal tragedy and Romantic techniques aside, he managed to create an unusual historical play filled with a strong social sense and with characters who far excel the Romantic stereotypes of the day.

E. Antonio García Gutiérrez (1813–1884)

Partly because of disappointment at not seeing his play *El trovador* produced, the author joined the army. When it was produced for the first time in 1836, he left his post without permission to see it.

García Gutiérrez composed some poetry and some *artículos de costumbres.* He authored some eighty plays, served as director of the National Library, and was elected to the Spanish Academy in 1862. Among his half dozen outstanding plays, one should mention his masterpiece, *El trovador* (1836), as well as *Simón Bocanegra* (1843), *Venganza catalana* (1864), and *Juan Lorenzo* (1865). He wrote in the usual manner of the Romanticists, employing historicolegendary themes, sonorous and declamatory verse, startling dramatic effects, dungeons, battlefield scenes, and unbridled passions, revealing a rich and vivid imagination.

In *El trovador,* combining prose and verse in five acts, García Gutiérrez reveals his outstanding ability to portray female protagonists. As in other dramas, he concentrates here on the power of love and vengeance. He used his play to deliver his sentiments about revolution and a liberal political and social message.

F. José Zorrilla y Moral (1817–1893)

This "spoiled darling" of Romanticism became a public favorite overnight when he recited his poetic composition at Larra's burial in 1837. He wrote voluminously, leaving volumes of lyric poetry, *leyendas,* and drama. Leading a haphazard bohemian existence, he unwisely married a woman many years his senior and was later widowed.

He went to Mexico, where Maximilian made him court poet and granted him a pension. He was enthusiastically received upon his return to Spain, and many honors were bestowed on him. Yet he spent his last days in poverty.

Zorrilla was an exuberant, often careless, and hasty writer, an inveterate improviser, and a shallow thinker; but perhaps his greatest literary sin was verbosity. Although genuine pearls appear in his work, one is dismayed at the amount of mediocre verse one must digest before coming across one of the loftier passages. He had the knack of versification, however, and regardless of his faults, he was capable of attaining great lyrical heights almost effortlessly. His theater is alive, passionate, and national in spirit. He wrote *comedias de capa y espada* in the Golden Age tradition, Classical tragedies, and historicolegendary plays based upon moving incidents from national history. Among the best of his more than thirty plays are *El puñal del godo* (1842); *El zapatero y el rey* (1840); and *Traidor, inconfeso y mártir* (1849), the latter of which is considered by many critics to be his best play. In three acts and verse, it revives the *sebastianista* theme as the mysterious central character, Gabriel Espinosa, is suspected of being King Sebastian of Portugal. José María Díaz is credited with having collaborated on the second act.

Zorrilla is remembered mainly, however, for one play, *Don Juan Tenorio* (1844). This world-famous figure, first dramatized by Tirso and used by others before Zorrilla, received his most successful reincarnation at the hands of the "troubadour poet." Zorrilla despised his own play for its obvious imperfections, which he himself pointed out, and sold it for a handful of *reales*. He referred to its *mal gusto* and *ligereza improvisora*. Yet it became the most successful play of the nineteenth century and is still played at the approach of All Saints' Day in many important Spanish-speaking centers. Despite its shortcomings, such as its improbabilities, inconsistencies, and other signs of careless craftsmanship, it has become an international institution and has delighted the common people for almost a century and a half.

Some of the appeal of this drama may be accounted for by the fascination of the main character himself, his charm and seductiveness, and the popularity of the theme. Equally attractive is the combination of adventure with a religious theme. Also, Zorrilla's don Juan may be more appealing to some than Tirso's, for he is more human and more generous, and his doña Inés is more attractive than her counterpart in Tirso's version. Finally, the conclusion of Zorrilla's drama, in which don Juan repents and is saved from damnation, may be more pleasant to contemplate than Tirso's ending, in which don Juan, repenting too late, is consumed by the fires of hell. Brisk, vigorous, colorful, filled with emotion, and melodiously versified, *Don Juan Tenorio* is one of Spain's best-known dramas.

G. Mariano José de Larra (1809–1837)

Angel del Río has pointed out that Larra was the opposite of Rivas. Rivas was Romantic in form and Classical in spirit, while Larra was Classical in form and Romantic in spirit. Best known as a composer of *artículos de costumbres* and a literary critic, Larra wrote one of the successes of the Romantic theater, *Macías* (1834). He had written a novel on the same theme, *El doncel de don Enrique el Doliente* (1834), and the play is a dramatization of the novel, but the theatrical production differs considerably from the novelistic account. Enrique Piñeyro considered *Macías*, which influenced both *El trovador* and *Los amantes de Teruel*, to be the first Spanish Romantic drama in verse, though Larra refused to label it as either Neoclassic or Romantic.

Larra had excellent gifts as a satirist and prosist, but he was not exceptionally endowed as a dramatist. He wrote several adaptations of French plays, mostly under the pseudonym Ramón Arriala. The best of them, which Larra defended as quite original, was *No más mostrador* (1831), a satiric comedy based on a work by Scribe.

H. Other Romantic Dramatists

Many others contributed to the Romantic theater in Spain. Some were total converts, some were lukewarm experimenters in their youth, some were Eclectics, others were writers of thesis plays, and still others wrote chiefly in altogether different genres. At one time in their careers, however, they tried the Romantic drama, an indication of how deeply Romanticism had permeated the literary fabric of the time. The following belong at least in part to Spain's Romantic theater: Mariano Roca de Togores (1812–1889), Tomás Rodríguez Díaz Rubí (1817–1890), Gertrudis Gómez de Avellaneda (1814–1873), Eulogio Florentino Sanz (1825?–1881), Patricio de la Escosura (1807–1878), Carolina Coronado (1820–1911), Eugenio de Ochoa (1815–1872),

Antonio Gil y Zárate (1793–1861), Manuel Bretón de los Herreros (1796–1873), and Ventura de la Vega (1807–1865).

THE REALISTIC THEATER OF THE NINETEENTH CENTURY

A. General Considerations

The Realistic theater of didactic intent existed before the Romantic movement became the leading literary movement, and outlived Romanticism by some fifty years. In the first half of the century the Eclectics dominated, combining Classical and Romantic ideas. In the transition period between Romanticism and Realism, playwrights largely abandoned historical dramas, though some continued to produce them with more attention to detail and psychological elements. With the rise of the middle class around 1850, a new type of social satire called *alta comedia* appeared. By the end of the century it had evolved toward the elegant modern comedy of Benavente.

Realists developed the drama of social satire and the thesis play, showing a decided preference for criticizing the weaknesses, foibles, and vices of their contemporaries. They also felt compelled to censure materialism in an age when money provided more luxuries and pleasures. In many cases the liberal and modern ideas expressed by an author through his characters offered a dramatic contrast with the traditional motives of honor and duty. In their thesis plays dramatists failed to find any real answers and often resorted to commonplace doctrines or even passionate outbursts.

B. Manuel Bretón de los Herreros (1796–1873)

Bretón, who wrote before, during, and after the Romantic movement, was immune to its effects. He cultivated instead a *costumbrista* theater related in spirit to the work of Mesonero Romanos. First a soldier and later a journalist, as a dramatist he was the best follower of the Moratinian tradition, without his master's precision but with more naturalness and comic force. Abandoning the strict Moratinian style, he took the first steps toward a Realistic comedy of manners and a drama of social satire but without serious philosophical pretensions.

Bretón was at his best when dealing with bourgeois customs, especially in a satiric and critical manner. Yet, never bitter, he exemplified a festive and pleasant spirit that allowed him to satirize without offending. In addition to composing more than one hundred original dramas, he translated copiously from the French theater and produced ten *refundiciones* of Golden Age dramas.

Among his best dramas are *Marcela o ¿cuál de los tres?* (1831), a comically satiric play dealing with the quandary of a girl who has to choose one of three unfit suitors, a situation that gives Bretón the opportunity to satirize middle-class types; and *Muérete y verás* (1837), a satiric play in which the rarity of true friendship is illustrated by the admonition: Die, and you will see who your true friends are. Other important titles are *El pelo de la dehesa* (1840) and *La escuela del matrimonio* (1852).

C. Ventura de la Vega (1807–1865)

Born in Buenos Aires, Vega came to Spain at an early age and soon achieved prominence. His early reputation stemmed from his translations and imitations of the Song of Songs (1825) and Psalms (1826). He adapted tragedies from the French, especially from Scribe, and wrote some historical plays, but his best work is in the Moratinian style, and he was most effective in the drama of social criticism. An Eclectic, he continued Bretón's work and initiated the *alta comedia,* later perfected by López de Ayala. Of fifteen plays, his best is *El hombre de mundo* (1845), a satiric portrayal of the life of the middle classes, anticipating somewhat the work of Benavente.

Also interested in a minor art form, Vega initiated the modern *zarzuela.* His *Jugar con fuego,* with music by Barbieri, can still be heard with pleasure.

D. Manuel Tamayo y Baus (1829–1898)

Born the son of actors and married to an actress, Tamayo showed an inclination for the theater at an early age and developed into one of the outstanding dramatists between Moratín and Benavente. An Eclectic, he tried every form of the drama among his more than fifty theatrical pieces: Classical tragedy, Romantic national dramas, and Realistic comedies of moral intent. He also adapted and translated foreign plays. Among his works are *Virginia* (1853), a five-act tragedy in verse about

71

honor and liberty; *La locura de amor* (1855), a Romantic historical play based upon the life of Juana *la Loca*, filled with sentiment and passion; *La bola de nieve* (1856), about the effects of unfounded jealousy; *Lances de honor* (1863), a thesis play about dueling; *No hay mal que por bien no venga* (1868); and *Los hombres de bien* (1870).

His masterpiece, *Un drama nuevo* (1867), a three-act tragedy, excels other plays of its time. It tells the story of Yorick, the clown of Shakespeare's troupe, who plays on the stage the part of the deceived husband only to find that he is playing the same part in real life. This play influenced Leoncavallo's opera *I Pagliacci*.

As a social critic, Tamayo continued the trend established by Bretón and Vega in satirizing the middle class. Particularly incensed by the Positivism and love of money in his day, Tamayo criticized them in *Lo positivo* (1862). His dramatic creed, he claimed, was to paint "el retrato moral del hombre con todas sus deformidades . . . y emplearlo como instrumento de la Providencia para realizar ejemplos de provechosa enseñanza."

E. Adelardo López de Ayala (1828–1879)

López de Ayala, whose work resembles that of his intimate friend Tamayo y Baus, also inherited the style of Bretón and Vega and refined it in his *alta comedia*. His artistic production consists of two distinct periods; he first wrote historical plays and then thesis plays. But even in his historical period he tried to develop "un pensamiento moral, profundo y consolador." He made this assertion in the preface to his first historical piece, *Un hombre de estado* (1851), in which he concentrates on the responsibilities of leadership and the virtue of duty.

His thesis plays, written to criticize and yet improve the lives of his contemporaries, emphasize moral themes, at times to the loss of dramatic impact. Some compare him with Juan Ruiz de Alarcón because of his careful attention to detail and skillful juggling of language and effects. His first such play was *El tejado de vidrio* (1856). In the better-known *El tanto por ciento* (1861), an attack on materialism, Positivism, and greed, López de Ayala preaches in favor of high public and private morals, insisting that true love is more important than money, a favorite concept of his. *Consuelo* (1878), his masterpiece, presents his one good character study (not his strong point because of his emphasis on a thesis) in the portrait of a woman who chooses wealth over love, to her sorrow.

F. José Echegaray (1832–1916)

Echegaray, a crowd pleaser, made concessions to public taste and ruled as undisputed king of the stage from 1874, with the appearance of his first play, *El libro talonario,* to the end of the century, when Benavente revolutionized dramatic literature. Echegaray, unloved by twentieth-century critics, was awarded the Nobel Prize in literature, which he shared with the Provençal poet Mistral. The award aroused a storm of protest in Spain among the writers of the younger generation who rebelled against everything for which Echegaray stood.

An important physicist and mathematician as well as a politician and statesman and the founder of the Bank of Spain, Echegaray wrote his first play at age forty-two and thereafter turned out one or two "hits" a year, producing some seventy plays. Though the critics kept pointing out his shortcomings, the public responded enthusiastically to his plays. Each premiere was received with noisy acclaim.

Though he is generally classified as a belated Romanticist, Echegaray attended the theater regularly in his student days in Madrid to see the Romantic works of Hartzenbusch and the Realistic ones of López de Ayala and Tamayo y Baus. These authors influenced his formation and development as a dramatist. His thesis plays, melodramatic and sensational, nonetheless depart from the usual Romantic technique by replacing the legendary and exotic with problems of the home and modern society. Echegaray also used the honor theme, placing his characters in agonizing situations in which they have to choose between duty and passion. About half of his plays were in verse, but he frequently used grandiloquent and sensational prose. He preferred to deal with strong emotions, and most of his plays end in tragedy and death. Although his plots were precisely engineered, Echegaray had little regard for logic or psychological verity, and he strained for effect in declamatory and exaggerated dialogue. His inflexible personages move about in a conventional world, harassed by a passion or *idée fixe* that leads to their own death or to someone else's. Creatures of his imagination, many of his characters border on the abnormal. His unyielding situations seem contrived, and his plays exhibit an

73

unusual patchwork of influences, among them Calderón, Romanticism, Naturalism, Ibsen, and social criticism.

The best of his day despite his faults, Echegaray had a lively imagination, a fecundity of invention, a keen sense of tragedy, and an unerring ability to portray the strong situation. His dramas created emotion and stirred audiences deeply, perhaps because he believed that "lo sublime del arte está en el llanto, en el dolor, y la muerte." Using honor, duty, and love, with a liberal sprinkling of adultery together with the time-worn fate motive, he filled his plays with feverish and exaggerated passions; but he also applied his art to the social problems and prejudices of his society.

Echegaray's two best-known plays are *O locura o santidad* (1877) and *El gran galeoto* (1881), the latter regarded as his masterpiece. The first of these, a combination thesis and honor play, relates the story of a quixotic protagonist whose sense of duty inclines him to return his wealth to its rightful owners. To forestall any such insanity, his own heirs commit him to an asylum. Typically, Echegaray insists upon the enforcement of honor even though the innocent will be hurt, and he exploits the dramatic situation skillfully. *El gran galeoto* deals with slander and frivolous gossip that destroy a marriage. Society as a whole is responsible, for as one of the victims says in the prologue, "el gran galeoto" is "todo el mundo." Filled with passionate outbursts and characters writhing in melodramatic agony, the play can only end in tragedy. Here again, Echegaray combines an honor tragedy, social protest, and Romantic passion.

Other important titles of Echegaray's production are *La esposa del vengador* (1874); *El puño de la espada* (1875); *El seno de la muerte* (1879); *La muerte en los labios* (1880); *El hijo de don Juan* (1892); *Mariana* (1892); *Mancha que limpia* (1895); and *A fuerza de arrastrarse* (1905).

G. Benito Pérez Galdós (1843–1920)

Although he was Spain's foremost novelist after Cervantes, Galdós unsuccessfully attempted to write for the theater in his early twenties. His first mature play, however, was not performed until 1892. Possessor of a keen psychological insight and the ability to create powerful characters, he nonetheless lacked the dramatic technique and feeling needed to create the perfect play. Many of his plays, dramatizations of his novels, by necessity develop more succinctly and clearly social theses involving justice, truth, and individual liberty.

Despite his relative failure as a dramatist, the strength, deep emotion, and sharp insight into human nature that characterize his novels are visible in his plays. *Electra* (1901), his most successful drama, reiterates a favorite theme of the author, the conflict between obscurantism and progress. *El abuelo* (1904), a stage adaptation of his novel by the same name, attempts to show the leveling power of love and that nobility is not a matter of birth but of spirit and heart, another favorite theme. Other plays are *La loca de la casa* (1893) and *La de San Quintín* (1894).

H. Lesser Dramatists of the Nineteenth Century

1. *Gaspar Núñez de Arce* (1834–1903), better known as a lyric poet, wrote a number of dramas, among them his masterpiece, *El haz de leña* (1872), recognized as the best historical play of the nineteenth century. The author, promoting religious tolerance, exhibits good psychological penetration and empathy in delineating the struggle between love and duty in the father (Felipe II) of a rebellious son (Carlos). Other plays are *Deudas de la honra* (1863) and *Quien debe paga* (1867).

2. *Joaquín Dicenta* (1863–1917) unsuccessfully attempted to apply Echegaray's violent emotion to proletarian themes. Credited with initiating Naturalism on the Spanish stage, Dicenta preferred themes such as those of an honest workman made a criminal by brutal treatment (*Juan José,* 1895) and a convict regenerated by love (*El lobo,* 1913).

Eugenio Sellés (1844–1926), with *El nudo gordiano* (1878), and *Leopoldo Cano* (1844–1934), author of *La opinión pública* (1878), could not equal Echegaray's lead. *Enrique Gaspar* (1842–1902), with his satire, Realism, and social consciousness, took a stride toward Benavente.

I. The *género chico*

In the second half of the nineteenth century the *zarzuela,* in its modern version a one-act operetta with music, song, and sometimes dancing alternating with dialogue, became immensely popular in Spain. Whether satiric, popular, or *costumbrista, zarzuelas* frequently depict in a comical vein low-life character types of Madrid. One of the most successful composers of *zarzuelas* was Francisco Asenjo Barbieri. Among writers of books are Ricardo de la Vega, Carlos Arniches, Javier de Burgos, and Vital Aza. Musicians include Valverde, Chapí, and Tomás Bretón. One of the best-loved *zarzuelas* is *La verbena de la paloma* by Ricardo de la Vega and Tomás Bretón.

TWENTIETH-CENTURY DRAMA

A. General Considerations

During the first thirty years or so of the twentieth century, Spanish drama took several directions, but the major innovators were Ramón del Valle-Inclán and Jacinto Grau. A number of writers contributed to a lesser degree. Despite the changes wrought by these dramatists, many of the nineteenth-century tendencies of the Realistic theater continued. Pérez Galdós wrote psychological dramas of the individual against society. Manuel Linares Rivas, theoretically a disciple of Benavente's, reflected more the nineteenth-century thesis play. Carlos Arniches, who began with the *género chico*, fused comic and tragic elements in full-length dramas, concentrating on the environment of Madrid and anticipating to a degree later experiments in the Theater of the Absurd.

The brothers Joaquín and Serafín Alvarez Quintero wrote about Andalusia, but their sentimental portraits, amiable reflections, and idealized pieces did little to advance the drama. Pedro Muñoz Seca entertained with exaggerated plays featuring comic types and absurd situations. Modernists such as Francisco Villaespesa and Eduardo Marquina wrote poetic theater, partly in reaction to Benavente's drawing room comedies. Marquina, more successful than Villaespesa, composed heroic dramas that emphasized traditional Spanish virtues and Spain's successful past, as well as some meaningful rural dramas.

Two members of the Generation of 1898, Unamuno and Azorín, wrote interesting dramatic works, the former dealing with problems of personality and Existential approximations of reality, the latter producing Surrealistic plays of the subconscious that anticipated certain aspects of García Lorca's work. Ramón Gómez de la Serna also attempted Surrealism with greater emphasis on sexuality. Finally, Gregorio Martínez Sierra, almost forgotten today, praised family values and good Christian women.

Benavente's immensely popular drawing room comedies, urban works, and provincial plays, done in a witty, ironic, though often superficial manner, undoubtedly made him a major figure. Yet, though he gave the death blow to Echegaray's melodramas, he contributed little to dramatic innovation. Ramón del Valle-Inclán was more important from a developmental point of view. He wrote universal, timeless plays, involving various archetypes. In his *esperpentos,* in which caricature did not disguise social concerns, he provided artistic deformations of traditional reality, thereby exhibiting aspects of the Theater of the Absurd. Jacinto Grau, who rejected commercialism for experimentation, attempted to synthesize various forms in his dramas and treated universal, eternal, transcendental problems, essentially tragic in tone.

The two major dramatists of the 1930s were García Lorca and Alejandro Casona, although a number of contributions were made by others, among them Rafael Alberti; Max Aub, who wrote before and after the thirties; Miguel Mihura, whose comic works were not performed until the 1950s; Jardiel Poncela, whose ironic parodies and self-mocking satires may be the most humorous of the century; and Miguel Hernández and Pedro Salinas, who, like Alberti, were more famous as poets.

In his theater, García Lorca combined his lyrical genius with Andalusian folklore, music, and dance to create symbolic dramas of archetypes and elemental passions. Though he flirted with Surrealism, he is best known for his rural dramas, in which he emphasizes the tragedy of inhibited personal liberty and, through symbols like the moon, the inevitable death that stalks us all. Casona excelled at the interplay of reality and fantasy. He believed in confronting reality and life, however painful, and stressed the impossibility of escape through madness or evasion. Among his other themes are concepts of punishment, redemption, and the power of true love.

A number of playwrights produced works in the 1940s and on into the 1950s and 1960s, extolling political, moral, or historical points of view in both serious and comic veins. Among these writers are José María Pemán, who began producing plays in the 1930s; Joaquín Calvo Sotelo; Juan Ignacio Luca de Tena; José López Rubio, whose major works appeared in the 1950s; and Victor Ruiz de Iriarte, whose works are elegant and witty.

The two major figures from the 1950s on are Antonio Buero

Vallejo and Alfonso Sastre. Buero's *Historia de una escalera* (1949) is one of the landmark dramatic productions of the twentieth century, and Buero continued to write dramas in the 1980s on historical, social, and moral themes and even in a fantastic and mythical vein. He uses a historical perspective to analyze current Spanish imperatives and believes in an open tragedy of hope. Buero is a master of technique and uses darkness and light, other arts, and Brechtian distancing to produce plays that almost always show compassion for human sorrows.

Alfonso Sastre has produced a number of somewhat revolutionary plays. In contrast with Buero's concept of *posibilismo,* that is, writing plays that can be produced even in a dictatorial society, Sastre prefers leftist dramas, even though they may not be performed, that is, *imposibilismo.* Most of his plays, unlike Buero's, present the audience with an Existentially closed situation. Though he is to an extent overly intellectual, Sastre supports the rights of individuals in a tragic, often inhumane world. He deals with moral responsibility, guilt, hate, love, and the pain of being part of humanity. Alfonso Paso, who was at first associated with Sastre's experimental theatrical group, wrote numerous dramas and popular tragicomedies, many of them in Mihura's ironic tradition.

Two other major playwrights of the 1960s, both of whom had to contend with the censorship of Franco's Spain, were Lauro Olmo and Carlos Muñiz, although writers from previous generations continued to produce plays. Olmo concentrated on the reality of a hypocritical society and themes like emigration. Muñiz wrote both Realistic and Expressionistic dramas that criticize the social situation, especially of the middle class.

Other writers one should mention include José Martín Recuerda, who began writing in the 1950s and was interested in both placid and revolutionary characters in an Andalusian setting; J. M. Rodríguez Méndez, who abandoned Realism to expose, through grotesque distortions, the reality of Spanish society; and Fernando Arrabal, who left Spain for Paris in the early 1950s and wrote most of his plays in French. Arrabal created a special Theater of the Absurd, or Theater of Panic, to use his own term. Also in the 1960s and 1970s a number of playwrights, because of censorship, wrote a kind of subterranean theater, often political allegories. The two best known of these underground dramatists are José Ruibal and Eduardo Quiles.

In the 1970s more experimentation took place, frequently involving foreign models, and with Franco's death in 1975, an explosion of previously forbidden sexual and libertarian themes appeared.

The 1980s saw continuing activity in the theater, with a variety of themes from homosexuality to history, combining reality and fantasy, exploring aspects of Surrealism and re-creating traditional literature. Buero Vallejo, Alfonso Sastre, Lauro Olmo, Jaime Salom, Antonio Gala, José Luis Alonso de Santos, Francisco Nieva, and many others continue to be active in the Spanish theater.

B. Jacinto Benavente y Martínez (1866–1954)

Benavente freed the drama from the moribund melodramatic tradition established by Echegaray. Among his 172 plays, Benavente wrote psychological, satiric, rural, fantastic, sentimental, historical, and even Surrealistic dramas, though many of his theatrical works seem to have more narrative than dramatic force, and his characters talk much but do little. After *El nido ajeno* (1894), his first successful play, he produced an even more merciless satire, *Gente conocida* (1896), which helped establish his reputation. In these early works, Benavente presents a succession of types whose shortcomings he pitilessly exposes. Only occasionally in his early plays does one encounter a noble person. Although most of his characters are hollow, hypocritical, and vain, at times Benavente curiously reveals compassion for the weaknesses of human beings. He attacked the aristocracy because, he said, it was more charitable to laugh at those with advantages than at the disadvantaged. Most of these dramas are conversational or drawing room comedies.

Between 1901 and 1904 Benavente produced eighteen dramas in an often malicious, skeptical, or cynical vein that dissect the hypocrisy of Spanish society. He wrote in an elegant but natural language and managed to create a few credible characters. Among the more interesting of these works we find *Lo cursi* (1901), an attack on the excesses of Modernism; *La gobernadora* (1901), an exposé of the corruption and lust for power in a provincial town; *La noche del sábado* (1903), a dissection of selfish ambition and a contrast between good and evil, a constant preoccupation of Benavente's; and *El dragón de fuego* (1904), a contrast between Oriental stoicism and Occidental materialism. One of Benavente's most incisive satires, *Los malhechores del bien* (1905), ridicules the abuses of false charity and religious hypocrisy.

Between 1907 and 1913, Benavente's twenty-five dramas revealed him as a more mature, confident, and versatile writer. In many of these dramas one finds a moral and humanitarian tone that is absent in some of his earlier works, and he emphasizes the necessity for the well-being and happiness of children. His father, a pediatrician, may have influenced some of his works, which reflect a deep knowledge of youngsters. Of this period, *Los intereses creados* (1907) is undoubtedly his best work, and it is considered by many to be his outstanding dramatic achievement. Benavente resorts to the grotesque masks of the Italian *commedia dell'arte* for his types. The ideas and sentiments, the vision of the world and life, differ little from his philosophy expressed elsewhere, but they have in this play a classic simplicity that is striking. Through their actions the puppets show us the hidden threads by which men are moved in life, the good and bad passions that inspire their actions. The rogue, Crispín, is the motivating force that sets off the various movements and puts them at the service of his master, Leandro. The contrasts that each man carries within himself are revealed, but the small and petty passions, vanities, and ambitions are treated with a satire of generous and humanitarian overtones that insists upon the power of love in human motivations, in spite of the creation of bonds of interest by Crispín for his idealistic master. Symbolically, Leandro represents the good, and Crispín, the wickedness of the human soul.

Two rural dramas complete the important work of this period: *Señora ama* (1908) and *La malquerida* (1913). The former attempts to define the Castilian spirit and soul. The latter reveals the consequences of the incestuous love of a father for his stepdaughter. Raimunda, the wife, struggles between hatred and pity for her husband because of this relationship and the murder stemming from it. In 1945 Benavente wrote a third, less successful, rural drama, *La Infanzona*.

Even though Benavente won the Nobel Prize in 1922, his plays after 1920 were largely unsuccessful. Probably the best of his works during his last thirty-four years were *Para el cielo y los altares* (1928), a prophetic work about approaching revolution; *La ciudad doliente* (1945), which in Pirandello fashion brings a novelist to the stage to discuss life with his own creations; and *Abdicación* (1948), a contrast between old and modern Spain. These years reveal the almost pathetic dichotomy between Benavente's own political and idealistic beliefs.

Benavente introduced a drama into Spain that in spite of its sometimes overlong conversations and discourses preaches the eternal truth that man cannot call himself free and happy unless he has dominion over his own soul. One might point to many characteristics he exhibits in his total works, such as elegance of style, ingeniousness in ideas, cynicism, subtle irony, skepticism, and tenderness. In his early criticism of society, he is less compassionate than he is later, but beneath his smile or irony we see a trace of kindness in all his works and an almost poetic and lyrical evaluation of life.

C. Ramón del Valle-Inclán (1866–1936)

Francisco Ruiz Ramón believes that Valle-Inclán's dramas are among the most revolutionary in the history of the Spanish theater. This, if true, may account for their lack of popularity until many years after the author's death. Among Valle-Inclán's plays are mythological works, farces, and *esperpentos*. He sought new paths constantly for theatrical expression and, while assimilating aspects of Symbolism and Expressionism, anticipated much of the Theater of the Absurd and produced a timeless and universal drama.

His first dramatic work, *Cenizas* (1899), is a reelaboration of *Femeninas* (1895), his first prose work. It treats the theme of adultery in a new manner and reflects the author's sensuality and the end-of-the-century perversity of some of his work. Most of Valle-Inclán's dramas are descriptive and project a narrative power, as, for example, in *El Marqués de Bradomín* (1907), a theatrical version of his *Sonata de Otoño* but with a different ending. In his *Comedias Bárbaras,* a trilogy of plays—*Aguila de blasón* (1907), *Romance de lobos* (1908), and *Cara de plata* (1922)—Valle-Inclán's interest in superstition and fascination with death continue. In these plays he reveals a masterful use of chiaroscuro. He uses archetypal and Freudian themes, at times with Nietzschean overtones, in his depiction of a protagonist, Juan Manuel de Montenegro, insatiably erotic, a Galician don Juan who lives in a disintegrating world of madness, violent conflicts, sex, and death. Montenegro represents an expiring feudal nobility and, in spite of his proclivities, exhibits a conscience and sense of nobility not shared by his sinful sons. Perhaps the most moving of these plays is *Romance de lobos,* which recounts the death of the protagonist. Among other plays, *El embrujado* (1913) again shows us a superstitious world ruled by fatality and death. *Divinas palabras* (1920) concerns a hydrocephalic dwarf, the focus of passion and death, and, combining cruelty and compassion with grotesque elements, anticipates Valle-Inclán's *esperpento* phase.

In the same year, *Luces de Bohemia,* his most famous *esperpento,* published in definitive form in 1924, appeared. The protagonist, Max Estrella, defined the new form as a concave carnival mirror in which the boundaries of the possible and the credible blur. Valle-Inclán attributed the invention of the *esperpento* to Goya and used the deforming mirror and its grotesque projections to come to grips with a more truthful and profound reality. The play deals with historical events between 1917 and 1920, and although highly stylized, it projects a painful Spanish reality. The author here anticipates the work of Beckett, Ionesco, and Adamov. Among Valle-Inclán's other *esperpentos* is *Los cuernos de Don Friolera* (1921), a grotesque, satiric, humorous commentary on Calderonian *pundonor.* Through a puppet show we see the negative aspects of humanity and the futility of trusting the Church, the government, or the military. *Las galas del difunto* (1926), a deformation of the don Juan myth, and *La hija del capitán* (1927), an attack on the dictatorship of Primo de Rivera, are other *esperpentos.* Grotesque elements are found not only in the *esperpentos* but also in many of Valle-Inclán's plays. Other Valle-Inclán plays include *Cuento de abril* (1910), *Voces de gesta* (1911), *La marquesa Rosalinda* (1912), and *La rosa de papel* (1924).

D. Jacinto Grau Delgado (1877–1958)

Jacinto Grau, one of the great renovators of the Spanish drama, never achieved much popular success, but he attempted, through his symbolic, intellectual theater, to return to the drama a dignity that commercialization had largely removed. As sources, he used Biblical themes (*El hijo pródigo,* 1918), the *romancero* (*El Conde Alarcos,* 1917), and the Classical drama (*El burlador que no se burla,* 1930). In view of his insistence upon new attitudes toward the theater and his attacks on producers and impresarios, it is not surprising that his plays were often boycotted in Madrid, though they were warmly received in other countries.

Even in his earliest efforts he revealed a subtlety, poetic vision, and dynamic style, concentrating thematically on the power of human love. Among his many important dramas are the following: *Don Juan de Carillana* (1913), about an older don Juan who falls in love with a mysterious woman who turns out to be his own daughter; *El señor de Pigmalión* (1921), an allegory of human selfishness involving puppets with almost human abilities who rebel against their creator; *El burlador que no se burla,* about a don Juan who knew all the secrets of a woman's heart but could not fathom those of death; and *La casa del diablo* (1933), quite similar to Sartre's *Les jeux sont faits* (1947), about people, after death, forced to suffer life again until they discover real love.

Grau, who exhibited a definite fondness for Existential themes, was a robust, virile, deep, human, and expressive writer. He promoted the view that true charity is love and all great love is charity. Having faith in humanity, he tried for a better world through combating the laws of nature that rule man blindly. In his plays he talked of free will, freedom through action, reality versus the ideal, the domination of women by men, the overwhelming power of sexual attraction, and salvation through love. Few dramatists in Spanish theatrical history are his equal in terms of maturity, ingenuity, philosophical depth, psychological analysis, character portrayal, and freshness in form, background, and language.

E. Other Dramatists of the First Thirty Years

1. *Carlos Arniches* (1866–1943) wrote over sixty original dramas and collaborated on a great many others. He started his career with the *género chico,* and his *sainetes,* together with his longer works, show that he was a comic genius with his linguistic experimentations. Among his best *sainetes* are *Las estrellas* (1904) and *Los milagros del jornal* (1924). Among his longer plays, which he labeled "tragedias grotescas," *La señorita de Trévelez* (1916) is his most famous. His work is a mixture of the comic and tragic, whatever the caricatures or grotesque situations may be, and it affords us a general social criticism of his country and time.

2. *Manuel Linares Rivas* (1867–1938) employs a satiric and moral tone in his examination of human weaknesses, often caused by laws or passing circumstances. His plays are quite similar to the thesis plays of the nineteenth century, and he concentrates on the prejudices and discriminations of his period. Almost forgotten today, his best drama is probably *La garra* (1914), about divorce and the need for tolerance.

3. *Serafín* (1871–1938) and *Joaquín* (1873–1944) *Alvarez Quintero* are responsible for important comic achievements set in Seville, where they grew up, and they fill their regional works with the sunshine and laughter of their native Andalusia. They

wrote the first of their more than two hundred plays in 1888 but had to wait until 1897 for their first dramatic triumph. For the next forty years, almost every theatrical season in Madrid had at least one play by the Quinteros. Almost one half of their dramas are of one act, but all are light, enchanting, and warmly humorous. Of their many plays one can cite *Los Galeotes* (1900), more serious than most of their works, and *Las de Caín* (1908). The Quintero brothers, witty and graceful, believed in a popular, polished, amiable, and realistic prose drama, preferably spiritually uplifting and optimistic.

4. *Pedro Muñoz Seca* (1881–1936) wrote a great number of *sainetes* in addition to longer dramatic works, but his major contribution was in the drama of intrigue, full of uncommon situations often verging on the ridiculous. He employs slang, puns, plays on words, caricature, parody, and dramatic tricks, producing a drama frequently labeled as *astracán*. He anticipates the grotesque in later Spanish dramas. Among his titles one can mention *La venganza de don Mendo* (1918).

5. *Gregorio Martínez Sierra* (1881–1947) learned much from Benavente, but he introduced a poetic note of idealism and love into his dramas. He portrays mainly the pleasant aspects of life in his search for beauty and demonstrates a faith in human nature. In his idealistic plays, virtue always triumphs, and good works achieve their reward. His wife, María de la O Lejárraga, an ardent feminist, collaborated with him in many of his dramas. This may account for the emphasis on family living, Christian morality, feminine values, and the sanctity of life. His plays include *El ama de la casa* (1910), about maternal love, and his masterpiece, *La canción de cuna* (1911), about the maternal love of nuns for a foundling abandoned at their convent.

6. *Miguel de Unamuno* (1864–1936), better known as an essayist, novelist, and poet, wrote a series of intellectual dramas with little action and sparse dialogue. As in his other works, in his drama he deals with man's essence, the problems of personality, the maternal instinct, and the classic themes of hate and envy. Among his better plays are *El otro* (1926), a work treating the Cain and Abel theme, and *El hermano Juan o el mundo es teatro* (1934), relating myth and reality in a new version of the don Juan theme.

7. *José Martínez Ruiz* (1873–1967), better known by his pen name, Azorín, wanted to change the nature and structure of Spanish drama, and in his attempt to create a Surrealistic theater, dealt with the temporal, the nature of illusion, and death.

As in his better-known essays, he concentrates on the nature of time. Some of his experimental plays are *Old Spain* (1926), a mixture of fantasy and reality, tradition and progress; *Brandy, mucho brandy* (1927), about the power of illusion and dreams; and *Angelita* (1930), involving magic and Christian themes.

8. *Ramón Gómez de la Serna* (1888–1963), better known for his novels and *greguerías*, also wrote plays, many of them somewhat Surrealistic, that concentrate on the theme of sexuality. One may mention among his titles *El drama del palacio deshabitado* (1909).

The poetic theater appeared toward the end of the first decade. The Machado brothers, Antonio (1875–1939) and Manuel (1874–1947), wrote seven plays in collaboration, five of them in verse. Their most successful was *La Lola se va a los puertos* (1929). Francisco Villaespesa (1877–1936), not too successful as a playwright, wrote *El alcázar de las perlas* (1911). The most important of the poetic playwrights was Eduardo Marquina (1879–1946), who wrote legendary and historical plays about a false and idealized Spanish past and some less successful rural dramas. His most famous are *Las hijas del Cid* (1908), a mixture of epic and lyric elements, and *En Flandes se ha puesto el sol* (1910), about the loyalty and self-sacrifice involved in the last days of the Spanish occupation of the Netherlands. In a second period he wrote *Teresa de Jesús* (1933), in which religious exaltation matches his earlier passionate nationalism.

F. Federico García Lorca (1898–1936)

Federico García Lorca, one of the truly great poetic dramatists of modern times, was born in Fuentevaqueros in Granada, a land where Moorish influences are everywhere present. He imbibed the spirit of the earth and Moorish climate in earliest childhood. These elements, combined with an uncanny ability to interpret popular traditions and folkways (but in unusual and daring imagery), were to persist throughout his entire work.

In 1919 Lorca wrote his first dramatic work, *El maleficio de la mariposa*, an allegorical and Symbolist play that was not well received at its first performance in 1920. In 1931 Lorca became the director of a student theater, La Barraca, which toured Spain and performed classics from Juan del Encina through Calderón. He wrote two farces, *La zapatera prodigiosa* (1930), about the consequences of a marriage of an old man and a young woman and the meaning of honor; and *El amor de don*

Perlimplín con Belisa en su jardín, finished in 1928 but not performed until 1931. *Mariana Pineda,* written in 1925 but not performed until 1927, is Lorca's only historical play. It is set during the reign of Fernando VII and tells of a heroine from Granada who sacrificed herself for independence and liberty. The Surrealistic *Así que pasen cinco años* (1931) is an allegory of lost time. *Doña Rosita la soltera o el lenguaje de las flores* (1935) is about frustration in a rigidly moral society and, like *Don Perlimplín,* about unattainable love. In 1933 Lorca also wrote *El público,* not published in a complete version until 1974, which in addition to its Surrealistic elements is an Expressionistic attack on the entire social order. Additionally Lorca wrote puppet plays: *El retablillo de don Cristóbal* (1931) and two others published posthumously, *Títeres de Cachiporra: La tragicomedia de don Cristóbal y la señá Rosita* (1949) and *La niña que riega la albahaca y el príncipe preguntón* (1982).

Lorca's most important dramatic work is a rural trilogy, *Bodas de sangre* (1933), *Yerma* (1934), and *La casa de Bernarda Alba* (1936). *Bodas de sangre* reflects Lorca's personal tragic view of a love triangle in which nature and human instincts are constrained by an unyielding social order. It concerns the abduction of a willing bride on her wedding day by Leonardo, her former sweetheart. The lovers are followed through the forest by the Bridegroom, aided by the Moon and Death, who describes the death of the two men. The *novia* looks for love and life but finds only death, and the family honor, a remnant of the sterile and artificial traditional Spanish code, can only result in tragedy. *Yerma* deals with sexuality, free will, and sterility, relating the tragedy of a childless wife in a loveless marriage who kills her husband and thus condemns herself to a barren existence. Almost an archetypal figure, Yerma, through her tragic act, rebels against the traditional forces that have hemmed her in. *La casa de Bernarda Alba,* not performed until 1945, resembles a Greek tragedy and emphasizes Lorca's favorite theme of the interplay between authority and liberty. Against the background of an impregnable, intensely white house and walls, we see the sterile existence of five unwilling virgin daughters beneath the tyrannical rule of a fanatically and hypocritically honor-oriented mother. Alba, whose name means white, represents the repression of a narrow, traditional, intolerant Spain.

Lorca used symbols on many levels, but certain images recur throughout his work, among them the moon, the bull, and the horse. Sometimes these are not symbols of tragedy, but for the most part they represent death or the dark servants of tragic fate. Death, accompanied by flowing blood, is served by a variety of pointed objects. In *Bodas de sangre*, the Moon asks for blood to warm herself. Tears and laughter, combined with a symbolic overlay and a poetic prose form, constitute basic elements of Lorca's dramas.

Lorca's principal roles are reserved for women, and his heroines are tragic creations who suffer from frustrations of various kinds. Tragedy accompanies them. In *Yerma*, the woman who cannot give life gives death. In *Doña Rosita la soltera*, death comes to the soul as a result of lost hope. In *Don Perlimplín*, death is the result of the realization of lost youth. In *Bodas de sangre* death is the only possible outcome, and in *La casa de Bernarda Alba* death follows quickly on the heels of sexual frustration and an overly rigid and artificial code of honor. In almost all these plays, the heroine either gives death or receives it. Quite often the women symbolize abstractions: Mariana represents liberty; Rosita, desolation; Adela, virginity; Bernarda, dominion; and Yerma, maternity.

In addition to the elementary passions that he portrays, Lorca employs to good advantage his knowledge of art, music, and the ballet, and his musical language casts an almost magical spell. His favorite colors include white and the pastel shades. His sounds are delicate, and his voices are usually subdued, but the quietness is often shattered by a cry of sorrow or a shout of joy. He utilizes pantomime, the chorus, songs, dances, and musical instruments.

Religious sentiment abounds in some of Lorca's plays, and his attitude ranges from tormented doubt to rebellion against traditional beliefs. Principally he writes about love and liberty, and he saw not only the tragedy of the women of Spain but also the tragedy of the disenfranchised everywhere. He pictured a society whose severe moral laws could lead only to tragic consequences, often for innocent, though frustrated, souls. Lorca witnessed the needs of those who, hemmed in by a dark forest of conventions and fears, sought to escape through love. It is their tragedy, the tragedy of the unloved, that Lorca wrote.

G. Alejandro Casona (1903–1965)

Alejandro Casona is the pseudonym of Alejandro Rodríguez Alvarez. Casona began his writing with poems in a Modernist vein, but he soon turned to the drama, while maintaining his lyrical base. He founded a children's theater, El Pájaro Pinto, and from 1931 to 1936 he served as director of the Teatro del Pueblo and Teatro de las Misiones Pedagógicas. Forced to flee the country by Franco supporters, he lived in Buenos Aires from 1939 to 1962, when he returned to Spain.

Some of his dramas are *La sirena varada* (1934), which won the Lope de Vega Prize; *Otra vez el diablo* (1935); *Nuestra Natacha* (1936), one of his few dramas without fantastic elements, which is a plea for social reforms in a Spain suffering from intolerance; *Prohibido suicidarse en primavera* (1937); and *La dama del alba* (1944), his best-known play, first performed by Margarita Xirgu in Buenos Aires. Death, La Peregrina, is a protagonist, who herself is a victim of her own tragedy but who nevertheless offers the only solution. This play, filled with light and color, Asturian folklore and legends, like almost all Casona's works mixes fantasy and reality with the theme of love and redemption. Still other plays are *La barca sin pescador* (1945); *Los árboles mueren de pie* (1949); and *El caballero de las espuelas de oro* (1964), a historical play based on the life of Quevedo.

Casona's works contain fantastic characters whose principal duty is to bring beauty to normal lives, but combined with this illusion is the constant preoccupation with truth and reality. In all his dramas he shows compassion for the weaknesses and difficulties of human sorrow. In some of his plays Casona seems preoccupied with the problem of suicide, but the predominant force that accompanies this fascination is always love, a love that saves and heals. In other dramas older characters provide the driving force as people who have fought the battles of life and have evolved a wonderfully comforting philosophy of work and love. Often Casona's characters seek to escape the world of pain and sorrow, but only in their adaptation, complete or partial, and a confrontation with reality can they find happiness. The sense of duty is strong in Casona, and ethical living and reality are synonymous for him. The Infantina in *Otra vez el diablo,* Sirena and don Joaquín in *La sirena varada,* the Amante in *Prohibido suicidarse en primavera,* and others weave a world of fantasy to defend themselves from the cruelty of the real one. Although they may escape temporarily through illusion, they can find true happiness only by facing up to their problems. Through sacrifice and duty and even suffering may come peace, for Casona repeats in many different keys the basic fact that only through facing the truth, no matter how bitter, can one be saved. He does not argue that illusion is bad, but his conclusion seems to be that the worlds of reality and happiness are synonymous.

His plays deal with Christian love, with individual moral values in a somewhat dehumanized world, with spiritual crises, with human warmth, with faith and optimism, and with social problems. But Casona also evokes the Asturian countryside, its people and their folklore and legends, in plays filled with a poetic mixture of dreams, mystery, and reality.

H. Other Dramatists of the Thirties and Forties

Many of the playwrights who published during the 1940s produced their best work in the 1950s and will be treated below, though an arbitrary decision is difficult to make.

1. *Pedro Salinas* (1891–1951) wrote fourteen theatrical pieces, two in three acts and the rest in one act. In his plays we see some of the same emphasis on love and beauty that is so much a part of his poetry, for which he is more renowned. Using an imaginative interplay of illusion and reality, which the poet himself called "realidad fabulizada," Salinas deals with the transfiguration of reality. Among his short plays are *La fuente del Arcángel* and *Los santos,* about Falangist cruelty and the meaning of innocence, sacrifice, and guilt. His two longer plays, *Judit y el tirano* and *El director,* stress the importance of being human and the problem of achieving happiness. His plays, written between 1936 and 1951, were published in his *Teatro completo* (1957).

2. *Enrique Jardiel Poncela* (1901–1952), also a novelist and short story writer, produced over a hundred works. He may well be the greatest Spanish humorist of the twentieth century. His somewhat grotesque theater involves ironic parodies and complex and self-mocking satires. One finds in his plays hunger, death, magic, ghosts, mystery, infidelities, madness, and both sexual and spiritual love. Jardiel Poncela sometimes employed cinematic techniques in his intricate and intellectual farces, which mix reality with fantasy, absurdities and caricatures with the sublime. His bizarre plots are filled with sudden appearances and disappearances. His plays after 1927 include *Angelina o el honor de un brigadier* (1934), a verse parody of the concept of honor; *Un marido de ida y vuelta* (1939); and *Eloísa está debajo de un almendro* (1940).

3. *Rafael Alberti* (b. 1902), who made his mark as a poet, wrote about a dozen plays, including an interesting adaptation of Cer-

vantes' *Numancia,* which he condensed and tried to make relevant for contemporary audiences. *El hombre deshabitado,* performed in 1931, borrows elements from Calderón's theater and is an Expressionistic and stylized modern allegory of paradise lost. Man, the protagonist, journeys through life, which he finds meaningless, and realizes that paradise is not for him. Though somewhat prolix, the work involves an avant-garde dance of the senses. Alberti's historical plays, *De un momento a otro* (1939) and *Noche de guerra en el Museo del Prado* (1956), deal with the Civil War. The first play tells the story of a family divided by ideological passion; the second deals with Goya, his paintings, and the interrelationships of the two war periods. *El adefesio* (1944), the second of a popular trilogy, reveals the influences of the *esperpento* and, some would say, of *La casa de Bernarda Alba.* The grotesque characters help Alberti focus on the bigotry, intolerance, and repression of his unhappy country.

4. *Max Aub* (1903–1972), who was born in France and died in Mexico, is better known as a novelist, but he may well be a major dramatist who deserves more recognition than he has hitherto achieved. The author of dozens of plays in a variety of styles, ranging from one to six acts, he may have influenced Lorca and Casona. In his early avant-garde period, his plays are, in varying degrees, erotic, Expressionistic, Existential, and Surrealistic, but whatever his intellectual abstractions, he always displays a social conscience. Aub constantly expresses his concern for human dignity, man's inability to communicate, and man's loneliness. His first work, *Crimen,* not produced until 1956 though written as early as 1923, concerns the relationship between subjective and objective truth. *Narciso* (1927) is a modern version of the myth of Narcissus.

His second period produced some Civil War dramas in defense of the Republican cause, the best of which is the somewhat allegorical *Pedro López García* (1936). Aub also wrote plays dealing with World War II, involving historical, political, and social preoccupations and such themes as individual dignity, human values, and the perils of living in a police state. In some plays he deals with the plight of Jewish refugees, and the play some consider to be his masterpiece, *San Juan* (1943), treats the tragedy of Jewish victims unwanted by any country and unable to disembark from their refugee ship. Although he uses reality and fantasy to good effect, his later plays show a more bitter reality. *Morir por cerrar los ojos* (1944), in six interesting acts, recounts the defects of French character in France's surrender to Germany in

1940. In 1950 he wrote one of his best psychological dramas, *Deseada,* called by the author "Fedra vuelta al revés." Aub continued writing plays throughout the sixties, including one about the Vietnam War, *Retrato de un general* (1969).

5. *Miguel Hernández* (1910–1942), a great poet who was less successful as a dramatist, wrote a kind of *auto sacramental, Quien te ha visto y quien te ve y sombra de lo que eras* (1934), about innocence, guilt, grace, and redemption. Hernández then turned to social drama, abandoning the verse of his *auto* for prose. *Los hijos de la piedra* (1935) is about an uprising of miners. Returning to verse, Hernández wrote another proletarian drama, *El labrador de más aire* (1937), and *Pastor de la muerte* (1937), about a popular hero and the defense of Madrid. In 1937 he published *Teatro de guerra,* consisting of four prose scenes, revolutionary in nature.

I. Antonio Buero Vallejo (b. 1916)

Antonio Buero Vallejo, who may be judged by future generations as the best dramatist of the second half of the twentieth century, served with the Republicans during the Spanish Civil War as a medical aide. Imprisoned until 1945, he came to public notice when he won two important prizes, the Lope de Vega Prize for *Historia de una escalera* (1949) and the Amigos de los Quinteros Prize for his one-act play *Las palabras en la arena* (1949), which treats the theme of adultery. It soon became apparent that Buero wanted to be both a witness and interpreter of the despair of modern man, and in his pursuit he reformed the concept of Spanish tragedy with his social conscience and his concept of tragic hope in a confrontation with tragedy. In his early dramas he showed the influence of Ibsen, but later, following Brecht, he tried, while involving the audience, to keep the spectator at a distance in the hope that he might later exhibit his own social awareness in promoting social justice and political and personal freedom.

Historia de una escalera shows us the interwoven drama of four families of modest means in 1919, 1929, and 1949. The three generations use as a focus for all their actions the stairway leading to their apartments, which reminds them constantly of their hopes and failures. Through a simple exposition of their daily pettiness and tragedy, Buero shows us people who manage to find only disillusion, disappointment, and death. In the end the son repeats the words of his unsuccessful father almost verbatim to paint a rosy future that the audience assumes will never occur.

91

Nonetheless, in this drama as in others, Buero sees hope in spite of apparent pessimism and defeat on the part of his protagonists. For him tragedy is a positive catharsis rather than a purification; it involves a sublimation of the human condition with moral and ethical implications, as hope helps revitalize faith and spiritual development. Although the message is clearer in other plays, in *Historia de una escalera,* in spite of the frustration, abulia, and lack of self-determination, man, responsible for his own development, can change through effort, and the younger generation can provide new vision and new hope.

En la ardiente oscuridad (1950) utilizes two of Buero's favorite themes, the inability of man to see reality as it is and the need to shed light on a socially repressive world. The play concerns an Institute for the Blind whose optimistic inmates are forced to see life as it is. Buero explores the meaning of truth and freedom, the individual's need for authenticity, and the relationship of physical and spiritual blindness. Some see political overtones in the play, but Buero protested that this drama has no thesis but simply explores what really motivates human beings. He again treated these themes in *El concierto de San Ovidio* (1962), about a group of grotesque would-be musicians, the destruction of their dream, and their rejection of tyranny. We see again a somewhat similar theme in *Diálogo secreto* (1984), about a color-blind art critic.

Many of Buero's plays explore the relationship between truth and fiction and in varying degrees employ myth, legend, and fable. Among these are *La tejedora de sueños* (1952), based on the Greek legend of Penelope and Ulysses; *La señal que se espera* (1952), about a musician's lost inspiration; *Casi un cuento de hadas* (1953), about the love of a beautiful princess for an ugly prince; and *Irene o el tesoro* (1954), about illusion and madness. In *El tragaluz* (1967), a play with a science fiction framework of time travelers from the twenty-third century who reflect on the tragedies of the Spanish Civil War, Buero, through a family's personal tragedy, pleads for individual liberty and dignity.

Buero stressed the theme of human suffering in *Hoy es fiesta* (1956), a collective tragedy involving the illusions, despair, and dreams of Madrid's lower classes. *Las cartas boca abajo* (1957) is a psychological play about human frustration. In *Aventura en lo gris* (1963), Buero deals with war refugees and the struggle between good and evil. In several plays Buero writes about historical figures who also struggled for individual expression and against repression and tyranny. In *Un soñador para un pueblo*

(1958), he depicts the eighteenth-century Esquilache, his dreams and his failure. In *Las meninas* (1960), he reflects his own artistic talent and interest in painting as he reinterprets historical truth and the life of Velázquez. He reiterates this interest in *El sueño de la razón* (1970), about Goya, his paintings, and the period in which he lived, a play that, according to some, reflects the intolerance and absolutism suffered under Franco. In *La detonación* (1977), he examines and reinterprets the life and times of Mariano José de Larra. Buero interprets his own prison experience in *La fundación* (1974). In *La doble historia del Doctor Valmy* (1976), he explores the use of torture as a political instrument and the themes of truth and ethical responsibility. In *Los jueces en la noche* (1979), he looks at terrorism, and in *Lázaro en el laberinto* (1986), he displays a kind of Freudian psychology.

Buero's total production won for him in 1986 the Cervantes Prize, Spain's most prestigious award. He was the first playwright so honored. Buero is a master of ironic devices, Brechtian distancing, chiaroscuro, and stage technique, but he achieved success because he showed a compassion for human sorrow, realized the difficulty of self-realization, and saw the possibility of spiritual development through suffering. Most of his plays had to be produced during the censorship of the Franco years, and so he had to practice what he called *posibilismo*, hoping his audience would interpret correctly the symbolic message underlying his dramatic works. Buero, in short, concentrates on the tragic aspects of modern man, the question of good and evil, the need for love and understanding in the contemporary, anguished world, and hope as a vital part of faith and the metaphysical justification of the world.

J. Alfonso Sastre (b. 1926)

By his birth date he belongs to a later generation, but as early as 1945 Sastre had already formed an experimental theater group for which he wrote short dramas. He protested against the conventions of the time and employed a variety of experimental techniques. His work, unfortunately, as in the case of Max Aub, has not been fully appreciated by Spanish critics. Part of this may be due to his insistence on *imposibilismo* as opposed to Buero's *posibilismo*, for he insisted on truthful dramas, even if that meant he could not have his works performed.

Critics often divide Sastre's production into three periods, the experimental plays between 1945 and 1950, the plays of the

93

1950s, and the epic theater after 1960. Many consider Sastre to be a revolutionary writer, and others find him too intellectual. He himself has labeled much of what he has written "theater of social agitation," as he stresses the rights of individuals in a static modern world; but he also rejects the label of a revolutionary with specific political ideologies in his attempt to portray the complexities and confusions of the twentieth century.

Sastre views tragedy as a kind of social sin, an artistic mechanism that tortures the spectator, who willingly accepts the distress as a means of catharsis. There are few happy endings in Sastre's closed Existential dramas filled with disillusioned characters, and he acknowledges that revolution may very well become reactionary; but his dramas also contain universal lessons and are not totally devoid of hope.

Escuadra hacia la muerte (1953), a kind of universal plea against war, shows us a frustrated and despairing humanity that has abandoned God and been abandoned by Him. A group of criminals sent to defend a strategic post murder their corporal and must then affirm or deny their individual responsibility. Other well-known works are *La mordaza* (1954), about tyranny and oppression, a criminal father, and his family; *Tierra roja* (1954), describing the revolt of unjustly treated miners; *Guillermo Tell tiene los ojos tristes* (1955), concerning a father's anguish and the price exacted for a people's freedom; *La sangre de Dios* (1955), dealing with faith and a professor who believes that God demands the sacrifice of his son; *El pan de todos* (1957), telling of an idealistic Communist who sacrifices his own mother and discovers too late that his Utopia is nonexistent; *Ana Kleiber* (1957), treating of a woman's need for and inability to accept love; *El cuervo* (1957), involving terror and mystery; *La cornada* (1959), about injustice, insensitivity, a bullfighter, and the loss of personal liberty; and *Asalto nocturno* (1959), his first experiment in epic theater, containing a murder, tyranny, and the consequences of repression.

Among Sastre's plays of the 1960s one finds *Muerte en el barrio* (1961), about the execution of a socially irresponsible doctor, and *En la red* (1961), about Algerian freedom fighters caught in a police net. Between 1965 and 1972, he published six plays, many of which contain narrative elements and which the author labeled "tragedias complejas." Sastre tried unsuccessfully to write a new kind of theater, rejecting Brecht, avant-garde movements, the *esperpento*, and Aristotelian tragedy, but involving elements of all of them. He shows a greater versatility in his dramatic structure and in his attempt to involve the audience in his revolutionary process. Among these works are *El banquete* (1965), whose theme of man's exploitation of man Sastre associates with *La cornada* and *La taberna fantástica* (1966), a kind of *esperpento* involving itinerant peddlers and society's relationship to the "outsider," not performed until 1985. Other titles of the 1960s are *Oficio de tinieblas* (1962); *La sangre y la ceniza* (1965), about Miguel Servet and the forces of repression, not performed until 1976, the year after Franco's death; and *Crónicas romanas* (1968), finally performed in 1982, which draws parallels between Numancia, Vietnam, and the contemporary world. In addition to perceptive essays, novels, and numerous adaptations of the works of a variety of dramatists including O'Casey, Brecht, and Lope, Sastre also has written some children's theater. His works of the 1970s include *Ejercicios de terror* (1970), finally performed in 1981; *El camarada oscuro* (1972); and *Ahola no es de leíl*, written in 1974 but not performed until 1979.

At first glance, Sastre's closed situation seems the opposite of Buero's, but even Sastre admits that at times tragedy may have a happy ending because absolute pessimism leads to deformity in the interrelationships between private anguish and public action. In spite of their emphasis on a social conscience, Sastre's dramas are incarnations of social problems of protagonists who live in an absurd world of false values, and as he deals with the universe of pain, poverty, and hunger, at times with black humor, he tries to maintain a delicate balance between a difficult social message and the metaphysical in plays that are boldly experimental.

K. Minor Dramatists of the Fifties

Although many of these minor dramatists wrote works in previous decades, they produced their best plays, for the most part, in the 1950s.

1. *José María Pemán* (1898–1981) produced his first play, *Isoldina y Polión*, in 1928 and continued writing dramas into the 1970s, but his most successful plays date from the 1950s. He wrote plays Classical in tone, such as *Antígona* (1946), *Electra* (1949), and *Julio César* (1955). His historical verse dramas, such as, for example, *El divino impaciente* (1933), about a sixteenth-century Jesuit, are reminiscent of Marquina's work. He also produced political dramas exemplified by *El viento sobre la tierra* (1957) and a series of moralistic, religious dramas, among them

Callados como los muertos (1952) and *En las manos del hijo* (1953). Pemán's best talent appears in his light, humorous pieces that he labeled "farsas castizas," the most successful of which was *Las tres etcéteras de Don Simón* (1958), a humorous, mysterious play set in Napoleonic times.

2. *José López Rubio* (b. 1903), a master of irony, satire, and sparkling dialogue, wrote humorous and often tender dramas about love, reality, illusion, and fantasy. The author of a play in 1930, he did not write for the theater again until *Alberto* (1949), about an imaginary character and repressed ambition. The 1950s gave us his best-known works: *Celos del aire* (1950), about jealousy and forgiveness; *Una madeja de lana azul celeste* (1951); *La venda en los ojos* (1954), which together with his masterpiece, *La otra orilla* (1954), about passion, selfishness, and love as seen from "the other shore," most resemble Casona's mixtures of the real and make-believe world; *La novia del espacio* (1955); *Un trono para Christy* (1956); and *Las manos son inocentes* (1958), about crime and remorse. Later plays are *Diana está comunicando* (1960); *El corazón en la mano* (1972); and *La puerta del Angel* (1986), begun fifteen years earlier.

3. *Miguel Mihura* (1905–1977), unlike Jardiel Poncela, Spain's other great comic genius, was more interested in human nature than in bizarre effects. Although he wrote for the entertainment of the majority and relied heavily on the incongruous, suspense, and comic situations, he also criticized the hypocrisy and false values of society and the price exacted from his characters by modern civilization. His first play, *Tres sombreros de copa*, written in 1932 but not performed until 1952, is still considered his masterpiece. Concerning the escape into illusion and a return to the everyday world, this satire on bourgeois materialism reveals an understanding of human weakness and the need for individual choices. *Sublime decisión* (1955) attacks male chauvinism and promotes women's rights in a late nineteenth-century setting. *Mi adorado Juan* (1956) describes a compromise between bohemian freedom and middle-class respectability. *Carlota* (1957) is about a woman victimized by her own deceit. *Melocotón en almíbar* (1959) treats of a nun's triumph over would-be robbers. *Maribel y la extraña familia* (1959) stresses the positive role of love in a prostitute's redemption. Other successful plays are *Las entretenidas* (1962), *La bella Dorotea* (1963), and *Ninette y un señor de Murcia* (1964).

4. *Joaquín Calvo Sotelo* (b. 1905) began his dramatic production in 1932 and has since written over three dozen plays. He

succeeded in the 1940s with *Cuando llegue la noche* (1943), *Plaza de Oriente* (1947), and *La visita que no tocó el timbre* (1949). Most of his works, whether farce, comedy, or the promotion of a thesis, deal with everyday problems of contemporary Spain. He has written about politics, social classes, international relations, and crises of conscience. Among his sometimes melodramatic works in the 1950s are *Criminal de guerra* (1951), dealing with the United States' occupation of Germany and moral responsibility; *María Antonieta* (1952); *El Jefe* (1953), regarding the nature of dictatorship; *Milagro en la Plaza del Progreso* (1953); *La muralla* (1954), his masterpiece, telling of a man tortured by his conscience, prejudice, and redemption through faith; *Historia de un resentido* (1956), regarding revenge and the struggle between good and evil; the Pirandellian *La ciudad sin Dios* (1957); *Una muchachita de Valladolid* (1957); and *La herencia* (1957), concerning the effects of the Spanish Civil War on the survivors. In the 1960s, Calvo Sotelo continued his prolific pace with many plays, among them *El proceso del arzobispo Carranza* (1964) and *El inocente* (1968). He began the 1970s with *El alfil* (1970).

5. *Victor Ruiz Iriarte* (1912–1982) continued the tradition of the *teatro de evasión*, exhibiting grace, tenderness, and humor in his sometimes sentimental plays involving reality and poetic illusion. He follows Casona in his management of weird and fantastic backgrounds. Although he wrote several dozen plays, beginning with *Un día en la gloria* (1943), he achieved his first real success with *El landó de seis caballos* (1950), about a poetic world where time can be frozen and illusion and love enjoyed forever. *El gran minué* (1950), called a "farsa ballet" by one critic, satirizes a European court of the eighteenth century, as the author discusses truth, morality, and philosophy. *Juego de niños* (1952), about a woman's effort to win back a faithless husband; *La guerra empieza en Cuba* (1955), a tender story of twins; *Una investigación privada* (1958); and *Esta noche es la víspera* (1958) are other plays of this decade. Some of his many plays of the 1960s are *El carrusel* (1964), *Un paraguas bajo la lluvia* (1965), and *Historia de un adulterio* (1968).

6. *Juan Ignacio Luca de Tena* (b. 1897) wrote over forty plays from 1918 through the 1960s. Most of his plays are light comedies, but he also has some historical dramas. Significant are *El cóndor sin alas* (1951), about relationships among social classes; *Pepe y Pepita* (1952); *¿Dónde vas, Alfonso XII?* (1957); and *¿Dónde vas, triste de ti?* (1959).

7. *Edgar Neville* (1899–1968) began writing in 1917, but with

the exception of an early work in 1934 he did not write seriously for the stage until about 1950. In 1952 his play *El baile* had an astonishing success. Among other plays are *Veinte años* (1954), *Adelita* (1955), *Prohibido en otoño* (1957), *Alta fidelidad* (1957), and *La extraña noche de boda* (1963).

8. *Alfonso Paso* (1926–1978) worked closely with his friend Alfonso Sastre in promoting experimental theater. He himself wrote over a hundred plays, mostly light comedies, at times with black humor, and also police dramas and what he called "social theater." He had a special talent for complicated plots. Given his extravagant drama, he inherited the mantle of Jardiel Poncela, but he could also create poignant scenes of people who suffered, loved, and dreamed. Some of his noteworthy plays are *Catalina no es formal* (1956), *El cielo dentro de casa* (1957), *Los pobrecitos* (1957), *Juicio contra un sinvergüenza* (1958), *Cosas de papá y mamá* (1960), and *Persecución de los cristianos por el emperador Nerón, según la idea y concepto que del hecho tiene el autor español Alfonso Paso* (1969).

L. *La Generación Realista*

A group of dramatists who followed the social concerns of Buero Vallejo and Sastre, in reaction against the *teatro de evasión* of López Rubio and others, have been loosely categorized, not to everyone's satisfaction, as belonging to the *generación realista,* sometimes also called the *generación perdida* or *generación del silencio.* Among its members are Lauro Olmo, José María Rodríguez Méndez, José Martín Recuerda, Carlos Muñiz, and Ricardo Rodríguez Buded. Antonio Gala, somewhat younger, also follows this generation's tendencies. The term *Realist* in no way implies a negation of illusion and fantasy in their inventive theater. Jaime Salom, who follows Alfonso Paso; José Ruibal, the leader of what was "underground theater"; and Fernando Arrabal, all important contemporary playwrights, do not belong to this generation.

1. *Lauro Olmo* (b. 1922), a master of popular language, treated social, ethical, and political problems, perhaps too forcefully. Many of his plays were censored by the Franco regime. Olmo has always held that the theater should deal with human beings and life, as evidenced by his masterpiece, *La camisa* (1962), to this day the play with which he is associated. The play deals with the problems of emigration because of poor economic circumstances in Spain. Olmo juxtaposes illusion and reality, though he

is unrelentingly realistic in his depiction of the impoverished classes living in shacks and the inability of the characters to escape their tragic circumstances. Juan, the protagonist, through his torn shirt, symbolizes a future hope, because for him leaving implies defeat. *La pechuga de la sardina* (1963), shown on television in 1982, depicts sexually frustrated women victimized by social hypocrisy and by the economy. Once more Olmo deals with the lower classes. *El cuerpo* (1966) calls for a sound mind in a sound body but is an ironic view of *machismo*. *English Spoken* (1968) (the title was written in English) shows us Spaniards returning home from abroad and the consequences. Among his other plays are *El cuarto poder* (1964), a kaleidoscopic, tragicomic play (to use his own description) about points of view, never performed; *Mare Nostrum* (1966), republished as *Mare vostrum* in 1982, about tourism and its effects; *La condecoración*, written in 1964 and finally performed, unsuccessfully, in 1977 as an outdated political denunciation; and *Pablo Iglesias* (1986), set in 1910 and concerning the first Socialist deputy. In the 1980s, aside from additional plays, Olmo wrote adaptations of *sainetes* by Arniches and others for television.

2. *Carlos Muñiz* (b. 1927) wrote first Realistic and then Expressionistic works involving social commentary about authoritarianism, revolt against the system, loneliness, and the demythification of history. His first play, *Telarañas* (1955), was unsuccessful. *El grillo* (1957), revealing Muñiz' compassion for the have-nots and concern over the lack of human progress, deals with the financial dilemma and dreams of an office worker, a frustrated victim of an unjust society. The play is loaded with symbolic sound imagery. *El precio de los sueños*, written before 1960 but not performed until 1966, deals with the force of middle-class opinion, attempts to escape reality, and the meaning of guilt. Muñiz' masterpiece, *El tintero* (1961), indicts the Spanish bureaucracy. Crock, the protagonist, scorned and deceived, an antihero victimized by a dehumanized world, must choose the consequences of freedom, an expression of individuality that ends in his death. In spite of the satire and the subject matter, it is quite poetic. *Las viejas difíciles* (1966) is an Expressionistic examination of society's persecution of victims and an implicit denunciation of hypocrites who would claim exclusive authority over what constitutes Christian morality. Muñiz has also written a number of one-act plays, among them *Un solo de saxófono* (1965), a kind of *esperpento* about racial discrimination. Aside from *El tintero*, his best work is *Tragicomedia del serenísimo*

príncipe don Carlos, written in 1972, published in 1974, and first performed in 1980. A demythification of Spanish history, the play recalls the works of Quevedo and Goya in its use of grotesque elements. Muñiz analyzes King Felipe II in a new way and describes him as a religious fanatic and hypocrite whose professed Catholicism led him to destroy his son.

3. *José Martín Recuerda* (b. 1922), like Lorca a native of Granada, deals with history and the cruelty and hypocrisy of society. He believes in the moral fight against injustice and the reality of charity. He examines the Spanish Civil War and its aftermath, conformists and nonconformists alike, the uses of power and its victims. He also decries the sexual repression he finds in his country. His plays are quite often Baroque, and he is fond of using the chorus as an added element. He is the only playwright to have won the Lope de Vega Prize twice, once for *El teatrito de don Ramón* (1959), about destroyed hopes and illusions, and again for *El engañao* (1981), a depiction of the life of San Juan de Dios, the sixteenth-century humanitarian whose views that the Church should return to a more primitive Christianity and practice charity clashed with the policies of Charles V and Church authorities. *Las salvajes en Puente San Gil* (1963) portrays a doña Rosita type, reminiscent of García Lorca's, and a group of defiant chorus girls who refuse to conform to the bigoted attitudes of the Church and narrow-minded, hypocritical conservatives. The author implies that the latter are the real savages. *Como las secas canas del camino* (1965) has some grotesque elements. The author describes the passion of an old schoolteacher for a student in a sterile town that serves as the demythifying symbol of an idealized rural life. *Las arrecogías del Beaterio de Santa María Egipcíaca* (1977) re-creates a Mariana Pineda, more historical than Lorca's. The convent, ostensibly turned into a prison for prostitutes, really holds political prisoners. Some of the female victims held for trial are almost mad. Victimized by the tyranny of Ferdinand VII, Mariana uses her body in the cause of liberty. Among other plays, *Caballos desbocaos,* published in 1978, concerns the aftermath of the Spanish Civil War and the carnival aspects of the transition from dictatorship to democracy. *Las conversiones* (1983), one of Martín Recuerda's few plays not set in Andalusia, deals with the reign of Enrique IV, his possible homosexuality, Juana la Beltraneja, and above all a youthful Celestina as she might have been.

4. *José María Rodríguez Méndez* (b. 1925) writes about alienation and isolation, especially of the poor. His first play, *Vagones*

de madera (1958), about the Moroccan War, deplores the indifference of society to the soldier's hardships and especially to his death. *La batalla de Verdún* (1961) portrays workers from the south of Spain who seek in vain for a better life in the north; they recall Olmo's individuals oppressed by circumstances. Rodríguez Méndez wrote many plays in the 1960s, among them *Los inocentes de la Moncloa* (1961), about alienated students; *El círculo de tiza de Cartagena* (1963), concerning the separatist movement during the first Spanish Republic; *La mano negra* (1965), a grotesque distortion of reality; *El vano ayer* (1966), about an unsuccessful revolt; and *Los quinquis de Madriz* (1967), according to the author a "reportaje dramático." It deals with the execution of a man for a crime he did not commit. In the 1970s his plays include *Flor de otoño* (1973), about drugs, homosexuality, and subverted values; and *Historia de unos cuantos* (1975), describing ten historical moments in Spanish history from 1890 to 1940 as seen by Marí Pepa, a street tobacco peddler. The inspiration of the *género chico* in this play is obvious. At times Rodríguez Méndez follows Valle-Inclán's experimentation with the grotesque; at others he is Existential; but he is always concerned for Spain's tragic history.

5. *Antonio Gala* (b. 1936) has worked in television and the movies. For some critics his plays may be a metaphor for Spanish society. The author can be poetic, humorous, or tender in turn in his portrayals of love, free will, duty, man's imperfections, and above all redemption. His works lend themselves to ambivalent visions and endings.

In his first play, *Los verdes campos de Edén* (1963), some alienated characters dwell in a cemetery crypt, and the author attempts to make a symbolic statement about redemption. *El sol en el hormiguero* (1966), a political, social, intellectual satire of a monarchy, parodies *Gulliver's Travels. Noviembre y un poco de hierba* (1967), depicting a Republican soldier in hiding and his death, is one of the best works dealing with the consequences of the Spanish Civil War. *Los buenos días perdidos* (1972) is about a strange family that takes refuge in a church. *¿Por qué corres Ulises?* (1975) may symbolize Spain's need to face life's choices and reality because it is out of step with the world. Ulysses has to abandon his self-created heroic myth and face reality. Other plays of the 1970s are *El cárcel en el espejo*, not performed but published in 1970, which in a Surrealistic manner treats of the possibility of new beginnings, human frustration, and love's changing perspectives; *Anillos para una dama* (1973), about

Jimena, the Cid's wife; and *Las cítaras colgadas de los árboles* (1974), about purity and Christian-Judaic relationships in the second half of the sixteenth century. Among his plays in the 1980s, *Petra Regalada* (1980) is his best known. The story concerns an eighteenth-century convent that became a brothel and a woman of flesh and blood who symbolizes not only personal truth and liberty but also the will of the people. Petra, rebelling against authority, is betrayed by a false redeemer and liberator but receives another chance for redemption when a feeble-minded admirer kills the tyrant. Still other plays include *La vieja señorita del paraíso* (1980); *El cementerio de los pájaros* (1982), about the paradoxical nature of liberty and the price it exacts; *Samarkanda* (1986); and *Séneca, o el beneficio de la duda* (1987).

Gala's social conscience impels him to write social criticism, but in addition to his analysis of the abuse of power, his themes include the lack of spiritual values, the demythification of history, and a kind of Existential hope reminiscent of the theories of Buero Vallejo.

M. Other Contemporary Dramatists

1. *Jaime Salom* (b. 1925), who writes in the vein of Alfonso Paso rather than under the inspiration of the *generación realista*, nonetheless gives testimony from time to time about contemporary Spain. In his quite moralistic early period, he wrote a number of murder mysteries. Later he became more interested in Biblical and religious themes, and finally in the woes of humanity. Among Salom's works (he began writing earlier but became known in the 1960s), mostly light comedies, are *Verde Esmeralda* (1960), *Viaje de un trapecio* (1960), *La gran aventura* (1961), and *Culpables* (1961). His first real success was *El baúl de los disfraces* (1964), dealing with romance and lost illusion and the inevitability of old age. A poetic fancy, it reveals the amorous adventures of an old man relived during one magical night. Another of Salom's successes in the 1960s was *La casa de las Chivas* (1968), which in somewhat blunt language shows us people thrown together by war, the problem of sexual promiscuity, and a moral conversion. *La playa vacía* (1965), an allegorical *auto*, examines the possibility of facing life, pleasure, death, and God. In the 1970s Salom wrote many plays, among them *Tiempo de espadas* (1972), a modern version of the Christ story involving the disciples and the Last Supper and promoting the idea that one cannot separate Him from the problems of modern civilization; *La*

noche de los cien pájaros (1972), concerning frustrated intellectual aspirations; *La piel de limón* (1976), about nudity, adjusting to different sociological, political, psychological, and sexual mores, and a plea in favor of divorce; and *Historias íntimas del paraíso* (1978), depicting Adam and Lilith, as equals, in the Garden of Eden. The 1980s brought other successes: *El corto vuelo del gallo* (1980), about Franco's father, who disapproved of his son's ideology; *Un hombre en la puerta* (1984), defining the need to face an ever-changing truth and choose one's future; and *Las Casas, una hoguera en el amanecer* (1986), recounting Bartolomé de las Casas' life in the years 1502 to 1515.

2. *José Ruibal* (b. 1925), master of the so-called underground theater, fills his works with complicated meanings, animal symbolism, and depictions of the use of power, disrespect for the animal world, and the dehumanization of man. He uses humor and irony to good effect, but he believes that theater essentially represents conflict. Ruibal started writing in the 1950s, and his one-act play *Los mendigos* (1957) is a satiric view of an imaginary country peopled by beggars who are subject to a repressive authority. In the 1960s he wrote, among other works, *El asno* (1962), about American imperialism and economic exploitation; *Su majestad la sota* (1965), in which the four kings of a Spanish deck of cards debate forms of government and the author makes known his views on oppressive power and the evils of totalitarianism; and *La máquina de pedir* (1969). His best-known work and the one that has evoked the most commentary is *El hombre y la mosca*, written in 1968 but not performed until 1983. This play has been compared with *Waiting for Godot*. A political parable, the play examines the psychology of dictatorship, the alienation and freedom of man, the universal versus the temporal, and the demythification of Spain. The play contains supernatural elements. Ruibal examines the ego of a dictator, his relationship to his double, and the petrification of a human being. Other plays include *Curriculum vitae* (1970) and *Controles* (1976), an abstract, symbolic play that makes a metaphoric use of animals.

3. *Fernando Arrabal* (b. 1932) is not universally accepted as belonging to Spanish literature, since most of his work has been written in French. Although fairly unsuccessful in his native country, he has achieved a worldwide reputation. He began writing a kind of Theater of the Absurd and initiated in 1962 what he called "Panic" theater, filled with confusion, chance, and Surrealistic elements. He wanted to cause psychic trauma in

103

the spectator through his combination of chaos and the erotic in his dramas. His plays became psychodramas and a kind of cathartic ceremony. Later in the 1960s he became more political. Most of his plays have not been performed in Spain, but when his masterpiece, *El arquitecto y el emperador de Asiria* (1967), was translated into Spanish and presented in 1977, it was not well received, perhaps for the perceived attack on the Church, God, and motherhood. The play is a poetic exploration of the problems of the human spirit and the mythical relationship of two symbolic personages. Other plays by Arrabal performed in Spain, including some from the 1950s, were *Los dos verdugos* (1958), *El cementerio de automóviles* (1959), and *Los hombres del triciclo* (1961), all translated from French and performed years later. His favorite play, *Y pondrán esposas a las flores* (1969), was published in Spanish in 1983, and two collections of his plays, *Teatro bufo* (1983) and *Teatro pánico* (1986), helped circulate his works in Spanish. Arrabal deals with suspended history, circular time, and illogical dialogues, and he utilizes themes like masochism, transvestism, and matricide. In spite of the grotesque elements involved in his plays, it is easy to see that Arrabal is preoccupied by the perils of what he perceives as a dehumanized technical world in which man's freedom and liberty are threatened by a mythical middle-class morality and responsibility.

Among other playwrights are Francisco Nieva (b. 1927), Andrés Ruiz (b. 1928), Luis Matilla (b. 1939), Eduardo Quiles (b. 1940), and Jerónimo López Mozo (b. 1942).

Part 4 **PROSE FICTION**

ORIGIN

The narration of fictitious human events that appear to be related to reality is an art as old as human imagination. Yet the novel as an art form lagged behind other genres and in all literatures appeared after verse had established itself. The earliest prose works in Spain appeared as late as the thirteenth century, long after lyric and epic poetry had blossomed. These early prose attempts were mostly survivals of ancient literature and tales carried in from elsewhere.

In tracing influences on the development of the Spanish novel, mention must be made of Old Testament stories like that of Joseph and his brothers, Greek novels of adventure, pastoral novels, and the short, picaresque, sometimes erotic Milesian tales that preceded them. The latter were popular in ancient Rome and were forerunners of medieval collections. The Greek novel peaked in the second and third centuries B.C. One of them, Heliodorus' *Aethiopica*, also called *Theagenes and Chariclea*, possibly inspired Cervantes' *Persiles y Sigismunda*. Most Greek tales recount the separation of lovers, narrow escapes from a long series of dangerous situations, a final reunion, and a happy ending. Roman novels, especially the *Satyricon*, which foreshadows the Spanish picaresque novel, and Apuleius' *Metamorphoses* or *Golden Ass*, which may have influenced Cervantes, are important for their discussions of social problems. The *Golden Ass*, in which a boy is magically transformed into an ass, teaches that whoever abandons himself to vice and curiosity forsakes his human condition and can be redeemed only by religion and mercy. The Oriental apologues, fables, and parables were also an important source of fictional motives. Originating mostly in India, these Oriental tales worked their way through Persia, then along the southern Mediterranean coast, and were brought into Spain by the Arabs. From Spain, the chief link between the West and East in the early Middle Ages, these stories made the rounds of all literatures. The fall of Toledo, a storehouse of fictional wealth, to the Spanish in 1085 and the Great Crusades resulted in increased importation of Oriental fictional motives, many dating back thousands of years, traceable in some cases to Sanskrit originals. Often they were joined together in a loose framework similar to that used by Juan Manuel in *El Conde Lucanor.* Oriental tales were mainly didactic and usually conveyed some moral lesson through humans in animal guise. Aesop's fables are an example of how this material was used by Westerners. Spanish authors used these Oriental apologues in their first attempts at narrative prose. Though they had no sustained plot, they contained the seed of the novel and were the single most important foreign influence on the development of Spanish narrative prose of the Middle Ages.

THE MIDDLE AGES

A. The *Exempla*

Spanish collections of short stories and Oriental apologues are called *exempla,* forerunners of the novel. They were short stories with a moral point, written between the thirteenth and fifteenth centuries, mingling Christian and Oriental morality. The following are the important Spanish collections:

1. *Disciplina clericalis,* Spain's first collection of Oriental stories, was written in Arabic, translated into Latin by its author and into Spanish by Pedro Alfonso, a converted Aragonese Jew of the early twelfth century whose real name was Rabbi Moisés Sefardí. The collection contains thirty-three apologues, each stating a moral principle or lesson in ethical conduct conveyed by bits of advice given by a father to his son. It was one of the most plagiarized books of the Middle Ages and was incorporated into the *Libro de los exemplos* in the fifteenth century by Clemente Sánchez de Vercial. It influenced Juan Manuel, Juan Ruiz, Timoneda, Boccaccio, and many others.

2. *Libro de Calila y Dimna,* the oldest fictional prose work in the Spanish language, was an anonymous translation from the Arabic ordered by Alfonso *el Sabio* in 1251. It relates how Dimna, a lynx envious of Senceba, an ox and favorite of the Lion, King of Beasts, turns the latter against Senceba, whom the king executes.

Repenting of his action, the Lion brings Dimna to trial and sentences him to death by starvation. The interest lies not in the plot but in the anecdotes introduced as illustrations, as Calila and Dimna discuss, philosophically and satirically, human beings and their illogical behavior. The fables are from Latin, Greek, and Hebrew sources, and especially from the Sanskrit *Panchatantra.* The apologues are alleged to have been authored by an Indian named Bildpai. Menéndez y Pelayo points out that the *Libro de Calila y Dimna* is important not only for its position in the chronology of the novel but also because of its significance in the history of the language. One of the oldest monuments of Spanish literature, it represents literary Spanish in its earliest stages.

3. *Libro de los engannos e assayamientos de las mujeres* (Book of the Deceits and Wiles of Women) was also of Indian origin. Known also by the title *Sendebar,* in 1253 it was ordered translated from Arabic into Spanish by the Infante don Fadrique, Alfonso *el Sabio*'s brother. Translated into every European language, it is known in English as the *History of Seven Wise Masters.*

Its setting is a trial at which a queen falsely accuses her stepson of attempted seduction. His advisers counsel him to remain silent for seven days, and at his trial seven wise men speak in his defense, illustrating in twenty-six stories the perfidy and vices of women. The queen retaliates with tales about the abuses of false counselors. On the eighth day the prince speaks for himself and is exonerated. The queen is condemned to death by fire. The stories are licentious and humorous, without being gross, and reveal the misogynistic attitudes of the Middle Ages.

4. *Barlaam y Josaphat* has a loftier tone than its predecessors and is ascribed to San Juan Damasceno (St. John of Damascus), although probably another John, a seventh-century monk in a monastery near Jerusalem, actually wrote it. The ultimate source is supposedly the Sanskrit *Lalita Vistara,* an account of Buddha's youth. Josaphat (Buddha), protected from all things that might cause sorrow, has allegorical encounters with old age, sickness, poverty, and death. Barlaam, his tutor, explains these things and converts him to the Christian faith. This Christianized form of the Buddha legend was most popular in the Middle Ages and influenced Juan Manuel, *El Caballero Cifar,* and the theater of France, Italy, and Spain. Lope used it in 1618 in his play *Barlaam y Josafá.*

Other collections of *exempla* are the *Libro de los gatos* (where *gatos* should probably read *cuentos*); Sánchez de Vercial's *Libro de los exemplos por a.b.c.,* containing some five hundred stories; and *Castigos y documentos,* attributed to both Juan García de Castroje-riz and Sancho IV of Castile.

B. The Medieval Novel of Chivalry

Some critics believe that the first Spanish novels of chivalry were imported from France, where the novel had evolved out of French epic poetry in which bards transformed their old Celtic epic heroes into knights-errant. Spaniards either translated or imitated these French novels, some of which passed through Italy on their way to Spain. The great Spanish novels of chivalry, the *Amadís, Tirant lo Blanch,* and the two *Palmerines,* which ap-peared in the Renaissance, were so thoroughly hispanicized that their originators could scarcely have recognized them.

Spanish novels of chivalry of the Middle Ages fall into four categories: The Carolingian cycle contains stories of Charle-magne, represented in Spain by *Maynete* and *Historia de Carlo Magno y de los doce pares.* The Arthurian cycle or Breton cycle deals with legends of King Arthur and the Knights of the Round Table in such works as *Demanda del Santo Grial* and the *Baladro del sabio Merlín.* The cycle of antiquity contains novels on Classi-cal legends such as the *Historia troyana,* which describes the siege and destruction of Troy as recorded by fourth-century chroni-clers. The cycle of the Crusades obviously deals with events, real or imagined, of the Great Crusades. The first and most famous of this type, *La gran conquista de ultramar,* written at the end of the thirteenth century, is the first example of the Spanish novel of chivalry.

C. *El Caballero Cifar*

El Caballero Cifar, ca. 1300, was the first original full-length novel in Spain and thus stands apart from all other chivalric novels of the Middle Ages. It contains adaptations of the life of Saint Eus-tace and resembles in part the Milesian tale, with its rambling plot and miscellaneous content, and in part the Arthurian leg-ends. Yet it is clearly Spanish in its moralizing, realism, use of popular speech, and the creation of the popular type, el Ribaldo, the forerunner of Sancho Panza.

It relates the adventures of Cifar, a knight persecuted by en-vious competitors. Exiled by his king, he and his family wander through foreign lands, and after many adventures, wars, separations, and the like, the family is reunited. Most of the rest of the book concerns the adventures of Roboán, one of Cifar's two sons. Part 3 of four parts is largely a collection of apologues.

El Caballero Cifar is the first novel to use superlatives, courteous phrases, popular language, dialogue, proverbs, and jokes, and probably the first to offer a prototype of Quijote's immortal squire. It is also the first novel of artistic prose and harmonious and elegant vocabulary. Cifar was also the first knight to adore his inaccessible lady fair.

D. *Amadís de Gaula*

This work circulated in the fourteenth century, but as its full impact lies in the Renaissance, it will be treated below.

E. Juan Manuel (1282–1347)

The first important name in Spanish prose fiction is that of Juan Manuel, grandson of Fernando III and nephew of Alfonso *el Sabio*. Many of his works have been lost, even though he deposited them for safekeeping in a Dominican monastery that he founded in Peñafiel.

Juan Manuel's masterpiece is *Libro del Conde Lucanor*, formerly known as *El libro de Patronio* (1323–1335), the finest narrative prose fiction produced in fourteenth-century Spain. Although it was written in four parts, only the first part is famous. Fifty-one times Count Lucanor asks advice from Patronio, an elderly sage, who gives him moral and ethical guidance in the form of stories. The Oriental influence is obvious in the use of stories dealing with various moral aspects of life, relationships among people, vanity, avarice, and other human shortcomings. Manuel's clear intention is didactic, and being intensely medieval, he shows little of the Renaissance enjoyment of life already felt in Spain. He is not without humor, however.

Manuel is considered the first Spaniard to possess a good personal and artistic prose style. He took his writing seriously and considered the pursuit of letters more befitting a gentleman than idle gaming. He polished his work, wrote in a grave, clear language, and was proud of his product. He chose words for their beautiful sound, always tried for clarity, sought multilevel meanings, and invented neologisms. He preceded both Chaucer and Boccaccio and was one of the most remarkable figures of the European Middle Ages. In his work is found the prototype

109

of *The Taming of the Shrew* and foreshadowings of Calderón's *La vida es sueño,* Alarcón's *La prueba de las promesas, The Prince and the Pauper, Faust, The Emperor's New Clothes,* and many other well-known titles. He did not intend to be original, but he adapted his sources so fully to the Spanish language and spirit that he gave his compatriots the best short stories they had for approximately three hundred years.

F. Alfonso Martínez de Toledo (1398–1470)

Perhaps the best satiric prose of the fifteenth century is to be found in *El corbacho o reprobación del amor mundano* (1438), by Alfonso Martínez de Toledo, Arcipreste de Talavera. Menéndez Pidal finds it important in its artistic use of popular speech in combination with its more artificial Latinized framework, syntax, and vocabulary, a duality that continued in Spanish prose from the Renaissance on. A second duality is found in its juxtaposition of a lofty and idealistic moral intent and the realistic details of the narrations that deal with some of society's most unsavory types. Of its four parts, the second is the most famous. It treats "los vicios, tachas e malas condiciones de las malas e viciosas mujeres."

Martínez was the first to give us the popular speech of women, whom he unsparingly condemned, and accurately described the customs, manners, dress, and styles of the time. He was the first to master the conversational style of writing and filled his pages with proverbs and folksy sayings. His tales are realistic and constitute a vigorous chapter in the antifeminine literature of the age. He portrayed every type of bad woman, furiously indicting them all. Only the good woman is missing. This monument to realism foreshadows *La Celestina* and *Lazarillo de Tormes* in many ways, particularly in its interest in the picaresque.

THE RENAISSANCE

A. Novels of Chivalry

Although the Renaissance ushered in the modern age, old traditions continued to live. An example of this is the spread of the novel of chivalry in which medieval heroes were transformed into knight-courtiers with the manners and ideals of Renaissance gentlemen. Novels of chivalry became the most popular and widely disseminated form of fiction in Spain in the fifteenth and sixteenth centuries. Although they existed earlier in other countries, Spain gave them permanence, produced the best-known knight, Amadís, and then brought the genre to an end. The Inquisition disapproved of them, scholars condemned them, and critics assailed their style and bad taste; but still all society devoured them. Their unprecedented popularity, some said, was due to an escapist urge in the Spanish people or to the nation's craving for adventure, which was in part being fed by the marvelous adventures in the New World. Others felt that the novels had an enervating effect on the people and wanted to ban them. In addition to the Carolingian and Arthurian cycles, the two important peninsular cycles were those of Amadís de Gaula and Palmerín. The vogue of the novel of chivalry lasted until realism returned with *Lazarillo de Tormes* in 1554. Don Quijote sounded their death knell when he laughed them completely out of existence in 1605. No novel of chivalry was written after that date.

Almost all the heroes of the chivalric novels are of illegitimate birth. The knight must sally forth to right wrongs and slay dragons to win the favor of his lady. At times he is aided by magic; at other times magic harms him. After many adventures he returns to be rewarded by his lady's smile. Often in the end he is recognized as the son of a king or nobleman, and he usually marries his lady.

Renaissance fiction was of loose construction, and novels ended either in a mystery or in such a way that the author or someone else could write a sequel. Thus, cycles of chivalric novels were born. Amadís, for example, had a son and a series of grandsons, and with them the adventures continued through a dozen volumes. The priest in the *Quijote* burns most of the worthless sequels, but he saved Amadís from the flames.

Chivalric novels are filled with absurdities, magic, enchantments, the hero's inevitable victory, and improbable incidents that have little attraction for modern readers, although most are acquainted with the gallant knight-errant and the charm of the Tristan and Iseult type of story. Yet all was not bad in the novels of chivalry, for they taught modesty, bravery, sacrifice, constancy in love, protection of the weak and oppressed, and fair play.

1. *Amadís de Gaula.* Whether this novel is of French, Portuguese, or Spanish origin has never been settled. The earli-

est allusion to Amadís, however, was by a Spanish poet, Pero Ferrus (Ferrandes), and López de Ayala's *Rimado de Palacio* testifies to a three-volume edition of his exploits circulating in Spain before 1350. The best redaction of the Amadís legend was made by a Spaniard, Garcí Rodríguez de Montalvo (also known as Garcí Ordóñez de Montalvo). All this makes a good case for a Spanish origin. Though the ultimate source of Amadís material is in the Arthurian legend, no one believes today that the Spanish version was a translation from the French. Unfortunately no medieval Spanish version was preserved, and the earliest known version did not appear until 1508, when Rodríguez de Montalvo gave us *Los cuatro libros del virtuoso caballero Amadís de Gaula.* This is the version that has lasted through the ages. In its portrayal of the perfect knight, it served as a code for good manners and virtuous conduct, thus greatly influencing the society of the time. It was translated into English by Southey and into French by Herberay and had an immense effect on the European novel. It adds to its fanciful wars against giants a bit of eroticism that differs from the emphasis of the more feudal English novels.

Rodríguez de Montalvo's *Amadís de Gaula* is Spain's best and most important novel of chivalry, and its renown has reechoed down through the ages. Spaniards, Italians, Frenchmen, Germans, and Englishmen used it freely as literary source material. Bernal Díaz del Castillo could only describe the incredible marvels of Mexico City in terms of the *Amadís.* This great novel went through many editions, represents the best Renaissance Spanish prose, and ranks as one of Spain's great contributions to the age.

2. *The Amadís cycle.* The first sequel to the *Amadís* was *Las sergas de Esplandián,* also written by Rodríguez de Montalvo. Esplandián was Amadís' son. Foulché-Delbosc explained that *sergas* refers to the paintings of knight-errantry that decorated the walls of the palaces of the day and is, therefore, synonymous with "adventures." Spaniards gave California its name because it reminded them of an island of that name described in *Las sergas.*

Feliciano de Silva, considered by Cervantes to be the best author of chivalric novels, was probably the most popular. He turned out a large number of "pot boilers," most of which are prolix and tiresome. Nevertheless, his success at home and abroad was enormous and attracted many imitators, including

Shakespeare and Spenser. His contribution to the Amadís cycle is *Amadís de Grecia.*

Juan Díaz committed the indiscretion of causing Amadís to die of old age and his beloved Oriana to enter a convent; but the adoring public would not countenance such treachery, and Amadís was promptly revived. As an immortal patriarch, he watched his offspring fight their way through an interminable series of adventures.

Scarcely anyone reads the *Amadís* today. But if the book has not been readable in all ages, it has the distinction of having engendered Spain's greatest novel, for without the *Amadís, Don Quijote* would very likely not have been possible.

3. *The Palmerín cycle* concerns the character who, next to Amadís, is the most important knight of the Renaissance. The first book in this cycle was the anonymous *Palmerín de Oliva* (1511), a poor imitation of *Amadís de Gaula.* The second in the cycle, *Primaleón* (1512), also anonymous, recounts, among other things, the adventures of Prince Edward of England (don Duardos), later dramatized by Gil Vicente.

Cervantes criticized chivalric novels harshly but praised the best of the Palmerín cycle, *Palmerín de Inglaterra* (1547), written by the Portuguese author Francisco de Morães (1500–1572) in 1544 but not published until 1567. The original was translated into Spanish and published by Hurtado de Toledo (d. 1590) before the Portuguese original appeared. Avidly read in Europe, *Palmerín* has a unity lacking in most of the other chivalric novels, beautiful passages, and detailed battle scenes. It influenced John Keats, among others.

4. *Tirant lo Blanch,* which recounts the adventures of a knight by the same name, was begun about 1460 and published in Catalan in 1490. The first three parts are by Johanot Martorell, the fourth by Martí Johán de Galba. It was translated into Spanish in 1511. Unlike other chivalric novels, it avoids the supernatural and emphasizes realistic and even obscene elements.

B. The Sentimental Novel

The sentimental novels treat the theme of love in an idealistic and sentimental manner and seem to be based on the personal lives of the authors. Their heroes are knights, and the important element is love, but surprisingly one finds discussions on the rights of women. These are among the earliest works to use let-

113

ters to develop plot and show a fusion of tradition and progress, of authority and liberty, typical of the Spanish Renaissance.

1. *El siervo libre de amor* (*ca.* 1440) is a somewhat allegorical, romantic autobiography by Juan Rodríguez de la Cámara (d. *ca.* 1450), also called Juan Rodríguez del Padrón. He championed women's rights and refuted *El corbacho*.

2. *Cárcel de amor* (1492) had extraordinary success, despite protests of the Inquisition and moralists like Luis Vives, and influenced two of Spain's greatest literary works, *La Celestina* and *Don Quijote*. Little is known of its author, Diego de San Pedro, except that he was probably Jewish and was in the service of don Pedro Girón. His famous novel had some twenty-five editions in the fifteenth and sixteenth centuries and over twenty foreign translations. Its influence at home and abroad was significant.

3. *Grimalte y Gradisa,* by Juan de Flores, an obvious continuation of the *Fiammetta,* was published in 1495. Flores' other famous novel is *Historia de Grisel y Mirabella,* written between 1480 and 1485. His novels were very popular, influenced Lope de Vega and Fletcher, and represent the culmination of the sentimental type.

4. *Cuestión de amor de dos enamorados* (*ca.* 1513) mixes prose and verse to recount the intrigues of the Spanish court at Naples and is sentimental, psychological, and historical at the same time. It is a *roman à clef,* and almost all its characters have been identified.

C. *La Celestina*

Known in its earlier editions as *Comedia de Calisto y Melibea* and *Tragicomedia de Calisto y Melibea,* it is now simply called *La Celestina.* Its author, Fernando de Rojas, was a converted Jewish lawyer who died in 1541. Some critics believe the dialogued novel to be a veiled attack by a *converso* on the discriminatory society of his day. Though there still is some controversy concerning *La Celestina*'s authorship, especially the five interpolated acts, it is now widely believed that Rojas authored all twenty-one acts.

The earliest known edition, published in 1499, contained sixteen acts. A 1501 edition adds a letter that claims that the author, on vacation, discovered the first act already written and added an act a day for fifteen days. The 1502 edition contains five additional acts. Rojas claimed to have written all but the first act, but modern consensus gives him the nod for all twenty-one.

Although the work is in the form of a drama in prose, it was never intended for the stage and is more novel than drama.

The chief sources of *La Celestina* are the works of Juan Ruiz and Martínez de Toledo. Celestina herself is an obvious outgrowth of Ruiz's Trotaconventos, and the language and atmosphere owe much to *El corbacho*. Many other literary figures, ranging from Ovid to Diego de San Pedro, probably influenced Rojas. In turn, *La Celestina*'s impact on European literature was tremendous. More than sixty-three editions appeared in sixteenth-century Spain alone, and translations were made into Italian, German, French, and English. It has been said that Shakespeare borrowed elements from it in writing *Romeo and Juliet*. In short, the importance of *La Celestina* on the modern novel can hardly be overestimated.

The plot is simple. Calisto, in love with Melibea, employs the services of an old crone, Celestina, and through her help enjoys the favors of the young lady. Sempronio and Pármeno, Calisto's servants who are in league with Celestina, fall out with her over the profits and kill her. In turn, they too are killed. After a midnight tryst with Melibea, Calisto falls from a ladder he used to scale her garden wall and dies from head wounds. Grief-stricken, Melibea hurls herself from a tower to join her lover in death. More important than the plot are the warm and human characterization, the language, the picaresque elements, the proverbs and folklore, the human passion, the tremendous realism, the richness and variety of the prose, and the originality of the form.

Celestina is a character of such magnitude that she dominates the entire work. A woman of many professions, she is a witch, a procuress in league with Satan, a former prostitute, a manufacturer of love potions, and a mender of broken virginities. She is quite wicked and greedy, but she does not envy or hate, and her one consistent philosophy is that life must be enjoyed. Though she seems to be evil incarnate, there is something likable about her attitudes toward life and her love for others. Sempronio and Pármeno are believable creations also, as are other minor characters.

La Celestina's language is remarkable, full of realistic dialogue, popular speech, and lively conversation. Each person speaks in a different manner, which gives a hitherto unknown flexibility to the work. Two levels of language are obvious, the cultured Renaissance speech of Calisto and Melibea and the common and popular language of the others. This duality once more illus-

115

trates the interplay between the ideal and the real in Spanish literature.

In style the work is again a two-level fusion of idealism and realism. Calisto's passion evokes the carnal realism of Celestina and the others. Melibea, the poetic creation, contrasts with the earthy Celestina. The romantic love of Calisto and Melibea, despite its carnal aspects, contrasts with the purely physical passion of Pármeno and Areusa. A lofty scene is followed by one of low life. The polished language of Calisto sets off the barbarisms of Celestina. To some extent the characters are symbolic also. Pármeno at first speaks as the voice of the Middle Ages, and Elicia is the voice of the Renaissance.

Rojas reveals his characters' human weaknesses of greed and passion. He tries to be objective but makes his moral sympathies clear when at the beginning of Act 1 he states that he composed the work "en reprehensión de los locos enamorados . . . en aviso de los engaños de las alcahuetas y malos y lisonjeros sirvientes." Despite the allegations of obscenity and immorality laid against it, *La Celestina* is an intensely moral book.

Despite its Classical references, overabundant for modern tastes, the work excels in its new psychological realism and its true portraits of human passion.

THE GOLDEN AGE

A. The Pastoral Novel

The pastoral novel developed in Spain in the second half of the sixteenth century. This type of fiction originated in Italy and was an artificial form of fiction intended for the aristocratic reader who had tired of knights-errant. Boccaccio's *Ameto* and *Ninfale Fiesolano* and Jacopo Sannazaro's *Arcadia* (1504) were the most famous early European pastoral novels. Pastoral literature attempted to re-create idyllic beauty with unreal rustic landscapes, false pictures of manners, courtly gallantry, and idealistic love. The majority are "key novels," and the shepherds represent real people, nobles in disguise, who wander about the countryside pouring out their love. The happenings are improbable, country life is idealized, and the novels are conventional, artificial, and lacking in verisimilitude as well as true emotion. They borrowed from the chivalric novels in the use of gallantry, magic, and chivalric love. The pastoral writers mingled poetry with their prose, and Classical eclogues, like those of Garcilaso, became a conventional part of later novels.

Italy did not provide the sole influence, for antecedents of the bucolic manner existed in Spain, namely in Galician-Portuguese lyric poetry, Berceo, the *cantigas de serrana* of Juan Ruiz, the *serranillas* of the Marqués de Santillana, and the *églogas* of Juan del Encina.

Los siete libros de la Diana (*ca.* 1559), the first and best Spanish pastoral novel, was composed by Jorge de Montemayor (*ca.* 1520–1561), a Portuguese Jew whose interesting life ended in a duel over a question of love. It ran through seventeen printings in the sixteenth century alone and influenced not only pastoral works of Lope de Vega and Cervantes but also Sir Philip Sidney's *Arcadia* (1590), Honoré d'Urfé's *Astrée* (1610–1619), and Shakespeare's *Two Gentlemen of Verona* (1595). The *Diana's* tedious plot is filled with frustrated loves, nymphs who come to the aid of lovers, magical love potions, and, of course, many tears. The novel is in elegant prose interspersed with pleasant lyrics. The story of Abindarráez y Jarifa was inserted into the fourth chapter, probably after Montemayor's death.

The *Diana* has the merit of brevity, and it captivated European readers. Its defects are its wearisome plot, cloying sentimentality, lachrymosity, and effeminate tone. Interestingly, Montemayor was probably the first to disguise women in men's clothing, a device that became popular later.

There were many imitations of the *Diana*, among them *Diana enamorada* (1564), by Gaspar Gil Polo, and Alonso Pérez's *Segunda parte de la Diana* (1564). Lope wrote *Arcadia* (1598), and Cervantes produced *La Galatea* (1585), both in the pastoral manner. The pastoral vogue lasted about a century, but by 1600 the public had tired of these unrealistic and artificial works and turned elsewhere for reading entertainment.

B. The Moorish or Historical Novel

These novels accentuate the Oriental effect, and although most are naïve, they are more readable than the pastoral or chivalric works. The "noble" Moor is idealized, although the Moors at this time were not generally admired or respected.

1. *Historia del Abencerraje y de la hermosa Jarifa*, an anonymous *novela morisca*, is the first of its kind and a precursor of the modern historical novel. Many consider it to be the outstanding short

117

fictional work of the sixteenth century. The story has come down to us principally in three versions, of which that of Antonio de Villegas in 1565 is considered the best. No agreement has been reached regarding its authorship or date. At any rate, it constitutes the earliest European nondidactic short story and shows a remarkable emotional and psychological penetration. It influenced many, including Cervantes, Lope, Chateaubriand, Hugo, Alarcón, and Washington Irving.

The plot tells of the capture and imprisonment of the courageous knight Abindarráez. He is released for three days to marry his beloved Jarifa. Upon returning to his captor, the latter is so impressed with his worth that he gives him his freedom.

2. *Historia de los bandos de los Zegríes y Abencerrajes,* usually called *Guerras civiles de Granada* (first part, 1595; second part, 1604), was written by Ginés Pérez de Hita (1544–1619). The first part, more novel than history, leads up to the fall of Granada. The second part, more history than novel, deals with the war against the Alpujarra Moors. The idealized portrait of the Moors as gallant knights was accepted as authentic by the rest of Europe, and it had a strong impact on other writers, among them Lope, Pedro Antonio de Alarcón, Washington Irving, Mlle. de Scudéry, Chateaubriand, Cervantes, Calderón, Martínez de la Rosa, and Mme. de La Fayette.

Much of Pérez de Hita's material came from the Moorish frontier ballads, some of which are interspersed throughout the book. The first volume tells of the kings of Granada, rivalries among the Moors, and the constant infighting between two factions, the Abencerrajes and the Zegríes. Pérez de Hita gave free rein to his fantasy and described the romantic legends and splendor of the Moorish capital in its last days. Although much is false and exaggerated, the feasts and other events seem quite realistic. Not a witness of the events he described, the author cleverly wove fact and fantasy, truth and legend, together so that they are quite often indistinguishable. This created a false impression of Moorish life that proved difficult to eradicate in later years.

C. The Picaresque Novel

The *pícaros,* upon whom the picaresque novel is based, were usually errand boys, porters, or factotums and were pictured as crafty, sly, tattered, hungry, unscrupulous petty thieves. They stole to escape starvation and were likable despite their defects.

The picaresque novel, a reaction against the absurd unrealities and idealism of the pastoral, sentimental, and chivalric novels, represents the beginning of modern Realism. It juxtaposed the basic drives of hunger, cruelty, and mistrust and the honorable, glorious, idyllic life of knights and shepherds. Hunger replaced love as a theme, and poverty replaced wealth.

Early picaresque novels were both idealistic and realistic, tragic and comic, and the authors attacked political, religious, and military matters. Some authors were sincere reformers, while others conveniently set off their sermons so they might be easily avoided. They reflected the poverty and unsound economic conditions of late sixteenth-century Spain. Spaniards were living in a dream world after the glories of the conquest of the New World. They flocked to the cities, the upper classes refusing to work with their hands, cultivate the land, or engage in business or commerce, all of which were viewed as degrading. Poor knights starved with the beggars. Thus, though comic elements are omnipresent, the sentiment is tragic—the tragedy of a Spain that was outwardly the most powerful nation in the world but inwardly on the path to decline and ruin. The picaresque genre faithfully portrays these tragic conditions.

The picaresque novel is autobiographical and episodic in nature, as the *pícaro* recounts his adventures in the service of one master after another. These novels rarely came to a conclusive end, and were sometimes continued in later volumes. They inherited a long tradition of satire and bourgeois humor dating as far back as first-century Roman novels. Foreign influences include Dance of Death poetry, the French *fabliaux,* Italian novels and short stories, and German collections. Antecedents in Spain are found in *El Caballero Cifar, El corbacho, El libro de buen amor,* and *La Celestina.* Spanish writers gave the picaresque genre an intensity and urgency, however, that was previously lacking and made their picaresque tales one of the landmarks of European Realism.

Usually the *pícaro* is of the lower classes. Forced into a life of servitude by the severity of the times, he drifts into a life of petty crime and deceitfulness in his struggle for survival. The tone of the novel is hard, cynical, skeptical, often bitter, and it often portrays the corrupt and ugly. Humor abounds, but it is only a step removed from tears, and what appears to be funny is tragic in a different light.

The *pícaros* ordinarily write in their old age about their experiences as idealistic youths. Yet they do not present the whole picture. In its emphasis on the seamier side of life, the picaresque novel twists and deforms reality. The *pícaro* lives by his wits and steals and lies just to stay alive. His many employers give the author the opportunity to satirize various social classes and to paint a portrait of a period full of living, brawling human beings.

1. *Retrato de la lozana andaluza* (1528), by Francisco Delicado, is the earliest preserved picaresque novel, but it does little justice to the genre as it paints a sordid picture of the corruption, licentiousness, and dissoluteness of Rome during the Renaissance.

2. *La vida de Lazarillo de Tormes y de sus fortunas y adversidades* (1554), known simply as *Lazarillo de Tormes*, is the first important picaresque novel. The question of authorship has not been decided, and most regard the work as anonymous. Its triumph was immediate and universal, and many native and foreign authors owe it a great debt. The Inquisition banned it in 1559, probably because of its bitter attacks on clerics. Since editions were being smuggled in from abroad, however, Felipe II ordered it purged of features that denigrated the clergy.

Lazarillo de Tormes has seven chapters in which the little anti-hero serves a blind man, a priest, an *hidalgo*, a friar, a seller of indulgences, a chaplain, and a constable before he settles down to a respectable position as town crier in Toledo. Each master contributes to the social commentary and to the realistic education of Lazarillo. The blind man opens his eyes to the cruelties of the world, the priest shows him miserliness and hypocrisy, and the others convince him of the essential depravity of man. The important third chapter reveals a starving *hidalgo*, symbolic of Spain, too proud to accept employment because of his noble blood and because work would be degrading. Yet he was willing to eat food begged by Lazarillo and thus become a parasite of a parasite. Lazarillo cannot afford this false pride, for he is a human animal who must search for something to eat in a world always against him and other underdogs who must survive by their wits.

Lazarillo's language, simple and rapid, is not vulgar and eschews crudities. Even when the humor is crude, the words are inoffensive. Antitheses, augmentatives, and personifications abound, along with an intimate tone in the constant use of possessive adjectives, as in expressions such as "Abro mi puerta, bajo mi escalera, subo por mi calle." Expressions such as "El bueno de mi padre" and "el bueno de mi ciego" add charm to the work.

Today it is difficult to visualize the revolutionary quality and temerity of *Lazarillo de Tormes*. Under Felipe II the risk of portraying Spain as it really was was great indeed. Imitations of the social satire of *Lazarillo de Tormes* did not appear until after the king's death. Most later writers of picaresque novels spoke more bitterly of life but added social studies, local color, and *cuadros de costumbres* to make their works more complete. As Spain became more decadent, the *pícaro* was perverted from a suffering human being into one who enjoyed crime for itself. As the seventeenth century wore on, crime, not hunger, became the *pícaro*'s chief guide.

3. Mateo Alemán (1547?–1614) composed the second most important picaresque novel, *Guzmán de Alfarache*, in two parts, published in 1599 and 1604. A proposed third part never materialized.

The *pícaro* in this novel leads a complete life, from youth to old age, and is portrayed more thoroughly as a character than Lazarillo. The social background is broader, albeit seamier, as parasites, criminals, and injustice are found everywhere. Cynicism, pessimism, and a profound conviction of the essential depravity of man permeate *Guzmán de Alfarache*, though occasional nobility shines through and the hero is saved by his Catholic faith. More popular at first than the *Quijote*, it went through some twenty-nine editions in five years and was translated into a number of foreign languages. The second part contains many beautiful scenes of Spanish life, but they must be searched for in the maze of long, moralizing passages and countless digressions, perhaps used to avoid censure and clerical censorship. *Guzmán de Alfarache*, like other picaresque novels, comprises a string of incidents held together by a central character, and one avoids the moral while watching with the author the heroes and villains of life from the *atalaya de la vida humana* (watchtower to view human life). This is also the subtitle of the novel.

4. *El libro de entretenimiento de la pícara Justina* (1605), known simply as *La pícara Justina*, has been attributed to the Toledan Francisco López de Ubeda and consists of an *Arte poética*, three prologues, and four books. It recounts Justina's adventures, which are quite difficult to follow. The book, in bad taste, is redeemed in part by its colorful and rich vocabulary and phraseology.

5. *Relaciones de la vida del escudero Marcos de Obregón* (1618) relates in autobiographical fashion the adventures of Vicente Espinel (1550–1624). This novel differs from the ordinary in its

lack of bitterness and in its refinement and appreciation of beauty. It has the marks of the Milesian tale and the usual digressions and moralizing. It is one of Spain's best picaresque novels and ranks along with *Lazarillo de Tormes*, *Guzmán de Alfarache*, and *El Buscón*.

6. *Vida del Buscón, llamado don Pablos* (1626) is simply called *El Buscón*. Considered by many to be Francisco de Quevedo y Villegas' greatest work, it represents the culmination of this type of fiction and is typical of its author's work. Quevedo is pitiless, almost grotesque, in describing the boardinghouses of Salamanca and a host of repulsive characters. He wrote in cruel, bitter, and somber tones, for he neither liked nor admired his fellow man. He exaggerated his realism to the point of caricature, a technique that resounded throughout Europe, and Quevedo's extremes had enormous effect. Life is portrayed as cruel and heartless, but if the crudeness, misanthropy, sarcasm, and repulsiveness of *El Buscón* are offensive, it attracts by its vigor and brilliance. The Baroque language is full of puns, conceits, and jokes despite the fact that Quevedo opposed Gongorism. Among his nonpicaresque works are the *Sueños*, a series of five visions in which he meets members of all strata of society undergoing punishment for their sins. This book is considered to be the bitterest social satire of the Golden Age.

Minor picaresque writers include Alonso de Castillo Solórzano (1584–1648), Alonso Jerónimo de Salas Barbadillo (1581–1635), and Luis Vélez de Guevara y Dueñas (1578–1644).

The vogue of the extremely popular picaresque novel lasted for approximately a century, from 1550 to 1650. Had Spain not entered upon its great decline, the picaresque novel could have developed into a realistic novel of manners, but it died along with other literary forms by the end of the seventeenth century.

The influence of the picaresque novel on Spanish and world literature was enormous. All the important Spanish novels were promptly translated into the other European tongues. They contributed as much as *Don Quijote* to the demise of idealistic fiction and proved once again that all views of life, the low as well as the high, can fascinate and that a realistic representation of life, even if it portrays the ugly, the grotesque, the unpleasant, the crude, and the repulsive, can be made appealing. This democratization of novelistic prose and the reinstatement of realism to fiction are two of the greatest contributions of the picaresque novel to literature.

D. Miguel de Cervantes Saavedra (1547–1616)

Cervantes lived at a time when Spanish letters had entered their Golden Age and all forms of the novel had flourished, setting the stage for the appearance of the master. Born in Alcalá, a great center of learning, Cervantes traveled widely over Spain with his father, a surgeon seeking better fortune. He thus came into contact with people of all types and classes. His education was sketchy, but he read widely in works of the Classical and Spanish authors. In Madrid he studied for a time with Juan López de Hoyos, who instilled in the youth a love of tolerance and freedom.

A poor lad of Cervantes' time had three career choices: he could emigrate or become a soldier or a priest. Cervantes chose the military and distinguished himself in the battle of Lepanto, in which he received three wounds. One of these deprived him of the use of his left hand, which gained him the title "El manco de Lepanto." This was always a source of pride for him. He fought in other battles, and after being honorably discharged, he set out for Spain. The ship on which he sailed, however, was taken by Barbary pirates, and Cervantes was held prisoner for several years in Algiers. Finally ransomed, he returned to Spain, wounded and poor but with a mind enriched by his experiences and hardships.

In Spain he obtained a government position as a purchasing officer for the Spanish Armada. His duties took him all over Spain, and once again he came into contact with various classes and types of people. Because of certain irregularities in his accounts and the defection of an untrustworthy subordinate, Cervantes was arrested and put in jail, where, it is said, he began writing *Don Quijote*. His family was suspected of some involvement in the murder of a nobleman outside Cervantes' house in Valladolid, but the charges were eventually dropped. The incident shows, however, the low esteem in which his family was held. Cervantes spent the last years of his life writing, and he had plans for many other works when he died of dropsy on April 23, 1616.

In most ways Cervantes was an ordinary man, but he had the spark of genius to produce great creative works. His first love was poetry, for which he had no talent even though he tried repeatedly to write poems. He tried his hand also at the drama and wrote some twenty plays of which only two were performed.

123

He did succeed with the *entremés* and wrote some of Spain's best. In them we see the same duality of materialism and idealism that would mark his fiction.

1. *La Galatea*, a pastoral novel, was written in 1583 and published in 1585. Cervantes completed only the first part, and until his death he thought his fame would rest on this work. He injected his double vision of life, the real and the ideal, into this novel and offered new elements such as blood and death and more vehement and tragic passion than appeared in the typical pastoral.

2. *Las novelas ejemplares* are much more closely allied with *Don Quijote*. In the prologue, Cervantes insists, perhaps to avoid difficulty with the Inquisition, that each *novela,* or short story, will teach some moral lesson. His twelve *novelas* can roughly be divided into romantic novels and novels of customs. In them he does not hesitate to paint vice and brutality, but he portrays them always in an artistic manner, and his occasional crude Naturalism is tempered by a delicate fantasy. Many of his heroes seem subject to moral compulsions to do the right thing.

His Romantic novels have too many digressions, tears, and false coincidences and take place in exotic settings such as the Orient or England. In the novels of customs, which take place in Spain, Cervantes unites his experiences, imagination, and prophetic vision into a unified whole. He takes a modern position on liberty and honor, and the true meaning of nobility and virtue for him differs greatly from the artificial Spanish *pundonor* of his time. He insists on virtuous matrimony and ethical and artistic harmony.

The value of these novels lies in the painting of the society of his time in many of its aspects, good, bad, and indifferent. The idea of a group of independent novels was almost unheard of in his day, but he tried to give them cohesion by promising that each would yield a profitable example and that the whole would provide tasty and honest fruit. Among the better novels are *La gitanilla, El casamiento engañoso, El coloquio de los perros, El licenciado vidriera,* and *Rinconete y Cortadillo.* Next to *Don Quijote,* these novels constitute Cervantes' best work.

3. *Los trabajos de Persiles y Sigismunda,* Cervantes' last work, was briefly more popular than the *Quijote,* despite its impossible plot, complicated movement, and overly perfect characters. The *Persiles* has value for its exoticism, its adventures to realize a perfect love, and occasional references to problems of the day. The prologue contains one of the most beautiful passages of Spanish

prose. Cervantes wrote it four days before his death and after receiving extreme unction.

Superficially, the *Persiles* resembles *Theagenes and Chariclea,* the Greek novel, and Cervantes admitted his indebtedness. He wrote it, he said, strictly as a "libro de entretenimiento" with no serious purpose in mind. It is subtitled *Historia septentrional,* the north being the land of romance and mystery, and he moves his characters from northern to southern climes, from misty seas and distant islands through Lisbon, Spain, France, and Italy. Numerous subplots enhance the interest of the novel, and for William J. Entwistle they are the outstanding value of the work.

Outstanding in the *Persiles* too are the brief, concise histories of the soul. Interspersed are discourses on history, love, honor, ignorance, women, and almost every other conceivable subject. The main characters, Persiles and Sigismunda, and the minor characters as well are perfection incarnate, model human beings. The one exception is Rosamunda, a minor character, who is lascivious and lewd, full of amorous desire, unable to resist vice and sensuality.

Critical opinion on this book is varied, ranging from Fitzmaurice-Kelly's frankness in condemning it a failure to Bell's finding it "a great work full of vital thought." Perhaps Azorín came closest in summing it up as a "libro admirable de un gran poeta."

4. *El ingenioso hidalgo don Quijote de la Mancha,* known affectionately simply as the *Quijote,* is Spain's greatest literary masterpiece. It has remained Spain's most popular book for 385 years, and a good case can be made for it as the world's best novel, since next to the Bible it is the world's most frequently published book.

Cervantes had failed to receive fame on the battlefield or as a writer, and when he set about the task of writing the *Quijote,* he was probably not clear in his mind what he intended to do, for the book grows in every way as it proceeds. He said that he would write his book as a chastisement of those authors of the pernicious, inane novels of chivalry and that his purpose would be "poner en aborrecimiento de los hombres las fingidas y disparatadas historias de los libros de caballerías." Viewed in this light, the *Quijote* is a parody on the novel of chivalry, establishing a precedent for the burlesque, which has been an integral part of Spanish literature ever since. But Cervantes despised only the excesses of the chivalric novels, and when he condemned them he saved from destruction some that convey idealism, bravery,

125

loyalty, and a sense of devotion to high causes. These virtues he wanted to preserve in an age when he could see them disappearing. His book, therefore, takes the form of the standard novel of chivalry, and don Quijote, who read these novels until his mind was turned, sets out into the world as a knight-errant in an age when knight-errantry has been dead for centuries. Accompanied by his squire, Sancho Panza, he fights and suffers for his knightly ideals as he attempts to right the wrongs of the world, to protect the weak and oppressed, to bring about what he called the "Golden Age," which to his mind was something like the "Kingdom of Heaven." He failed, to be sure, to reform the world, but he never relinquished his ideals, never retreated in the face of danger, hardships, suffering, or disappointment, and although he failed, he was quite sure that the effort had been worth making. Could Cervantes have intended to represent Spain in the character of don Quijote? The analogy holds, for Spain, too, had set out to reform the world and had failed, but felt the effort had not been in vain.

To attempt to limit this great book to one theme is folly, for many themes abound therein, and it is much more than a pseudonovel of chivalry, parody, or allegory. Within the larger work are found the inserted tales that represent every fictional type of the age—the Moorish, the pastoral, the Italian, and others—and Cervantes fused them all into a harmonious whole. Perhaps the basic question of the author is, What is reality? Cervantes asks why one cannot create one's own reality, a higher reality in the fields of religion, art, and politics, and suggests that though the world may think the idealist mad, he may find a higher satisfaction within himself. And as one sympathizes with Quijote's splendid idealism and watches him in one failure after another, one wonders whether it is not reality, after all, that is at fault. Cervantes also makes the point that truth is relative, and what are windmills to the realist may be giants to the idealist.

The *Quijote* appeared in two parts, the first published in 1605 and the second in 1615. From the title itself one can perceive the dualism of the novel and the interplay of the real and the ideal. The name Quijote is a fanciful invention, and La Mancha was a well-known province of Spain, but *ingenioso* was a new and exotic word in Cervantes' time. Quijote, a typical *hidalgo*, of whom there were many, remembered a glorious Spanish past and was moderately well-off. Exactly as Cervantes failed in real life, so Quijote was to fail, for the lot of a truthful "madman" is not an enviable one. The "real" world he wanted to bring back had never existed, and he discovered that, unfortunately, one cannot live continually in a Utopian or poetic world. In his "madness" he was on a higher level than reality, but eventually he had to accept an imperfect world. The tragedy of Quijote is the tragedy of reformers, and perhaps in the end he does not fail as he abandons his noble attempt and idealism. Madariaga said that while Hamlet represents the pressure of society on the individual, don Quijote represents the pressure of the individual on society. Man must always strive to create through the use of his imagination, but even when that ability disappears at death, his Christian ideal of *hacer bien* continues. Cervantes satirizes everything and everybody, but he does it with kindness.

The *Quijote* is the complete novel of humanity, for the two characters, don Quijote and Sancho Panza, represent the two most common types to be found anywhere. Quijote is the idealist and the reformer, unselfish, long-suffering, striving for the good of mankind. Sancho is the utter realist, self-centered and desirous of satisfying first his own animal needs, hunger and thirst. Together they represent every man, and Cervantes seems to say that to be whole each person needs some attributes of both.

Sancho is the opposite of Quijote as the work begins. He sees windmills, not giants, but under the constant vigilance of Quijote he ascends to a somewhat idealistic level, though he always keeps his materialistic base. When he returns home, he is unable to explain his idealism to his wife, for the gulf between them is too wide; and when Quijote finally recognizes himself as Alonso Quijano, it is Sancho who begs him not to die but to remain steadfast to his ideal and sally forth once more into the world. Though Sancho is never loath to receive the material benefits of life, in the end he has himself became somewhat of a *caballero*, sharing his master's idealism.

Cervantes sees goodness in all the world. For him, the evil are often good, for he does not judge by outward forms. He causes his characters to reveal their kindness and goodness, if they have it in them (Cervantes insists that beneath the ugliest exterior may lie the most Christian soul), and don Quijote makes those around him enter his world rather than entering theirs. Although their motives vary, everyone strives to enter Quijote's poetic world. Believing in the reality of the book of chivalry, Quijote insists on righting wrongs, but as the novel progresses he assumes Christ-like attributes and expresses the need of the world for a new idealism, Christian knight-errantry, and *hacer bien.* He incarnates the chivalrous perfection of liberality, generosity, and faithfulness. The world judges him mad, but Quijote insists that the exterior is less important than the reality of imagination. In fact, this supposed madman gave lessons in sanity to the very ones who mocked him.

In 1614 a second volume appeared, written by an unknown, Alonso Fernández de Avellaneda. It seems the very antithesis of the original and has little merit. It did spur Cervantes on to write his own second part, in which he deals somewhat charitably with Avellaneda despite his distortion of Quijote and personal attacks on Cervantes.

Cervantes' own second volume, published in 1615, contains less action and more conversation than the first volume, and the characters take on a deeper symbolic meaning. The psychological and spiritual qualities have greater impact, and it becomes clear that Sancho and Quijote, instead of being opposites, are more nearly identical in their dedication to an ideal. Here Quijote lives the entire life of a man, of all men. He and Sancho discuss religion, philosophy, in short, life itself, but as the end of the *Quijote* approaches, the less the immortal pair have need of speech. Quijote's creative imagination dies as he begins to recognize inns as inns instead of castles, but his ideals continue. As Waldo Frank has said, though the knight gives us countless reasons for disliking him, Cervantes ends with love and we with veneration.

The book's construction is fairly loose, and when Cervantes thought of something new he simply added an episode to the framework. Almost seven hundred characters from all walks of life, from the noblest to the basest, parade before us. Cervantes was such a master stylist that the Spanish language is sometimes referred to today as *la lengua cervantina*. He used many stylistic devices, but no single one or any combination of them can explain the poetry, beauty, and majesty of the work.

Perhaps the merit of the *Quijote* lies in a kind of interior harmony and combination of multilevel attributes. For some it is a comic work. Others see in it a new style, while still others see a great moral value or the conflict between the ideal and the real. Romanticists see Quijote as the supreme individualist, the man against the world. For others, Sancho is as great as Quijote in moral and ethical force. Many great novelists have copied some aspect of the *Quijote,* including Flaubert, Fielding, Balzac, and Galdós. Marx, Tolstoy, Turgenev, Goethe, Ben Jonson, Dostoyevski, Alexander Hamilton, and Thomas Jefferson read it.

Dostoyevski classified it as the supreme work of fiction that represented the highest expression of human thought.

Other works have better plots and finer technique, but none has achieved such an equal balance or has come so close to the wellsprings of human nature and endeavor. Cervantes' book has gone through some one thousand editions, and many more editions will appear in the future. Sansón Carrasco put it in perspective in Chapter 3 of the second part: "Los niños la manosean, los mozos la leen, los hombres la entienden y los viejos la celebran."

E. Minor Novelists of the Seventeenth Century

The post-Cervantes period was one of decadence. Novels were second-rate: the plots were frivolous and artificial, the writing was of a sophisticated superficiality, and the humor lacked the depth, pace, and meaning of Cervantes'. In addition to Lope de Vega, mention may be made of the following novelists: Francisco Lugo y Dávila (1615–1669); Gonzalo Céspedes y Meneses (1585?–1638); and María de Zayas y Sotomayor (1590–1650), the only woman among the minor novelists.

THE EIGHTEENTH CENTURY

The eighteenth century did not produce great literature. The Neoclassic tradition produced even less in the novel than in poetry and the drama. Only two names merit mention as novelists in this age, Torres Villarroel and Padre Isla.

A. Diego de Torres Villarroel (1693–1770)

This mysterious and enigmatic figure left home at the age of twenty, lived with a hermit in Portugal, performed as a bullfighter and dancer, and returned home to study medicine, which he did not practice. After a couple of lucky predictions in some almanacs he published, he became famous, was known as something of a magician, and was hired to drive goblins out of the houses of Madrid. He entered the competition for the chair of mathematics at the University of Salamanca in 1726 and strangely won over all his opponents. He was publicly acclaimed as a scholar until he became a priest in 1745.

Torres wrote in many fields, but his best-known work is his

129

autobiographical picaresque novel in which the adventures recounted may have been based on his own experiences. The full title of this book is *Vida, ascendencia, nacimiento, crianza y aventuras del Dr. Don Diego de Torres Villarroel* (1743). He takes the reader through a series of picaresque episodes, during which he serves a number of masters, and in so doing gives an accurate and sprightly commentary on the life of his times.

B. José Francisco de Isla de la Torre (1703–1781)

Padre Isla, a Jesuit, wrote the most famous novel of the eighteenth century, indeed the only pure novel worthy of mention, *Historia del famoso predicador Fray Gerundio de Campazas, alias Zotes,* usually called simply *Fray Gerundio.* The two parts of this work appeared in 1758 and 1768 under the pseudonym Francisco Lobón de Salazar. The work's value lies in its satire of the abuses, education, Baroque preaching, pedantry, and *mal gusto* of society in the eighteenth century. Fray Gerundio incarnates the type of preacher who could not read yet knew how to preach, having been taught all the trappings of Gongorism by his tutor, Fray Blas. Popular in its time and widely read by the educated aristocracy, it aroused the wrath of the clergy, who felt the sting of ridicule in Isla's unmasking of their defects.

Padre Isla, largely forgotten now like most writers of the eighteenth century, made several translations. One of them, the *Año cristiano* by Father Croiset, which contains short lives of saints, is still read in some Spanish homes. No translation succeeded better, however, than the one published in 1787–1788 of the French work of Lesage, the four-volume *Aventuras de Gil Blas de Santillana,* an eighteenth-century picaresque novel with a Spanish flavor. This translation by Padre Isla outlasted *Fray Gerundio,* and it was the only picaresque novel that many ordinary readers had encountered up to that time. Fortunately, Padre Isla's skillful translation is better than the original.

THE NINETEENTH CENTURY

A. Romanticism

Spanish Romantic novelists imitated Sir Walter Scott, the dominating figure of the time, but Manzoni's novels were also known in Spain, as were those of Chateaubriand and James Fenimore Cooper. In 1830 Ramón López Soler (1806–1836) wrote one of the first Spanish historical novels in imitation of Scott, *Los bandos de Castilla: o, El caballero del Cisne*. Larra produced *El doncel de don Enrique el doliente* (1834), based on the legend of Macías. Successful in its period, like other historical novels it has not stood the test of time. Espronceda wrote *Sancho Saldaña* (1834), but his true forte was poetry. The best Spanish Romantic novel was *El señor de Bembibre* (1844), by Enrique Gil y Carrasco (1815–1846).

The pseudoarcheological novelistic prose of the Romantic age failed to give rise to a permanent figure, but Manuel Fernández y González (1821–1888) devoted a lifetime to this type of novel and wrote over three hundred of them. The number of such novels printed in the first half of the nineteenth century attests to their popularity. Although nothing of permanent value came from these works, it must be said that the Romanticists' appreciation of landscape was passed on to the Realistic novelists of the second half of the century, who developed it with greater skill and made it an important part of their art.

B. *Costumbrismo*

Flourishing in the years preceding Romanticism and representing a continuation of the realistic prose manner, *costumbrismo* proved to be one of the most popular literary forms in the first half of the century and was cultivated even by some confirmed Romanticists. The realistic portrayal of manners, customs, and characters reached a minor peak in short prose sketches (occasionally in verse) depicting various social backgrounds.

The oppressive censorship of Fernando VII's despotic reign delayed the arrival of Romanticism in Spain. The *artículo de costumbres* was tolerated, since it was thought to be innocuous, although a very definite shift in tone is noticeable after the death of Fernando and the establishment of a liberal government. The *costumbrista* literature has, of course, an inherent value, but more important, the *costumbristas* probably laid the groundwork for the regional novel. In fact, the first such novel was largely a stringing-together of *cuadros de costumbres* on a negligible plot. Viewed in this light, the nineteenth-century regional novel was an outgrowth of the *costumbrista* manner. Another school of thought, however, feels that one reason for the comparative lateness of the development of the novel in Spain in the nineteenth century was that the *artículos de costumbres,* by serving the purpose of fiction and satisfying readers, may have delayed it.

C. The Regional Novel

One of the highlights of Spanish literature is the regional novel of the second half of the nineteenth century. Developing out of *costumbrismo* and the rich realistic manner of earlier centuries, the regional novel represents a reaction against the passions, artificiality, and sentimentality of Romanticism. In the early years of the regional novel, writers depended on their own tradition and native forebears for example and subject matter. Later, influences from France drifted across the border, and a few Spaniards attempted Naturalism but tempered it with typical Spanish warmth and subjectivity.

Since the novel was concerned with life in various areas of Spain and since the novelists were interested in portraying that life down to the smallest detail, it was natural that they should limit themselves to descriptions of the regions of the land they knew best. Galdós was the only writer who was able to invade all regions of Spain with success. The regional novel, however, was not merely a collection of *cuadros de costumbres* haphazardly joined together by some sort of plot, for it soon outgrew its infancy and blossomed into one of the great novels of Spanish literature.

1. *Cecilia Böhl von Faber* (1796–1877), better known by her pen name, Fernán Caballero, produced the first well known regional novel, *La gaviota,* in 1849. She wrote it first in French and then translated it into Spanish, which may account for some of the stylistic maladroitness. *La gaviota* lacks a realistic technique, though it does convey an image of life in a definite historical time and place. The story of the gifted peasant girl whose lovers die and who loses her beautiful singing voice is essentially Romantic. Nevertheless, Fernán Caballero carefully observed popular customs and used a realistic tone. As she said, "La novela no se inventa, se observa." Her work suffers from an excessively moral tone and from her sentimental idealization of the picturesque. Also we see in her work the theme of Antonio de Guevara's *Menosprecio de corte y alabanza de aldea.* As in Pereda's later novels, the city to Fernán Caballero is a "den of iniquity" where the lovely heroine is beset by all kinds of evil temptations.

Among her other novels are *Clemencia* (1852), *La familia de Alvareda* (1856), and *Un servilón y un liberalito* (1857). Her realistic portrayal of Andalusian customs was a welcome relief after the vagaries and artificialities of the Romantic novel, in spite of her old-fashioned ideas and prejudices, lack of imagination, reactionary manner, and faulty style. To her credit is her democratic interest in common people and her insistence upon the importance and value of simple things and a wholesome life. Her chief claim to distinction is that she was the first to write a regional novel.

2. *Pedro Antonio de Alarcón* (1833–1891), one of Spain's greatest humorists, was from Andalusia. As a young man he was a radical revolutionary, but he later became a conservative and a staunch defender of religion. He was elected to the Cortes and, in 1877, to the Royal Academy.

His works can be divided into long and short novels, short stories, travel books, and miscellaneous writings. His four full-length novels are *El final de Norma* (1851), *El escándalo* (1875), *El niño de la bola* (1880), and *La pródiga* (1881). *El final de Norma,* a youthful work about the love of a violinist for a singer, against the setting of fantastic and romantic adventures in the north, achieved an undeserved popularity, and the author himself declared it to be "naïve, childish, fantastic . . . commonplace."

In *El escándalo,* Alarcón offers a strong defense of the Catholic religion and attempts to prove that immorality and religious inconstancy inevitably bring tragedy. Because it deals with religious matters, it has been his most controversial book, eliciting glowing praise and hearty condemnation. The exceedingly complicated plot tends toward Romanticism, as do most of his semirealistic works.

Alarcón's fame rests largely, however, on his shorter novels, *El capitán Veneno* (1881) and *El sombrero de tres picos* (1874). The former concerns a misogynist tamed by his sweet and charming nurse, who uses psychology to get her man.

El sombrero de tres picos, his most famous work, has served as the basis of operas in French, German, and English and ranks on par with Cervantes' *Novelas ejemplares.* It is based on a ballad theme, *El molinero de Arcos,* and is little more than a short story. Its humor, fast pace, and intriguing characters make it an ever-readable work. The best features of Spanish Realism are combined with the rich picaresque tradition of the Golden Age, and critics speak of its "comic vigor," "popular flavor," and "lively dialogue." This delightful tale relates how a miller, "tío" Lucas, fearing that his wife is playing him false with the aged Corregidor, seeks revenge with a visit to the latter's wife. Three years later the Corregidor loses his position and dies in jail as a patriotic Spaniard. Frasquita and "tío" Lucas live to a ripe old age. Alarcón, in this little gem of the storyteller's art, clothes a folk tale in elegant style without sacrificing its popular charm.

Alarcón's *Historietas nacionales* (1881) contains his best-loved short stories, *El libro talonario, La buenaventura,* and *El afrancesado. Cuentos amatorios* (1881) and *Narraciones inverosímiles* (1882) are other volumes of short stories. Because of their conciseness, greater clarity of dialogue, and lack of didactic goals, Alarcón's short stories are superior to his novels, most of which are melodramatic, labored, and too moralistic to have lasting appeal. Since his works have characteristics of both movements, he is often considered a bridge novelist between Romanticism and Realism. He also left three travel books, three volumes of war correspondence, a play, two collections of essays, and an autobiography, in which he reveals his bitterness because of adverse criticism.

3. *Juan Valera y Alcalá Galiano* (1827–1905), an Andalusian of aristocratic origin, embarked on a long diplomatic career that took him to Lisbon, Rio de Janeiro, Russia, and Washington. A cosmopolitan linguist, he had a wide knowledge of Classical literature. His "salon aristocracy" and obvious refinements wear on the reader, as do his often simple and cloying plots. He wrote largely for an intellectual elite of which he was a member.

Valera's most famous novel is *Pepita Jiménez* (1874). Its epistolary form lent itself to introspective monologue, at which Valera was adept. The plot concerns the mental and emotional turmoil of a young seminarian who is won from the priesthood by the beautiful young widow Pepita Jiménez. In most of his novels, including *Pepita Jiménez,* Valera is concerned with human conduct, and his works are nearly always analytical. Valera points out that the mysticism of Luis, the young seminarian, is false and founded on youthful, romantic notions, that man is not called on to lose his body in order to save his soul, and that God can be served in a number of ways.

Doña Luz (1879), a reversal of *Pepita Jiménez,* deals with the platonic love of a girl for a priest. The novel is filled with the same kind of philosophical and religious discussion found in the earlier work.

Valera's collected works run to some forty-six volumes. The most important are *Las ilusiones del doctor Faustino* (1875), which was for Valera his most real creation and "un compuesto de los vicios, ambiciones, ensueños, escepticismos, descreimientos, concupiscencias . . . que afligieron a la juventud de mi tiempo"; *El comendador Mendoza* (1877), which deals with the adventurous life of Fadrique in Spain, Peru, and finally in the French Revolution; and *Juanita la larga* (1895), which concerns an old man's love for a young girl and contains nostalgic recollections of youth and childhood.

Valera won admittance to the Royal Academy in 1861, largely as a critic and poet. He was recognized as one of the best literary critics of the nineteenth century, and his readers admired his solid Classical and cultural background, rational outlook, common sense, good taste, and natural, simple, and lucid analyses. His prose was direct and elegant but without affectation.

Valera, whose style was cold yet undeniably beautiful, believed in "art for art's sake," since for him the highest function of literature was to create something beautiful and pleasant. This philosophy was in direct contrast with that of some Realistic novelists, who felt that the intentional avoidance of unpleasant things was a betrayal of the artist's responsibility to portray reality in all its aspects. Much of what Valera wrote does not fit into any neat classification. He exhibits pleasure and charm, Classical tranquility, and yet, from time to time, a light Romantic vein. In his novels he liked to deal with constants and with what he felt were experiences common to all. Thus his works contain psychological analyses and usually deal with an inner action of universal scope. He did not accept many doctrines, but he had faith in life and in the value of living it; joy, not despair, was his goal. In the analyses of his characters' souls, he often became too interested in his procedure, and his dialogue is not always suited to the character for whom it is intended. The lack of action in his works makes his novels discursive rather than dramatic. Yet he is not artificial, as he stresses harmony of style rather than warm life.

Valera, described as both pagan and Christian, was at times somewhat mystical in his works. His characters, most of them Juan Valera in thin disguise, are virtually without exception discreet, elegant, and cultured. His plotting, with almost inevitable Hollywood endings, leaves much to be desired. Nevertheless, he is psychologically penetrating and reflects realistically his beloved Andalusia within the obvious limitations of his overly optimistic view of life and the world.

Valera's short stories are often based on historical anecdotes. Usually he does not explain unnecessarily or give too much factual background. He preferred to use folklore material, not because it was popular but because it was traditional, for he disliked the former and respected the latter. He wrote historical, fantastic, moral, and legendary stories, often incorporating his own moral viewpoint.

4. *José María de Pereda y Sánchez de Porrúa* (1833–1906), the most regional of the nineteenth-century novelists, portrays effectively his native region of Santander and the *montaña*. He represents better than any other writer the evolution of the sketch writer into the regional novelist. Whereas Andalusia seems a product of recent history, the northern part of Spain, comparatively more isolated, conserved much of the spirit of the Middle Ages. Pereda was a typical product of that traditional, conservative life of the north, and his works reflect this background.

Pereda emphasized the evils of contemporary life, especially in large cities with their demoralizing and corruptive influences. He stressed the glories of the monarchy, the Church, and the patriarchal way of life. Consequently he preached for a return to the good simple life of the country. In line with this philosophy, he injected into his works the language of the peasant folk, the salt of the earth, and he continually emphasized tradition and rural aristocracy.

His first fiction, *Escenas montañesas* (1864), is mostly a series of sketches, but it is important as one of the earliest Realistic works and sets the pattern for much of Pereda's later work, which emphasizes the countryside instead of plot. It contains natural dialogue and regional impact and demonstrates that Pereda is essentially a *costumbrista,* as were all the Spanish Realists of this time to some degree.

Pereda's first long novel was *El buey suelto* (1878), an exaggerated tale that decries bachelorhood and deals with the problems of marriage. Pereda's skill with words is reflected in the stylistic beauty of this book, but the plot is trivial. *Don Gonzalo González de la Gonzalera,* a satire on revolutions and politicians that appeared in 1879, defends the old traditions in which Pereda was interested. *El sabor de la tierruca* (1881) exhibits freshness, purity, and rustic tranquility, combined with beautiful descriptive power. *Pedro Sánchez* (1883), judged by Pardo Bazán and Clarín to be a good novel, deals with corruption in Madrid and describes Pereda's student life there. He returns here to one of his favorite themes, the joy and peace of rural life, away from the toil and turmoil of the monstrous city.

De tal palo, tal astilla (1880) was, according to some opinions,

Pereda's answer to *Gloria* by Galdós. Menéndez y Pelayo agreed that this was a thesis novel and that the fervently Catholic Pereda had abandoned to a certain degree "la observación desinteresada." Surprisingly, the extremely conservative Pereda and the liberal Galdós were good friends.

Pereda's two most popular works were *Peñas arriba* (1895) and *Sotileza* (1884). The former, containing his best descriptions of the *montaña* district, stresses again the need for a return to the simple life and has an almost mystical attitude toward nature, painted with masterful strokes. It relates how a young city dweller, at first contemptuous of country life, is able to find happiness only by becoming a part of that life himself. In *Sotileza*, Silda, or Sotileza, an orphan girl, has three suitors from different social levels. Pereda shows that he can deal with various types, including drunks and degraded men and women, though his contrast of the pure Sotileza with the rough fisherman seems overly Romantic. In *Sotileza*, reputed to be the best novel of the sea by a Spaniard, Pereda gives us a striking picture of the life, the fine virtues, and the miserable physical existence of the Santander fisherfolk together with their struggles against the sea.

Pereda studied details with an almost scientific detachment, which caused some to comment on his Naturalistic technique at a time when Naturalism was not highly regarded in the literary world. Pereda himself felt that Naturalism was *hediondo*. Sincere in his beliefs, he defended his ideas valiantly. He was a painter of nature in all its aspects—simple, grand, savage, or gentle. He was above all a descriptive artist, not a good psychologist or storyteller, and he tended to moralize too much. His enormous vocabulary, archaic words, Latinisms, religious emphasis, and excessive regionalism make for heavy reading. In consequence, his popularity with modern readers has suffered, but he was undoubtedly one of Spain's most admired Realists.

5. *Benito Pérez Galdós* (1843–1920) is the greatest Spanish novelist of the nineteenth century and the only one who deserves to be ranked with great European novelists like Balzac, Dickens, and Dostoyevski. One wonders why he has not yet taken his place in world popularity among these giants, and one can conjecture that in part it is due to bad translations and in part to antagonisms he aroused in his own country. His stern, somewhat fanatically religious mother caused him some anxiety, and many see in his well-known creation doña Perfecta a portrait of that severe old lady. Galdós' family was fairly well-off, and he studied at English schools in his native Canary Islands.

137

Though he studied law in Madrid, he was far more interested in newspaper work and writing articles than in attending class. His mother sent him to France to try to reform him, but his trip there simply convinced him that his true vocation was writing and gave him a closer acquaintance with the novels of Balzac.

On his return to a Madrid of *tertulias,* plots, counterplots, and revolutions, Galdós found himself in his element. He spent his time visiting buildings, studying architecture, listening to sermons—all of which would be grist for his mill later in his novels. He visited poor tenement houses and the lower districts to study life. He wrote for some of the best newspapers of the day, attempting even in these early journalistic efforts to analyze and evaluate the Spain he loved. Galdós, undoubtedly the giant of Spanish letters, championed the liberal causes, a factor in delaying his entrance into the Royal Academy until 1897 and its refusal to recommend him for the Nobel Prize. When he died, the masses mourned the only novelist of the time who truly understood them.

Although he was disheartened by the lack of dignity and intelligence of his environment, he optimistically insisted on the possibility of a better world and a better Spain. He believed in a God of love and not of wrath. He disliked artificial, restrictive, and bigoted codes, but he was, notwithstanding, a religious man. After an unsuccessful attempt called *La sombra,* he published·*La fontana de oro* (1870), a historical account of the liberal and revolutionary period of 1820–1823. In a vein reminiscent of the Generation of 1898, he discussed the deplorable and backward state of his country and its future possibilities.

In 1873 he began his first series of historical novels, the *Episodios nacionales.* In all he wrote five series, a total of forty-six volumes (the final series of ten was never completed), beginning with the battle of Trafalgar and covering the history of Spain for the next seventy years. He stopped writing historical novels in 1879 (after the first two series) but recommenced in 1898. Galdós shows a remarkable ability to synthesize historical figures with his fictional characters, and he combines this talent with an evocative picture of the broad canvas of Spanish politics, customs, and history.

Galdós wrote seventy-seven novels and twenty-six plays. His works are difficult to classify since some are Realistic, some Romantic, some Naturalistic, some psychological. Joaquín Casalduero classifies Galdós' novels into categories such as historical, abstract, Naturalistic, spiritualistic, and mythological, but critics usually divide them into Novels of the First Period and the so-called Contemporary Spanish Novels.

The novels of his first period, *Doña Perfecta* (1876), *Gloria* (two volumes, 1877), *Marianela* (1878), and *La familia de León Roch* (two volumes, 1879), in spite of Romantic overtones, try to carry out Galdós' ideas expressed later in his speech upon entering the Royal Academy. There he insisted that the novel had to be the image of life, the reproduction of human beings—their passions, large and small weaknesses, souls, bodies, language, physical and spiritual attributes, and possessions. Indeed, as with the *Comédie humaine* of Balzac, there is a unity in his work, both in the characters who reappear from novel to novel and in the thread of love, justice, tolerance, and humanity that runs throughout his entire production.

Galdós wrote naturally, which occasioned the comments of uninformed critics that he had no style—the same kind of criticism offered to the works of Dickens, Balzac, Cervantes, and Dostoyevski. His vocabulary is one of the largest among writers, but his special words and phrases do not detract from the overall impact. All the Galdosian characters live in an internal contradiction (the same duality we have seen so often). Like Cervantes, whom he resembles greatly, Galdós often shows us a most horrible man or woman, claiming that this is the stuff of which we are all made, that we must thus love our fellow men with a true Christian love, and that even the most abject personalities may have positive moral values.

The early novels involve the continuing analysis of various hypocrisies, the struggle between science and religion, the conflict between different faiths, and the meaning of beauty and true charity. *Doña Perfecta* concerns a progressive, modern, and broad-minded nephew from Madrid who meets a tragic death at the orders of his aunt in a struggle with a bigoted, reactionary, and tradition-bound town. Pepe Rey, the nephew, believes that men can be led upward through education. With his science, he believes in God (perhaps a *Krausista* influence on Galdós), while doña Perfecta, despite superficial appearances, does not believe, at least not in a tolerant Christian God. *Gloria*, too, treats a religious theme; it tells of the tortured, tragic love of a noble English Jew and a fine Spanish Catholic girl. Their son, Jesús Nazarenito, the symbol of the power of love, is the hope for the future. Here Galdós adopts a rational attitude in an attempt to unify humanity. *Gloria*'s appearance created almost a national crisis, and for months the book was discussed, condemned, and

139

praised. The dramatic appeal of the novel lies in the conflict between true love and the force of traditional belief, and though the ending is inevitable, the call to love and tolerance overshadows it.

Marianela, his most lyrical novel, seems like a quiet interlude after the torrential passions of his previous works. It is an idyllic story of the pathetic love of an ugly orphan girl for a handsome and attractive blind lad whom she serves as a guide. The love ends with the death of the girl when the boy recovers his sight, forgets the lovely soul that had made him love her, and shrinks from the ugly body. Marianela, representing imagination; Paul, rationalism; and Teodoro Golfín, the doctor who restores Paul's sight, science, are symbols of the various stages through which civilization has passed. When science supplants imagination as the guide of man, poor Marianela must die. The novel bears an obvious similarity to Cervantes' comparison of creative imagination and life. *La familia de León Roch* shows how excessive religiosity and religious differences can wreck a marriage.

In the novels of the contemporary period, Galdós deals with all aspects of life of all social classes and analyzes the vices of Spanish society. His masterpiece is *Fortunata y Jacinta* (1886–1887), in four volumes. Basically the work contrasts two women: Jacinta, the wealthy middle-class wife, and Fortunata, the mistress from the lower class. The principal parts of the novel consist of the varying relationships between these two, though Galdós fills his book with a whole host of types, rich and poor, among them the pathological Maxi, Fortunata's husband. Galdós was interested in mental illness and pathological types and shows a surprisingly modern knowledge of them. Jacinta is sweet, refined, and angelic, and Fortunata is generous and warmhearted but of stronger passions. Fortunata gives Juanito Santa Cruz the child that Jacinta would have liked to bear; a favorite theme of Galdós is that the common people are virile, whereas the upper classes are decadent and thin-blooded. Maxi sums up the conflict between the ideal and the real in his contention that spirit and thought cannot be stilled by physical limitations. *Angel Guerra* (three volumes, 1890–1891) emphasizes spiritual and personal ideas of Galdós and treats the themes of humility, abnegation, salvation, and divine mercy. Angel Guerra (perhaps Galdós himself) sees a vision of a better world and dies when he comes into contact with the concrete reality of Spain and humanity (note again the Cervantine influence).

La desheredada (1881) and *Misericordia* (1897) are excellent samples of Galdós' Naturalistic work. Isidora, of *La desheredada*, is a maladjusted, emotionally unstable woman of refined tastes. Gradually her habit of self-delusion grows, and she sinks into moral degradation. The novel bears a certain similarity to Zola's writings, as Galdós describes Madrid slums and the effects of heredity and mental degeneration in Isidora's family. *Misericordia*, set against the background of the lower classes in Madrid, beautifully sums up Galdós' ideas of true charity. Again we observe the Cervantine theme that in the ugliest and simplest body one can find great moral and aesthetic values. Galdós, in addition to treating the concept of forgiveness and including a message of hope, seemed to be preaching the possibility of conciliation between classes based on human understanding and uniting the degenerate aristocracy with its remaining ideals to the vitality of the masses.

Among the countless other novels are the four *Torquemada* books (1889–1895), of which the first, *Torquemada en la hoguera*, is the best. These works study the psychology of avarice.

Love, in its Christian sense, as the only solution for humanity, appears to be one of Galdós' strongest themes. Galdós sought unity in a mad world, harmony among various classes and people through tolerance and understanding. His world is one of hope for a better future. Unlike the twentieth-century grayness and agony of Existential novels, his novels breathe a note of idealistic optimism as opposed to the later pessimistic intellectualism. Galdós is not naïve, however, in his hopes. He portrays humanity with all its vices and crudity, its passions, its tragedies, and its comedies, but he insists that through love of one's neighbor, tolerance for the weakness of others, and liberty for the individual (hence his protests against political, social, and religious abuse), man can triumph.

Psychologist, moralist, philosopher, and Christian, Galdós was the only novelist of his time who truly tried to amalgamate modern philosophy and science with social justice and the spiritual and religious needs of man. Galdós sought not only the meaning of human nature but also in his eternal quest the meaning of life itself.

D. Naturalism

The next movement in fiction of any importance was Naturalism. The Naturalistic approach to life originated with Comte and Darwin and was employed by Zola in his *roman expérimental,*

141

where he attempted to show us life under laboratory conditions. The basic difference between French and Spanish Naturalism is that Spaniards cannot depersonalize themselves enough to be truly objective, to look at life with cold eyes and unyielding hearts, and they incorporate the warmth of their souls and the passion of their emotions. French Realism, according to Flaubert, tried to see reality in the coldest and most objective manner possible, eliminating all sentiments and emotions of the author. The Realistic rationalism, accentuated even more in Zola's pseudoscientific materialism, accumulated details about the more bestial tendencies in man. Spanish Naturalism, on the other hand, was more spiritual, as it tried to give an impression usually without excessive emphasis on detailed imagery. Nevertheless, by the end of the nineteenth century, French Naturalism had made inroads into Spain, especially in some of the novels of Emilia Pardo Bazán, but the vogue was not to be a lasting one.

In the 1880s in Spain a continuing polemic appeared in the newspapers and reviews on the meaning and impact of Naturalism. Critics and authors discussed determinism, impersonality of style, and whether authors had to experience the series of events they were describing. The critics were about evenly divided and saw in Naturalism either the repugnant, pessimistic, and immoral or a new era of freedom and a new direction for the novel.

While it is true that most of the Spanish Realists to a greater or lesser degree partook of certain aspects of Naturalism, most of them rejected either completely or in part the materialistic determinism of the French movement. The experimental novel, Palacio Valdés said, led to fixed results with which he could not agree. Pardo Bazán objected to the extremes of the movement and condemned Zola's overly deterministic philosophy, though she defended him as an artist. Most writers reacted variously to the label Naturalist, but whether they accepted or rejected it, all refused to confine themselves to disagreeable things in human beings.

1. *Leopoldo Alas* (1852–1901), who used the pseudonym Clarín, was one of the most important literary critics of his day. His fame as a novelist comes from a long novel, *La Regenta* (1884–1885), a dissection of a rainy provincial town where the three principal occupations are playing cards, gossiping, and discussing sex. The heroine, Ana Ozores, torn between imaginary mysticism and erotic desire, is one of the most powerful characters of the nineteenth-century Spanish novel. She finally

yields her favors to one of the town citizens and brings death to her husband and ruin to herself. *La Regenta* spares nobody in its bitterness and seems to follow Zola's technique more closely than any other Spanish novel, although Clarín was not by any means a total convert to the French school.

Clarín's method differed sharply from that of the French. He objected to vulgar language, was opposed to Positivism, and knew almost nothing of science. His characters exhibit a free will far removed from the deterministic aspects of French Naturalism. Although Ana was frustrated sexually, she was considered to be an extremely cold type. She goes through agonies trying to resolve her struggles, but she is inevitably driven to certain predetermined actions. *La Regenta* excoriates the envy, intrigue, false erudition, and mental stultification to be found in Vetusta, Oviedo, and thus in all Spain.

Su único hijo (1890) describes the atmosphere of a romantic period of Spain's life and predates the Generation of 1898 in its evocation of city characters who have a plan to regenerate Spain. In his short stories Clarín resembles Galdós greatly in his use of humor and tenderness. His later works also reveal a lyrical and idealistic note.

For some critics, Clarín must be considered the creator of the modern short story in Spain. Here he displays his analytical and critical gifts in combination with his keen sense of humor. His stories follow no definite pattern and are of every type imaginable—humorous, satiric, patriotic, fantastic, Realistic, erotic, idealistic, and religious. Among his many collections are *El Señor y lo demás son cuentos* (1893), *Cuentos morales* (1896), and *El gallo de Sócrates* (1901).

Clarín was much influenced by *Krausismo* in forming his ethical and moral judgments. Also he acknowledged his debt to one of his teachers, don Francisco Giner de los Ríos. As a professor at the University of Oviedo, he interested himself in philosophy and law, but his reputation rests on his newspaper articles, his critical works, and his fiction.

2. *Armando Palacio Valdés* (1853–1938) has some purely Naturalistic works, such as *La espuma* (1891), an attack on the vices of the aristocracy and a satire on their rottenness and their oppression of miners. Another novel of this type is *La fe* (1892), an attack on religious hypocrisy and false religiosity. Although his other works have certain aspects of the Naturalistic technique, Palacio Valdés really belongs to an earlier and happier period. He used Naturalism much as the earlier Eclectics in the drama

143

had used the best elements of Romanticism and Neoclassicism. Though for many years he was considered a leader of the Spanish Naturalistic movement, he was never a whole-hearted convert. He shows a predilection for science, it is true, and he examines society carefully, looking at its vanities, its intrigues, and its imaginary and real piety. But even when he discusses horror, it is only as it rises naturally and not because of any abiding belief in determinism. Nor does he hammer away at the unpleasant or base in life.

El señorito Octavio (1881), Palacio Valdés' first novel, deals with the love of a sentimental country boy for a countess. *Riverita* (1886), set in a small village on the northern coast and in Madrid, reveals his personal experiences and his childhood. Fishermen, bullfighters, politicians, and sailors pass through the book. *Maximina,* its sequel, appeared in 1887 and is also somewhat autobiographical. *La alegría del capitán Ribot* (1899), which preaches a philosophy of resignation, takes place against a background of Valencian customs.

The adjective *pleasant* comes to mind in discussing Palacio Valdés. He arouses no great emotions, though some critics have pointed to the profundity of one of his better novels, *Marta y María* (1883), a study of two sisters, one worldly and the other mystical, in which the author voices a preference for the former. Here Palacio Valdés contrasts the inner, contemplative, religious life with the active life. Local color abounds as he adequately paints the region he knows quite well and weaves his plot through episodes from the Second Carlist War. He stresses the harm religious excesses and fanaticism can do; yet he does not attack Mysticism, but only its cold imitators.

Another of his well-known novels is *José* (1885), a novel of the sea that deals with Asturian fishermen. Again the author brings in authentic local color from a region he knew well. *José* clearly pictures the stormy life of fishermen, their sorrows and their difficulties. José, the hero, must struggle against the sea, nature, and human intransigence. Although the work is Realistic, it is also an idealization of the humble fisherfolk and pictures them as simple, devout, hardworking, long-suffering, honorable people. Some have detected an almost epic quality in Palacio Valdés' treatment of these unsung heroes.

Palacio Valdés' best-known work is *La hermana San Sulpicio* (1889), a regional novel set in Seville that concerns a young nun who leaves the convent to marry. The book is particularly interesting for its local color, found in the descriptions of strange types in boardinghouses and the spirited, brave qualities of the Andalusian. *Sincere, joyous,* and *picturesque* are adjectives customarily used in describing this work. *La aldea perdida* (1903) reiterates an old theme, and the author, like many before him, yearns for the good old days when the village was a haven of rest, a Utopia. Materialistic progress, says Palacio Valdés, brings discontent instead of happiness.

Palacio Valdés handles sadness, humor, Realism, idealism, and religion in a rather conventional and even *cursi,* though pleasant, manner. When one compares him with Galdós or even with Clarín, his pleasant superficiality is immediately apparent. He offers no deep insights and usually employs simple themes, but he varies his geography. Wherever he sets his novels, the sites are full of color. His characters are true to life, and he often analyzes them with humor and irony. He is especially good with women characters: Laura in *El señorito Octavio,* Marta and María, Ventura and Cecilia in *El cuarto poder* (1888), and, of course, "la hermana San Sulpicio." He often displays an excessive sentimentalism. He is saved, however, by sincerity, truth, beauty, and clarity; and for him beauty and truth, which he loved, exist and can be found in nature. He himself believed that in writing novels, plot, length, setting, and especially character, whether simple or complex, were important. Palacio Valdés enjoyed great success, largely because of his simple and clear style that is easy to read, because his criticism did not offend, and because he was often sensitive, loving, and warmhearted.

3. *Emilia Pardo Bazán de Quiroga* (1852–1921), a countess, was the regional novelist of Galicia. Though she was of an extremely conservative family, she was occasionally more open-minded than Pereda. She was not allowed to read French novels, which may in part account, at least at a subconscious level, for the fact that such a staunch Catholic should have accepted French Naturalism even partially. In about 1879 she became interested in Zola and the Naturalists, and in the prologue to *Un viaje de novios* (1881) she suggested that Spain needed a new kind of novel similar to that being written in France, though she warned against too servile an imitation. Apparently Zola's *L'Assommoir* impressed her greatly, and she was attracted by the techniques of closer observation of life and the possibility of greater objectivity. But as she said, she disapproved of the systematic selection of the repugnant. In 1883 she treated the question of Naturalism at length in a series of newspaper articles under the title *La cuestión palpitante.* Along with her Naturalistic pictures, Pardo

145

Bazán gave us, in keeping with the truth after which she strove, an analysis of the part played by religion in the life of man, pointing out its many positive and consoling virtues.

Her first work, *Pascual López* (1879), is a somewhat puerile, although occasionally colorful, story of a medical student. It contains an artificial striving for stylistic effect through formalized archaic language. *Un viaje de novios,* in spite of the author's apparent objections to sordid details, treats of the physiological incompatibility of a dissipated old man and a naïve adolescent girl. *La tribuna* (1882) is a study of popular customs about the *cigarreras* in Coruña. Critics are almost unanimous in regarding this as a Naturalistic novel composed in accordance with the principles of Zola. *El cisne de Vilamorta* (1885) is another Naturalistic work. In *Una cristiana* (1890) and several later works, Pardo Bazán lays great emphasis on the spiritual forces in life rather than on environment or heredity, and in *La Quimera* (1903), one of her richest novels, she examines the roles of inspiration and imagination in the aspirations of artists.

Pardo Bazán's two most famous works are *Los pazos de Ulloa* (1886) and its sequel, *La madre naturaleza* (1887). In *Los pazos de Ulloa,* a novel of the decaying feudalism of Galicia, the author describes the beautiful countryside, but its grandeur contrasts with the creeping decadence of the humans inhabiting it. The treatment of the effects of environment and heredity and the importance attached to determinism make this a Naturalistic work.

The sequel, *La madre naturaleza,* represents a further deterioration and degradation of the family of the marquis, whose children, Perucho, a son by Sabel, and Manolita, a daughter by Nucha, are driven to a momentary incestuous love, encouraged by a luxuriant natural surrounding.

Even though these two works contain many sordid episodes, drunkenness and adultery in the first volume and incest in the second, the technique seems more Realistic than Naturalistic. Pardo Bazán longed for membership in the Royal Academy but was never appointed, probably because of her sex, since her literary excellence and conservative attitudes would have caused her little difficulty in that body.

In analyzing Pardo Bazán, one must remember her ultraconservative upbringing. She had strong feelings, many of them intolerant. She condemned bullfighting and the Spanish peasant, hated the Arabs and the Jews, and felt that the salvation of Spanish women lay in their copying European models and being educated to their privileges. Her fatal blind spots, perhaps the product of her somewhat unhappy life, detract from her work. Though her Zolaesque works, such as *La tribuna* and *El cisne de Vilamorta,* have been forgotten except by literary gravediggers, *Los pazos de Ulloa* and *La madre naturaleza* will continue to be read.

Pardo Bazán stands as a unique figure in an age when the novel was dominated by men. Surpassed by Galdós, Pereda, and Valera in most aspects of the novelist's art, she was nevertheless the equal of the best of them in the grace of her style and the coloring of her phrases. Her language is considered to be among the purest of her time in spite of the regional quality of her work. Her women are beautifully portrayed. Indeed, their very perfection points up the weakness of her male characters, although she did manage an occasional good masculine portrait in her rural novels. She only rarely sought to idealize or embellish her characters, however. She maintained that she wanted to represent the truth and to portray her characters as they were. She surpassed most of her contemporaries as a storyteller, and her short stories rank with the best Spain has produced.

4. *Luis Coloma* (1851–1914), a Jesuit, is of minor interest. Considered a disciple of Fernán Caballero's, he shared her enthusiasms and prejudices. In addition to *Cuadros de costumbres populares* and a series of fictionalized historical sketches, Padre Coloma left a number of novels. Those of lesser importance are *La Gorriona* (1887), about a countess mixed up in politics; *Por un piojo* (1889), on Christian charity; and *Boy* (1910), a story of aristocratic intrigue. His best novel was *Pequeñeces,* which appeared in 1890. In this book, a bitter censure of Madrid society, Coloma created what many considered a *roman à clef,* and the pastime of the season was to attempt to identify the principal characters. Frankly Naturalistic in his treatment of the immoralities in Madrid society, Padre Coloma probably intended the work as a satire, but his purpose is weakened by his didactic intent. *Pequeñeces,* based on real-life characters, is a combination of sermon and satire, in which Coloma discloses that something is rotten in Spanish society. It is a pessimistic book that paints the ugly and the grotesque and attacks the moral defects of the aristocracy.

5. *Vicente Blasco Ibáñez* (1867–1928), chronologically a part of the twentieth century, belongs through his ideas, style, and technique to the Realistic and Naturalistic schools of the nineteenth century. In his early work he was the regional novelist of Valencia, which has prompted many critics to maintain that the fe-

cund, beautiful landscape influenced him to be exuberant, generous, energetic, strong, and passionate. Blasco was by nature a person of impulse, and his imagination was rich and luxuriant. His parents reared him as a devout Catholic, but through his political activity he achieved a reputation as an anticlerical revolutionary, suffering exile and imprisonment many times for his attacks against the government.

The work of Blasco's first and essentially regionalistic period comprises *Arroz y tartana* (1894); *Flor de mayo* (1895), about a street where he lived in his youth; *Cuentos valencianos* (1896); *La barraca* (1898), considered by most to be his masterpiece; *Entre naranjos* (1900); and *Cañas y barro* (1902). Most of these novels reflect in vivid colors the Valencian landscape in almost epic measure. *La barraca,* a great monument to Realism, combines the picturesqueness of Valencia with the sordid story of the miserable life of the peasant in his struggle against superstition, injustice, and rapacious landlords. Blasco, as might be expected, reveals great compassion for the have-nots of the world. The work of his second period consists of social novels, sometimes called novels of protest or rebellion, that cover various areas of Spain. Among these, the best is *La catedral* (1903), an anticlerical novel about traditional Spanish religion. *El intruso* (1904) analyzes the Jesuit power in Spain. *La bodega* (1905), a politically oriented study of social life in Andalusia, echoes anarchistic ideas against the rich class and stresses the evil of alcohol. *La horda* (1905) discusses low society in Madrid, the beggars, thieves, and gypsies.

He has countless other novels, too numerous to analyze here. Two other famous works are *Sangre y arena* (1908) and *Los cuatro jinetes del Apocalipsis* (1916), both of which had successful screen versions, as did five of his other novels. *Sangre y arena* concerns a bullfighter and the national institution of bullfighting, which Blasco attacks. Made famous in the United States through the motion picture version, the work concludes that the real villain is the crowd that clamors for blood. In this novel, as in most of the works Blasco wrote after 1906, he emphasizes character and psychology. It is also a novel of customs in its Realistic sketches of Spanish life.

Blasco had planned a cycle of novels on his American adventures, but he had completed only one, *Los argonautas* (1914), when the First World War and especially the battle of the Marne inspired him to write *Los cuatro jinetes del Apocalipsis*. Blasco understood the consequences of a German victory and foretold the intervention of the United States. The first part describes life on an Argentinian ranch, but in the second part Blasco reproduces photographically the scenes of violence, pain, and misery brought on by the war, analyzes pitilessly the immorality of fighting, and senses the coming of a new era in human affairs. He intensely expresses here the hates, desires, horrors, and beauties of being human. This novel won for him a widespread international reputation.

His many other postwar novels need not be mentioned here. Some of his novels have been dramatized and presented on the stage. Many critics claim that Blasco was an improviser, and they fail to grant him his positive virtues. He presented brilliant scenes of nature and life. He spoke sincerely and passionately of human problems, and in spite of stylistic defects and often indelicate expressions, this most underrated of writers has, with a truly dramatic impact, painted rich and powerful descriptions in bold and moving colors.

THE TWENTIETH CENTURY

A. General Considerations

It is erroneous to think of the year 1898 as marking any crisis in Spanish letters, and in this respect the slogan invented by Azorín, "Generation of 1898," originally "Generation of 1896," is a misnomer. Ganivet, one of the leaders of the movement, died in 1898. The war with the United States and Cuba simply substantiated writers' ideas of the need for a renaissance of spirit and letters. The young writers of the time, independently and in different ways, examined the Spanish status quo and found it wanting. In their soul-searching, they examined many different possibilities for the salvation of their country. Some of these men were interested in practical reforms, others in new artistic ideas, and this dichotomy accounts for some of the confusion in classifying writers as members of the generation or as Modernists. Some were conservative, and some were revolutionary, but all were united in a negative reaction to the corruption, decadence, and mediocrity they saw around them. They protested against the legacy of the nineteenth century and sought the restoration of some eternal values, a change from Spain's insularity, and educational reform.

Among the members of this generation, Valle-Inclán and Pío Baroja were primarily famous as novelists, but Unamuno, Azorín, and Ganivet, better known as essayists, also produced important novels. Although some of Azorín's novels, in their philosophical examinations of spiritual and intellectual problems, resemble essays, they foreshadow later important fictional developments.

After the Generation of 1898, classification by generation becomes quite difficult, and disagreement exists about which writers belong to which generation and, indeed, whether such divisions are legitimate. Part of the problem is that authors belonging to the same age group may follow different cultural paths in their fiction and thus may belong to different literary generations.

The Generation of 1914, a kind of extension of the Generation of 1898, includes novelists who are more elitist, intellectual, and lyrical, though there is only a tenuous link between the artistic novels of writers like Miró and Pérez de Ayala and those of members of the following generation. Among other novelists of the Generation of 1914, Wenceslao Fernández Flórez, Ricardo León, and Concha Espina represent a more conservative, traditional, Catholic point of view.

The Generation of 1925, also known as the Generation of 1927 (though for the novel some prefer to call it the Generation of 1930), seems more European than Spanish. The writers employed avant-garde techniques to produce incoherent, depersonalized, and absurd narrations with little plot or characterization. They rejected the traditional Spanish novel and attempted to create new forms. They followed the "dehumanized" aesthetic of Ortega y Gasset, and to an extent Jung and Freud, and experimented with Surrealism and imagery. The older members of this generation, like Gómez de la Serna and Benjamín Jarnés, though culturally belonging to it, chronologically fit as well into the previous generation. Some of the most important writers of the Generation of 1925, like Aub and Ayala, changed their style later to concentrate on the human. Others, like Ramón Sender, the best known of the group, never really accepted the metaphoric, dehumanized types of writing, though, like Ayala, who experimented with Surrealism and ironic humor, all the authors were interested in technique and new forms of communication. Many of these writers, as well as almost all of the members of the following two generations, were obsessed by the Spanish Civil War and its consequences.

The Generation of 1936, which includes among its members some of Spain's most famous twentieth-century figures, like Cela and Delibes, reacted against the depersonalized fiction of the previous generation. Cela and others are said to belong to a *generación destruída, generación astillada,* or a variety of similar appellations. Credited with beginning the *tremendismo* movement after the Civil War, Cela initiated a new kind of Naturalism with strong Existential overtones, involving cruelty and violence or boredom and anguish, together with an insistence on the more negative aspects of life. Laforet's *Nada* and Romero's *La noria* fall into this *tremendista* category, though the most important representative of this kind of writing is Cela's *La familia de Pascual Duarte* (1942).

The Generation of 1950, sometimes called the *generación herida* because it was traumatized by the war, includes many of Spain's greatest contemporary writers, among them Goytisolo, Matute, Benet, and Martín-Santos. In their early writings some members of this generation wrote Objectivist novels that supposedly contained no value judgments, though the apparent photographic and uncommitted realism of these novels scarcely disguises the social and political concerns of the authors. Rafael Sánchez Ferlosio's *El Jarama* (1956) is Objectivism's outstanding example. The 1950s and early 1960s also saw the appearance of a number of Existential novels, combining previous trends with a continuing Neorealism. Many of these writers later reacted against Neorealism in favor of new aesthetic preoccupations.

Luis Martín-Santos' *Tiempo de silencio* (1962) succeeded the Spanish Realistic novel as a new kind of fiction. In addition to looking at reality in a different way, the new novelists attempted fresh kinds of linguistic and literary Baroque elements. Goytisolo and Benet experimented with myth, Structuralism, Formalism, point-of-view narration, intertextuality, ironic parody, and eventually textual literary discourse as its own reality. Thematically they explored personality, sexuality, and power, but in a new way.

The Generation of 1968, more international than any previous group, reacted once more against the moral values of their elders and against what they saw as oppressive tradition. These writers began publishing in the late 1960s, continuing through the 1970s and beyond. They include José María Guelbenzu and Ana María Moix. While avoiding a return to Neorealism, neglected after Martín-Santos' breakthrough, their experimental novels focus on interpersonal relationships and the development of character, though it is difficult to generalize about their subjective, unique, personal contributions to fiction.

The innovative fiction classified rather loosely under the heading "The New Novel," a designation that came to mean all anti-Neorealistic fiction, took still another step forward with the publication in 1975 of Juan Goytisolo's *Juan sin tierra,* labeled by some as a "self-referential" novel because it analyzes the process of its own creation. Some prefer the terms *self-conscious narration* or *metafiction.*

The writers of the Generation of 1950 (as well as some from the Generation of 1936) continue to publish important works. Gonzalo Torrente Ballester (b. 1910) published *La saga/fuga de J. B.* (1972), a parody of the experimental novel; *Fragmentos de apocalipsis* (1977); and *La isla de los jacintos cortados* (1980), all highly acclaimed. Still other writers continue to experiment—J. Leyva (b. 1938), for example, with mixtures of Kafkaesque techniques and Surrealism and attempts at the demolition of narrative discourse itself.

B. The Generation of 1898

1. *Miguel de Unamuno* (1864–1936), famous primarily as a philosopher, essayist, and poet, wrote dramas with Existential implications and a series of novels exemplifying his ideas about life and death. Like Azorín, another famous essayist of the Generation of 1898, Unamuno is not primarily noted for his fiction, but with the passing years its stature has been enhanced. In his novels as in his essays, Unamuno works with problems such as the meaning of existence and the anguish and struggle in faith and life. His characters fight against destiny and seek to live their own lives, independent of their creator, but Unamuno rarely allows them this freedom. Most of his novels, therefore, are histories of passion and tragedy based on conflict, and his themes include those of love, death, envy, will, maternity, and faith. Unamuno put himself and his own personal interior struggle into each novel, as he did in his other writings, and scorned realistic detail except in his first work, *Paz en la guerra* (1897), which treats the Carlist siege of Bilbao in 1874. Nonetheless, even this novel reflects his inner self. Unamuno calls his book "una historia anovelada," and it does have the appearance at times of a chronicle rather than a novel, despite its lyrical overtones.

His second novel, *Amor y pedagogía* (1902), the first that Unamuno classified as a *nivola* ("relatos acezados de realidades íntimas"), concerns a father's disastrous attempt to create a genius son through eugenics. Unamuno's conclusion seems to be that science cannot answer our doubts or anxieties or our need for immortality and a concomitant God. When critics could not agree that this work was a novel, Unamuno declared that if he did not write *novelas*, he would write *nivolas*.

Unamuno's next *nivola*, *Niebla* (1914), predates Pirandello's *Sei personaggi in cerca d'autore* in creating fictional characters who are independent of their creator. Here too Unamuno faces completely for the first time his own central problem, the immortality of the soul and the meaning of existence. Augusto Pérez, the protagonist, searches out Unamuno to discuss whether to go on living. He dies, but before doing so, he explains that men die not from great sorrows or joys but from small incidents that envelop them like a mist.

Abel Sánchez (1917), subtitled *Una historia de pasión*, is a tragic and personal drama of hate and envy that Unamuno thought was "acaso la más trágica de mis novelas." It deals with the tragedy of the uncontrollable envy of a man, Joaquín Monegro (Cain), who is in reality a more capable man than his object of envy, Abel Sánchez, who nevertheless easily triumphs in every encounter. When Joaquín has a chance, as a doctor, to kill his hated rival, he puts forth every effort to save him. We are finally tempted to love Joaquín, the real man, in his anguish and struggles and to dislike Abel for his smug complacency.

Una historia de amor (1911), a novelette, is one of Unamuno's minor works, but *Tres novelas ejemplares* (1920) exhibits the Existential aspects of his writing. The most interesting of these exemplary novels is *Nada menos que todo un hombre*, which deals with the reality of personality. Alejandro Gómez, the protagonist, personifies indomitable will, but even he cannot overcome the ultimate and final opponent, death. The other two novels of this collection are *Dos madres* and *El marqués de Lumbría*. *La tía Tula* (1921) deals with one of Unamuno's favorite themes, the maternal instinct, in this case that of a virgin aunt, Gertrudis.

San Manuel Bueno, mártir (1931), republished in 1933 in more definitive form, is undoubtedly the high point of Unamuno's fiction. A fictional statement of "the tragic sense of life" and filled with ambiguities, the novel delineates a devoted priest's vain struggles to find his faith and belief in eternal life. He remains a priest to help his parishioners and to preserve their illusions of a better world. During a church service, as the congregation fervently recites the Creed, he dies before reaching the words that state the belief in the resurrection of the flesh and everlasting life.

La novela de don Sandalio, jugador de ajedrez (1933), with an interplay of fantasy, dream, and reality, concerns the meaning of Existential authenticity and explores the life of an imaginary gambler who may, nevertheless, have a real existence and who "se ha puesto fuera de sí para mejor representarse."

Unamuno once declared that he dealt with *agonistas* and not *protagonistas*. His characters in facing their problems seem to lack free will, whatever their obsession. Most of them are introverted and concerned with metaphysical problems, and most symbolize some incarnated passion. All Unamuno's work bears more or less directly upon the problems that he himself faced in life, including that of immortality. However paradoxical or contradictory his novels may be, they almost always reveal his ontological preoccupations. He gave most of his attention to the inner drama of the individual, whose life, for Unamuno, was a novel. His dramatic intensity, whatever the intellectual discussion, strikes a note of reality and sincerity. His penetration into the souls of his antirealistic characters, into the subconscious level, offers more to the reader than the pitiless materialism of a modern world.

2. *Ramón del Valle-Inclán* (1866–1936), born Ramón María Valle Peña, who insisted that style was the important thing in literature, resembles D'Annunzio in his play-acting. For some he appeared indifferent to the problems of Spain, but he was not, though it is true that in his earlier works he most nearly approaches the prose ideal of Modernism with his harmonious and musical style. Like Unamuno, he wrote dramas, short stories, and poetry, as well as essays, and in all these genres he reveals himself to be a stylist. Indeed, words fascinated him, and he was obsessed by the musical power to be expressed in prose, which may account for his constant experimentation in style.

Artistically, Valle-Inclán went through various phases. Born in Galicia, a land of superstition, legend, and dreams, he includes in his early short stories, principally *Jardín umbrío* (1903) and *Jardín novelesco* (1905), much of the mystery, mistiness, lyricism, and tragedy of his native province. Even here he experiments with points of view, delayed action, and special description to create an atmosphere of mystery, terror, or superstition. In his first works he is sensual, erotic, and at times morbid. The most famous works of this period, perhaps of his entire production, are his *Sonatas,* four refined, sensual, beautiful books named for the seasons of the year, which represent the various stages of the love life of the Marqués de Bradomín. In spite of his emphasis on the aesthetic problem and on the past instead of the future, he is an author of the Generation of 1898 in his reaction against the old literary traditions of his country. Subtitled *Memorias del Marqués de Bradomín,* these erotic *Sonatas* offer an elegant and ironic view of life through the incidents of that Galician gentleman's life. The author, elegant and ironic, glorifies the pleasures of the flesh, combining the almost licentious character of these works with a nearly mystical feeling. His musical, sonorous, lush prose fully justifies the musical titles of these works, as he suits his adjectival description to the season.

The *Sonata de otoño* (1902) describes "sensaciones de recuerdos, rosas que se deshojan, tristeza de lluvia," and relates how Bradomín seduces Isabel while Concha, the marquis' sweetheart, dies a few feet away in another room. Though published first, it represents the third season. *Sonata de primavera* (1904) is filled with "sol de abril, graciosa ondulación, fragancia de rosales," and concerns the marquis' attempt to seduce María Rosario, who is about to become a nun. *Sonata de estío* (1903), filled with "pasión voluptuosa, olor marino, resplandor rojizo de la selva que arde, la naturaleza lujuriosa y salvaje," tells of "la niña Chole," who is incestuously involved with her father while becoming also the mistress of the marquis. While the *Sonata de primavera* represents the awakening of love in an Italian villa, and the second represents the fulfillment of love in tropical Mexico, the third and fourth *Sonatas* return to Spain for their setting and represent the waning years of man's life. Thus *Sonata de invierno* (1905) talks of "causa perdida, sensación de frío y de fin, desilusión de la muerte," and recounts how Bradomín almost seduces his own daughter. Style, especially aesthetic refinement, is important for the author, and he concentrates on the use of musical words, cadence, harmony, and rhythm in his depiction of the eternal themes of love, death, and religion.

Flor de santidad (1904) concerns Adega, a shepherd girl full of ingenuous and naïve devotion, who welcomes a traveler as a reincarnation of Jesus and gives herself to him. The novel is full of credulity, hunger, tenderness, and superstition.

A second phase in Valle-Inclán's production is evident in his trilogy on one of the Carlist Wars, in which he seems more interested in the popular spirit and discusses regional and popular types. The trilogy consists of *Los cruzados de la causa* (1908), which relates how the Marquis of Bradomín tries to obtain a cache of arms hidden in a convent and tells of the death of a young recruit who deserts his post; *El resplandor de la hoguera* (1909), a series of episodes that attempt to reveal the full effects of a civil war on a country; and *Gerifaltes de antaño* (1909), in which a ferocious and fanatical priest is allowed to escape capture because his extreme behavior helps the very enemy he seeks to defeat. In these novels a number of strange types appear who stand out against a background of war. Even though the author strives for concision of expression and demands the right adjective for the mood or sound of the moment, he is not completely absorbed here in the descriptive process and demonstrates his narrative power.

In his last phase, Valle-Inclán concentrated on the popular and historical and depersonalized where possible, creating grotesque types and prose *esperpentos* filled with disharmonies. He had planned a cyclical series of nine novels to be entitled *El ruedo ibérico*, dealing with the period 1868–1898, but he finished only two, *La corte de los milagros* (1927) and *Viva mi dueño* (1928), about the court of Isabel II. A third, *Baza de espadas*, was published posthumously in 1958. Pedro Salinas called *El ruedo ibérico* "la cima de todo el arte valleinclanesco" and pointed out its dramatic and theatrical esperpentic qualities. Valle-Inclán rejects, in these works, the current values held dear by Western civilization.

His most interesting work from a technical standpoint is a *tour de force*, *Tirano Banderas* (1926), a novel of dramatic, almost hallucinatory, intensity. In this work, Valle-Inclán uses a variety of chronicles and Mexican stories for his themes and heroes, and he cleverly constructs his novel to take full advantage of his ability to dominate time. One detects Impressionistic passages as the author pursues his notion that man is a grotesque puppet, a distorted reflection of an imperfect mirror. He poses the problem of the tyrant, Santos Banderas, who refuses to live by democratic processes and who inevitably destroys his own people. The novel is essentially a dramatic and exotic *esperpento*.

Valle-Inclán, then, glorified words and music and combined them beautifully with a pictorial and plastic imagery, evoking sensations, moods, and emotions. But in the *esperpento*, a deformation of style, he also depicted the grotesque and ridiculous in modern life. In all his writing he set a new standard for prose excellence that has been felt since his time.

3. *Pío Baroja y Nessi* (1872–1956) produced almost seventy novels, in addition to essays and other writings. His Basque

background reappears constantly in his work, as does his life as a vagabond. His medical studies also gave him knowledge of the abnormal and pathological, which he reproduced in his novels. In his early works one sees clearly the influence of Schopenhauer and Nietzsche, and the author also clearly reflects a Socialistic and anarchistic approach to social values.

Baroja, uninterested in the "closed novel," as he explained in the prologue to *La nave de los locos* (1925) and in his *Memorias* (1948), reproduced his version of life, for him a haphazard series of confused events without any preconceived plan. This view accounts for his structural inconsistencies and digressions, but it allowed him to reproduce the panoramic canvas of life itself. Often his plots, as well as his action, are illogical, and one becomes lost in all the threads of the interconnected lives, though at times his interpolated anecdotes are more interesting than the central plot. Since his novels represent all of life, he does not focus on the interior man as did Unamuno, and often his characters seem to be two-dimensional. He creates an air of movement and activity by the sheer number of characters. His most typical work deals with a man of action or adventure, often a vagabond, for whom an unhappy fate awaits. This dynamism exceeds in importance either characterization or plot. Many of his works are autobiographical, and many are picaresque. One finds in his works anarchism, skepticism, irony, bitter humor, and disillusion, but he can be sentimental and lyrical at times. He sympathizes with the weak and abandoned of the world, but he offers no solutions to their problems. As a man of 1898, Baroja criticizes Spanish decadence and sees no salvation through art, religion, or social conscience. Baroja is excellent at creating atmosphere, a mass picture, and the tapestry of life itself, but one looks in vain for profound psychological development.

His first volumes deal with Basque regional life. Among these are *La casa de Aizgorri* (1900), his first full-length novel; *El mayorazgo de Labraz* (1903), about a blind hero suffering from abulia, or lack of will, one of the constants in the writings of the Generation of 1898, but who recovers enough to decide to live the life of a vagabond; and one of his best-known novels, *Zalacaín el aventurero* (1909), about a Basque from the wrong side of the tracks who lives and loves until he is shot smuggling arms into Spain.

Baroja was a prolific writer and continued to produce almost up to his death. He prepared his novels frequently in cycles or trilogies and also wrote one tetralogy. His cycles are *Tierra vasca,*

La vida fantástica, La lucha por la vida, El pasado, La raza, Las ciudades, El mar, Memorias de un hombre de acción, Agonías de nuestro tiempo, La selva oscura, and *La juventud perdida. La lucha por la vida,* one of his most important trilogies, portrays the low life of Madrid in a picaresque manner. The three novels involved are *La busca* (1904), *Mala hierba* (1904), and *Aurora roja* (1904). The hero of these novels pokes fun at the Church, has little respect for the most cherished institutions, and skeptically views the hypocritical conventions with which man has surrounded himself. Baroja here glorifies the individual in his fight against the "haves" of the world. As he describes the miserable lives of his many characters, one senses his desire for the social rehabilitation of society's victims. *Paradox, rey* (1906), the third volume of *La vida fantástica,* completes the adventures, begun in the first volume, of Paradox, a bohemian living in a Madrid garret. As in *Zalacaín,* the hero appears to be a symbolic projection of the author as he discusses a mythical Utopia founded by a well-meaning international group of adventurers. They succeed in forming a better society, which is destroyed finally by a hypocritical, cruel, and supposedly civilized government. One finds in this work many of Baroja's favorite ideas on liberty, war, science, art, education, institutions, religions, various nationalities, and especially women, for him generally negative creatures. As always he poses as a moral skeptic and views Western values pessimistically. The novel includes some of Baroja's most striking lyrical interludes.

One of Baroja's preoccupations in his novels is Spain—its present and possible future and its relationship with the rest of the world. *Camino de perfección* (1902), *La ciudad de la niebla* (1909), *César o nada* (1910), and *El mundo es ansí* (1912) emphasize the Spanish problem through a variety of tortured protagonists. In the first of these novels, Fernando de Ossorio reflects the spiritual crisis of the end-of-the-century Spaniard. In *César o nada,* César Moncada, a Nietzschean character, strives for political success, but he settles for a rich wife instead. He caricatures the petty world of the intriguers, the bored ones of which, according to Baroja, high society consists. Of all his works bearing upon the Spanish situation, however, *El árbol de la ciencia* (1911) is the most pessimistic. The protagonist, Andrés Hurtado, has serious discussions on the problems of knowledge, suffering, and life. He studies medicine, falls in love, and commits suicide when his sweetheart dies. Some say that Andrés is Baroja himself.

A remarkable series of novels, *Memorias de un hombre de acción,* consists of twenty-two volumes. These novels are often compared with the *Episodios nacionales* of Galdós. The protagonist, Eugenio de Aviraneta, the perpetual conspirator, acts out his life against the historical background of the nineteenth century. The action moves so rapidly and is so episodic that the reader has difficulty in following the historical sequence.

Baroja's later novels were not well received by critics, with the possible exception of *El cura de Monleón* (1936) and *El cantor vagabundo* (1950), though one can mention a number of titles, among them *La familia de Errotacho* (1931) and *Las noches del Buen Retiro* (1934).

In his novels Baroja presents a procession of social outcasts—thieves, prostitutes, anarchists, and degenerates—but he shows them for the most part as victims of a cruel society that is responsible for their sorry plight. He condemns a world that creates evil and maintains different standards for different levels of society. He is not exactly a social crusader, for he does not preach to the reader, but he speaks out bravely and sometimes dips his pen in acid. Like Unamuno, Baroja rarely gives free will to his characters. He forces them to mouth his own ideals, his pessimism, his anarchy. Yet in a sense they are his opposites and a kind of idealistic creation of what he would have liked to be. Pío Baroja was essentially interested in living and describing what he felt was real life and not the fiction of art. For him that reality was usually summed up by the individual, not by the rules and regulations of any organized government.

Baroja's most characteristic note is undoubtedly his sincerity, especially when discussing the underprivileged and the maladjusted individuals of modern life. Unfortunately, he was just as sincere in his antidemocratic, anti-Semitic beliefs, often in corrosive portrayals. His heroes rarely succeed, either through the accidents of an absurd world or through loss of ambition; but his prejudices aside, he hated the injustice, cruelty, and hypocrisy that he found everywhere and attacked them indiscriminately. In spite of their abulia, his characters resist being swallowed up by the civilized maw. Baroja has some good people in his works, and he revealed his understanding and humanity in discussing them, but he continued believing that life is basically illogical and irrational. Nonetheless, he succeeded in giving us what Azorín called "un gran fragmento auténtico de la realidad española."

4. *José Martínez Ruiz (Azorín)* (1873–1967) is much more fa-

mous as an essayist, but he wrote sixteen novels and some short stories. His novels are autobiographical and fragmentary and have only a slight plot. Lyrical in nature and Impressionistic, they emphasize the countryside, though in a later phase Azorín also wrote experimental, almost Freudian novels. In *La voluntad* (1902), his second novel, Antonio Azorín describes the country-side and talks of life, time, eternity, and the regeneration of Spain. The author is also the protagonist of *Antonio Azorín* (1903) and *Las confesiones de un pequeño filósofo* (1904). All these works involve episodic description, interior soul states, and an Impressionistic and aesthetic appreciation of the surroundings. Although little happens, Azorín finds importance and value in minute details, more realistic for him than great historical events. In 1915 he published *El licenciado vidriera,* later changed to *Tomás Rueda* (a reprise of sorts of Cervantes' novel). *Don Juan* (1922) paints a new kind of don Juan who resists temptation and seeks salvation. *Doña Inés* (1925) is the story of a woman who identifies with a historical ancestor. It involves a kind of reincar-nation and the idea of circular time.

In his efforts to dominate time and space, Azorín wrote a se-ries of Surrealistic novels, attempting to explore states of mind and the perception of reality: *Félix Vargas* (1928), later changed to *El caballero inactual; Superrealismo* (1929), later changed to *El libro de Levante;* and *Pueblo* (1930).

In his last phase he became interested in the concept of fic-tional artistic creation, producing *El escritor* (1942) and *El en-fermo* (1943). In other novels—*Capricho* (1943); *La isla sin aurora* (1943), quite Surrealistic; *María Fontán* (1944); and *Salvadora de Olbena* (1944)—he experimented with fantasy and escape from external reality, with mixed results.

The Azorín whom people remember is the one who described the countryside extensively, dominated time, and wrote in an exquisite, evocative style. He anticipated the modern novel of authors like Robbe-Grillet in eschewing narration in the Classi-cal sense, as he gave us his own version of existence and reality.

5. *Angel Ganivet* (1865–1898), more famous for his *Idearium español* (1897) and other essays, wrote two novels, *La conquista del reino de Maya por el último conquistador español, Pío Cid* (1897) and *Los trabajos del infatigable creador Pío Cid* (1898), the latter of which was much more important. Ganivet produced a kind of metafiction. He comments on his own novel, and the narrator is not the author. His two novels, philosophical in nature, are lyri-cal, autobiographical, and intellectual exercises in which the pro-

tagonist, suffering from abulia, satirizes civilization and vainly attempts to activate will in others, something he himself cannot achieve.

C. The Generation of 1914

1. *Ramón Pérez de Ayala* (1880–1962) wrote short stories, poetry, and essays that reveal his understanding of Spanish life, but he is primarily famous as a novelist. In some of his early works he traces the crisis of Spanish conscience developing from 1898, especially in *Tinieblas en las cumbres* (1907), *La pata de la raposa* (1912), and *Troteras y danzaderas* (1913). He took the latter title from the Arcipreste de Hita. The protagonist, the alter ego of the author, is Alberto Díaz de Guzmán. In these novels, sensual episodes are interspersed with philosophical discussions. The first one treats of young prostitutes who climb a mountain to see an eclipse; the second concerns Alberto's recovery from his mountain adventure and his soul-searching in an attempt to realize the dignity inherent in man as opposed to self-pride, immorality, and wickedness. *Troteras y danzaderas* describes the literary world of the poets, the cafés, and the boardinghouses in Madrid and contains caricatures of Valle-Inclán and Ortega y Gasset. The novel speaks on a variety of subjects such as theater, education, and Spanish politics; and disillusioned Alberto concludes that Spain has produced only "procuresses and dancing girls."

AMDG (1910)—*Ad majorem Dei gloriam* is the Jesuit motto— concerns Alberto's experiences in a Jesuit school and the meanness and injustice he encounters there. The author depicts the narrow, cold corridors, the fears of the boys, and the love of the young hero, Bertuco (Alberto), for the Virgin and his doubts about God. In spite of Pérez de Ayala's obvious passionate involvement, he strives for careful, objectively detailed descriptions.

Pérez de Ayala wrote three short "poematic novels," to use his own label: *Prometeo, Luz de domingo,* and *La caída de los Limones,* all published in 1916. *Promoteo* shows us human beings controlled by illogical circumstances in a world where evil triumphs, and the author once more emphasizes his link with the Generation of 1898 through his description of the pernicious effects of *caciquismo,* the political boss system. He also stresses "the lyric spirit," the power to live fully, to identify with humanity, to be tolerant and just. The second "poematic" novel concerns the

161

rape of a bride-to-be as the author stresses the essential depravity of man. In the third novel, Arias, a criminal, is destroyed by his own weakness.

Two of Pérez de Ayala's other novels, *Luna de miel, luna de hiel* and its sequel, *Los trabajos de Urbano y Simona,* both published in 1923, are uproariously funny. The protagonist, Urbano, reaches adulthood in complete innocence about life but in the course of a year learns the meaning of virility. The author attacks bourgeois prudery but also reveals his genuine sympathy for human beings.

Pérez de Ayala's two masterpieces are *Belarmino y Apolonio* (1921) and *Tigre Juan* and its second part, *El curandero de su honra* (1926). *Belarmino y Apolonio,* an intellectual *tour de force,* depicts Belarmino, an introvert and philosopher who is fascinated by the power of words, and Apolonio, a dramatist and extrovert who must express himself at all costs. Apolonio's son runs off with Belarmino's daughter. Their marriage is prevented, and the daughter is driven to prostitution. The boy becomes a priest, redeems his former sweetheart, and manages to reconcile Belarmino and Apolonio. The author handles the characters as though they were components in an orchestra and at the same time displays his tremendous vocabulary and evocative, moving sentences. Words meant power to Pérez de Ayala, as they do for Belarmino; words are important in a life-like drama where men meet and overcome their destinies, achieving communication with each other and reconciling reason with faith. The author's plea for tolerance and justice seems strongest here.

Tigre Juan, which involves a kind of counterpoint or simultaneous narration, treats the themes of don Juan and Spanish honor. Juan, a misogynist, does not know how to channel his passion into positive action. His wife flees with Vespasiano Cebón but soon discovers that only Juan can offer her the love she needs. Tigre Juan learns to laugh and love, and his wife, Herminia, especially with motherhood, forgoes her fears. Tigre Juan's happiness is complete when his son is born, and he forgets his Calderonian fantasies about honor as Herminia forgets Vespasiano in her discovery of her husband.

In turn ironic, humorous, metaphysical, and Existential, Pérez de Ayala deals with the problem of time, the tragic sense of life, and life's relationship to art and creates different planes of reality. Through suggestion and implication or direct observation and description, he produced novels that are dramatic and objective as well as lyrical and subjective. He bridged the gap between the poet and dramatist in his creation of a complete world peopled by real and imaginative characters who reflect aspects of his own soul and the reality of the outer world.

2. *Gabriel Miró* (1879–1930) in a sense anticipates the *nouveau roman,* though his narrative rhythms and style are unique. In his short stories and novels he displays an impeccable aesthetic, lyrical sense of the beauty and harmony of language, and he depicts objects and landscapes with a painter's eye. Although of another generation, he reflects the spirit of the artistic endeavors of the Generation of 1898, especially of Valle-Inclán and Azorín. At times his works, through their psychological analyses, remind one also of Proust and Joyce. Among his works are *Del vivir* (1904), his first novel, written in a Modernist vein; *Las cerezas del cementerio* (1910), his first full-length novel; *Libro de Sigüenza* (1917), about Miró's alter ego, a sensitive, Impressionistic, personal work that seems to be as much an essay as fiction; *El humo dormido* (1919), again almost a group of poetic essays; *Nuestro padre San Daniel* (1921); *El obispo leproso* (1926); and *Años y leguas* (1928). His most polemical novel, *Figuras de la pasión del Señor* (1916–1917), is an unorthodox, though reverent, interpretation of the life of Jesus. Miró's insistence on the metaphorical, Impressionistic, and symbolic creates at times a tone of artificiality, but the author can also describe cruelty and physical suffering. He himself lost his orthodox faith, though Catholic doctrine and liturgy fascinated him. He deals with transcendental themes in some of his works and combines sensuality, mysticism, and spiritual anguish in a special way, but he always insists on personal and ethical responsibility.

3. *Ricardo León* (1877–1943) wrote novels that contain order and religion, harmony and music, and Classical, mystical visions of beauty, but they lack pace and depth. Most of the characters are Ricardo León in a thin disguise. *Casta de hidalgos* (1908), his first and best novel, talks about the perils of abandoning traditional values, as the protagonist, at his death, sadly reviews his defeated ideals and wasted life. *Comedia sentimental* (1909); *Alcalá de los Zegríes* (1909); *El amor de los amores* (1910), which pleads for spiritual over human love; *Los centauros* (1912), about the political and social life of a provincial capital; *Amor de caridad* (1922); and *Cristo en los infiernos* (1941) are among his other novels. León, a conservative enamored of the old and traditional, represents a moral Catholic view. Much like Pereda, he favors the old slow-moving way of life, more conducive, in his opinion,

to peace of mind, creative work, and moral growth. Variations on these themes prove to be monotonous for most readers, but León's craftsmanship, especially in his use of words and musical harmonies, helps retain an ever-narrowing circle of readers.

4. *Concha Espina* (1869–1955) wrote a number of short stories and seventeen novels. She effectively interprets women's emotions in many of her novels. Nonetheless, the same feminine character recurs, in various guises and under different names, often in an autobiographical manner. Frequently sentimental, the author alternates between resignation and hope. In some of her novels she shows a social preoccupation; more often than not she is melancholy and pessimistic. She displays a striking ability in her use of popular language. Her first novel, *La niña de Luzmela* (1909), contrasts virtue and evil. Her most famous novel, *La esfinge maragata* (1914), describes a special region of León, its manners, customs, and traditions. Another good novel, *El metal de los muertos* (1920), deals with the hardships of Spanish miners. *Altar mayor* (1926) shared the National Prize of Literature, but it is not one of her better novels. In *La virgen prudente* (1927), she rejects the traditional role of women, and in *El más fuerte* (1947), she presents psychological realities of family conflict.

5. *Wenceslao Fernández Flórez* (1885–1964), who became a friend of Franco's, was well known as a humorist and reactionary journalist. At times Naturalistic, he was usually ironic in his depiction of sexual, political, or patriotic themes. Among his novels are *La procesión de los días* (1914); *Volvoreta* (1917), about first love; *Ha entrado un ladrón* (1920); *El secreto de Barba Azul* (1926); *Una isla en el mar rojo* (1939); and *El bosque animado* (1943), probably his best novel, which contains oneiric and magical elements.

Other writers of the Generation of 1914 include Manuel Ciges Aparicio (1873–1936) and Manuel Azaña (1880–1940), the president of the Second Spanish Republic, whose *El jardín de los frailes* (1927) is a lyrical novel about rigid religious education and the rebellion of students against the system.

D. The Generation of 1925

1. *Ramón Gómez de la Serna* (1888–1963), whom some place in the Generation of 1914, wrote numerous essays, critical works, biographies, and articles, well over a hundred books in all. He is primarily known for a special literary form he created, the *greguería,* a short statement of reaction to the incongruities, triviali-

ties, and grotesqueness of life, "lo que gritan los seres desde su inconsciente." He wrote several volumes of *greguerías* beginning in 1910. One associates the author with the absurd, the morbid, the grotesque, and the erotic. Many of his novels are fantastic or Surrealistic, and some are filled with intrigue. Although he wrote allegorical, Baroque novels that avoided social contexts, he also wrote about the emptiness of life and even the atom bomb.

El doctor inverosímil (1921), first published in 1914 in a different format, deals with a psychiatrist who fancies himself a medical Sherlock Holmes. Another of his well-known novels is *El torero Caracho* (1926), about the life and death of rival bullfighters. He labeled a series of his novels as "nebulous," for example, *El incongruente* (1922), a Surrealistic novel involving time and space, and *Rebeca* (1936), about a dehumanized but erotic quest for the ideal woman. Other titles include *El caballero del hongo gris* (1920); *Cinelandia* (1923), about Hollywood parties and promiscuity; and *Piso bajo* (1961), his last novel. Gómez de la Serna in some of his novels recalls Unamuno's love for the conceptual and Azorín's love for inanimate objects, and he had a unique way of combining subconscious associations without losing his poetic and lyrical gift for imaginative detail.

2. *Benjamín Jarnés* (1888–1949) was one of the novelists whose experimental techniques made him a stylistic if not a chronological member of the Generation of 1925. He emphasized the erotic and the sexual, but his experimental techniques, inspired by Ortega y Gasset and the *Revista de Occidente,* overshadowed any thematic material in his eleven novels. Art reigned supreme in his fiction, and his protagonists lived in a subjective world insulated from reality, which the author handled without passion or sentiment. Jarnés explored the relationship between myth and reality, utilized aspects of Surrealism and dream states, made use of irony, the mirror image, and points of view, and engaged in Pirandellian encounters with his characters, even entering his novels to foretell the plot. He created an early type of metafiction and the self-referential novel.

El profesor inútil (1926) is a metaphorical, psychological narration about the ambiguous relationship between the narrator and his world. *El convidado de papel* (1928); *Paula y Paulita* (1929); *Locura y muerte de nadie* (1929), about a search for identity in a depersonalized world; *Escenas junto a la muerte* (1931), describing agonizing over life and death in a carnival atmosphere; and *La novia del viento* (1940) are other novels.

165

3. *Rosa Chacel* (b. 1898) wrote short stories, autobiography, essays, and poetry, was an ardent disciple of Ortega y Gasset, and tried to write a novel to substantiate his theories, though ironically her fame as a novelist was only fully recognized in the 1980s. Her first novel, *Estación: Ida y vuelta* (1930), written in the winter of 1925–1926, has almost no plot and is an ironic, humorous attempt to reproduce the conflicts in a man's mind. She uses double personality in her cerebral novel and explores the relationship of author, narrator, and nameless characters. *La sinrazón,* her second novel, written in the 1930s though not published until 1960, also explores mental processes and the power of individual will. Later Chacel changed her technique somewhat but continued Baroque experimentation. *Teresa* (1941) is a fictional version of the story of Teresa Mancha, Espronceda's lover, and is filled with an anxiety for love. *Memorias de Leticia Valle* (1946) concerns an artificial memoir of a twelve year old. In 1976 the author began an autobiographical but fictional trilogy with the first volume, *Barrio de maravillas,* about two children at the turn of the century. The second volume, *Acrópolis* (1984) carries the action up to the Second Spanish Republic and depicts the intellectual, moral, and aesthetic ferment of the 1920s. The third volume, *Ciencias naturales* (1988), deals with Chacel's exile years. Chacel calls her work "esbozos de almas perdidas en el laberinto de la libertad." In 1987 she was awarded the Premio Nacional de Letras Españolas in recognition of her lifetime achievement.

4. *Juan Antonio de Zunzunegui* (1900–1982) revealed in his early short stories and novels the influence of Ramón Gómez de la Serna, especially in his unusual imagery. He published a number of short story collections and short novelettes, but he was at his best in his long novels. His Realism smacks more of the nineteenth century than of the twentieth, and he attempted to write historical works somewhat reminiscent of Galdós' *Episodios nacionales.* Many of his novels center around Bilbao—the bay, the port, the streets and customs—though he also has a number of works set in Madrid.

Chiripi (1931) is about the rise and fall of a soccer player. *El chiplichandle* (1939) portrays an interesting, picaresque Basque. *¡Ay—estos hijos!* (1943), probably his best novel, relates the story of a Bilbao family. *El barco de la muerte* (1945) concerns an avaricious undertaker killed by an enraged town; *La quiebra* (1947) treats of the power of money. *La úlcera* (1949) is about a frustrated man who devotes his life to his ulcer and dies when a young doctor cures him. *El supremo bien* (1951), the author's own favorite, insists that life is God's greatest gift to man. *La vida como es* (1954) uses underworld slang most effectively in its treatment of thieves and pickpockets. These are but a few of Zunzunegui's novels published in the 1950s. Some of his novels from the 1960s and 1970s are *Don Isidoro y sus límites* (1963), about loneliness and old age; *Un hombre entre dos mujeres* (1966), a story of incest and a son who accidentally kills his mother; *Una ricahembra* (1970); *La hija malograda* (1973); and *De la vida y la muerte* (1979), about drugs, greed, and money.

Zunzunegui wrote about middle-class Spain, often in a humorous, sentimental, moral, or satiric manner. At times he gave us a depersonalized evaluation of reality, but he was excellent at creating authentic characters, often types defeated by life. A sharp observer, Zunzunegui was also a good psychologist. Among his themes are society's materialism, religious hypocrisy, the lack of Christian charity, and the futility of striving for power and false goals. Although he tempered his photographic realism with occasional fantasy, he is more the heir of Galdós, whom he greatly admired, and Baroja than he is typical of the Generation of 1925 as generally defined.

5. *Ramón Sender* (1902–1982) wrote short stories, plays, biography, poetry, and innumerable articles in addition to his novels. He is without a doubt the most important member of his generation and one of the best novelists of the century. His wife and other members of his family were killed during the Civil War, and he left for America. Sender rejected the metafiction of his generation, although he used the mythical and symbolic for political and social preoccupations.

Imán (1930), based on his war experiences in Morocco, reveals the eternal horror of war and the indifference of Spanish citizens to the suffering of their soldiers. *Orden público* (1931), which recalls his experiences as a prisoner, is the first novel of a trilogy, *Los términos del presagio*. *Viaje a la aldea del crimen* (1934), the second volume, relates the cruelty of the Civil Guard, and the third volume, *La noche de las cien cabezas* (1934), attacks Spanish corruption. *Siete domingos rojos* (1932) depicts the left-wing and radical movements in Spain and resembles strike novels of the United States of the 1930s. His next novel, *Mister Witt en el Cantón* (1935), won the National Prize for Literature. Psychological and ironic, Sender retreats historically to 1873 and the attempt at popular government in Cartagena. Amid the political activities, Mr. Witt senses with uneasiness his approaching old

167

age and his wife's potential interest in younger men. *El lugar del hombre* (1939), appearing in a later edition as *El lugar de un hombre,* is a sardonic portrayal of human relationships. A man, supposedly murdered, is returned to society with ensuing complications. Sender, in this poetic novel, reiterates that one must respect the dignity of man and humanity.

In 1942 Sender, who has a number of works set in the New World, published one of his finest novels, *Epitalamio del prieto Trinidad,* about a revolt of a Mexican penal colony in the Caribbean. A novel of "dark and towering symbolism and fantastic terror," it is an allegory of monsters who wished to become men, along with an analysis of moral, immoral, and spiritual characters. The 1940s also marked the appearance of his *Crónica del alba* (1942), an autobiographical recounting of happy memories in a village in Aragón, of a severe father and a talkative sister. The work carries us through the tenth year of Sender as a boy, and Pepe Garcés, as he lies dying, practices a kind of total recall. The same title was used for the 1966 nine-part expansion and reworking of *Crónica del alba* and other novels previously published separately: *Hipogrifo violento* (1954), *La Quinta Julieta* (1957), and *El mancebo y los héroes* (1960), together with five other separate parts.

Sender thought that his *La esfera* (1947), first published in a different version as *Proverbio de la muerte* (1939), was his most serious novel. In this philosophical novel, Sender engages in an agonizing search for the true path and meaning of life, but in his metaphysical searching one sees still his plea for social justice and his belief that immortality for the individual exists only insofar as he is part of all mankind. Another of his best novels, *El rey y la reina* (1948), takes place in Madrid during the Civil War, and some strange characters explore man-woman relationships.

Sender published a number of novels in the 1950s, among them *El verdugo afable* (1952), an Existential, symbolic novel of strange dreams and moral responsibility; *Los cinco libros de Ariadna* (1957), in which the author expresses his hatred of totalitarianism; and *Los laureles de Anselmo* (1958). More important, he published the novel *Mosén Millán* (1953), which he later revised as *Réquiem por un campesino español* (1960), undoubtedly his masterpiece. In this story of a priest who betrays a young man, Paco el del Molino, which leads to his death, we see the suffering of the Spanish people. Sender also explores the problem of culpability and the true meaning of Christianity as separate from the sacramental duties imposed by the Church. Paco, unlike the priest, understood the need for social reform and true charity. The novel is a poetic, agonized examination of man's cruelty to man.

Sender continued to publish novels in the following decades. Among his sixty-four novels, other noteworthy ones are *La aventura equinoccial de Lope de Aguirre* (1964), one of a series of historical novels; *En la vida de Ignacio Morel* (1969); *El fugitivo* (1972); *Adela y yo* (1978); and *Epílogo a Nancy* (1983), about an American girl whose adventures in Spain he first published in 1962 as *La tesis de Nancy*. In 1984 his novels about Nancy were published as *Los cinco libros de Nancy*.

In his novels Sender searched for charity, tolerance, kindness, and idealism. He could in turn be satiric, humorous, highly symbolic, or Existential. As might be expected, the Civil War affected him greatly, and it undoubtedly sharpened his preoccupation with the destiny of man and a true Christian ethic. He believed in human potential, and this faith in man, coupled with his protest against social injustice plus a real sense of the metaphysical and the marvelous, make him one of the most authentic Spanish fictional voices of the century.

6. *Max Aub* (1902–1972) was a short story writer, poet, and dramatist. He clearly shows in his early novels the influence of Ortega y Gasset, whose ideas he later criticized. Without surrendering his imaginative and lyrical abilities, he broke with the avant-garde idea in 1934, with the publication of *Vida y obra de Luis Alvarez Petraña*, to concentrate on the human and political. This novel, about frustration and suicide, is an accusation against the Vanguard movement. *Las buenas intenciones* (1954), dedicated to Galdós and written in a more traditional style, is about a dutiful son who sacrifices his happiness for his mother and ultimately dies at the hands of Falangists. Mention should also be made of *La calle de Valverde* (1961), about Spain under Primo de Rivera.

As a novelist Aub is primarily known for *El laberinto mágico*, the general title for a series of novels, epic in nature, combining narrative, sketches, and historical and fictional figures. *Campo cerrado* (1943) analyzes Spanish political reality up to the early part of the war; *Campo de sangre* (1945) deals with political incidents in different city settings and involves the concept of treason; *Campo abierto* (1951), set in a time before that of *Campo de sangre*, again gives us a varied geography; *Campo del moro* (1963) involves the last days of the war in Madrid in 1939; *Campo francés* (1965) depicts the fate of Spanish Republicans in France; *Campo de las almendras* (1968) is about Republican refugees waiting to escape. These novels involve rapid action, monologues, documents, and moral disquisitions and reveal the heroism of the Spanish *pueblo*.

Aub also wrote a series of fictional biographies, among them *Josep Torres Campalans* (1958), the story of an imaginary Catalan painter based on apocryphal documents, letters, and drawings. These biographies and *El laberinto mágico* far outweigh in importance his early Vanguard novels, *Geografía* (1928) and *Fábula verde* (1933).

In his early works Aub engaged in Baroque verbal games. He later wrote what he called "realismo transcendente," with characters who engaged in long discussions of ideas and self-analysis. He used a variety of techniques, including cinematic elements and temporal and spatial shifts. His principal themes involve man and his problems—religious, Existential, and political. Although Aub had an active social conscience, he portrays a world of despair and betrayal, with occasional hope, but essentially one that is a cold and alien labyrinth that leads nowhere.

7. *Francisco Ayala* (b. 1906), a novelist, short story writer, essayist, and literary critic, left Spain in 1939, returning after Franco's death. His early fiction, filled with ironic and almost playful contradictions and literary allusions, is intellectual, aesthetic, and Baroque. His first novel, *Tragicomedia de un hombre sin espíritu* (1925), is based on the supposed manuscript of a solitary victim who forgoes madness for survival. His second novel, *Historia de un amanecer* (1926), lacks the parody of his first one, though it is ironic and imaginative. Ayala abandoned fiction until 1944, when he once more began writing short stories (nine volumes to date). Among them, *Los usurpadores* (1949), about corruption and redemption, fanaticism, and the role of power, and *El jardín de las delicias* (1971), an experimental, Existential mosaic combining essay and art forms, have elicited the most critical attention.

Ayala's two most famous novels are *Muertes de perro* (1958) and its sequel, *El fondo del vaso* (1962). In the first novel he deals with a Latin American dictatorship and its fall. Pessimistic and satiric, Ayala speaks of humanity's propensity for evil through the narrator, the cripple Pinedito, who combines memoirs, diaries, and letters to tell us the story of the life and death of the dictator, Antón Bocanegra. Almost an *esperpento*, the novel is filled with corruption, cruelty, and degraded human beings. In the sequel, not as tragicomic or allegorical as the first one but with continuing moral preoccupations, Ayala, through the narrator, José Luis Ruiz, who attempted vainly to vindicate the dictator, gives us a kaleidoscopic view of a disintegrating world.

Ayala uses dreams, points of view, parody, and literary allegory to present, though not solve, man's problems. Ayala, a master of stylistic techniques, writes about alienation and aberration, and though he is a concerned intellectual, he views society and the world as morally bankrupt. In 1988 he won the Premio de las Letras Españolas.

8. *Others.* Arturo Barea (1897–1957) is best known for *La forja de un rebelde,* an autobiographical trilogy published in its Spanish version in 1951 and dealing with events at the turn of the century through the Spanish Civil War. Sebastián Juan Arbó (b. 1902) has written sixteen novels. His *Sobre las piedras grises* (1949) won the Premio Nadal in 1948. It is a psychological study of a humble municipal employee.

Antonio Espina (1894–1972) wrote *Pájaro pinto* (1927), among other works. José Díaz Fernández (1898–1940) published *El blocao* (1928), his best-known work. Joaquín Arderius (1890–1969) has several novels, among them *La espuela* (1927). César M. Arconada (1898–1964) published, among other titles, *La turbina* (1930). Still other novelists of this generation include Juan Chabás, Claudio de la Torre, Andrés Carranque de Ríos, Andrés Benavides, and Mauricio Bacarisse.

E. The Generation of 1936

1. *Gonzalo Torrente Ballester* (b. 1910), besides being a dramatist, short story writer, and critic, is one of Spain's major twentieth-century novelists, though he was not well known until 1973. His first novel, *Javier Mariño* (1943), concerns a young Spanish intellectual in Paris. *El golpe de estado de Guadalupe Limón* (1946) combines literary history and myth, as the author, with black humor, examines the struggle for power and the stupidity of man. There are references to Napoleon, a legendary heroine, feminine intrigue, and attempts to overthrow a dictator. It burlesques the Falangist revolt through the use of parody and caricature. Torrente wrote a trilogy, *Los gozos y las sombras,* whose three volumes are *El señor llega* (1957), *Donde da la vuelta el ave* (1960), and *La pascua triste* (1962). Pueblanueva is the village setting for a kind of return myth that involves the question of Existential authenticity through the struggle of a psychoanalyst and an industrialist. Set between 1934 and 1936, the novel de-

picts the conflict between decadence and tradition on the one hand and modernity on the other.

Don Juan (1963), one of his major novels, fuses the don Juan theme with that of the Wandering Jew, condemned to live forever and essentially a man who confronted God. The protagonist, in Paris in the early 1960s, meets don Juan's servant in a theological bookstore. The servant claims to be the original one and as a diabolical emissary has special powers. The author includes a play within the novel as the narrator, perhaps the author, relates the true/false story of his life before the events depicted in Tirso's play.

La saga/fuga de J. B. (1972), structured like a musical fugue involving counterpoint of melody and rhythm, utilizes myths of various kinds, historical figures, and structural intricacies to parody modern novelistic techniques that the author uses. J. B., grammarian and literary specialist, converses with a variety of nebulously real, foreign alter egos as he is reincarnated on various planes and in different times in search of his identity.

Fragmentos de apocalipsis (1977) involves a novelist's notebook that describes the process of artistic creation in some fragmentary notes. The novel incorporates Surrealistic juxtaposition of time and space, fantasy and prophecy, the social and political, but is essentially a novel about writing a novel. Lénutchka, who represents the creative conscience of the author, helps him write the work. In combining legends and myths to write history as fiction, the protagonist seeks to change history, but in the end it may all have been a dream.

Another major novel is *La isla de los jacintos cortados* (1980). Again the notebook of a narrator to his beloved, who participates on one level, is involved. The protagonist tries to deny Napoleon's existence but includes intertextual references to the author's don Juan, commentary on creativity, voyages to the past, and attempts to live that past as present.

Among his other novels are *Offside* (1969), a parody of a world of art, sex, and crime; *La princesa durmiente va a la escuela* (1983), actualizing the legend of Sleeping Beauty; *Dafne y ensueños* (1983), dealing with Napoleon, his favorite theme; *Quizás nos lleve el viento al infinito* (1984); and *La rosa de los vientos* (1985), involving a discovered manuscript and the relationship of fantasy to history. In most of his works, Torrente Ballester deals with the relationships of literature and reality, the author's role in creating character, and the self-referential novel. He uses fantasy, parody, humor, and literary theory both in his work and as the target of his criticism. He discusses philosophy, aesthetics, and history and postulates the equal validity of all levels of reality.

2. *Camilo José Cela* (b. 1916), the acknowledged leader of the *tremendista* school though he denies its existence, utilizes bloody deeds and environmental factors with Existential overtones in his creation of a group of memorable if abnormal characters who reflect the anguish of modern life. He was awarded the Nobel Prize for Literature in 1989.

La familia de Pascual Duarte (1942) is one of the three or four most important novels published after the Spanish Civil War. A condemned criminal, Pascual, for whom we come to feel a certain compassion, relates his sad life. Pushed by circumstances, he kills his dog, horse, sister's lover, and finally his mother. The author seems to imply that good and evil are not absolute values, but Pascual's primitive ideas about justice follow from those of a supposedly civilized world. The novel reflects the brutal and violent situation of a fratricidal Spain.

La colmena (1951) utilizes the technique Dos Passos and Huxley made famous. The novel deals with fools, prostitutes, poets, homosexuals, and the downtrodden poor who frequent doña Rosa's sordid café. Intended as a slice of life, the novel involves hundreds of characters who suddenly appear and disappear. These unhappy beings carry on with little hope against a background of misery, rationing, and hunger, and their gray and hateful lives in the cells of the hive are viewed by a candid camera. The author chooses three days in 1942 in an area of Madrid to reflect on repugnant vices, repulsive passions, and man's existential insecurity.

San Camilo, 1936, whose full title is *Vísperas festividad y octava de San Camilo del año 1936 en Madrid* (1969), is Cela's third major novel. In it the author uses some autobiographical elements and explicit sexual language. A scatological deformation of Spanish history, the novel reflects the author's subjective account of events preceding the Civil War in July 1936. Cela uses a variety of technical resources—interior monologues, stream of consciousness, and the whorehouse as a kind of symbolic center—to confront his conscience in a Spain of horror, anguish, and repressed sexuality.

Oficio de tinieblas 5 (1973) is a kind of Surrealistic adventure involving sex, love, and death. The number 5 is used because several other novelists had previously used the title *Oficio de tinieblas*. The novel, sung by a choir of invalids, is a parody of

Spain's official propaganda, and it explores the sadistic, erotic, and religious aspects of a powerful and monstrous Spanish state. Cela, in over a thousand prose fragments, explores time and space.

Mazurca para dos muertos (1983), a highly symbolic novel, explores the role of the narrator, the veracity of history, the period between 1936 and 1940, and the relationship of sexuality and death. Typically Galician in environment and vocabulary, the novel is a poetic evocation of persons and places, though it is replete with murders and death. The story of the rivalry of two clans, the novel involves two murders, but the reader must learn about them through repeated conversations in the novel, since Cela himself will not clarify events. The title relates to Gaudencia, a blind accordion player in a brothel who played the mazurka on the two crucial occasions.

Another important novel, *Cristo versus Arizona* (1988), is set in Arizona between 1880 and 1920 and includes events such as the gunfight at the O.K. Corral. This novel stresses again Cela's themes of brute force and elemental passions, according to him so much a part of the human equation.

Among Cela's other novels are *Pabellón de reposo* (1943), about life in a sanatorium for tubercular patients; *Nuevas aventuras de Lazarillo de Tormes* (1944); *Mrs. Caldwell habla con su hijo* (1953); and *La Catira* (1955), set in Venezuela. Cela, an editor, publisher, critic, poet, and short story writer, has also written a series of travel works, especially about rural existence. Among these is *Viaje a la Alcarria* (1948). Many of Cela's novels have a lyrical note, but he is at his satiric best in depicting the ugliness and brutality of his country. His world, perhaps a deformation, is one of violence, cruelty, despair, and death, and his characters include pedophiles and prostitutes plus a variety of handicapped citizens.

3. *José María Gironella* (b. 1917) has written memoirs, essays, short stories, and travel literature. His first novel, *Un hombre* (1948), won the Premio Nadal. *La marea* (1949) is a historical, political treatment of World War II and an analysis of the lack of humanity, the false pride, and the racial pretensions of the Germans.

This author is primarily famous for his Civil War epic, *Los cipreses creen en Dios* (1953), originally intended to be the first part of a trilogy but later conceived by the author as the beginning of a new kind of *Episodios nacionales* from the Second Spanish Republic on but with the Spanish Civil War as the central preoccupation. The first volume of this vast canvas, covering April 1931 to July 1936, is set in Gerona, and through the Alvear family, especially the protagonist, Ignacio, we meet not only the middle class but all Spanish social classes with all degrees of political and economic beliefs—reactionaries and liberals, priests and Communists. In the second volume, *Un millón de muertos* (1961), Gironella narrates what happened between July 1936 and April 1939, telling us about Ignacio's war experiences, his family, their psychology and persuasions. In mixing historical with fictional creations, Gironella tries to recapture the inner ambience of his compatriots. *Ha estallado la paz* (1966) continues the story of the Alvear family between 1939 and 1941 and tells of their return home and Ignacio's continuing search for truth.

Gironella suffered a nervous breakdown, and the first novel he wrote upon recovering was *Mujer levántate y anda* (1962), about Myriam, a complex character, erotic, impulsive, and masochistic, who learns finally about positive values. A study of good and evil, the novel involves symbolic characters: a psychoanalyst, representing good, struggles for her soul against a nuclear scientist who represents the satanic aspects of life. Among Gironella's other novels are *Condenados a vivir* (1971), about two Barcelona families in the period between 1939 and 1967 and the world of pop music, sexual activity, and the generation gap. *Los hombres lloran solos* (1986), the fourth part of his so-called *Episodios nacionales*, analyzes the aftermath of the Civil War and the impact of World War II, and *Cita en el cementerio* (1983) and *La duda inquietante* (1988) also show Gironella's continuing obsession with the Spanish Civil War and its aftermath.

Sometimes prolix, at times banal, Gironella in his total output has created an impressive, extensive treatment of the Civil War in Spain.

4. *José L. Castillo-Puche* (b. 1919), primarily a Catholic moralist, is also an Existential writer. Hécula is the microcosm in which he reflects on sad war memories and sexual repression, often with a humor that is sometimes grotesque but never cruel. His earlier novels are quite Realistic; his later works are Baroque. In his early works Castillo-Puche treats the struggle between religious vocation and a Realistic acknowledgment of life, the ambivalent emotions of Civil War survivors in Hécula, and, typically, in *Con la muerte al hombro* (1954), a fusion of past and present in a spiritually wounded protagonist who seeks escape from his ties to Hécula.

Paralelo 40 (1963) is about Genaro, an anarchistic agitator from

Madrid, and the relationship of a period of his life with Spanish historical events and religious preoccupations. The novel includes emotions involving American soldiers, orgies, prostitution, and race relations. *Como ovejas al matadero* (1971) examines religious preoccupations in a Catholic ambience, the taking of vows, and the madness of one of the newly ordained priests. *Jeremías el anarquista* (1975) uses monologues, dialogues, memories, and author-protagonist-narrator relationships in a story of a terrorist in New York. The author comments on motivations for leaving the priesthood in what he calls a "crónica negra de curas españoles metidos a conspiradores en Nueva York."

Castillo-Puche's most important work to date is a trilogy, the first volume of which is *El libro de las visiones y las apariciones* (1977). The author uses first and second person, dream and reality, and neologisms and proverbs to recall the horrors and divisions of the Spanish Civil War. He analyzes the emotional reaction of a child to the environment, based on recall of memories and terror, a visionary, nightmarish, unreal world in Hécula, a village of prayer, liturgy, and fear of eternal damnation but not forgetfulness. *El amargo sabor de la retama* (1979), the second volume, carries on the pseudoreligious fantasies in Hécula, and the third volume, *Conocerás el poso de la nada* (1982), concludes the author's negative view of a dogmatic and intolerant Catholicism as the Existential narrator faces his life as a child in Hécula, his mother's death, and his seminary experience.

The author has started another trilogy, *Bestias, hombres, ángeles,* the first volume of which is *Los murciélagos no son pájaros* (1986), in which the protagonist painter, worried about a possibly inherited insanity, examines his own dreams and hallucinations to lay bare his own homosexuality, hypocrisy, and human shortcomings.

5. *Miguel Delibes* (b. 1920) is one of the major writers of the twentieth century. He is a novelist, essayist, short story writer, journalist, and author of travel books and works on hunting and fishing. In his early novels he deals with everyday life, eschewing the experimental forms involving temporal fragmentation and the like, but he handles popular dialogue, humor, irony, and even caricature with an uncommon mastery. His first novel, *La sombra del ciprés es alargada* (1948), a Premio Nadal winner, is the pessimistic history of a young orphan who confronts society, solitude, nature, and death. *Aún es de día* (1949) concerns a deformed lad in a sordid environment who sacrifices his happiness for the sake of an unborn child. *El camino* (1950), one of his most

popular novels, is filled with poetic anecdotal incidents about the adventures of some boys who must decide their future. Delibes evokes a Castilian village through flashbacks of an eleven year old the night before he leaves for the city. Other novels of the 1950s are *Mi idolatrado hijo, Sisi* (1953), related from multiple viewpoints, which is a psychological analysis of an egotistical father unable to accept his son's death; *Diario de un cazador* (1955), winner of the National Prize for Literature, which tells about the protagonist's passion for hunting, man's relationship to nature, and the rural life; *Diario de un emigrante* (1958), a kind of sequel set outside Spain; and *La hoja roja* (1959), an Existential study of an insignificant life, loneliness, solitude, and death.

Las ratas (1962) is one of Delibes' sharpest attacks on the deficiencies of Spanish society. He depicts the hunger, backwardness, and neglect of a forgotten village and the harsh struggle for life of the Castilian peasant. In 1966 the author published what many consider to be his masterpiece, *Cinco horas con Mario,* a kind of long interior monologue of a wife who, through free association and a chaotic time frame, converses with the corpse of her dead husband. Delibes, through the vain, materialistic, shallow, and bigoted Carmen, may be giving us a portrait of the bourgeois Spanish mentality. He contrasts her self-justification of her own less than admirable adultery and her prejudices with the intellectual achievement of more liberated Spaniards. His even more experimental novel, *Parábola del náufrago* (1969), subverts and degrades the language itself in a depiction of an authoritarian society. The novel can be read as a kind of allegory about universal man trapped in a nightmarish Orwellian technological world where personal dignity and identity are crushed by the omnipotent, bureaucratic, dehumanizing state. Delibes employs oneiric, hallucinatory, and Kafkaesque imagery.

In the 1970s and 1980s Delibes published a number of other novels. Among these are *Las guerras de nuestros antepasados* (1975), about violence as a Spanish heritage, narrated through taped conversations of the protagonist with a psychiatrist; *El disputado voto del señor Cayo* (1978), contrasting the rural wisdom of a patriarch with the knowledge of professional politicians; *Los santos inocentes* (1981), exalting the virtues of primitive man; and *377A: madera de héroe* (1987), a family history about events before and after the Civil War and the social and political milieu of the times.

In general Delibes is concerned with the decline of rural Castile in the face of a somewhat suspect progress, and his charac-

177

ters who leave the land usually suffer dire consequences. He has sympathy for the disinherited of the earth and deplores the physical and spiritual abuses of the wealthy against the poor. He is an excellent psychologist, especially in dealing with adolescents, but he excels also at the portrayal of old age and the prospect of impending death. Aside from his despair at the destruction of rural Castile and its values, he examines man's relationship to nature, his alienation, and the depersonalization of modern man, whose misfortune may sometimes be mitigated by faith.

6. *Carmen Laforet* (b. 1921) lived in the Canary Islands until shortly after the end of the Civil War and became famous almost overnight with the publication of her first and best novel, *Nada* (1945), the first winner of the prestigious Premio Nadal. *Nada* is the story of Andrea, a young girl who comes to Barcelona to live in the home of her maternal grandmother. The young girl, living with the weird and eccentric family of neurotic women and unhappy men, struggles for identity and physical and spiritual independence. A *tremendista* and Existentialist novel, *Nada* reflects the discontent and feeling of alienation of an entire generation, and the harsh reality, the dirt and the poverty, the frustration, solitude, and hate mirror aspects of Spanish reality. In her depiction of the voyage from adolescence to adulthood, the author uses mythical symbolism and temporal patterns.

Laforet's short novels and later full-length works have never equaled her first success. *La isla y los demonios* (1952), with autobiographical data about her own life in the Canary Islands, discusses Marta, another version of Andrea, in her attempts to escape home and gain independence. Her clashes with her family lack the nightmarish atmosphere, hypocrisy, suicide, and personal hells that Andrea's family experiences. Nonetheless, the demons, representing the seven deadly sins shared by the characters, reflect the superstition, murder, and passions evoked by the Spanish Civil War. The heroine rejects one of the demons, sexuality, for freedom. Laforet's third novel, *La mujer nueva* (1955), depicts the protagonist Paulina and her conversion to Catholicism, perhaps a reflection of the author's own conversion in 1951. *La insolación* (1963), scheduled to be the first volume of a trilogy, *Tres pasos fuera del tiempo*, again describes the coming of age of an adolescent, a sensitive and alienated teenager who finally achieves independence. The second volume, tentatively titled *Al doblar la esquina*, and the third, *Jaque y cuento*, have not yet appeared. Laforet has also written a number of short story collections as well as several volumes of travel literature.

7. *Elena Quiroga* (b. 1921), starting with an early realism in a Galician setting, elaborated her fiction with a series of experimental techniques involving dramatized narrators, multiple perspectives, multiple points of view, interior monologue, cinematic views, stream of consciousness, and a variety of sensory imagery. Her first novel, *La soledad sonora* (1949), treats of a woman who marries without love, remarries thinking erroneously that her first husband had died in the Civil War, and eventually renounces both men.

In the 1950s she wrote *Viento del norte* (1951), a Premio Nadal winner, about an older man who marries a young girl and the resulting problems; *La sangre* (1952), portraying four generations whose activities are viewed and narrated by a chestnut tree, the family telluric symbol; *Algo pasa en la calle* (1954), which in a series of flashbacks reveals the character of Ventura, a dead man, during the viewing of his corpse by other members of the family, who themselves had led existentially frustrating and inauthentic lives; *La enferma* (1955), about a solitary woman in a small fishing village, rejected by a lover the town has never forgiven; *La careta* (1955), depicting the post–Civil War generation and specifically a young boy who saw his parents killed (he was responsible for his mother's death), unable to communicate, face his guilt or God, or come to grips with his false heroic role; and *La última corrida* (1958), a psychological analysis of three types of *toreros* and the world of bullfighting.

Among Quiroga's later novels, *Tristura* (1960) is about a motherless girl living with relatives, the frictions involved in the household, the girl's mistreatment, and her aunt's hypocrisy. In a kind of sequel, *Escribo tu nombre* (1965), Tadea is again the protagonist, this time in a convent school. The author dissects the false vision of the world created by an indifferent educational system. *Presente profundo* (1973) is the story of two women told from multiple perspectives, about their existential anguish, unhappy childhoods, and eventual suicides.

Quiroga, an Existential novelist, is masterful in her portrayal of youthful rebellion; the lack of communication among human beings; the uncertainty, emptiness, loneliness, and alienation found in the modern world; the conflict between love and hate, reality and illusion; and the process of self-deception. She deals with the impact of grief and guilt, of solitary beings victimized

179

by the hostility of the world, who seek, often in vain, for a communion with an understanding God.

8. *Other novelists* of the Generation of 1936 include the following:

a. *Alvaro Cunqueiro* (1911–1981), a well-known poet, excelled at magical, oneiric universes of memory, myth, and legend. One of his best novels is *Un hombre que se parecía a Orestes* (1968), a Premio Nadal winner.

b. *Angel María de Lera* (1912–1984) wrote largely on social themes and the materialism of his society. He deals with alienation and solitude, especially of adolescents. Among his seventeen novels, his tetralogy, consisting of *Las últimas barreras* (1967), *Los que perdimos* (1974), *La noche sin riberas* (1976), and *Oscuro amanecer* (1977), has received the most favorable critical attention.

c. *Ignacio Agustí* (1913–1974), who helped found the Premio Nadal, is known primarily for his five-part saga, *La ceniza fue árbol*, dealing with a Catalan family, beginning with *Mariano Rebull* (1944) and ending with *Guerra Civil* (1972).

d. *José Suárez Carreño* (b. 1914) won the Premio Nadal for *Las últimas horas* (1950), which set the tone for early Neorealist and Existential novels.

e. *Luis Romero* (b. 1916) has written short stories, travel books, and a variety of novels, the best known of which is *La noria* (1952), a Premio Nadal winner.

f. *Pedro Lorenzo* (b. 1917) experimented with a unique style reminiscent of Miró and Azorín. He published his first novel in 1943 but later developed a series of novels published as a unit in 1975 as *Novelas del descontento*, whose protagonist is the antihero Alonso Mora.

g. *Dolores Medio* (b. 1917), short story writer and novelist, won the Premio Nadal with *Nosotros los Rivero* (1953), about a protagonist, her alter ego, and the process of going from adolescence to adulthood in time of war. Among other novels are *Diario de una maestra* (1961), about her work as a rural teacher; *La otra circunstancia* (1972); and *El fabuloso imperio de Juan sin Tierra* (1974), involving a kind of magical realism.

h. *José Luis Martín Vigil* (b. 1919), poet, essayist, and priest, has written more than thirty novels beginning with *La vida sale al encuentro* (1955) and continued through the 1980s. He concentrates on the preoccupations and problems of the young and adolescents, usually from a moral, social, or religious point of view.

i. *Tomás Salvador* (b. 1921), one of the most prolific members of this generation, has written historical, Existential, and fantastic novels in a writing career of almost forty years. Among his many works one should mention *Cuerda de presos* (1953).

Also worthy of note are Darío Fernández Flórez (1909–1977); Segundo Serrano Poncela (1912–1976); Enrique Azcoaga (1912–1985); Ricardo Fernández de la Reguera (b. 1916); Mercedes Salisachs (b. 1916); Cecilio Benítez de Castro (b. 1917); Concha Alós (b. 1922); and Ramón Pinilla (b. 1923).

F. The Generation of 1950

1. *Luis Martín-Santos* (1924–1964), a psychiatrist, is deservedly famous for his *Tiempo de silencio* (1962), universally acknowledged as the novel that closed out the period of Neorealism and traditional chronology and that marked the beginning of a new stage in the development of the novel.

Tiempo de silencio uses counterpoint, interior monologue, free association, multiple levels treated simultaneously, intertextuality, and mythology. Baroque, and with shifting narrative perspectives and narrative voice, the novel uses parody and irony (Martín-Santos has a devastating assessment of Ortega y Gasset) to demythify Spain, at times with nihilistic, despairing, or angry tones. The novel rejects technology and scientific apparatus as solutions for human oppression and death, and Existentially the author claims that man cannot really know or act in an authentic manner. Martín-Santos twists reality in his mixture of the poetic and scientific to produce what he called "realismo dialecto," a kind of ethical aestheticism. He uses psychiatry, anthropology, and psychoanalytic symbolism in his exploration of the mental processes of his protagonist, but he also mirrors the tragic life of Spaniards of all classes in postwar Spain (in a geography of middle-class, aristocratic, tenement, and whorehouse buildings), living in an absurd world and victimized by science, the Church, and their own sexuality.

Through Pedro, a weak-willed research scientist trapped by conscience, the author shows us the price that society exacts from failures who still believe in human values and who must pay with their "time of silence." Pedro, active in cancer research, needs a special strain of mice he can obtain only through Muecas, who has stolen a pair from the laboratory and managed to breed them. Muecas asks Pedro to save Florita, his pregnant daughter, from a botched abortion, and when she dies Pedro is

181

discharged. He plans to marry Dorita, granddaughter of the owner of the boardinghouse in which he lives, but Florita's vengeful boyfriend kills her.

In 1975 *Tiempo de destrucción,* which Martín-Santos had never finished, was published. It attacks institutions that impede individual liberty and again involves an alienated protagonist.

2. *Jesús Fernández Santos* (1926–1986) started as a Social Realist, but later, without totally abandoning the traditional or embracing all the new narrative techniques, he achieved a special blend of fictional elements. He wrote a great number of novels, the first of which, *Los bravos* (1954), depicts *caciquismo* in a rural community filled with hate, hostility, unhappiness, and stagnation. Though technically an Objectivist novel, it pleads for tolerance and justice. Among other novels of the 1950s and 1960s are *En la hoguera* (1957), depicting an unfortunate protagonist dogged by fate; *Laberintos* (1964), about Madrid intellectuals and their Existential problems; and *El hombre de los santos* (1969), portraying an alienated protagonist, unable to escape Civil War memories, who has to abandon his artistic career.

In the 1970s Fernández Santos published *Libro de las memorias y de las cosas* (1971), the story of the Brethren, a Protestant sect in the 1880s in Spain; *La que no tiene nombre* (1977), an intertwining of a medieval allegory with contemporary lives, concerning three time periods, personal memories, incest, and a mixture of history and legend; and *Extramuros* (1978), in which the author tries to penetrate the historical period of seventeenth-century Spain to narrate a tale of passion, human solitude, and the conflict between a convent world and the outside one. The outside world is attracted by a false miracle invented by two lesbian nuns to save their convent. As in other novels Fernández Santos treats here of the power of time on individuals.

In the 1980s up to his death, this author published a number of novels, among them *Cabrera* (1981), a historical novel in a nineteenth-century setting, involving an anonymous protagonist in a concentration camp on a small island near Mallorca. Replete with ethnic groups, women good and bad, and other characters, this novel about the Napoleonic invasion of Spain conveys the horror of war. *Jaque a la dama* (1982) treats of anti-Semitism and political liberty; *Los jinetes del alba* (1984) continues Fernández Santos' investigation into Spanish history, the effects of war, and the meaning of solitude. *El Griego* (1985) is about El Greco's life as seen from different points of view and by different characters. *Balada de amor y soledad* (1987) concerns the protagonist's psychological problems set against the background of an ecological crisis.

In general Fernández Santos concentrates on history as narrative, seeking to recover and re-create the past, its psychology and language. An Existentialist, he treats of solitude but also of religion, unhappy children, nature, and human sexuality.

3. *Ana María Matute* (b. 1926), as with many members of her generation, was indelibly marked by the Civil War, its horror, cruelty, and death. She is equally famous for her short stories and her children's stories. She deals with the rivalry among brothers in a world where the innocent dream futile dreams. But she exhibits a feminine viewpoint and evinces a strong maternal instinct. She tells her stories of children and adolescents, lonely and alienated victims of adult incomprehension, with lyrical intensity and uses a series of techniques—temporal jumps, free association, flashbacks, and at times deforming devices—to mirror the emotions of her protagonists. Her fiction also emphasizes Existential themes of loneliness and isolation with occasional escapes into fantasy.

Her first published novel, *Los Abel* (1948), involves the Cain and Abel theme and the disintegration of a family. *Fiesta al noroeste* (1953), a novella, concerns a childhood victim attempting to find solace and revenge as an adult and also the antagonistic relationship of stepbrothers. *Pequeño teatro* (1954), written much earlier, is about corruption and frustration in a fishing village. *En esta tierra* (1955), a revised version of a censored novel, *Las luciérnagas* (1955), deals with a young girl's coming of age in Barcelona during the war. Matute's first great triumph, however, was with *Los hijos muertos* (1958), involving autobiographical reminiscences of children suffering in an adult world and their later disillusion. She deals with three generations, examining the rivalry and betrayals repeated from generation to generation.

The author's trilogy, *Los mercaderes*, undoubtedly her masterpiece, consists of *Primera memoria* (1960), *Los soldados lloran de noche* (1964), and *La trampa* (1969). In the first volume, a Premio Nadal winner, she uses flashbacks from the perspective of Matia, a fourteen-year-old girl, to show Matia's dramatic awakening to the sordid and hypocritical adult world. Dominated by her grandmother and a cruel cousin, Matia allows the incarceration of Manuel, an innocent lad. The implicit Christian aspects of self-sacrifice and betrayal reflect the Biblical symbolism. In the second volume, about the uselessness of war, Manuel, recognized as the heir of Jorge de Son Mayor, his father and the mysterious adventurer of the first volume, encounters Marta, also a victim of cruelty and vanity. Both are killed by a Nationalist tank. In *La trampa,* Matia, returning for her grandmother's one hundredth birthday celebration, accentuates the frustration, both metaphysical and real, of Spanish women. We see the degradation and continuing hatred dividing Spain during the war's aftermath. Matia, now an adult, has led a solitary life, tortured and melancholy, and Borja, largely unchanged from the first volume, wants to inherit his grandmother's estate. Bear, Matia's son, becomes involved with Mario, a political activist, and becomes the avenging instrument against one who earlier had betrayed Mario's father. Again we see the Existential anguish of the characters and the continuing degeneration in Spain after the Civil War. In 1971 Matute published *La torre vigía,* set in the Middle Ages and mirroring a magical, sensual world of a youthful protagonist and his apprenticeship.

4. *Rafael Sánchez Ferlosio* (b. 1927) has published only three novels aside from his short stories. His first, *Industrias y andanzas de Alfanhuí* (1951), a mixture of fantasy and realism, offers us a kind of mythological interpretation of a boy who represents the human soul and perhaps the writer's own self-awakening to art and truth. Following the picaresque model, the story is about a boy who serves a variety of masters in various places. The thirteen episodes are essentially antiurban and stress the harmony of man and nature through a series of events involving animals and a continuing allegory.

The novel that made Sánchez Ferlosio famous and that influenced an entire generation of writers, *El Jarama* (1956), a Premio Nadal winner, though considered the supreme Spanish Objectivist work, nonetheless uses poetic and almost Surrealistic elements. A group of city workers spends a Sunday on the banks of the Jarama River at the same time that an older group of citizens frequents a bar-restaurant overlooking the river. The novel covers a time frame of sixteen hours and five minutes as we witness the boring, gray lives, the banal and even vulgar conversation of the group. One member drowns, but those who remain seem no more alive. Time and history fuse and flow like the river: immutable, it mirrors the lack of values in the endlessly repeated monotonous details of the group's existence.

El testimonio de Yarfoz (1986), supposedly edited by the author from a manuscript written by an engineer, claims that the manuscript was in turn only part of a larger historical work written by another writer. Sánchez Ferlosio examines the relationship of fiction and history, and the protagonist wants to relate and preserve the truth for future generations concerning his friendship with the self-exiled Prince Nébride.

5. *Juan Benet* (b. 1927) is a writer of short stories, novelettes, and some dramatic works, as well as his more famous novels. Benet, unlike most members of his generation, did not begin with Neorealism. Most of his novels are set in Región, perhaps a microcosm of a static Spain, a mysterious, cold, and lonely area where fantastic, chaotic, and paradoxical happenings occur involving the Spanish Civil War and its aftermath. His first novel, *Volverás a Región* (1967), leads the reader astray through a series of illogical sequences. Occurring between 1925 and 1939, the novel concerns an inveterate gambler, Gamallo, who even gambles away his love, María. Later, as a colonel, he launches a successful attack on Región. Years afterward the colonel's daughter visits Doctor Sebastián, the head of a sanatorium in Región, hoping to recapture the memory of a sexual fulfillment with María's son during the Civil War. Sebastián is killed by a patient, and the daughter is shot by Numa, a mysterious guardian of Región. In one way or another the characters try to relive the memories of their past, but they are hemmed in by a closed circle of moral and physical ruin and a fate from which there is no escape and that reason is unable to control.

Among his other novels, *Una meditación* (1970), set between 1920 and 1960, is one long paragraph of first-person narrative that deals with the efforts to remember on the part of both author and characters in order to recapture a past reality. *Un viaje de invierno* (1972), the third part of the Región trilogy, is a reprise of an attempted return and the ensuing fatality. The author again obfuscates by using contradictory sequences and by relating the novel to the Demeter-Persephone myth. *La otra casa de Mazón* (1973) concerns the progressive decadence of a once-rich family and the ruin and decay in a Región-like region. *En el estado* (1977), set outside Región, deals with grotesque characters in an isolated town who all lead frustrated and unhappy lives. *Saúl y Samuel* (1980), again in Región, reflects the solitude, guilt, life, and death involved in Falangist-Republican rivalries during the Spanish Civil War. *Herrumbrosas lanzas,* done as a collection of books (I–VI, 1983; VII–XII, 1986), involves Civil War attacks, Región, and characters from earlier novels. In 1989 Benet published *En la penumbra.*

Benet plays with time and memory, examines Existential

problems, shows us portraits of ruin and decay in a world where communication is impossible, and, using self-parody, stresses the importance of attempted recall for the solitary and alienated individuals who live in a deterministic universe. Benet loves dualities—instinct versus reason, present and past—and to achieve his special effects he uses a Neobaroque language, often with technical vocabulary and foreign languages. Whatever the art or allegory, one can conclude that he is really talking about life under Franco and the sadness of Spanish life in the twentieth century.

6. *Juan Goytisolo* (b. 1931), an author of short stories, novelettes, travel books, literary criticism, and autobiography, came to the attention of critics with his first novel, *Juegos de manos* (1954), about a group of youngsters who decide to kill a minor political official, choosing for the task one of their more sensitive youths. The chosen one, David, unable to murder, is himself killed by another member. The novel typifies Goytisolo's early works about adolescents who are frustrated and paralyzed by guilt or other inadequacies and the process of growing from childhood to adulthood. Among other works more or less in the Neorealistic vein are *Duelo en el paraíso* (1955), about an orphan during the last weeks of the Civil War who is killed by other refugee children in a violent reproduction of the adult world; *El circo* (1957), a farce that dissects both adult and juvenile delinquents and has a protagonist living in a self-induced dream world and accepting responsibility for a murder he did not commit; *Fiestas* (1958), four interwoven stories about poor Murcians who live, suffer, and die in a poverty-stricken section of Barcelona; *La resaca* (1958), concerning a Church holiday and the hypocritical role of the Church, indifferent to the misery and death surrounding it; and *La isla* (1961), a grim picture of adult cynicism and sexuality and a gross materialistic world, formed in part by tourists in Spain.

In spite of their social impact, these novels, though traditional in structure and using objective descriptions of a bigoted and intolerant Spain, foretell, through lyrical and stylistic devices, the future novelist. After Martín-Santos' *Tiempo de silencio*, Goytisolo abandoned Social Realism to stress a new kind of language and to mirror the disintegration of human relationships in a world without myth and values. Plot and character came to be secondary elements in a text that served as its own reality. Nonetheless, these novels continued a criticism of the Catholic Church, a defense of personal liberty, especially sexual, and

Goytisolo's ambivalent view of life, consisting of executioners and victims. His novels, mirroring Structuralist and Formalist beliefs, used sentences that were not sentences, foreign languages, anaphoric techniques, collages, and Baroque redundancies in an effort to destroy the language that represented established institutions and traditional literary values. In 1966 he published *Señas de identidad,* the first volume of what some see as a trilogy along with *Reivindicación del Conde don Julián* (1970) and *Juan sin tierra* (1975).

Señas de identidad concerns Alvaro Mendiola, who attempts through memory to recapture the past. A descendant of a family of industrialists and landowners whose values he despises, he tries to find his authenticity and a cause in which he can believe. *Reivindicación del Conde don Julián* reverses the legend of the traitor who helped the Arabs in their invasion of Spain. The protagonist, through an interior monologue, again invades Spain in his imagination and destroys all its religious, political, literary, and sexual pretensions. The novel involves a series of "happenings" that include rape, sodomy, and the destruction of literary classics. The novel uses free association, dream, revery, and a protagonist-narrator who renounces his country of disparate masks. Though the novel may be viewed as a kind of dream, it nonetheless is a very real protest against Spanish social and political shortcomings. *Juan sin tierra,* one of the earliest of the self-referential novels that explores the process of creating the very novel being written, is Goytisolo's strongest attack on the Spanish language. The author also attacks all Western civilization and the reproductive act itself through hate and perversion as he mirrors a series of conscious and subconscious hostilities. A spatial, temporal, fantastic travelogue, an erotic and linguistic aggression against the world and specifically against frozen and petrified cultural and linguistic codes, the novel employs multiple points of view, monologues, and most of the so-called newer narrative techniques.

Among later novels, *Makbara* (1980) attacks capitalistic society, consumerism, and woman as a kind of deformed creature, though the mother figure (his own was killed in a Civil War air raid) permeates much of his fiction. The story line involves the outcast hero and a rebellious angel exiled from heaven. *Paisajes después de la batalla* (1982) continues the sexual preoccupations and other themes of tourism, capitalism, and the like, especially the problem of authorship, narrator, author, hero, and protagonist. The novel uses the life of Lewis Carroll, instead of Count

187

Julián through a solitary protagonist who molests little girls. *Las virtudes del pájaro solitario* (1988) concerns a complex dialogue involving the works of San Juan de la Cruz and *sufí* poetry. The novel is a collage of intertextual material and demands careful reader participation to decipher the roles of the many narrators and themes, which range from the mystical to ecological disaster.

7. *Luis Goytisolo* (b. 1935), in *Las afueras* (1958), a collection of seven thematically related stories, writes a Neorealistic novel of alienated and difficult lives of members of the working class. *Las mismas palabras* (1962) examines a week in the empty lives of middle-class youths in Barcelona and its suburbs. Goytisolo is best known, however, for *Antagonía*, a tetralogy that is one of the most ambitious undertakings of the last two decades. The author studies alienation, political impotence, and the process of growing up in Barcelona, satirizes Spain, and caricatures the Communist party. But the tetralogy is also a self-referential novel, as well as a history of Barcelona in the 1950s and 1960s, involving changing narrators, the past and future, and various narrative levels.

Recuento (1973), the first volume of *Antagonía,* explores the relationship of language to literary text. In addition to commentary on the art of writing, the author explores the sexual metaphor to explain aspects of Spanish culture and history. The character-writer believes that the reader could write another novel on the novel being read. A kind of self-parody, it concerns the maturation process of Raúl, the narrator, and the relationship of his novel to his own reality, which involves joining and leaving the Communist party and a love affair. *Los verdes de mayo hasta el mar* (1976) inquires into the nature of writing once again, and the creator becomes authentic through his own creativity. Set in a seaside resort on the Catalonian coast, the novel includes sexuality, myth, and a kind of visionary allegory about a drifting ego. The third volume, *La cólera de Aquiles* (1979), again examines difficult human relationships and the nature and function of sexuality. Matilde Moret, the protagonist, is writing the novel. A rich lesbian, she attempts to destroy her lover's relationship with a man through a series of notes and creates a novelist who invents a fictional protagonist in a novel. A sort of battle of the sexes, the novel examines the intricate relationship of domination to sexuality. The fourth volume, *Teoría del conocimiento* (1981), again contains an interpolated novel and tape transcriptions of two characters, as Goytisolo once more analyzes contemporary Cataluña and the act of creation. Among other novels are *Estela del fuego que se aleja* (1984), a continuation of the metafictional mode, about a protagonist who writes a novel whose protagonist also wants to live and write a novel about a protagonist who is his own creator; and *La paradoja del ave migratoria* (1987), depicting the making of a film and the fusion of reality and unreality.

8. *Other writers* of the Generation of 1950 include the following:

a. *Ignacio Aldecoa* (1925–1969), one of Spain's best short story writers, wrote *El fulgor y la sangre* (1954), about the Civil Guards and their families, and *Con el viento solano* (1956), portraying the murder of one of the Guards. His *Gran sol* (1957), concerning a sea voyage of thirteen fishermen, is, after *El Jarama*, probably Spain's best Objectivist novel. *Parte de una historia* (1967) examines urban versus rural values. Aldecoa used archetypal symbolism to good effect.

b. *Carmen Martín Gaite* (b. 1925) wrote her first novel, *Entre visillos*, in 1958. It is a Neorealistic study of young people and provincial prejudices in postwar Spain. *Ritmo lento* (1963) treats of a youth in a psychiatric center who rejects societal pressures to conform. *Retahílas* (1974), her own favorite, written in the new linguistic and experimental vein, concerns a kind of psychoanalytic encounter between a man and a woman. The entire novel, which explores the authenticity of woman's role, consists of the conversation. Probably her best novel is *El cuarto de atrás* (1978), dedicated to Lewis Carroll. The protagonist falls asleep while reading Todorov, and a self-invited guest in black appears. The author-narrator-protagonist, in her dialogue with this fantastic entity, reveals her thought processes and efforts to recapture her childhood and lost time.

c. *Alfonso Grosso* (b. 1928) deals with a varied world of promiscuity, homosexuality, Civil War antagonisms, and the tragic dimensions of life. He contrasts two classes of society, the very rich and the very poor. The poor lead gray and hopeless lives, as empty as those of the upper classes in their pursuit of amusements through fast cars and sexual encounters. Death is a constant in his work. A thoroughly Baroque writer, he nonetheless combines the social with his techniques of interspersed dialogues, interior monologues, time jumps, and free association. He has written a number of novels, the early ones of documentary realism. *La zanja* (1961) examines life in rural Andalusia; *Un cielo difícilmente azul* (1961) is about *caciquismo* in an Andalusian village; and *Testa de copo* (1963) portrays tuna fishermen and the incarceration of an innocent victim.

El capirote (1966) concerns a hapless worker crushed by a falling religious statue. *Inés Just Coming* (1968) is filled with *cubanismos* and American scenes, especially sexual, of life under Fidel Castro. *Guarnición de silla* (1970) deals with philosophical introspection and an Existential universe whose inhabitants express no societal values. In 1981 Grosso published *Con flores a María*, a revised version of the unpublished *La romería* (1962), which together with *Testa de copo* and *El capirote* was to have formed a trilogy. Other novels include *La buena muerte* (1976), about a homosexual priest and decadent aristocrats; *El correo de Estambul* (1980), about the Middle East; *Toque de queda* (1983), a novel of intrigue set in Uruguay; and several volumes of *Giralda*, published in 1982, 1984, and 1985.

d. *Carlos Rojas* (b. 1928), one of the best contemporary novelists, has not yet received the critical acclaim he deserves. For him writing is more than a semantic game, and he explores themes of fratricide and tyranny, acknowledging man's inclination toward evil but accepting the possibility of an increasing tolerance. In early novels he explored the problems of power and alienation plaguing the human condition. From about 1963 on he has dealt more with the problem of identity and metaphysical and religious themes. He uses complex levels of language that reveal a total understanding of Cervantine style. In addition to themes of a search for lost liberty and social justice, Rojas examines the relationship of literature and art and their further ties to the historical through time. Among his many novels are *De barro y de esperanza* (1957), his first, in which he fuses history and literature; *Adolfo Hitler está en mi casa* (1965); *Auto de fe* (1968), an ambitious reconstruction of the reign of Carlos IV fused with Lazarus' narration of events after the Crucifixion; *Aquelarre* (1970), which uses myth, witchcraft, and Goya's paintings as reflections of contemporary events; *Azaña* (1973), an evocation of the Spanish Republic and the real and metaphysical Azaña; and a trilogy using as a character Rojas' alter ego, Sandro Vasari. The volumes are *El valle de los caídos* (1978), *El ingenioso hidalgo y poeta Federico García Lorca asciende a los infiernos* (1980), and *El sueño de Sarajevo* (1982). The first novel deals with historical themes that transcend immediate reality as it fuses the lives of Ferdinand VII, Franco, Goya, and Sandro Vasari. The second volume evokes a García Lorca created by the Vasaris in a manuscript sent to Rojas, also a character in the novel. A kind of metafiction, the novel speculates on the life and death of Lorca, whose spirit lives in a constantly re-created hell. The third novel again gives us a historical view of Goya's life and times through a gathering of ghosts in a Spanish monastery.

e. *Juan Marsé* (b. 1933) wrote his early works in the Objectivist vein, but he achieved recognition with *Ultimas tardes con Teresa* (1965), ostensibly still a work of Social Realism but also a parody thereof. Through a picaresque protagonist, the author satirizes Spanish society. *La oscura historia de la prima Montse* (1970) involves a narrator who is a distorted version of the author and deals with repressed sexuality and the Catalonian bourgeoisie. *Si te dicen que caí* (1976) is an allegorical novel, a kind of global vision of post–Civil War society, and a continuing satire of a social structure that inhibits love and freedom. It is more complicated and complex than previous novels and, aside from its pictures of prostitution and sexuality, is a re-creation of the author's childhood. Other novels include *La muchacha de las bragas de oro* (1979), involving the relationship between an old Fascist writer and his niece who helps him type his memoirs; *Un día volveré* (1982), a kind of sequel to *Si te dicen que caí;* and *Ronda del Guinardó* (1984). The author uses irony to good effect in his novels, whose major themes consist of sexuality, guilt, alienation, and social criticism. He experiments with temporal planes, interior monologues, and the like.

Also worthy of note are Antonio Ferres (b. 1924); Francisco Candel (b. 1925); Armando López Salinas (b. 1925); José Manuel Caballero Bonald (b. 1926); Juan García Hortelano (b. 1928); M. García Viñó (b. 1928); Luisa Forellad (b. 1929); Antonio Martínez Menchen (b. 1930); José María Carrascal (b. 1930); and Daniel Sueiro (b. 1931).

G. The Generation of 1968

1. *Ramón Hernández* (b. 1935) excels in depicting the deforming power of a materialistic society and individuals trapped by forces they are unable to control. He insists on the centrality of mental functioning, and his dehumanized victims, at times almost schizophrenic and at times truly mad, attempt to distinguish the real from the unreal. Essentially an Existentialist, Hernández views each individual as representative of humanity in his search for authenticity. He employs many of the modern tech-

niques—direct and indirect discourse, interior monologue, temporal dislocations, disguised narrative voices, and arbitrary typography and syntax.

His first work, *El buey en el matadero* (1966), was reissued in 1979 as *Presentimiento de lobos* and deals with hypocrisy and the role of social and economic power. *Palabras en el muro* (1969), also reedited and republished in 1984, details the dehumanization of prison life through the suffering of three prisoners. Hernández explores the prison honor code and the monotony, hopes, dreams, madness, and death involved through a constant interior mental recall by the prisoners. In *La ira de la noche* (1970), the author attempts to reproduce the chaotic thoughts of the protagonist, Walia, whose madness was triggered by a child's death. The arbitrary narration flows from the disordered mental processes of the protagonist. In *El tirano inmóvil* (1970), Hernández again describes an imaginary, grotesque, and absurd reality through the deformed protagonist who must confirm his own authenticity through the destruction of an oppressor. *Invitado a morir* (1972) again takes up Hernández' theme of a dehumanized protagonist, a neurotic executive who lives an inauthentic life ruled by obsessive detail and corporate bureaucracy. He commits a cold-blooded murder for which he must pay the price, just as he is beginning to understand his own self-realization. *Eterna memoria* (1975), again a mental recall, is an antiwar novel that defends individual liberty against the absurdity of modern life. The protagonist, already dead on the dissecting table, relates what is happening. *Algo está ocurriendo* (1976) deals once more with the disoriented and irrational thought processes of a protagonist who realizes his own self-limitations.

Hernández has written several other novels. *Pido la muerte al rey* (1979) is related by the occupant of an insane asylum who was sent there as a result of a false accusation of terrorism and was subsequently tortured, an act that caused him to go mad. He asks the king to allow him to expiate his supposed crime, because, in a society of violence and injustice, we are all guilty. *Bajo Palio* (1983), a combination of myth, fantasy, and reality, deals with a caudillo's widow who seeks the resurrection of her dead husband in an attempt to stop time and return to a vanished past. *El ayer perdido* (1986) presents a narrator already dead and thus outside time who relates his life story. *Sola en el paraíso* (1987) concerns solitude, old age, and victimization in a city beset by dogma and prejudice.

2. *Esther Tusquets* (b. 1936) in 1978 published the first volume of a trilogy, *El mismo mar de todos los veranos,* an exploration of the relationship between sexuality and textuality and character participation in the creative process. In her analysis of female sexuality as a positive force, the author uses both Freudian and Jungian archetypes and at the same time uses negative phallic metaphors to show her rejection of patriarchal power. The erotic themes emphasize the Existential process, as her female characters seek their authenticity through sexual activity. Quite often the author contrasts childhood fairy tales and Greek myths with the suffering or frustration involved. Tusquets uses minute details, often repetitive, in her exploration of events. The protagonist in this first volume, a university professor alienated from her mother and daughter as well as from a promiscuous and sexually aggressive husband, seeks a genuine love through a lesbian relationship with a student, which serves also as a kind of compensation for the suicide of a potential male savior who might have satisfied her intimate needs.

The second volume, *El amor es un juego solitario* (1979), includes some of the same characters. Elia, unsatisfied existentially, engages in an affair with Ricardo, who sees in her not only his first guide to sexual experience but also a source of power. Clara, the young woman in love with Elia, seeks escape through fantasy. The novel, aside from the sexual emphasis, especially on the pleasures of the female body, also explores childhood and loss.

The third novel, *Varada tras el último naufragio* (1980), again involves Elia as well as Eva, a feminist lawyer, and her husband. Clara also appears in a homosexual role. In spite of matrimonial crises, Elia rediscovers her love for her son and rejects sexuality as a final solution. The trilogy deals with upper-class Catalan society in the late 1960s and the 1970s and treats a series of heterosexual, bisexual, and lesbian relationships. In spite of the subject matter, the treatment is both lyrical and tender.

Other titles about the same Barcelona bourgeois world are *Siete miradas en un mismo paisaje* (1981) and *Para no volver* (1985).

3. *Jesús Torbado* (b. 1943), a journalist, scriptwriter, short story writer, and author of travel works, wrote a prize-winning novel, *Las corrupciones,* in 1965 about disillusioned youth, their self-deception, love, and attempts to escape from their situation and to find their authenticity. Among other novels, *En el día de hoy* (1976), filled with the political spirit of rebellion and disillusion, ends in 1940 with German planes flying overhead. The thesis of

193

the novel is that the Republicans won the Civil War and that Franco had to flee to America. Finally, says the author, any kind of political power by definition creates a series of victims. *Moira estuvo aquí* (1971) is a modern reconstruction of the myth of the three Fates who govern human destiny, specifically Lachesis, pursued by the protagonist, who in the process becomes a hippie, a social situation repeated from an earlier novel. *Historias de amor* (1968) is about hippies, drugs, and sexuality. *El día de hoy* (1976) won the Planeta Prize. *La ballena* (1982) concerns a group of retired people of different occupations who find a whale on a beach. This starts a process of struggle over ownership and ends up involving the government, the Church, a group of Fascists, and the Civil Guard. Through the lives of the protagonists we come to understand the shortcomings of authority and the author's satire of modern society.

4. *José María Guelbenzu* (b. 1944), the author of this group who has received the most critical acclaim, in his early novels used a variety of linguistic experiments, attempting reversed sentences, special sounds, fragmentation, arbitrary divisions, and typographical arrangements. Though he never accepted Neorealistic tenets, he employed fewer of these techniques in later novels. Guelbenzu is specifically interested in personal relationships, and his complex characters, alienated and anguished, search for authenticity and identity. His work often involves imaginary or oneiric elements and a reality viewed from different perspectives. This search for individuality in a conformist society involves autobiographical elements of infancy and youth.

His first novel, *El mercurio* (1968), explores the sterility of postwar Spain. *Antifaz* (1970), his second, mirrors a confused generation, frustrated people seeking to satisfy desire and achieve an authentic existence in an absurd world. Guelbenzu uses two interweaving conflictive love stories on two narrative planes. *El pasajero de Ultramar* (1976) is an exploration through memory as part of a search for authenticity by a stoic protagonist who seeks strength within himself. *La noche en casa* (1977) tells of an unwilling courier involved with a terrorist group. He meets a former love, also on a trip, and spends a night with her, united with her by surprise and memory. The novel employs a great deal of intertextuality. *El río de la luna* (1981), a kind of recapitulation of previous themes, is a five-part novel of protagonists doomed to the very failures from which they are fleeing. The novel, which uses counterpoint, interior monologue, parody, and burlesque, depicts the sordid existence under

Franco of characters who explore childhood reality and fantasy and who engage in compulsive sexual adventurism. Fidel, an abulic character, meets Teresa, an old love, after fifteen years. Entering a bar, he encounters a strange character who relates the story of a youth lost in a labyrinth, and José, that adolescent, has a nightmare that in part involves the narration being lived. The author explores alienation and sexuality, desire and death. *El esperado* (1984) relates, against a Civil War background, the story of a fifteen-year-old boy's first trip from home, his first love, and the rites of passage in an adult world complete with adultery, violence, and murder. Guelbenzu published *La mirada* in 1987.

5. *Ana María Moix* (b. 1947), a poet and short story writer, deals with her own unhappy childhood and, in her tales of lack of communication and deception, uses different narrative levels, flashback, and other techniques to describe an essentially alienated postwar Barcelona society. Her novels deal with people who love, despair, remember, and aid the author in her recall of deception and dream.

Julia (1969) has a protagonist who searches in vain for acceptance by her mother and a university professor mother figure. A victim of a sexual attack in her childhood and the recipient of a special education by her grandfather, Julia seeks escape through fairy-tale fantasies. She feels more and more dominated by Julita, herself at the age of five; her schizophrenic experience eventually leads to an unsuccessful suicide attempt. Moix employs a good deal of Freudian theory in her recall of the homosexuality of the protagonist's brother, lesbianism, and a general feeling of powerlessness. Julia finally acknowledges Julita in her attempt at self-liberation in the Franco Spain of the 1950s and 1960s. *Walter, ¿por qué te fuiste?* (1973), a kind of sequel involving episodes from *Julia*, deals with Julia's cousin Ismael, whose recall of the past involves family and an alienated group of youngsters living in a repressive society. In love with Lea, who taught him and Julia about sexuality, he searches for her in vain, substituting for his dream girl a centaur circus companion who dies during his search. The ten-year-old Ismael and Julia had been impressed by Walter, Lea's mysterious lover, who disappointingly turned out to be a seminary student.

6. *Other writers* include Francisco Umbral (b. 1935), Pedro Antonio Urbina (b. 1936), Raúl Guerra Garrido (b. 1936), J. Leyva (b. 1938), Manuel Vázquez Montalbán (b. 1939), Germán Sánchez Espeso (b. 1940), José María Merino (b. 1941),

195

Lourdes Ortiz (b. 1943), Eduardo Mendoza (b. 1943), Terencio Moix (b. 1943), Marina Mayoral (b. 1944), Cristina Fernández Cubas (b. 1945), Juan José Millas (b. 1946), Vicente Molina Foix (b. 1946), Montserrat Roig (b. 1946), Soledad Puértolas (b. 1947), and Rosa Montero (b. 1951).

Part 5 LYRIC POETRY

THE MIDDLE AGES

A. Origin

Considerable evidence indicates a flourishing primitive Castilian lyric, but very few examples of such poetry have been preserved. Contrariwise, much early lyric poetry in the Galician language has been preserved, and Galician was, indeed, the preferred language for lyric expression during the Middle Ages even for Castilian poets. Consequently, Galician poetry dominated the peninsula from the twelfth to the fourteenth century. It was not until the end of the fourteenth and the beginning of the fifteenth century that the Castilians began to use their own language to compose lyric poetry. The *Cancionero de Baena* (1445) represents the work of the first genuine Castilian school of lyric poets. Thereafter Spanish replaced Galician as the preferred language for lyric expression.

It is sometimes difficult to classify medieval poetry as narrative, epic, or lyric, for in some poems elements of each can be found. Rigid categorization is therefore frequently unsatisfactory. The general types of medieval poetry are Galician-Portuguese, narrative-lyric, primitive Castilian, Spanish-Arabic, and epic.

B. Galician-Portuguese Lyric Poetry

The courtly love poetry of France, brought to Spain by French troubadours, strongly influenced those writing in the Galician-Portuguese tongue. (Galician and Portuguese were the same in the Middle Ages.) Though it has been traditional to regard Provence in southern France as the place of origin of most of the lyric poetry of Europe, new light has been thrown on a possibly more distant origin through studies of Spanish-Arabic poetry. Nevertheless, if the Provençal poets did not invent this style of poetry, they at least refined it and disseminated it over Europe.

Provençal poetry was erudite, artificial, and highly refined. It showed a reversal of erotic values: the lover, formerly adoring his lady, now felt unworthy of her. The object of the lover's attention was a married woman, and the consummation of his love was viewed as altogether impossible, unsought, and undesirable. This agonizing situation led to a poetry of lament, melancholy, and complaint. It was brilliant and technically excellent, but also frequently tedious. The poet's sadness and frustration were not taken seriously, however, but were rather devices for exhibiting verbal virtuosity and technical skill. Love became a game, a kind of religion that was intended to have a chastening, uplifting, civilizing effect. Provençal lyric ignored the sensual love one finds later in the Middle Ages in works of writers like Juan Ruiz.

As early as the twelfth century, Galician, Portuguese, and Catalan poets began to imitate the Provençal courtly lyric. In Galicia, however, where life was more primitive, it did not entirely supplant the native folk poetry. As a result, Galician poetry, strengthened by Provençal techniques and skills, developed along two lines: the Provençal courtly love poetry and the native peasant poetry, represented by the *cossante* and the *danza prima*.

The Galicians preserved their poetry by means of *cancioneiros*. The principal ones are *Cancioneiro da Vaticana, Cancioneiro da Ajuda,* and *Cancioneiro Colocci-Brancuti*. The principal types of poems written in the Galician tongue were *cantigas de escarnio,* satiric songs, frequently bawdy and obscene; *cantigas de amor,* amorous laments; and *cantigas de amigo,* love songs.

C. Primitive Castilian Lyric Poetry

The Castilian-speaking people composed lyric poems in the age when Galician poetry dominated the peninsula, but unfortunately they did not collect and save the poems. Most have perished, as has almost all their epic poetry. Some early poems, such as the *serranillas,* the May songs, the watchman's songs, shepherds' songs, and songs for important occasions like Christmas, have been rescued from oblivion by later writers, such as Berceo, Juan Ruiz, the Marqués de Santillana, and the playwrights of the Golden Age. The influence of these early lyrical efforts may also be found in the *coplas, villancicos,* and other folk poems that are composed by Spanish-speaking people today.

D. The *Jarchas*

When S. M. Stern was studying Hebrew *muwassahas* in a synagogue in Egypt, he found that a number of them ended with a few verses that were not in Hebrew but in *mozárabe,* a Romance dialect spoken in southern Spain as early as the tenth century and probably much earlier. Eventually Stern found some twenty of these charming little poems called *jarchas (jarchyas, kharjas)* and soon afterward discovered an Arabic *muwassaha* with its *jarcha.* Following Stern's lead, Emilio García Gómez discovered a similar number of *jarchas* attached to Arabic *muwassahas.* Later on, other students of primitive peninsular poetry increased the number, until today we have more than sixty of these poetic jewels. A number of other scholars have studied and are still studying the *jarchas,* which are fraught with problems owing to the fact, in part at least, that they are written in Hebrew and Arabic characters, without vowel signs, and the scribes often omitted diacritical marks that identified consonants. Some *jarchas* were written completely in Arabic or in Mozarabic, while in others Arabic words are mixed in with the Mozarabic or vice versa, making transcription even more difficult. Another problem is that the original copyists of these refrains were transcribing into Hebrew and Arabic characters a language that they did not know, and thus they were prone to make errors. Since Stern's original discovery, a number of scholars have worked at correct readings of many *jarchas,* and as time goes by they are getting closer to a satisfactory transcription of many of them into modern Spanish.

The discovery of this poetry created great excitement in the literary world and has been compared in importance with the deciphering of the Rosetta Stone, the discovery of the Dead Sea Scrolls, or the invention of the telescope by Galileo. These may seem like exaggerations to all but philologists and students of the primitive Castilian lyric and the origins of European lyric poetry; but Menéndez Pidal seems to put it into context when he states that the discovery of the *jarchas* is doubtlessly one of the most important in the twentieth century, since they antedate by a century or more any examples of Spanish literature previously found and precede the Provençal courtly lyric by many years, making them the oldest lyric texts of Europe. Dámaso

199

Alonso concurs that it is now known that the Spanish *jarchas* precede all other European poetic texts by a century. All this destroys the theory that Spanish lyric poetry was late in appearing and lagged behind epic poetry. Linda Fish Compton holds that "although the *jarchas* are the oldest known secular lyrics in any Romance language and occupy a significant position within the mainstream of Western lyrical poetry, the exact relationship of these lyrics to the poetry of Europe and the Middle East has not been clearly determined."

The *muwassaha* (*muwashshah*), a very popular and widely used verse form, was invented in the tenth century. It is not yet clear who created this poetic form, but credit is usually given to Muqaddam de Cabra, a Mozarabic poet living in southern Spain, though none of his poems have been preserved. It was to the *muwassaha* that the *jarchas* were appended. The earliest *muwassahas* and *jarchas* yet discovered date back to the eleventh century. Another verse form of Hebrew and Arabic origin is the *zéjel,* used by Spanish poets through the centuries. Evidence points to the popular origin of the *muwassaha,* and it is theorized that the *jarcha* (the word means "exit") is the quintessential expression of the sentiment of the main body of the poem and was taken from the primitive Spanish popular poetry, forming the metrical and thematic basis upon which the *muwassaha* was constructed. In other words, the poet began with the *jarcha* as a theme and built his *muwassaha* upon it, attaching the original *jarcha* as the final verses. Critics do not unanimously support this theory, however, and some feel that the *jarcha* (also called *markaz*) was a thematic appendage to a *muwassaha.*

The *jarchas* usually run from two to four lines (thirty-two syllables) of verse and are almost without exception amorous in nature, spoken by a young girl who candidly and often quite ardently laments the absence of her lover while her mother or sisters listen or advise. These devices were common to the *cantigas de amigo* of the Galician-Portuguese poetry. Speaking of her intense feelings of love, the girl occasionally mentions the admirable attributes of her lover. In short, the *jarcha* with its accompanying *muwassaha* may have marked the beginnings of European lyric poetry. The Arabs had cultivated this genre centuries before invading Spain, and professional poets were retained at court by Arabic kings. The concept of platonic love as found in Provençal poetry was known to the Arabs, and as Brenan points out, the notion of love as obedience and suffering is of Arabic origin. As evidence gathers, we may eventually learn that European lyric poetry originated in Moslem Spain and not in Provence after all. Even now the evidence for such a conclusion is strong.

The Spanish Arabs also collected their poems into books, the best known of which is that of the Cordovan poet Abencuzmán (Aben Guzmán), whose poetry recounts his own experiences and is audacious in nature, anticipating the amorous adventures of Juan Ruiz and resembling much of the goliardic poetry of the European Middle Ages.

Alfonso *el Sabio* used the *zéjel*, as did Juan Ruiz, and examples of it are found in the Galician-Portuguese collections, the *Cancionero de Baena*, other fifteenth-century Spanish collections, and even in works as late as those of Lope de Vega. It is a verse type that may have affected all the poetry of Europe in one way or another and thus may form a link in the chain of popular choral dance songs dating back into forgotten time.

E. Conclusions Concerning Origins of Lyric Poetry

Much conjecture remains about the origin of Castilian lyric poetry. In the light of present evidence, however, the following conclusions seem valid. The people of southern Spain who spoke a dialect that eventually emerged as Spanish produced a lyric folk poetry dealing with their everyday cares and occupations, but they did not record it. Learned men declined to use the vernacular for their lyrical efforts, turning instead to Galician. Provençal poetry, possibly borrowing its philosophy of love and its concept of the professional poet from the Spanish Arabs, dominated peninsular poetry for two centuries. Spanish-Arabic and Hebrew popular poetry in the form of the *muwassaha* with its *jarcha* and the *zéjel* provide the earliest preserved examples of literary Spanish and influenced Spanish poets for centuries in both spirit and manner.

F. Lyric Poems and Poets

1. *Razón de amor,* also known as *Razón feita de amor* and *Aventura amorosa,* a charming little anonymous piece in the Provençal style, is the oldest preserved complete lyric poem in Spanish. Written early in the thirteenth century, it is probably a descendant of the Galician *cantigas* and contains gentle talk of love between a *doncella* and her poet-lover, who remains disconsolate when she departs. It is a pleasant, delicate poem, but as impor-

201

tant as its intrinsic merit is the fact that it clearly reveals a connection between the Galician-Portuguese school and Castilian poetry. After the love colloquy of the *Razón de amor*, the poet continues with a burlesque medieval debate between water and wine entitled *Denuestos del agua y del vino*. The two portions are not too skillfully joined but are not entirely incompatible with one another.

2. *Alfonso el Sabio* (1221–1284), whose school of scholars produced enormous historical and legal works, was also a poet who wrote the best Marian poetry of the Middle Ages in his *Cantigas de Santa María*. The 430 poems of this collection are mostly narrative in nature and recount miracles, tales, and poems of praise concerning the Virgin Mary. The entire book, except for one poem in Castilian, is written in the Galician-Portuguese dialect, despite the fact that Alfonso was a Castilian monarch.

3. *Gonzalo de Berceo* (1198?–1274?) was the earliest poet to write in Spanish whose name has been recorded. Fortunately, he preserved among his songs a sample of the primitive lyric of Castile, the watchman's song *Eya, velar*. Though often a plodder, he wrote at times with a sweetness, naïveté, simplicity, and genuine lyrical feeling that has elicited praise from twentieth-century poets.

Berceo wrote for the people and thought of himself as a *juglar* and not an erudite poet, though he used the *cuaderna vía* extensively. He declared that he would write in *romance paladín*, the common language of the people, and, perhaps jokingly, discounted the merit of his poetry, which in his view was worth at least a glass of good wine. He sprinkled the clichés of the *juglares* liberally throughout his poems. He was a learned man with a large vocabulary, but he employed rustic humor and viewed life in an uncomplicated way. From his some 13,000 lines of verse emerges an accurate portrayal of the sentiments of the people of his day.

Berceo did not invent; he merely imitated. His poems, almost exclusively religious in nature, recite the lives of saints and the miracles of the Virgin, and his uncomplicated religious faith, childlike simplicity, candor, and truly popular flavor have endeared him to many generations of Spaniards. His major works are *Vida de Santo Domingo; Milagros de nuestra Señora*, containing his best poetry; and *Vida de Santa Oria*. Especially attractive in the *Milagros* are the genuine lyricism of the opening lines, Berceo's love of nature and sympathy for the poor, oppressed, and unfortunate, and the realistic details and speech patterns.

4. *Juan Ruiz, Arcipreste de Hita* (1283?–1350?) rose in the first half of the fourteenth century as a major star in Spain's poetic constellation. His volume of poetry, named by modern critics *El libro de buen amor,* is ranked by everyone as one of the major works of Spanish literature.

We know very little of the life of this man. If we judge him by portions of his writings, we find that he was a pleasure-loving priest who personified the morals and spirit of an age not noted for its morality. Though he apparently yielded to the temptations of the flesh, his religious poems exhibit a sincerity and devotion that cannot be denied. For unknown reasons, he was imprisoned for thirteen years, possibly because of wayward behavior or failure to comply with orders from his superiors. It is supposed that he composed parts of his masterpiece during that long, tedious time.

If we are to believe what Ruiz says, *El libro de buen amor* does not represent his entire literary output. He wrote, he says, so many poems that they could not be contained in *diez pliegos* (about 240 pages), but unfortunately this poetry has disappeared. Among them, however, were poems of all kinds: dancing and street songs for Jewish and Moorish girls, songs of jest and mockery, songs for night-prowling students, for blind men, for beggars, and for many others.

El libro de buen amor is a miscellany of poems probably written at different periods of the archpriest's life, with a great variety of themes. The poet's personality, liberally injected into his poems, unifies the haphazard collection, which proceeds without transitions. The volume opens on a very serious note with a prayer to be delivered from prison. Then follows the author's explanation of the true intention of his book. There are two kinds of love, he says: *loco amor,* the sinful, worldly love of the flesh, and *buen amor,* the love of God, which is much to be preferred over the former. His book will teach the dangers in *loco amor.* Since most mortals are sinners, however, those who wish to practice *loco amor* will find some interesting ways of doing so in his pages. His other stated purpose is to instruct those who wish to write verse, and he exhibits an uncommon variety of meters.

After this introduction, he plunges into the prime matter of his book, love, and relates in a frank way his own love affairs in which he is far more often a failure than a success. Interspersed are encounters with don Amor, who advises him concerning his love interests; animal fables that have didactic intent; disquisitions on the mortal sins; a lengthy description of the battle between Lady Lent and Sir Flesh; devout religious hymns; and miscellaneous poems on a variety of themes.

In addition to the unique figure of the archpriest himself, other eternal characters emerge to become prototypes of Spanish literature: Trotaconventos, the ancestress of all go-betweens, and her replacement, don Furón, the original *pícaro*. These and many minor characters pass before the reader's eyes, contributing what very well may be the most interesting part of the book: the portrait of the life and society of the time.

In the fourteenth century, morals had relaxed, faith had weakened, and a pagan spirit filled the air. Opinion varies concerning whether Ruiz had a moral purpose in mind or was serious in stating his preference for *buen amor*. Some have understood Ruiz to be an austere moralist who objected to the moral laxity of his day, a sincere reformer who offered himself as a scapegoat for the sins of his fellow men. Others portray him as a pagan sensualist interested in glorifying only nature and passion. The truth probably lies somewhere in between. He was not obsessed with moralizing and at times was very much on the side of *loco amor*. In the next moment, however, he might show himself to be a repentant and devout man of God.

A keen satirist but at the same time a kind, understanding human being, he could see, understand, and accept people's weaknesses. He sympathized with sinners; he was more amused than offended by their vices, some of which he shared, and could generously forgive them. His satire, therefore, lacks the indignation and wrath of the strict moralist and shows love rather than condemnation. And with a sudden shift from human concerns, he could write a hymn to the Virgin with extraordinary spiritual fervor or compose a sincere learned disquisition on the evils of sin.

Stylistically Ruiz's unorganized collection of poems represents a great advance over preceding poetry and the culmination of the lyric writing of the Middle Ages. Unfettered by rules, Ruiz improvised with loquaciousness, verbosity, spontaneity, naturalness, and humor. He added new words to the language, showed good adjectivization, musical quality, and keen feelings for nature. He loved women, describing their movements, sounds, voices, and even the state of their souls, something new in the Middle Ages. His language ran the gamut from street words and popular utterances to the holiest expressions. He used hyperbole, free verse, and surprising metaphors, employing more than sixteen different meters and all the metrical combinations known at the time. Yet he preferred the *cuaderna vía,* which he infused with the throbbing pulse of life. His sources range from Church devotional literature to Ovid's *Art of Love* and the drama, from *Pamphilus de amore* to folklore and Aesop's fables. In short, he drew from the entire tapestry of the life of his time.

Juan Ruiz, an archpriest and yet a man of the people, towers above other writers of the Middle Ages. He represents the culmination of medieval life and foreshadows the coming Renaissance. He fused all the poetic elements of his time, interjected picaresque elements, and made use of allegory. His *joie de vivre,* his indulgent attitude toward human weaknesses, and especially his poetic genius make him one of Spain's greatest literary figures. He foreshadows coming generations, for in him lay the seeds of *La Celestina* and the picaresque novel.

5. *Pero López de Ayala* (1332–1407), the outstanding figure in poetry in the second half of the fourteenth century, has been called Spain's first Humanist, for the Renaissance had touched him. He lived through the reigns of five kings in a very troubled era, wrote their history as an eyewitness, and regarded his task not merely as the recording of events and names but as a judgment. Though he supposedly wrote his masterpiece, the *Rimado de Palacio,* while in military prison, he probably composed it at different times in his life. Like *El libro de buen amor,* it is a compilation of poems on miscellaneous themes that range from disquisitions on religious topics to bitter social satire.

No reader has ever been confused concerning the intention of the *Rimado de Palacio,* for López de Ayala saw the abuses, vices, crimes, and dishonesty of his day and set out to expose them, criticize them, and, if possible, reform them. Not all his work is social satire, however. He opens with poems of a religious nature but then plunges into criticisms of life on all levels as he attacks the Church, the pope, the schism of Avignon, kings, government, nobility, Jews, shopkeepers, feudal barons, warfare, injustice, and all the vices—hypocrisy, vanity, dishonesty, bribery, misery, and corruption. He inveighs bitterly against them all, thus becoming the model of satiric style of the Middle Ages.

His personality was diametrically opposed to that of Juan Ruiz. The latter was cheerful, joyous, pagan at times in spirit, lighthearted, humorous, gay, and loving. He saw man's weaknesses, vices, and sins but was not shocked. Rather he sympathized with and forgave his fellow men. López de Ayala was disillusioned, formal, embittered, moralistic, dismayed, and even angered by the meanness of human conduct and the evil in men's hearts. He denounced them indignantly. He was correct, noble, dignified, melancholy, and of sincere religious conviction, a man of the palace who could not share the epicurean tastes of Ruiz or tolerate human weakness.

López de Ayala, a proto-Quevedo, stood in the middle of a sorry era of civil war, treacherous politics, and lax morals. He was of a sensitive nature and was tragically grieved and disillusioned by the vice and corruption he saw all around him. Having felt the breath of the Renaissance, he stood on the threshold of modernity. Significantly, he was the last important author to use the *cuaderna vía*.

6. *Cancionero de Baena* was compiled around 1445 by Juan Alfonso de Baena for Juan II. The late fourteenth century and most of the fifteenth was truly a transition period in which the Galician-Portuguese that had long dominated lyric poetry and the love game of the Provençal poets was supplanted once and for all by the Castilian language and the innovations of the Italianate school of Dante and Petrarch.

Baena's *Cancionero* contains poems from several generations of poets, from the reigns of Pedro I through Juan II. As a whole the poets are at best mediocre and, with rare exceptions, their poetry is insipid and lacking in real poetic feeling. Nevertheless, the collection shows the evolution of poetry from the Galician to the Italianate schools. There are nearly six hundred poems by more than fifty authors in the *Cancionero*. Included is work of Enrique de Aragón (1384–1434), better known as the Marqués de Villena, who was one of the initiators of the poetic movement in Castile and the author of an *Arte de trobar* (1433). Later, Juan del Encina added to the increasing accumulation of literary criticism with his *Preceptiva*. This critical activity indicates that the poets were conscious of their responsibility and were genuinely interested in improving their art.

The efforts of Baena's poets to refine the language and adapt new verse forms made possible the superior verse of two major poets of the fifteenth century, the Marqués de Santillana and Juan de Mena. The best-known of Baena's poets still writing in the Galician manner was Alfonso Alvarez de Villasandino (1350–1428), also called de Toledo and de Illescas, who dominated the *Cancionero* by sheer weight if not by talent. Francisco Imperial reacted against the frivolity of the love verse of the *escuela trovadoresca* and sought his models in Dante and Petrarch. Though there were some traces of allegory before Imperial, he popularized it and is credited with having introduced the Italian hendecasyllable to Spain. The *Cancionero de Baena* was the first collection of Spanish poetry, and a few poetic treasures have been found in it over the years.

THE LATE MIDDLE AGES

A. General Considerations

By the turn of the fifteenth century Castilian had replaced Galician as the language for lyric poetry. The nearly sterile formulas and traditions of the troubadouresque love game, which had never really captivated the Castilians, fell into disuse. This plus the importation of new ideas from Italy produced two major poets in the first half of the fifteenth century, the Marqués de Santillana and Juan de Mena.

In the second half of the century political unrest was terminated by Ferdinand and Isabel. The queen patronized Latin studies, foreign Humanists came to Spain, and Elio Antonio de Nebrija (1441?–1522) wrote the first grammar of a modern language. Lyric poetry continued to flourish. The allegorical school followed the lead of Juan de Mena, and a refined and metaphorical courtly poetry developed in a different direction. This period witnessed the rise of a third major poet, Jorge Manrique, and the satiric *Coplas del Provincial* and the *Coplas de Mingo Revulgo* were written about this time. With the fifteenth-century poets, the Middle Ages ended, and Spain was prepared for Juan Boscán and Garcilaso de la Vega to usher in the Renaissance.

B. The Marqués de Santillana (1398–1458)

Iñigo López de Mendoza, Marqués de Santillana, the son of Diego Hurtado de Mendoza, also a poet, represented the height of literary culture and Humanism during the reign of Juan II. The *Proemio e carta al condestable de Portugal* (1449), in prose, was the first attempt at literary criticism in Spain. In this essay he gives his opinions about poetry. He asserted that poetry should be useful as well as beautiful and that poetry falls into three categories: sublime, or the poetry of Greek and Latin writers; mediocre, that written in "vulgar"; and infamous, or the disorderly

207

folk poetry of the lower classes. His other important prose work, *Refranes que dicen las viejas tras el fuego,* indicates that the Marqués de Santillana had a lively interest in folk literature and did not believe "disorderly folk poetry" was so infamous after all.

The poetry of don Iñigo falls into two groups: that written in the manner of the Galician-Portuguese school, and that in the manner of the allegorical Dantesque school. Of the two, the first is the most appealing, for there one finds the *canciones, decires, villancicos,* and *serranillas* whose folk feeling is ingeniously combined with refined delicateness and grace. Santillana's simplicity and freshness, gentleness, and even exquisiteness of expression reach their peak in the *serranillas,* the best known of which is *La vaquera de la Finojosa.* His *Comedieta de Ponza* imitates Dante as it recounts naval battles in allegorical style, the manner also used in his *Infierno de los enamorados.* Most important are his forty-two *Sonetos fechos al itálico modo,* reputed to be the first sonnets written in Spanish.

C. Juan de Mena (1411–1456)

Juan de Mena's entire life was devoted to letters, and thus he became Spain's first professional writer and scholar. A native of Córdoba, he studied at Salamanca and later went to Rome, where he imbibed the Renaissance spirit at its fountainhead. Upon Mena's return to Spain, Juan II named him secretary of Latin letters and royal historian, an appointment that allowed him ample time to pursue his studies and writing.

Mena's poetry falls into two groups: the light, short, frequently amorous verse distinguished for its musicality and perfection of form, possibly the product of his youth, and the verse written in *arte mayor* style in imitation of the allegorical-Dantesque manner with the added feature of Cordovan *cultismo.* In his shorter poems he is not particularly serious, but in the Italian manner he is grave, profound, religious, and patriotic.

The *Laberinto de Fortuna* (1444), his masterwork, is sometimes called *Las trescientas* since it contains approximately 300 (actually only 297) strophes of *arte mayor.* This verse form is an eight-line strophe of twelve-syllable lines containing four marked rhythmic accents and divided in half by a caesura. The *Laberinto* is aptly named, since it leads the reader through a maze of allegorical experiences that are often tedious; nevertheless, it contains a few passages that have endured the test of time. The poem's true merit lies in its fluent versification, descriptive force, and patriotic fervor, as Mena glorifies Spanish heroes who died in defense of the *patria*.

Borrowing from Latin, Mena initiated a renovation of poetic vocabulary that would influence the seventeenth-century *gongoristas*. Mena is the first of the *culto* poets for several reasons: about 80 percent of Góngora's *cultismos* are found in his work; he favored the rotund, ornate style; he addressed a cultured minority and scorned the *vulgo;* he introduced Latinisms in both vocabulary and syntax; and he sometimes intentionally obscured his writing, often using mythological references. Whether these characteristics are considered shortcomings or not, we must acknowledge that the Spanish language and poetic style were enriched through Mena's efforts.

D. Jorge Manrique (1440?–1479)

Jorge Manrique, born into an illustrious family that included the Marqués de Santillana and Gómez Manrique, a dramatist, was first and foremost a soldier. He died a hero's death at the age of thirty-nine fighting for the Catholic Sovereigns in an assault on the stronghold of Garci-Muñoz.

Jorge Manrique's poetic output is slight, and he would be forgotten were it not for his *Coplas*, an elegy written at the death of his father. But these forty strophes of *pie quebrado* verse (two eight-syllable lines followed by a four-syllable line) are probably the best-known verses in Spanish poetry. It is curious that an unknown poet with no special preparation and whose thoughts had been commonplace since Biblical times should write an immortal poem. But it was Manrique's fate to be shocked by his father's death into crystallizing and condensing into one poem all the important sentiments of the Middle Ages. Under the stress of emotion, he was able to say what everyone else was saying, but better.

The complete title of his poem is *Coplas a la muerte del Maestre don Rodrigo, su padre*. Its themes are meditation on the transitory nature of worldly things and a nostalgic longing for the past; the *ubi sunt* motif; and a eulogy of Manrique's father and an account of his death.

Jorge Manrique was the last poet of the Spanish Middle Ages. He was unaffected by poetic schools and nearly obsessed with the idea of death. He was a restless man, yet tranquility and repose are the keynotes of his poetry. His *Coplas* have been imitated, translated (into English by Longfellow), and set to music.

They are still found in every anthology, for their basic ideas are commonplace: death is the great leveler, you can't take it with you, worldly things are fragile, virtue conquers time for it is forever remembered. Manrique lamented the death of his father in his *Coplas,* but he also lamented the passing of an age.

E. The *Cancioneros:* The Minor Poets

The late fourteenth and fifteenth centuries teemed with poets. Their poetry, for the most part justly condemned to oblivion, has been preserved in anthologies called *cancioneros.* In addition to the *Cancionero de Baena* (1445) are the *Cancionero de Stúñiga,* compiled for Alfonso V of Naples, the *Cancionero general,* compiled by Hernando del Castillo in 1511, and the *Cancionero de burlas provocantes a risa,* which appeared in 1519.

Minor poets of the fourteenth and fifteenth centuries are Pero Ferrús, the first to mention Amadís; Macías, called El Enamorado, whose tragic life story inspired works by Santillana, Lope, and Larra; Gómez Manrique, uncle of Jorge; Antón de Montoro, a Jew who wrote sharp, satiric verse; Pero Guillén de Segovia; Juan Alvarez Gato; Garci Sánchez de Badajoz; Rodrigo de Cota; Juan de Padilla; Fray Iñigo de Mendoza, a favorite of Queen Isabel's; and Fray Ambrosio Montesinos.

THE RENAISSANCE

A. General Considerations

Ordinarily we regard the sixteenth century in Spain as the Renaissance age, but rumblings of it had been heard long before in the works of Juan Ruiz, Juan de Mena, and others. The movement was well under way during the reign of Ferdinand and Isabel.

We must also observe that the sixteenth century embraced two quite different periods. The Early Renaissance, characterized by the Humanistic, liberal Italian spirit, occurred during the first half of the century. The Late Renaissance, marked by the spirit of the Counter Reformation, orthodoxy, and a stifling of the pagan spirit, rationalism, and Protestantism, occurred during the second half. A free spirit and Boscán's and Garcilaso's Italianate poetry typified the first period. The second period showed the involution of the nation following the Counter Reformation and Felipe II's isolationist policy and was characterized by the poetry of the Mystics, Fray Luis de León and San Juan de la Cruz.

The political chaos of the first two-thirds of the fifteenth century, which occasioned the satiric and libelous writings of the time (*Coplas del Provincial* and *Coplas de Mingo Revulgo*), ended with the political stability and strong central government created by the marriage of Ferdinand and Isabel and the uniting of their kingdoms. This absolute monarchy set the nation on its way to its most glorious hour, as Spain became the dominant world power whose influence was felt in the remotest corners of the globe. It also brought linguistic unity to the nation, as Castilian became the national tongue.

The two major influences on Spanish literature of the Renaissance were Humanism and Italianism, both nurtured under Ferdinand and Isabel. Greek and Latin writers were emulated, and Italians were extensively imitated. Universities were founded, and the joyous spirit of the Renaissance abounded. Rationalism began to gain a foothold, and the teachings of Erasmus influenced learned circles. A hard core of objectors, however, opposed the new style and strove to reject the foreign imports and retain the traditional Spanish short verses and popular motives.

Italian influence was nothing new to Spain, but in the opening years of the sixteenth century it grew apace and dominated a school of poetry led by Boscán and Garcilaso. Neoplatonism was the philosophical fad and contributed to the growth of Mysticism in the second half of the century. The humdrum poetry of the fifteenth-century *escuela trovadoresca* died, and poets now spoke of their innermost personal sentiments. Pastoral, bucolic poetry triumphed, and even though shadows of the courtly love poetry lingered, Spain was on the threshold of its greatest literary age.

The literature of the second half of the sixteenth century reflects a changed attitude in the Spanish people. When Charles I failed in his attempted reconciliation with the Protestants, he made Spain the champion of Roman Catholicism. After the advent of the Counter Reformation, Spain was closed off from the rest of Europe, turned in upon itself, and declined to join the march to modernity through the new rationalism and the scientific method. Desirous of sharing in the new Renaissance spirit but able to accept only those aspects of it compatible with a strict and rigid orthodox Catholic faith, Spaniards were left in an ambiguous situation that accounts largely for the retention of so much of the Middle Ages in Renaissance Spain and the great flowering of Mystic literature in the latter part of the sixteenth century.

The Italian Renaissance spirit was not to be denied, however, and it grew rapidly in the lyric as well as in the drama and the novel. From the Italians the Spaniards learned new meters and themes and a whole new attitude toward life. The drab and monotonous became bright and colorful. The innovations in lyric poetry at this time marked a profound change in the genre and had an effect on its character and destiny noticeable down to the present day.

In summary, the major trends of the sixteenth century are as follows: Boscán and Garcilaso establish the Italianate school, which dominates until about the middle of the century. Castillejo and others react in favor of tradition, and poetry splits into two camps identified with regions of the country, namely Andalusia (Sevilla) and Castile (Salamanca). Hence we find the Salamancan school of poetry, headed by Fray Luis de León, and the Sevillian school, headed by Fernando de Herrera. In addition, poetry takes a third direction, that of Mysticism, represented by Fray Luis de León and San Juan de la Cruz.

B. The Italian School

1. *Juan Boscán Almogáver* (1493?–1542), a Catalan who forsook his native tongue to write in Castilian, engaged in a variety of literary activities and was clearly more than a dilettante. One of his major contributions was his translation of Castiglione's *Il Cortegiano,* which aided in educating the noble *cortesano* and in completing the process, begun under Ferdinand and Isabel, of transforming him from a rebellious country baron to a polished gentleman.

In 1526 the Venetian ambassador, Andrea Navagero, persuaded Boscán to try to adapt to Spanish the Italian meters and strophes, which he deemed superior. Unsuccessful at first, Boscán persevered, and sustained by his friend Garcilaso, he eventually naturalized to Spanish the iambic hendecasyllable (different from the hendecasyllable *de gaita gallega* used earlier by Spaniards), the sonnets and *canzone* of Petrarch, Dante's *terza rima,* and the octaves of Ariosto.

Boscán was of mediocre poetic talent, with little inventiveness or emotion, and was often dry and prosaic. His contribution was rather in the field of stylistic innovation at a time when it was needed. The metrical changes he wrought in Spanish verse have brought him everlasting fame, for seldom has one man single-handedly had such a great influence on the literature of his country. Though he was unable to write great poetry himself, he gave to others the tools to do so, especially to Garcilaso de la Vega, whom he influenced strongly.

2. *Garcilaso de la Vega* (1501?–1536), the "perfect courtier" and the "faultless poet," has always been a favorite. He was the ideal courtier; handsome, intelligent, talented, and aristocratic, he knew Latin and Italian and was a favorite of the ladies. He served Carlos V as a soldier and was killed at the age of thirty-five leading his troops in an assault on a fortress in southern France.

His great love, Isabel Freyre, who scorned him and married another, inspired some of his poetry, published in 1543. The matchmaker queen forced him to marry Elena Stúñiga, but his love for Isabel remained. His total literary production is small: thirty-eight sonnets, three eclogues, two elegies, five *canciones*, one epistle, and a few other poems. With Boscán and especially with Garcilaso, sobriety, grace, and elegance returned to poetry after a momentary flirtation with the *culto* style in Spanish poetry when the Italians first became known in Spain. Garcilaso was an expert craftsman and balanced his language skillfully between the popular and the pedantic and artificial.

The universal admiration of Garcilaso, which continues today, was not awakened by any originality of ideas. He freely and frankly borrowed from Italian and Classical masters. His originality lies in his expressing for the first time universal poetic themes that were not typically Spanish. What charmed his readers, however, was his fluent, facile manipulation of the language and verse. For the first time a genuine musicality appeared in Spanish verse. He created linguistic harmonies unsurpassed to this day. His harmony and technical perfection together with an elegance and extraordinary sweetness were unknown up to his time and have seldom been found since. A reverence has been granted to Garcilaso that few men have known.

His principal themes are love and nature. His prevailing mood is nostalgic melancholy, to which he adds a tenderness and gentleness that belie his adventurous life as a soldier. His best work is *Egloga primera,* occasioned by news of the death of Isabel Freyre. The autobiographical nature of this poem in which the characters represent Garcilaso and Isabel makes the poem more attractive to those who find Garcilaso lacking in substance.

213

The second eclogue narrates the history of the house of Alba, and the third describes the nymphs of the Tagus along with two shepherds named Alcino and Tirreno. Neither compares in quality with the *Egloga primera*, but the verse is strikingly cadenced. Garcilaso's sonnets surpassed any that preceded them, for no one before him and few since could compete with Garcilaso's virtuosity and uncanny ability with the language. Had he not devoted himself to the pastoral manner and to foreign concepts and ideas, turning instead to native Spanish themes with his miraculous power of expression and control of rhythm and harmony, he would seldom if ever have been equaled.

3. *Gutierre de Cetina* (1520?–1557?), an apt pupil of Garcilaso's, was also fond of poetizing, soldiering, and making love. Born into a noble family, he became the friend of many notables of his day, including Diego Hurtado de Mendoza and Jorge de Montemayor. In 1547 he went to Mexico. Ten years later he was seriously wounded and possibly died in a duel.

His one poetic theme was love. He was a fluent, melodic versifier, capable of sweetness, freshness, and beautiful thoughts reminiscent of Garcilaso, but he had a touch of sobriety and humor not found in the latter. He was also influenced by Ausías March and especially Petrarch.

He wrote 244 sonnets, 11 *canciones,* 5 madrigals, and one of the first Spanish anacreontics. His madrigals comprise his best work, and he is especially remembered for the one that begins "Ojos claros, serenos."

Other followers of Garcilaso's are Hernando de Acuña (1520?–1580?), known for characterizing Felipe II as "un monarca, un imperio, y una espada," and Diego Hurtado de Mendoza (1503–1575), immensely important in local and international politics and as an eclectic poet combining Italianism with Traditionalism. Gregorio Silvestre (1520–1569), a musician, began by speaking ill of the Italian style but eventually accepted it.

4. *Francisco de Figueroa* (1536–1617) nearly achieved the *vida retirada* that Fray Luis yearned for, when he retired to his native city while still young. As a young man in Italy, he devoted himself enthusiastically to Italian letters and language to the point that he was able to compose poetry in that language. He also composed poems with alternating lines of Spanish and Italian. He was renowned for his amatory and bucolic verse in Garcilaso's manner and earned the epithet *divino* from his contemporaries. He was dominated by the Italian school and devoted to Garcilaso, but before he had finished, the pastoral theme had

faded in popularity. One of his best accomplishments was his use of the *verso suelto,* which he managed as well as any of his contemporaries. Typical of his work is *Los amores de Damón y Galatea* and the sonnet *A los ojos de Fili.*

C. The Traditionalists

Cristóbal de Castillejo (1490?–1550?), the most persistent in resisting the Italian manner, is in some ways reminiscent of Juan Ruiz. At the age of forty, ordained in the priesthood, he fell in love with Ana Schaumburg, who did not share his passion. The impossibility and frustrations of this love coupled with ill health and homesickness inspired much of his poetry.

Despite his cloth, Castillejo was liberal in his thought. His poetry, filled with feminine names and amorous sighs, was banned by the Inquisition until 1573, when an expurgated selection saw the light of day. Through his poetry runs a mischievous, merry note, at times bittersweet, at other times erotic, reminiscent of his spiritual kinsman the Arcipreste de Hita. *El borracho convertido en mosquito* illustrates this lighter side.

Though a fair poet, he is best remembered for having led the Traditionalists, who objected to the importation of foreign models for fear that Spanish poetry might lose its distinctive character. His best-known poem is *Contra los que dejan los metros castellanos y siguen los italianos.* His crusade was ineffectual, for the Italian manner triumphed by the end of the sixteenth century, but the victory was not easy or ever complete. Cervantes and Lope at one time supported the native Spanish manner, and some of its medieval verse forms lived on, notably the *quintilla,* the *décima,* and the *romance.* With Lope, Quevedo, and Góngora in the seventeenth century, the two manners are fused, and the struggle is over.

THE LATE RENAISSANCE: SALAMANCAN AND SEVILLIAN SCHOOLS OF POETRY

A. General Considerations

The second half of the sixteenth century saw several schools of poetry, each centered around some outstanding poet. The southern poets, residing mostly in Seville, followed Fernando de

Herrera and formed the Sevillian, or Andalusian, school. The northern poets looked to Fray Luis de León of Salamanca for leadership and created the Salamancan school. A third group, also guided by Fray Luis, wrote Mystic poetry.

The Salamancan school is noted for its sobriety, concise language, unadorned expression, and the insistence of matter over form. It produced dignified, serious, and restrained poetry, concerned more with ideas than the manner of expressing them.

The Sevillian school reflects the exuberance, the wealth, the gaiety, and the lack of restraint of its native city. Its poetry exhibits an abundance of adjectives—especially those of color—attention to form over matter, and the use of neologisms and syntactical innovations. The poems are rhetorical, sensual, often passionate, and ornate. These poets wanted to create a language for poetry different from that used for prose, thus continuing the trend established by Juan de Mena and forming a link between him and the *cultistas* of the seventeenth century.

B. The Salamancan School

1. *Fray Luis de León* (1527–1591) is undoubtedly one of the most impressive Spanish writers of all ages and clearly a lyric poet of the highest order. He joined the Augustinian Order in 1544 and was graduated with a degree in sacred theology from the University of Salamanca. Those against whom he competed for a professorship there, which he won, denounced him to the Inquisition for having questioned the accuracy of the Vulgate translations of the Bible and having translated the Song of Songs into Spanish. They also expressed doubts regarding his orthodoxy, with references to the fact that his great-grandmother had been a Jewess. Fray Luis was arrested and spent almost five years in prison, but he was finally released with a judgment of not guilty.

He admired Horace, who had found peace and solace, and Fray Luis longed for the same in the hope of escaping the turmoil, envy, competitiveness, intrigues, and competition among the professors at the university. His longing for a peaceful existence is reflected in his famous poem that opens with the lines "¡Qué descansada vida / La del que huye el mundanal ruido!" Called the Christian Horace, he sought refuge in nature, where he found peace in God's greatness and the beauties and mysteries of the universe. This facet of his work illustrates the Mystic strain in his personality, though his Mysticism did not ascend to the heights of that of San Juan de la Cruz.

Fray Luis did not regard his poetry highly and did not intend to publish it, but it was saved from oblivion by Quevedo in 1631. Fray Luis thought his prose writings to be of far more importance, but they are greater only in bulk. Among them are *De los nombres de Cristo* (1583) and *La perfecta casada* (1583). His fame rests primarily on his poetry.

The deep seriousness, quiet sobriety, gravity, and freedom from artifice are the most appealing features of Fray Luis' poetry. His language is simple and unadorned; his poetry is intellectual, not passionate, and reveals his desire for spiritual elevation and escape from reality through nature, a feeling he conveys to his reader. He sought in solitude and communion with nature the harmony of the universe.

His poetic output amounts to about forty poems, which in clear, direct, unaffected style reveal a masterful combination of perfect form with depth of thought, a rare combination among Spanish poets. He recommended "plain living and high thinking." Three of his best-loved poems are *Vida retirada, Noche serena,* and *A Francisco Salinas.* The latter is dedicated to an organist in whose music Fray Luis felt his forgetful soul might rediscover its divine origins. He demonstrates eternal values in all his works, which have lasted through the centuries and are still favorites in the twentieth.

2. *Pedro Malón de Chaide* (1530?–1589) joined the Augustinian Order and was a disciple of Fray Luis'. His major contribution was his very highly rated prose work, *La conversión de la Magdalena.* Of special interest to the student of literature is its prologue, in which the author assails the novel of chivalry and worldly books of poetry, condemning even Boscán and Garcilaso. He also offers an excellent defense of the Spanish language, which he considered second to none. His few poems are sprinkled throughout his *Conversión* as a relief from the prose. Most of them deal with Biblical themes, often paraphrases of Psalms. They show him to be a poet of talent of whom his model did not need to be ashamed.

3. *Benito Arias Montano* (1527–1598) was one of the great cultural figures of the Renaissance. Because Arias knew nine languages, including Hebrew, Chaldean, and Sanskrit, Felipe II appointed him professor of Oriental languages at El Escorial. He was learned in all-important fields of study and accompanied

Martín Pérez de Ayala, Bishop of Segovia, to the Council of Trent, where he impressed many with his learning and intelligence. Felipe II asked him to direct the edition of the *Biblia Regia de Amberes,* which he concluded in eight volumes from 1569 to 1572. His poetry won for him the reputation of being one of the principal imitators of Fray Luis, and like the master, he also attempted his own version of the Song of Songs, *Paráfrasis sobre el Cantar de los Cantares.*

4. *Francisco de la Torre* is a shadowy figure, for less is known of his life than of that of any other Spanish writer. Lope de Vega attested to his existence, as did a few others, but documentary evidence is totally lacking.

Quevedo published his poetry in 1631 but confused him with Alfonso de la Torre. Luis Josef Velázquez reprinted his poems in the eighteenth century but ascribed them to Quevedo under the pseudonym Francisco de la Torre. Others have surmised that he was a Portuguese named Almeida.

There is no such confusion concerning the merit of his poetry. He was one of the best writers of the Salamancan school and left excellent samples in many sonnets, *canciones,* odes, *endechas,* and eclogues. His principal traits are simplicity of expression, good taste, elegance, gentleness, pleasant imagination, and a melancholy reminiscent of Garcilaso. In matters of technique he leaves little to be desired.

5. *Soneto a Cristo crucificado,* an anthology favorite that has been translated into the major European tongues, has been attributed to many persons of the sixteenth century, including Santa Teresa, San Juan de la Cruz, San Francisco Javier, and even San Ignacio de Loyola, but no convincing proof of its authorship has as yet been adduced.

C. The Sevillian School

1. *Fernando de Herrera* (1534–1597), a Sevillian, was the leader of the Andalusian school and so highly regarded that he was called *el divino* by his contemporaries. He devoted himself exclusively to a life of study and letters but did take minor orders as a convenience. He took part in the first-known *tertulias* at the home of Alvaro Colón y Portugal and there fell passionately in love with Leonor de Milán, Condesa de Gelves. This unrequited love, the source of most of his amorous verse, never got beyond the poem-writing stage but provided the needed spark for his inspiration.

Herrera's other theme was patriotism. His *Canción por la victoria de Lepanto* and others like it are better suited to his fiery disposition, which won him few friends, than the quieter love poems. His patriotic poems are passionate, exuberant, full of sound and fury, fancy rhetoric, strong images, and surging rhythms. We see the true spirit of the Sevillian school in this heroic, epiclike poetry. Herrera used neologisms and hyperbaton and sought the unexpected metaphor and the colorful adjective. By imitating the Bible, he achieved a striking effect in the Lepanto poem, probably the most majestic in Spanish literature. Herrera, grandiloquent, a lover of pomp, and a true Sevillian, nearly completed the task begun by Juan de Mena of creating a vocabulary peculiar to poetry. His mission was to improve, uplift, and ennoble Spanish poetry. He symbolizes strength and rugged power, and his patriotic fervor, though sometimes verging on bathos, is noble and touching. He presages the seventeenth century with his ornate style and attention to form and is doubtlessly one of the major influences in the rise of Gongorism. But he also saw merit in the Italianate trend set by Boscán and Garcilaso, and he edited the latter's poetry in *Anotaciones a las obras de Garcilaso de la Vega* (1580).

2. *Juan de Mal Lara* (1524–1571), though not a poet, influenced the birth of the Sevillian school since some of its better-known members, including Herrera, attended his school of "Gramática y Humanidades." He inclined his students to the *estilo ampuloso* of the Sevillian school. Aside from this influence on his students, his greatest contribution to letters is his collection of Spanish proverbs, *Filosofía vulgar* (1568), which he studied with great erudition and illustrated with stories, apologues, and tales of his own invention. This work illustrates once again the popular note running throughout Spanish literature.

3. *Baltasar del Alcázar* (1530–1606) ranks as the best Spanish poet of light verse that is gay, convivial, and amatory. He is also one of Spain's best epigrammatists. After successful years of study, he took up arms and served in the navy. Later in life he held important governmental posts. After the death of his wife, he became so entangled in love affairs that he had to flee. In 1590 he withdrew to his home in San Juan de la Palma, his health failing and his fortune dwindling. Yet at the age of seventy he wrote a sprightly poem to Isabel.

As a poet he disdained fame and glory and used his poetry only for delight and recreation. His forte was the festive style, but he tried the amatory and religious also. At his best, he displays a pleasant epicureanism with an attractive underlay of humor. His *Cena jocosa* is his best-known piece. Also typical is his *Secreto para conciliar y sacudir el sueño* as is the poem with the intriguing title *A una vieja que se halló un pedazo de espejo en un muladar y lo quebró*. He was a master at the language, perfect in writing *redondillas,* and his *joie de vivre* shines through his work, making the most mournful smile.

D. Mysticism

Mysticism was late in reaching Spain, having flourished elsewhere in Europe in the medieval period. Adapting the symbols of the Italian and popular tradition, Mysticism reached its peak in Spain in the second half of the sixteenth century, surfacing later from time to time in varying degree. Most Mystic literature is in prose. The Mystic poets include Fray Luis de León, Pedro Malón de Chaide, Benito Arias Montano—all of the Salamancan school—San Juan de la Cruz, and Santa Teresa de Jesús.

No single theory can explain the origin of Spanish Mysticism, although it can be traced as far back as the thirteenth century, when Raimundo Lulio (Llull in Majorcan), working as a missionary among the Spanish Moors, acquainted himself with the complicated conceits and rich imagery of Arabic poetry and used concepts and sentences that parallel those of San Juan de la Cruz, Spain's most ardent Mystic. The likeliest explanation, however, of the rise of Mysticism in Spain is that it provided an outlet for Spanish energy, intellectuality, and spirituality within the framework of orthodoxy after the Counter Reformation had cut Spain off from the developing rationalism of Europe. All foreign heretical ideas were forbidden, and under Felipe II's censorship and control of thought, men forsook the experimental, scientific method and again, as in the Middle Ages, concerned themselves with immortality, reward, punishment after death, scorn for worldly things, and especially longing for spiritual union with God. Interpretations independent of the Church were stifled, and Renaissance paganism and Erasmism disappeared.

The Mystic writers were members of religious orders, but much of what they wrote was concerned with mere asceticism, that is, fasting, meditation, penance, prayer, and the like, which were intended to purify the body and soul so that union with God might be possible. Not all ascetics, however, achieved the lofty Mystical goal of union with the Divine and spiritual marriage with God. If this goal was reached, the Mystic then attempted to describe his feelings in poetry, but it was difficult to communicate, concretely, ineffable experiences. It is here, however, that the Spanish Mystic differs, for he manages to maintain a balance between idealism and realism, and the rapture experienced during the union with God is tempered by the strong feeling of reality and practical immediacy that the Spaniard never loses. Thus the Spanish Mystics come closer than anyone else to communicating the total Mystical experience.

1. *San Juan de la Cruz* (1542–1591) was the last great figure of Mysticism in Spain and represents its highest flights. His poetry is the most intense and metaphysical, the most abstract and pure, of all Mystic poets. He joined the Carmelite order, and inspired by Santa Teresa's reforms, he attempted to carry them out in his own branch of the order. Other members disagreed, kidnapped him, and threw him into a prison in Toledo where he languished for nine months, half starved and ill treated. In a vision, the Virgin directed his escape by means of a rope made from a blanket. Brenan believes that the immense joy San Juan felt as he escaped from the dark prison into the Andalusian countryside prompted the poet's best verse, all written within a few months after his escape.

His poetic production is extremely small, consisting chiefly of three major poems: *Noche oscura del alma, Canciones entre el alma y el esposo,* and *Llama de amor viva.* San Juan takes off where others stop and reaches higher levels of ardor, lyricism, and Mystical experience than any other Spanish poet. In him is an inner fire, a metaphysical tension that we glimpse but that his words cannot express, making him difficult sometimes to understand. The ineffability of his experiences caused him to erupt in numerous exclamations and to use symbols and comparisons to try to express his sentiments. Recognizing the reader's difficulties, he wrote long prose treatises in which he explained phrase by phrase what he meant, a rare if not unique occurrence among poets.

2. *Santa Teresa de Jesús* (1515–1582) made her chief contribution in prose, but she left a few poems that have much merit. Perhaps her contribution to Mystical poetry lies more in the inspiration she gave to Fray Luis de León and San Juan de la Cruz than in her poetic writings. In 1982 some lost poetry of this famous woman was found.

THE BAROQUE AGE: THE SEVENTEENTH CENTURY

A. General Considerations

The Baroque literary style dominated Spain in the seventeenth century and was felt also throughout Europe. Whereas the sixteenth century conceived spatial beauty in terms of geometrical balance, the seventeenth emphasized broken, uneven masses. The sixteenth century strove for clarity, the seventeenth sought embellishment, obscurity, and ornamentation.

The Baroque style, called Gongorism in Spain, had been present in Spanish poetry from the days of the Galician-Portuguese school through Juan de Mena and Herrera, growing steadily in complexity and reaching its peak with Góngora in the seventeenth century. Many theories have been advanced concerning its origins: critics assert that it resulted, variously, from the exaggerated use of metaphors by the Cordovan Moors, the efforts of grammarians to enhance the language, the repressive effect of the Church, Felipe II's censorship, and the reaction of the sensitive, artistic types to the incipient decadence of the nation. Whatever the origins may have been, the Baroque period conveys a melancholy tone, a pessimism, and a feeling that life is an unreal dream. Old themes—war, love, fame, religion— were sterile, and no new ones arose to replace them. For lack of ideas, poets turned to complicating the language and style of their poetry, avoiding the simple and natural and gradually adding greater stylistic complexity, ornamentation, and obscurity. Góngora's *Soledades* have astonishingly little substance but incredible embellishment and linguistic complexity.

In Spain the Baroque style consisted of two different but not incompatible manners, *culteranismo* and *conceptismo*. When Góngora published his controversial poetry in 1612, the literary world split into two camps, and the struggle between *culteranistas* and *conceptistas* began.

B. *Culteranismo*

Culteranismo is a deliberate obscuring of style. Specifically, the *cultistas* wanted to create a poetic vocabulary different from ordinary language. To do this they borrowed and invented neologisms from Latin and Greek; distorted syntax, separating words

222

that go together by logic, agreement, or custom, a practice called hyberbaton; used other devices, such as the suppression of the definite article, the use of hyperbole, ellipsis, and all the rhetorical figures of Latin poetry; invented audacious metaphors and epithets and made it a practice not to call things by their names but to give them others; and made abundant references to Classical mythology, exotic geography, and anything else that might make a strange impression.

The *cultistas* aimed to dazzle the reader and to shine by a display of verbal technique and fireworks. Some regarded their products as tasteless, absurd, and contrived and were horrified by some of the words they invented or borrowed. It is to their credit, however, that through their high artistic standards they enriched both language and diction.

C. *Conceptismo*

Culteranismo is an aesthetic, sensory manifestation. *Conceptistas*, giving greater significance to meaning, insisted that the manner in which something is said is not so important as what is said. They sought out brilliant thoughts, turns of phrase, striking comparisons, unexpected associations of words, and extraordinary subtleties of thought. This tendency can be traced back to the Provençal poets and still affects Spanish literature.

Whereas the *cultistas* heaped words and images upon one another, the *conceptistas* avoided too many words. In order to express their brilliant mental concepts they employed cleverly turned metaphors, antitheses, puns, paradoxes, and conceits. The latter, which became the identifying mark of the manner since it so perfectly characterized what they were trying to do, is a fanciful or extravagant notion clothed in metaphorical guise. *Culteranismo*, which developed into a school, was basically a manner of writing. *Conceptismo* was a mode of thought rather than a style and did not form a school. Both tendencies together compose the Baroque style of Spain.

D. Luis Carrillo y Sotomayor (1583–1610)

At one time it was thought that the Cordovan poet Carrillo was a great influence on Góngora, but Dámaso Alonso has shown that the latter was already infected with the Baroque virus and did not need Carrillo's example. The latter summed up nicely,

223

however, much of the doctrine of *culteranismo* in *El libro de la erudición poética* (1611). He disdained the ordinary reader and pleaded for the poet to direct himself to a select, enlightened few. He urged changes in the forms and meanings of words and demanded that the poet not concern himself with common or base things. He also wrote some good poetry, and Gracián considered him to be the first *cultista* of Spain. His death at twenty-seven years of age cut short his career, and one can only speculate about what he might have done had he lived longer.

E. Minor Poets Between Herrera and Góngora

Herrera and the Sevillian poets had added color, ornamentation, and inflation to their Renaissance heritage. By the time Góngora had fully developed the *culto* style, he had refined and altered significantly Herrera's legacy. Between these two giants appeared lesser poets. Pedro Espinosa's anthology, *Flores de poetas ilustres de España* (1605), contains works from the Antequeran or Antequeran-Granadine school. Pedro Soto de Rojas was another noteworthy poet of the day. The Aragonese school, eclectic in nature but more inclined to the Renaissance manner, included the Argensola brothers, Lupercio and Bartolomé, and Esteban Manuel de Villegas.

F. Luis de Góngora y Argote (1561–1627)

Góngora had a charming, attractive, and sometimes mischievous personality that made him a popular figure. He took minor orders and was commissioned to travel all over Spain. In 1617 he was ordained and appointed chaplain of honor to Felipe III. But already in 1609 symptoms of the disease arteriosclerosis had appeared, and a stroke caused his death in 1627.

Until Dámaso Alonso proved otherwise, it was thought that Góngora's poetic production consisted of two distinct styles, a simple, direct manner, popular in flavor, and the *culto* style of the *Soledades.* Up to 1612 (some say 1610) the popular style dominated and was characterized by short poems, *letrillas, romances,* and sonnets. Then supposedly the poet made an about-face, changed his manner completely, and wrote the highly obscure, Gongoristic verse of the *Soledades* and the *Polifemo.* Dámaso Alonso has shown, however, that Góngora was a *cultera-*

nista from the time he began to write and that his later style merely contained such a profusion of *culto* ingredients that it only appeared different from his earlier manner. The two periods, therefore, are different only on a quantitative basis, not on a qualitative one.

The Góngora of the first period has always been popular, and some of his early poems were "hits" in their day and still are. The more difficult works of his later years were often called "literary insanity" up to the time of Dámaso Alonso's studies, but opinion has now changed. Góngora's star has been in the ascendancy in the twentieth century, for the Spanish poets of the 1920s who appreciated his poetic wizardry have resurrected him as one of the greatest Spanish poetic talents of all time.

Góngora invented nothing new in the *Soledades*. He simply massed the elements of the *culto* style together in such profusion that he achieved a density unequaled by any other poet. The cramming of obscure elements into his poetry makes it difficult to read, but when it is deciphered one finds Góngora's astounding imagination, expressiveness, and genius truly amazing.

Góngora's detractors attacked him for what they considered to be poor taste and excesses. They decried his use of new names for common things: hair became *oro;* anything white became *alabastro, nieve, nácar, plata;* a bird became a *cítara volante;* a piece of a wrecked ship was a *pino;* water became *cristal,* and grass *esmeralda.* By this process of substitution, the poet moved away from reality and stylized nature as *marfil, claveles, plata, rosas, lirios, cristal, fulgores, miel, nieve,* and so on. Thus, he nearly accomplished the dream of Spanish poets since Juan de Mena, for by expressing the distinctive quality of a thing rather than using its common name he created in effect a poetic language. Also, he discovered the subtle or unexpected relationships between things and then devised metaphors to describe them.

The use of hyperbaton also makes Góngora difficult to read. Consider the following example from *Angélica y Medoro:* "y la que mejor se halla / en las selvas que en la corte / simple bondad, al pío ruego / cortésmente corresponde." Unscrambled, these lines read "y la simple bondad, que se halla mejor en las selvas que en la corte, corresponde cortésmente al pío ruego."

His rich and unusual metaphors, chromatic effects, decorative, lush imagery, and extraordinarily uncommon thoughts and comparisons leave the reader amazed if not perplexed. He employed other complicating devices, such as antithesis, chiasmus, oxymoron, litotes, and allusions to unfamiliar geography and Classical mythology.

His *Soledades*, finished about 1613, constitute his masterpiece in the *culto* manner. He apparently intended to write four parts to the *Soledades* but completed only one and most of another. They are in the pastoral style with a trivial plot; but the poet embroiders them extensively and clothes them in two thousand lines of verse. Góngora's artificial *culteranista* world contains no part of nature that is ugly, evil, or distasteful. The *Soledades* come close to being pure poetry, but one can still discern the brilliance of the poet's metaphors, the ingenuity of his thought, the abundance of color, and the musicality of his verse.

Other works in the *culto* manner are the *Fábula de Polifemo* (*ca.* 1613), his *Panegírico al Duque de Lerma* (1609), and the *Fábula de Píramo y Tisbe* (1618). Absorbed with embellishment and unconcerned with the great emotions of love, hate, war, and religion, the second Góngora holds little appeal for readers seeking content, philosophy, emotion, or at least some new contribution to man's understanding of life. Some reassessment of this occurred, however, in 1961, four hundred years after Góngora's birth. Others find the greatest possible expression of beauty through words in his verse and ask for nothing more. He was an extraordinary genius before whom few readers can remain neutral.

G. Minor *Cultistas.* Followers of Góngora

Góngora's highly affected poetry split the poets of the nation into two camps. Humanists denounced his "licentious metaphors." The *cultistas* were called "swans," and their opponents called themselves "geese." A host of poets followed Góngora's example. Since the *culto* poetry was directed to the cultured literary elite, not to acclaim it might stigmatize one as a dolt or a cultural beggar. Some poets, whose reputations were already secure, objected to the style, but a few adopted it themselves.

Among the noteworthy poets writing in the *culto* manner were Rodrigo Caro (1573–1647), Juan de Tassis y Peralta, Conde de Villamediana (1582–1622), Hortensio Félix Paravicino y Arteaga (1580–1633), Juan de Jáuregui (1583–1641), Pedro Soto de Rojas (1585–1658), Francisco de Rioja (1583–1659), and Gabriel Bocángel Unzueta (1608–1658). The *Epístola moral a Fabio,* considered by some to have been written by

Andrés Fernández de Andrada, was extravagantly praised as the best poem of the seventeenth century.

H. Francisco de Quevedo y Villegas (1580–1645)

Quevedo's chief literary contributions were in prose, but he attempted other genres as well. His poetry runs the gamut from love poems to some of the funniest burlesques ever written. He also left serious poems on moral and philosophical problems revealing his deep reaction to the spirit of his times.

Quevedo's poetry shows him to be a clever wit opposed to the *culteranista* style. He hated the fancy words and inventions of the *cultistas* and campaigned for clarity and moderation in language. To provide good models for aspiring poets, he published the poetry of Fray Luis de León and Francisco de la Torre. Yet Quevedo was unable to avoid some of the excesses of the style he criticized and sinned on the side of *conceptismo* and involved ideas. His satire was sharp, sometimes bitter, often funny; but even in his most comical moments one can discern his characteristic melancholy and disillusionment.

In *Aguja de navegar cultos*, Quevedo pokes fun at the *cultista* manner and the less-gifted "perverters of good taste," but to think of Quevedo as simply a witty opponent of Gongorism is to see only one side of the coin. He was a deeply philosophical poet who showed the melancholy and disillusionment of the Baroque period. His suffering and tragic life are apparent in his bitterness and satire. He deplored the political failures and decadence of his nation and criticized the softening of the Spanish spirit, the degeneration of the monarchy, and the abuse of power by the *privados*. He pessimistically lamented these things but had no solutions to offer. Hence his hopelessness and frustration were but a reflection of his nation. He felt that man was essentially depraved with little hope for salvation. His sonnet *Miré los muros de la patria mía* expresses some of these ideas.

Quevedo was an ascetic and a stoic and viewed the vanities of life as one might expect. He shared the view that life is a dream and expressed it in these lines from one of his sonnets: "¡Fue sueño ayer: mañana será tierra! / ¡Poco antes nada; y poco después, humo!" Typical of his political satire is his poem *Epístola satírica y censoria* directed against the Conde-Duque de Olivares. He wrote love poems directed to a certain Lisi, religious poems, and burlesque-satiric poems such as *Poderoso caballero es don Dinero*.

227

Quevedo had a brilliant intellect and felt more strongly than any other writer of his time, except perhaps Gracián, the need to write something startling, to express some rare thought or extraordinary idea. He caricatured reality with his hyperboles but was a writer of great depth and strength, rated by some as the best in the language. His knowledge was vast. A formidable enemy and a demolishing satirist, he never shrank from hard words or unpoetical, even indecent, expressions; yet few would accuse him of bad taste or crudeness. He embodies as nearly as any one man can the spirit of the Baroque age.

I. Lope Félix de Vega Carpio (1562–1635)

Lope so dominated the drama of his time that we forget he is one of Spain's greatest lyric poets as well. With the exception of Góngora, Lope managed better than anyone else to synthesize the Renaissance spirit with the Baroque style. He declared himself an enemy of *culteranismo* but could not escape it. He combined the popular spirit with learned poetry and produced poetic miracles. His *romances, letras para cantar,* and *villancicos* are the most attractive part of his lyric poetry. The *romances,* especially, express his personal feelings, loves, hates, and passions, all displayed with extraordinary verbal magic. His sonnets, too, are often autobiographical and range in theme from worldly to divine love.

His poetic production is scattered throughout his works. There is scarcely a drama without a sonnet, and everywhere one finds lyric jewels in the popular vein embedded in his writings. He was the voice of Spain, embodying the popular spirit and possessing the real *duende* that few Spaniards have. With spontaneity, grace, and movement, he could be witty, tender, brilliant, festive, sincere, pious, satiric, humble, or anything else. There was no end to his inventiveness and sorcery with words.

Lope wrote longer poems, such as *La Dragontea* (1598), *Jerusalén conquistada* (1609), and *La Gatomaquia* (1634). He also wrote eclogues and epistles that reveal sincere and deep feeling; a poem on the occasion of his son's death, *Canción a la muerte de Carlos Félix;* and a didactic poem on how to write dramas, *Arte nuevo de hacer comedias* (1609). He remains unchallenged as one of Spain's greatest lyric geniuses. People said in his time: "Creo en Lope todopoderoso, poeta del cielo y de la tierra," a remarkable tribute to one whose name is still spoken with admiration and respect.

THE EIGHTEENTH CENTURY: NEOCLASSICISM

A. General Considerations

Lyric poetry, like other literary forms, deteriorated in the eighteenth century. The *culto* style was unmanageable, except in the case of a very few poets, such as Gabriel Alvarez de Toledo and Eugenio Gerardo Lobo. Good taste, restraint, and artistic feeling perished. As a consequence, no lyric poet of stature appeared until the latter decades of the eighteenth century, when a fresh wind began to blow across the poetic landscape.

As a corrective, Ignacio de Luzán (1702–1754) wrote his *Poética* (1737), a sort of Neoclassic manifesto, in which he pleaded for moral purpose and didactic intent in literature and insisted that literature must edify as well as entertain. He admitted, however, that lyric poetry might be written solely as a delight. He abhorred the excesses of Gongorism and recommended clarity and common sense, curbing the imagination, verisimilitude, and the imitation of nature. Feijóo also believed in rules and precepts as the cure for disorderly writings, but like Luzán he recognized a certain indefinable *no sé qué* about a good poem that makes it appealing in spite of rules or lack of them. Other *preceptistas* also felt that the disorderliness, *culteranismo,* and *conceptismo,* with their turgidity, obscurity, and staleness, would have to be reformed by the imitation of Classical models. Consequently they proposed to purge undesirable elements through the imposition of Neoclassicism, characterized by imitation of French and Classical models; moderation, common sense, avoidance of excesses, dominance of reason; and clarity of style and expression. The poetry that resulted from these correctives was very correct but cold, prosaic, unpopular, and uninspired.

In the second half of the century, poets of merit began to appear, and in accord with the custom of the times, they organized themselves into academies and *tertulias,* the most important of which were the *Arcadia Agustiniana* in Salamanca, the *Academia del Buen Gusto* and the *tertulia* at the Fonda de San Sebastián in Madrid, and the *Academia de Buenas Letras* and the *tertulia* of don Pablo de Olavide in Seville. From these academies grew two schools of poetry: the eighteenth-century Salamancan school, inspired by the work of Fray Luis de León, and the Sevillian school, inspired by Herrera and others. In addition, two authors cultivated the fable, and Moratín and Cadalso

229

did not really belong to any of the schools. Toward the end of this era evidence of nineteenth-century Romanticism began to appear.

B. The Fabulists

In an age when one of the prime functions of poetry was instruction, it was natural that the fable should have been cultivated. Tomás de Iriarte and Félix María Samaniego were two who did this.

1. *Tomás de Iriarte* (1750–1791) was in many ways a product of the Neoclassic age, for he loved and admired culture, was a renowned polemicist, and believed in the didactic mission of art. In 1782 he published his *Fábulas literarias,* well-written fables in many different meters, with the express purpose of exhibiting the author's notions concerning the defects of the literature of his time, his only target. He refers more or less covertly to known authors, asserting his ideas regarding the function of literature and the responsibilities of writers as well as the rules for writing well. Typical of his fables is an all-time favorite, *El burro flautista.*

These fables touched off an immediate reaction, notably from Juan Pablo Forner and Félix María Samaniego. Literary polemics were very much the style at this time, and good talent was spent on unrewarding arguments. Iriarte wasted much energy and time in such pursuits. In addition to his fables, Iriarte wrote a long didactic poem, *La música* (1779), and two excellent comedies of manners, *La señorita malcriada* (1788) and *El señorito mimado* (1788).

2. *Félix María Samaniego* (1745–1801) wrote his *Fábulas morales* (1781 and 1784) at the request of his uncle for the education of students at the Seminary of Vergara. His intention was to impart moral lessons, and he modeled his fables after Aesop and La Fontaine. In a way they recall those of another fabulist of former years, Juan Ruiz.

C. The Madrid Poets

1. *Nicolás Fernández de Moratín* (1737–1780), an important Neoclassicist, failed with his drama. In lyric poetry, however, he could not resist the charm of Spanish tradition and paradoxically, considering his negative attitude toward the theater of Lope and Calderón, wrote poetry in the Golden Age manner,

producing what some have called the best poem of the eighteenth century, *Fiesta de toros en Madrid.*

2. *José Cadalso y Vázquez de Andrade* (1741–1782), sometimes listed among the poets of the Salamancan school, wrote his poetry in the Neoclassic manner—anacreontics, eclogues, and bucolics. He traveled through Europe and became acquainted with foreign literatures and languages. Upon his return to Spain he followed the profession of arms and became a colonel in the cavalry. At the same time he was writing for the stage, but his tragedy *Sancho García* (1771) was a failure. He went to Salamanca, where he met Meléndez and other poets. His poetry was published in 1773 in the volume *Ocios de mi juventud* under the name José Vázquez. He is better remembered for his prose writings than for his efforts as a poet.

D. The Eighteenth-Century Salamancan School

1. *Fray Diego Tadeo González* (1733–1794), an Augustinian monk, idolized Fray Luis de León and established the eighteenth-century Salamancan school of poets. His group was called *Arcadia Agustiniana,* and its members adopted pastoral pseudonyms. Their poetry in the pastoral mode resurrected a jaded and outmoded manner, but Fray Diego's intention to restore poetry is to be admired. His enthusiasm for Fray Luis must have affected the only real poet of the lot, Meléndez Valdés, a plus for Fray Diego's work. Strangely, the best-known poem of González is *El murciélago alevoso,* which has been criticized, perhaps unjustly, for its alleged display of sadism and cruelty.

2. *José Iglesias de la Casa* (1748–1791) was a better priest than a poet, though he did manage to write some memorable *letrillas* reminiscent of Góngora and Quevedo. He was at his best when writing about the customs and manners of his time, as was his contemporary Ramón de la Cruz.

3. *Juan Meléndez Valdés* (1754–1817), a member of the *Arcadia Agustiniana,* was influenced by Cadalso and Jovellanos. As a Francophile, he fled to France when the French regime in Spain collapsed, and he died there, of hunger, his doctor said.

Meléndez began writing poetry in the pastoral manner but contrived with his superior artistry to make it pleasing to the senses, exhibiting great sensibility with light, happy verses. He used Garcilaso and Fray Luis as models and showed spontaneity, grace, and fluidity, embellishing his poetry with a thinness and delicateness that make it appear almost fragile at times. He wrote a play, *Las bodas de Camacho* (1784), and a didactic ode, *La gloria de las artes* (1781).

In later life, Meléndez turned philosophical, and a melancholy note coupled with a sensitivity to pain, deception, and sorrow and a Romantic sentimentalism crept into his poetry. He tried odes like those of Jovellanos but could not match him. His greatest talents were undoubtedly his descriptive power and genuine poetic sensibility, which outweigh his defects of monotony and shallowness. He represented the varied currents of the eighteenth century and foreshadowed the rise of Romanticism.

4. *Gaspar Melchor de Jovellanos* (1744–1811) is important not for his poetry but for his role as a statesman, social scientist, educator, and patriot. His important writings are in prose.

As a poet, Jovellanos, known as Jovino to his friends in the Salamancan school, wrote in the typical manner of that group, composing anacreontics, idylls, and the like, which seem a little incongruous with his sober personality. In his epistle *A mis amigos de Salamanca,* he urged his friends to forsake the shallow pastoral, amorous themes in favor of philosophical and moral ones. His own *Epístola de Fabio a Anfriso* (1779) strikes a melancholy, pessimistic note that would recur later in Romantic poetry. In the end, he showed that he was largely interested in poetry as an educational tool.

E. The Later Salamancan Poets

French Neoclassicism produced a very correct but cold lyric poetry in Spain. Poets soon reacted, however, against its emptiness and formalism and showed definite signs of a pre-Romantic style that included sentimentalism, emotionalism, and a more florid and rhetorical language. They became interested in exotic themes and were attracted to solitude, suffering, nocturnal scenes, intimate feelings, and violent, vehement, passionate, exclamatory modes of expression. In short, the Salamancan poets of the last few years of the eighteenth century helped usher in Romanticism.

1. *Nicasio Alvarez Cienfuegos* (1764–1809) exhibited many of the characteristics of the pre-Romantic poet. He abandoned Neoclassicism and gave expression to melancholy and sentimentalism in an inflated style. The titles of some of his poems reveal his Romantic disposition: *Mi paseo solitario, A un amigo en la muerte de un hermano, La escuela del sepulcro.*

2. *Manuel José Quintana* (1772–1857), a very important political figure, belongs chronologically to the nineteenth century, but temperamentally and ideologically to the eighteenth. He passed through the storms of Romanticism without taking sides and became the tutor of Queen Isabel II, who later crowned him poet laureate.

Though Quintana wrote drama and prose sketches of famous Spaniards, posterity remembers him for his poetry. Like Luzán, he believed literature should serve some useful end, and his main themes were liberty and progress. He remained loyal to his *patria* when the French invaded, and his patriotism, expressed in his actions as well as in his poetry, has endeared him to his countrymen. His odes *Al combate de Trafalgar* (1805) and *A España después de la revolución de marzo* (1808) passionately expressed love for his country with a virility and fire reminiscent of Herrera. Other poems were devoted to progress—to printing, for example, and to medical advances. He was Classical in every respect, except in moderation and restraint. He reacted with emotion, not with the intellect, and in this sense can be regarded as a forerunner of Romanticism.

3. *Juan Nicasio Gallego* (1777–1853), a priest of liberal politics, conformed largely to the Neoclassic manner but surmounted its coldness and intellectuality in his best poem, *Al dos de mayo*, in which he preserved in bold imagery and high rhetoric the same day that Goya immortalized on canvas. Gallego's poetry, enthusiastic and occasionally emotional, contains a foretaste of Romanticism.

F. The Sevillian School

The Sevillian school emerged from the *Academia de letras humanas*. Though its adherents ostensibly adhered to the Neoclassic code, they felt that beautiful poetry did not necessarily have to conform and that genius could not be bound by rules. This and their belief that the poet could express his own personality are clear signs of the coming Romanticism.

1. *Alberto Lista y Aragón* (1775–1848) is better remembered as a great teacher than as a poet. A man of vast culture, he stood halfway between Neoclassicism and Romanticism, admired the moderation and good taste of Fray Luis, and attempted to draw his young Romantic pupils, like Espronceda, away from the excesses of Romanticism. Yet his own poetry's vague sentimentality and melancholy allied him with that movement.

233

2. *José María Blanco y Crespo* (1775–1841) forsook his priesthood, went to England, and changed his name to Blanco White. He is the only Spanish poet to write well in English, a fact proven by his sonnet *Mysterious Night*. He also wrote in Spanish, of course.

3. *Minor poets* of the Sevillian school are Félix José Reinoso (1777–1841), José Marchena (1768–1821), and Manuel María Arjona (1771–1820).

THE NINETEENTH CENTURY

A. Romanticism

The many attempts to define Romanticism confirm the difficulty of doing so. Sainz de Robles defines it as an artistic revolution against what he termed the rigidity, the coldness, the regulations, the antinationalism, the cerebralism, the pagan aestheticism, the religious incredulity, the preponderance of the objective over the subjective, the declamatory emphasis, and the artistic impersonality of Neoclassicism. He lists Romanticism's characteristics as contemplation of nature, intimacies of natural life, revival of the Middle Ages, the cult of the individual, rejection of the rules of Boileau and Luzán, the national against the foreign, subjective lyricism against epic objectivity, anarchy of inventiveness and procedure, the intimate connection between art and life, and absolute emancipation of the *yo*. Victor Hugo put it much more succinctly in the preface to *Hernani,* where he stated that Romanticism was simply "liberalism in literature."

As we have seen, the eighteenth century witnessed the return of Romanticism in Meléndez Valdés' nature sentiments. Although dates cannot be firmly fixed for its triumph as the dominant literary taste, we can conclude that the nation was prepared well in advance of the outburst that occurred in 1833 with the return of the *emigrados.*

Spanish liberals had had to leave Spain under the despotic reign of Fernando VII, during which time a rigid censorship had succeeded in holding the nascent Romanticism in check. The expression of liberal ideas and the rebelliousness and individuality that characterized Romanticism were dangerous under Fernando's oppressive, absolute monarchy. On Fernando's death, however, the scene changed. María Cristina, the Queen

Mother, called back the exiled liberals, or *emigrados,* for she needed their support to hold the throne against Carlos, Fernando's brother.

Many of the Romantic poets and dramatists, who as liberals had been obliged to leave Spain, breathed abroad the Romantic atmosphere of England and France, where the movement was already fully grown. When they returned after the 1833 amnesty, they brought the new literary rage with them. Romanticism was nothing new to Spain, however, for it had always been an undercurrent in Spanish literature. The nineteenth century revived what was typically Spanish rather than creating something new. The battle that raged in other European countries between Classicists and the Romantic revolutionaries was neither fierce nor prolonged in Spain. The public was happy to revive a characteristic feature of their tradition and was not interested in literary quarrels. What the nineteenth century witnessed was the intensification and concentration of the elements of Romanticism to such a degree that other traditional characteristics of Spanish literature were subdued momentarily and suppressed. The undercurrent now became a flood on the surface and swept everything before it.

The moderation and restraint of Neoclassicism were gone. Rules and precepts ceased to exist for the poet, who recognized no authority and no codes of behavior. Poets demanded absolute freedom and believed their primary function was to be expressive, not necessarily beautiful. Their poetry was often one of dreams in which they lost sight of reality. A melancholy, pessimistic, sometimes despairing note pervaded their poems, as they observed that the reality that surrounded them did not conform to their dream world. Poets became interested in exotic themes, such as Oriental potentates and their courts, and in the noble Moor, idealized in somewhat the same fashion as Rousseau had idealized the American Indian. Fatally attracted to the sepulchral, the mysterious, the funereal, tempestuous seas, rugged mountains, yawning abysses, ruins, nocturnal scenes, and landscapes, poets revealed through their vocabulary their interests and feelings, and used an abundance of terms such as *sórdido, fúnebre, hórrido, gemido, tétrico, lúgubre, melancólico, espectro, tremendo, ¡Ay!, sombras, histérico, languidez, duda, suspiro,* and *lágrimas.* Poets were impassioned, unrestrained, and pessimistic, and emotionalism replaced reason in their poetry.

The poets of Romanticism, with few exceptions, were dramatic or narrative poets and did their best work in the *leyenda* and the drama. The Romantic fervor lasted only a short time in Spain. As the lingering scent of Romanticism weakened, writers interested themselves in more serious questions, and a group of so-called philosophical poets appeared, headed by Campoamor and Núñez de Arce. A third direction that poetry took in the second half of the century was that represented by Bécquer and Rosalía de Castro, who, although perhaps classified temperamentally with the Romanticists, actually represented a movement of transition to the modern schools of poetry. Finally, the *costumbrista* poets of the last years of the century brought the experimental period to a close as the age of Modernism approached.

1. *Angel de Saavedra, Duque de Rivas* (1791–1865) won his acclaim primarily in the drama. As a poet his genius lay in narrative style rather than in the lyrical vein, as exemplified in *El moro expósito* and the *Romances históricos*. In his earlier work, Rivas tried the Neoclassic manner and dedicated a series of poems to beautiful shepherdesses. Although he has some interesting descriptions of nature, his most sincere poetry is that dedicated to Olimpia, a girl he fell in love with in 1819, that reveals the poet's nostalgia and the pain and pleasure of a lost love. His own rules for Romanticism at best can be termed mild: quicken the reader's interest in the narrative; suit style to argument; adapt style to the person speaking; make use of color; use historical customs; use clear expressions; and versify well.

In addition to his love themes and nature, which could be either pastoral or tempestuous (in *El faro de Malta,* for example), Rivas concentrated on religious and nationalistic and patriotic themes. His love of Spain, intensified by the homesickness and sorrow of exile, is one of the truly admirable traits in his lyric poetry. He also has some moral poems and uses the theme of the stylized noble Moor in some of his *romances*. Most of his poetry after 1835 is less noteworthy as part of his total production.

2. *José de Espronceda y Delgado* (1808–1842) enjoys the reputation of having been Spain's greatest Romantic lyric poet. Everything about this man was Romantic except his manner of dying. At the age of fifteen he joined a group of young conspirators called Los Numantinos. Arrested and later, in 1827, exiled, he met Teresa Mancha in Lisbon, fell in love with her, and induced her to abandon her husband in London and live with him. His life with Teresa was a tempestuous one. Meanwhile, between 1829 and 1835 he became involved in a series of military uprisings, both in France and Spain.

It would be convenient to classify Espronceda's poetry into two types: lyric and narrative. To the first type belong the shorter poems, such as *Canción del pirata,* and to the latter belong *El estudiante de Salamanca* and *El diablo mundo.* Such a classification, however, is not altogether valid, for there is much in the longer poems that is lyric—the *Canto a Teresa,* for example—and something of the epic in the shorter ones.

Espronceda personifies in his life and work what we might term the "Romantic frenzy." He was vehement and passionate, a born rebel who wanted to convert his dreams to reality. He was outraged by restraints and could tolerate them neither in his art nor in society, an attitude fully revealed in his *Canción del pirata.* There, in a moment of exaltation, he dreams of being a pirate, a rebel outside the law and society, who is his own law, feared by all, and who laughs at dangers and his enemies. Here one finds revolution and anarchy, scorn for the established order, and a plea for individualism and liberty.

Neither reality nor women nor anything else conformed to what the poet expected or wanted, and from a moment of exaltation, as in the *Canción del pirata,* we see the pendulum swing to the opposite pole, where the poet confesses that his desire is eternal and insatiable and that he believes only in the peace of the sepulcher. As Bonilla so well put it, the four principles of Espronceda's philosophy are doubt, the first principle of thought; pain, the positive reality of life; pleasure, the world's illusion; and death, the solution to every problem. Combined with these are skepticism, irony, and sorrow.

Although Espronceda has been labeled "the Spanish Byron," and although the Spanish poet knew English and admired Byron, there are few direct influences of the one on the other. Both were skeptical, liberal, and pessimistic regarding life, which they found to be largely an illusion. Espronceda had much more of a social conscience and was patriotic. In any event, Espronceda's poetic sensibilities were far too great for him to be a servile imitator.

After an early series of poems written in the Neoclassic vein between 1828 and 1833, including some dedicated to friends and others involving themes of exile, politics, country, and freedom, he wrote his best-known poems, all included in the 1840 edition of his poetry. In addition to the *Canción del pirata,* the consummate expression of individual liberty, he wrote *El mendigo,* another cynical vision of the world; *El reo de muerte* (he was opposed to capital punishment); and *El verdugo.* In these poems, dedicated to the disillusion of the passing years, Espronceda combines realism with idealism and shows his sympathy for the outcast, the unfortunate, and the misunderstood. Perhaps the most pessimistic of these lyric poems is *A Jarifa en una orgía,* in which he identifies himself with the prostitute as a social outcast.

El estudiante de Salamanca, a kind of *leyenda* that handles the don Juan theme in a new way, synthesizes all the tendencies in Espronceda's works up to that time. His don Félix, unlike the other don Juan prototypes, is a disillusioned materialist who discovers that life is a fantasy and death is the only reality. The poem uses a great number of poetic meters and chiaroscuro to good effect.

El diablo mundo, his longest poem (never completed), can be considered his masterpiece. It was conceived as an epic of mankind, a vast undertaking to show man's struggles, deceptions, triumphs, and longings; but the poem is quite uneven, rising to great poetic heights at times but falling lamentably at others. Its *mal du siècle* tendencies are combined with a jumble of ideas, but the salient thought seems to be that life is senseless, after all, if all it has to offer is one deception after another. The plot relates how the protagonist, Adam, is miraculously restored to youth and, with the mind of a child, unspoiled by experience, goes through one disillusionment after another. Despite its standard Romantic philosophy, however, the poem has some exceptionally well-conceived and well-executed passages, for if Espronceda was not a philosopher, he was a great versifier. The introductory scene of *El diablo mundo* has been compared in majesty with the opening scene of *Faust.* It and the second canto written to the memory of Teresa are masterpieces of Romantic poetry. The *Canto II; A Teresa; Descansa en paz* has no connection with the rest of the poem and was intercalated by the poet with the typical Romantic comment: "Este canto es un desahogo de mi corazón; sáltelo el que no quiera leerlo sin escrúpulo, pues no está ligado de manera alguna con el poema." He expresses the typical Espronceda themes of delirium, despair, lament for lost youth, and the pleasure of dreams of glory. *El diablo mundo* also emphasizes that man becomes spiritually old quickly and looks forward to death; the hero's idea of life bears no similarity to that of the masses; a young, dreaming soul is easily deceived and abandons real love for deceptive illusion; man indulges in blind and purposeless dreaming for an unattainable ideal; and dismal grief is man's lot, and the world will not grieve over one more corpse.

In his Romantic poetry, Espronceda served as the catalytic agent to fuse a large number of poetic tendencies awaiting expression, much as Rubén Darío did later. Rivas was the national, historical Romantic, but Espronceda represents the highly personal, subjective, revolutionary poet. In a sense, whether one doubts his sincerity or not, he carried on the humanitarian and libertarian spirit of the eighteenth-century French philosophers, conveyed to Spain by Hugo and others, but he was restless and undisciplined, original in his experimentation with meter and lines, if not in his themes. His characteristic note is doubt, almost desperation. When a bit of life and radiance creeps in, as in *El sol*, he fears that his happiness will be temporary and that the dark night will soon cover the radiant life. Despite the unevenness in his poetic output, Espronceda was the best poet of the century down to Bécquer.

3. *José Zorrilla y Moral* (1817–1893) often liked to refer to himself as a troubadour: "Yo soy el trovador que vaga errante." This sobriquet suits him in many respects, for like the troubadours of old, he had a native faculty for versifying and a gift with words that made writing poetry effortless for him. In Madrid in 1837 he became famous overnight when he stepped forward at Larra's funeral and read some of his verses written for the occasion.

Zorrilla's works are not intimate or personal. Sometimes called the Lope de Vega of the nineteenth century for his facility, he was more plebeian and less cultured than either Rivas or Espronceda. His basic inspiration seems to have been national, with a spirit more authentic, indeed, than that of Rivas. He conveyed emotion and a feeling of beauty but was overly fond of sensational imagery and even vulgarity. His characteristics are those of Romantic poetry in general: love of the medieval and national tradition and religion, as well as all the other trappings of the movement, such as boisterous nature, nocturnal scenes, tempests, exotic castles, shadowy figures, and ruins.

In the tradition of the troubadour, Zorrilla's poetic talent was more narrative and descriptive than it was lyric. He could describe what he saw or imagined much better than what he felt. He was a great storyteller, and his evocative power is not to be denied. Consequently, his best Romantic poetic work is in the longer narrative poems called *leyendas*. Even in his shorter poems he was not concerned with themes that produce lyric poetry. His verses often have a vagueness, a sentimentality, a melancholy, and diffuseness that are typical of the emotional atmosphere of Romantic lyric poetry; but atmosphere was about all that interested Zorrilla. The total result is that Zorrilla has little depth. In style he was so fluent and wrote so easily that he sins on the side of verbosity.

But in spite of his defects, he was a master versifier and developed wonderful music with words that please the ear. Typical of his short poems are his *Orientales,* and among these are *Dueña de la negra toca, Corriendo van por la vega,* and *Mañana voy, nazarena.* Zorrilla is still a favorite with the general public, forever captivated by his troubadouresque style, the music of his lines, and his rhythms.

4. *Juan Arolas* (1805–1849) became a priest over his parents' protests but had no true calling. His frustrations and unfulfilled longings made his life unhappy, and he died insane at the early age of forty-four.

His poetry, which is largely a reflection of the state of his mind, is conveniently divided into four thematic groups: religious, amatory, chivalresque, and Oriental. Significantly, the poems on religious themes are the least attractive of all in spite of their undeniable sincerity. His chivalresque poems revive great heroes of the past with all their splendor and color. His sensual love poems are somewhat autobiographical, for Arolas' love was not a game, as played by poets of earlier ages, but something very personal. His *Orientales,* showing influences of Victor Hugo, are acclaimed as his best lyric effort and are perfectly in keeping with the Romantic tradition. Here we find sultans and pirates, Oriental courts, rich color, voluptuousness, mellowness, and languidness. His Orientalism, based on his imagination, is exotic, sensuous, colorful, and imaginative and soars far above that of Zorrilla and at times even that of Espronceda. His poetry was published in two collections: *Poesías caballerescas y orientales* (1840) and *Poesías religiosas, orientales, caballerescas y amatorias* (1860).

5. *Gertrudis Gómez de Avellaneda* (1814–1873) was born in Cuba, of a Spanish father and a Cuban mother, but she came to Spain when she was twenty-two. She was highly regarded by poets of her day. She admired the Romanticists, especially George Sand, and was a personal friend of all the Spanish poets. Her life was one of suffering, disappointment, and anguish, all reflected in her poetry.

She left an extensive work of half a dozen huge volumes, including dramas, novels, and lyric poetry, some of which she wrote under the pseudonym Tula. She is best remembered for her poetry, in which she was eloquent and passionate, as well as sincere. Her two principal themes were love, both divine and human, and religion, although she did write some poems on nature. Typical poems on these topics are *A la cruz, A él,* and *Al sol.* She wrote a poem on Niagara, *A vista del Niágara,* as did her fellow Cuban Heredia, the Venezuelan Pérez Bonalde, and the North American William Cullen Bryant. Her cadenced verses forecast the coming of the moderns.

Her best poetry contains Byronic desperation of a love scorned. Her religious poetry, to which she may have been propelled by her frustrated love, is quite orthodox. Though she shows deep and sincere feeling, nonetheless she has little concern for humanity except as an expression of Christian charity on her part.

Among her many novels are *Espatolino* (1844), *Guatimozín* (1846), and *Sab* (1841). Her legends include *La montaña maldita* and *El aura blanca. Alfonso Munio* (1844), her best play, tells of a love triangle in Toledo in 1142. Avellaneda later changed its title to *Munio Alfonso.* Other plays are *El Príncipe de Viana* (1844) and the Biblical dramas *Saúl* (1849) and *Baltasar* (1858). The robustness of her versification and the gravity of her thought prompted Nicasio Gallego to say of her: "Es mucho hombre esa mujer," but nevertheless the Spanish Academy in a stormy session refused to seat a woman.

6. *Carolina Coronado* (1820–1911) wrote tenderly idealistic, intensely sentimental poetry with delicateness, sweetness, and Romantic melancholy. She did not use the inflated rhetoric or sonority of so much Romantic poetry. In the beginning she was content to write about small wonders of nature, like flowers and butterflies, but later in more profound fashion she expressed her own feelings at once amorous and mystical. She attempted the novel without success. Her best-known poem is *El amor de los amores,* inspired by the Song of Songs.

7. *Nicomedes Pastor Díaz* (1811–1863) wrote poetry that is melancholy and gently pessimistic in tone, with a dreamy vagueness that is in keeping with the poetic tradition of his native Galicia. Typical poems are *A la luna* and *La mariposa negra.* He was affected by the Romanticist's interest in the macabre and could contemplate as well as any other his dead sweetheart and the hopelessness of his fate. He posed as an austere ascetic who felt society could be redeemed. He thought the poet's mission was to be a social and religious high priest and refused to separate the poet from the politician.

8. *Other poets* of Romanticism are Gabriel García Tassara (1817–1875); Patricio de la Escosura (1807–1878), who also wrote Romantic novels; Antonio Ros de Olano (1808–1886), born in Venezuela, who was a close friend of Espronceda's and wrote the prologue for his *El diablo mundo;* Enrique Gil y Carrasco (1815–1846), author of the most famous Romantic novel, *El señor de Bembibre,* who also wrote a number of excellent nature poems, among them *La gota de rocío* and *La violeta;* and *Juan Martínez Villergas* (1816–1894), author of mordant, satiric verses, who also attempted the novel and the drama.

B. The Transition: Second Half of the Nineteenth Century

The term post-Romantic has often been applied to the poetry that appeared after the Romantic movement had spent itself and was no longer the dominant force in literature. This designation, however, is not fully applicable to the period that dates roughly from 1850 to Rubén Darío's *Azul,* which appeared in 1888, for many of the poets classified as Romanticists lived and wrote Romantic poetry long after 1850. Two of the greatest poets of the century, Gustavo Adolfo Bécquer and Rosalía de Castro, are sometimes so designated, but because they are more than Romanticists and form the link between Romanticism and Modernism, we shall include them here as transitional poets. Although the Romantic tradition extended into the second half of the century, no definite trend developed in lyric poetry until the advent of Modernism in the last years. In addition to the Romantic note that continued, trends toward philosophy, skepticism, religiousness, and *costumbrismo* appear in the works of Campoamor, Núñez de Arce, Medina, and Gabriel y Galán. The age, one of experimentation, found poets reacting against the excesses of Romantic imagination and exuberance with the evident intent of bringing poetry back to earth and making something useful of it. This eclectic period closed when Rubén Darío descended upon the peninsula and carried everything before him.

1. *The philosophical poets* include the following:

a) *Ramón de Campoamor* (1817–1901), known as the Spanish Homer, enjoyed a tremendous vogue in the nineteenth century. His popularity with the people gave him a ranking out of proportion with his true merit. In Campoamor's time the middle class and the general public believed that they had inherited the role of connoisseur formerly enjoyed by the aristocrats. With every man a literary critic, standards of culture and good taste degenerated. Campoamor was able to give the public the kind of poetry they wanted, a homespun philosophy with ironic, sometimes sarcastic comments on life, easily memorized. He reacted against Romanticism and adopted as his guide "el arte por la idea" in his *Poética* (1883). Humor abounds in his poetry, but it is often piquant and cynical.

He prided himself on having invented new poetic forms to which he gave the names *dolora, humorada,* and *pequeño poema.* The *humorada* is a very brief composition, usually of two lines, sometimes four, with philosophical intention and characterized by irony and skepticism. Campoamor's were collected in *Humoradas* (1886) and have been called "sculptured, chiseled expressions of thought." The *dolora* (*Fábulas morales y doloras* [1846]) is a dramatized *humorada,* combining concision with philosophy, a kind of tiny drama with ideas, reflecting the mediocre and commonplace. The *pequeño poema* is an amplification of a *dolora.*

Opinions on Campoamor's work have been highly contradictory. Some have seen him as highly original, and others find nothing but platitudes in his poetry. Some consider his verse attractive, and others have called it doggerel. A fair judgment would not condemn him too harshly or praise him too highly, recognizing his ability as a versifier and his ingenuity in crystallizing thought, often in a delightful way, but at the same time admitting his lack of creative ability and failure to reach the stature of a truly great poet. His most famous poem, *¡Quién supiera escribir!,* is a three-part dialogue in which an illiterate girl attempts to dictate to an obtuse priest a letter intended for her distant lover.

b) *Gaspar Núñez de Arce* (1832–1903), like Campoamor, reacted away from the emotion of Romanticism and wrote ideological poetry. There are two strings to his harp, namely philosophy and politics. He summed up his poetic creed himself when he wrote: "La poesía debe pensar y sentir, reflejar las ideas y las pasiones, los dolores y los gozos de la sociedad . . . No debe limitarse a cantar como el pájaro." In line with this serious purpose, Núñez de Arce deals with the philosophical and moral problems of his times and reflects better than any other poet of his day the nineteenth-century struggle between religious faith and science. To illustrate his philosophical reflections, he composed poems on great intellectuals of the past who were either confronted by similar situations or were considered nonconformists and original thinkers. *La visión de Fray Martín* (1880) deals with Martin

Luther. Other poems deal with Raimundo Lulio, Dante, and Lord Byron.

This poet yearned for the orthodox religious faith, but the discoveries of a rationalistic science would not allow him to justify it. From this conflict grew a sort of pessimism quite different from the Romantic kind. He also studied the problems of philosophical doubt. He is perhaps best loved today for his political poems in a declamatory style reminiscent of Quintana. *Gritos de combate* (1875) reveals his attitudes as a statesman and politician and reflects his disillusionment in the people's abuse of democracy, his hope for the future, and his belief in progress and political and religious freedom.

c) *Minor philosophical poets* include Ventura Ruiz Aguilera (1820–1881), whose *Ecos nacionales* (two volumes; 1849 and 1854) illustrate his concern with social and political questions; and Manuel del Palacio (1832–1906), good at the epigram and much like Campoamor in his ability to wrap up a clever thought in a few words. He claimed to be the first to write the so-called *sonetos filosóficos,* serious at the beginning but with a humorous twist at the end.

2. *The transition poets* include the following:

a) *Gustavo Adolfo Bécquer* (1836–1870) authored poetry that has risen in popularity and esteem with twentieth-century poets and critics, in contrast with that of Campoamor and Núñez de Arce, which has suffered. Many now feel that Bécquer's poetry, although slight in quantity, is the greatest poetry of the century, principally because of his ability to foresee and to predict, in a sense, the modern schools of poetry. He is perhaps the purest Romanticist of all Spanish poets, for unlike Espronceda, he reveals no pose or showmanship in his sadness. But there is more than Romanticism in Bécquer, as will be pointed out.

Christened Gustavo Adolfo Domínguez Bastida, Bécquer was orphaned at an early age, and he was left in the care of his godmother. At eighteen he went to Madrid in search of literary fame but did not find it. He took a number of jobs, married unhappily, and left three children at his death. Because of a serious illness, Bécquer retired to Veruela with Valeriano, his favorite brother, to recuperate. They spent a year there, and Bécquer wrote several works. Bécquer died at the age of thirty-four, exhausted by tuberculosis. He never knew the acclaim of the public as Espronceda, Campoamor, or Zorrilla did, and his poetry reflects his sad, impoverished, sick life. Luis González Bravo, Isabel II's minister who had promised to publish Bécquer's *Rimas,* was deposed by the revolution in 1868, and the manuscript was lost. Bécquer rewrote the *Rimas,* and it was published posthumously in 1871. Some variation of number and order exists, but the standard order in most editions is that of Bécquer's friend, Narciso Campillo.

Bécquer's fame rests on this one small volume. These love poems constitute what one might consider a spiritual autobiography of the poet. At the outset we see an almost ecstatic yearning for poetry. He sees his love in nature and in his imaginary muse in the form of a woman. He finally meets his woman of flesh and blood and becomes desperately enamoured of her. At first she is cool to his love, but he manages to win her affection. His rapture ends with the hint of a bitter quarrel and his dismissal as she refuses to recognize him. His love continues, however, as he tries in vain to win her once more, and he consoles himself with the thought of approaching death. The *Rimas* close with meditations on death and nature, together with an expression of fears and desires. Some critics have felt that the *Rimas* are a running, true commentary on the poet's love for Julia Espín y Guillén, the daughter of a music professor, who later married an influential politician.

Throughout the seventy-six little poems (some say seventy-nine or eighty, for no authentic edition exists), the poet is deeply subjective and sentimental. He represents a kind of purification of the exaggerations of Romanticism. The style is effortless and natural; the keynote is simplicity. He avoids altogether the rhetoric and inflation of Núñez de Arce and all other preceding poets and makes use of suggestiveness that the Symbolist poets did not discover until the end of the century. The simplicity of style, the musicality of the verses, the theme of love, and the appeal of Bécquer's sentimentality and melancholy have made him a great favorite.

In his poetry as in his prose legends, Bécquer's world is one of half shadows, uncertain shapes, and suggestions of feelings and sentiments. There is nothing solid, but the poet carries the reader with him as he combines music with delicate and fugitive words and almost intangible, unutterable feelings. His poetry is full of sighs, dry leaves, smoke, gilded threads of spider webs, and wispy fog. There is a total effect of immense sadness, almost desperation, and above all resignation and tenderness. His poetry exhales suffering. As one critic has said: "He has caught the subtle vibrations of an ethereal music."

Aside from their intrinsic merit, Bécquer's poems have had a great influence on the development of modern poets. Dámaso Alonso has said that Bécquer is the "punto de arranque," the starting point, of all contemporary Spanish poetry. "Cualquier poeta de hoy," he says, "se siente mucho más cerca de Bécquer (y en parte, de Rosalía de Castro) que de Zorrilla, de Núñez de Arce o de Rubén Darío." This closeness in spirit to Bécquer is due in large part to the fact that Bécquer was really the first to see the difference between the traditional, pompous, rhetorical Spanish poetry that had been written up to his time and the new style of short, unadorned, simple poetry. Bécquer himself made very clear the distinction between the two types.

In the second type, his own, which he called "the poetry of poets," he points out the direction that modern Spanish poetry will take, showing the coming generations how to write poetry that insinuates and suggests, that brushes lightly against you and then departs. Bécquer attempted to convey the interrelationship of reality and dream, and in his poetry, pure affect related to sight and touch, he tried to define his inspiration, the "children of his fantasy."

Jorge Guillén feels that had Bécquer lived as long as Zorrilla or Núñez de Arce, he would have been Spain's greatest lyric poet of the nineteenth century. Juan Ramón Jiménez, Rubén Darío, and others truly appreciated him, and modern critics agree that he is the principal precursor of Modernism. To understand Bécquer's poetry is to understand more about our contemporaries. This poet could indeed be called the prophet of twentieth-century Spanish poetry.

Bécquer's best prose work, *Leyendas* (1860–1864), is a group of delicate, rhythmic, Romantic legends in the style of Hoffmann and Poe. Almost all are set in a medieval atmosphere of ruins, monasteries, and churches. The supernatural, a magical sense, and fantasy were his strong points. Among his well-known legends are *Maese Pérez, organista; Los ojos verdes;* and *La ajorca de oro. Desde mi celda,* a collection of literary letters written from the Monastery of Veruela in 1864, describes the countryside and the persons he met. This, too, is touched with the subjective magic and poignant message of all his work.

b) *Rosalía de Castro (1837–1885)* had a life that, like Bécquer's, was sorrowful and unhappy. Like Bécquer she was disillusioned and melancholy, and like him she died a victim of a terrible sickness. Like Bécquer she made poetry a personal, unashamed outpouring of sentiment and tried to express with words what cannot be uttered but only suggested. The musicality of her verse, the tenderness, the vagueness, the symbolism and imagery, and the suggestiveness and intuition have endeared her to twentieth-century poets, who have found in her, as in Bécquer, pure poetry—simple, unrhetorical, interpreting an atmosphere and reflecting a state of soul but never describing in the traditional manner. Her fame, which was slight in her own lifetime, has increased steadily since her death. Brenan judges that she would be the greatest poetess of modern times had she written all her poetry in Spanish.

Born out of wedlock (her father was a priest), Rosalía was raised until her ninth year by a peasant woman. From her peasant relationships as a child she absorbed the spirit of Galician folk song that she used so beautifully later. At nineteen she went to Madrid to live. There she met the poets and writers of her day and began to write herself. City life, however, had little attraction for her, and she grew immensely homesick for her native soil. She could find no beauties in the Castilian landscape, which augmented her *soidade* ("homesickness"). Perhaps because of this she became interested in a young Galician writer living in Madrid, Manuel Martínez Murguía, whom she later married. Her husband mistreated her, and her health failed as she struggled constantly against poverty to rear and educate her five children. Her emotional conflicts, occasioned by shame over the irregularity of her birth and the disfiguring effects of her disease, cancer, caused her finally to withdraw from the world and to see no one during the last years of her life. She died in her beloved native land at the relatively young age of forty-eight.

Rosalía de Castro wrote many novels, among them *La hija del mar* (1859) and *El caballero de las botas azules* (1867), but she is essentially a great poetess. Much of her poetry was written in Galician, not used for poetry for many centuries, but she knew the folk song that had preserved the vagueness, melancholy, and suggestiveness of Galician poetry. Her Galician volumes, *Cantares gallegos* (1863), intensely personal, and *Folhas novas* (1880), filled with deep despair and melancholy, prepared the way for her last volume, in Spanish, *En las orillas del Sar* (1884), a collection of poetry written over many years, some shortly before her death. Slow and painful cancer caused her concern, and the poems reveal her longing for the relief of the life beyond death as well as a love and yearning for her native land. We see the past days that will never return as she expresses her deep feeling for Galicia, its nature, customs, and the miseries and suffering

of the poor. The poems reflect the counterpoint, through nature, of hope and despair, approaching spring and fatal winter.
She reflects both an inner and outer reality, the autumn light,
night and pain, a desire for happiness, and a kind of mystical
union with the universe. Tormented, feeling unloved, and ex-
periencing the shadow of impalpable desires, she awaited an approaching death.

The poetess experimented with meter, harmonies, assonance,
and varied lines of poetry. Her poetry, completely personal, is
modern in its anticipation of the suggestiveness of the Symbolists. In her nostalgic poetry she repeatedly drifts in dreams back
to her native land where shapes are indecisive and the essences
of things are intangible. Along with Bécquer's, her poetry is the
purest of the transition period that stretched from Romanticism
to Modernism.

3. *The costumbrista poets* include the following:

a) *José María Gabriel y Galán* (1870–1905), schoolteacher and
farmer, represents a direction that is altogether different from
that taken by other poets of the transition period. In him we find
an expression of regionalism and *costumbrismo* as he describes
life in his isolated little archaic town in Extremadura. He had a
sincere, deep feeling for the country life and Spanish Catholic
tradition preserved by the Castilian peasants. He anticipated the
coming Generation of 1898 with his appreciation and glorification of the Castilian landscape but fell short of their artistic tastes
and standards. He was fond of the rustic sayings of the people,
extolled the simplicity of rural life, used dialect in some of his
poems, and optimistically bore sorrows and burdens. His best
side is the descriptive one. His best-known poems are *El ama*, for
which he became famous overnight, and *El cristu benditu*. Among
his collections are *Castellanas* (1902) and *Religiosas* (1906).

b) *Vicente Medina y Tomás* (1866–1936), journalist, soldier,
schoolteacher, and poet, who hailed from Murcia, is another re-
gionalist. His first book of poetry, *Aires murcianos* (1898), was edited by Azorín and was well received by known literary figures,
among them Unamuno and Clarín. Medina had but one style—
a regionalistic, rustic type of poetry expressed in simple language flavored with frequent use of dialect. His chief defect,
consequently, is monotony, for he could only repeat himself
rather than give new dimensions to his muse. He created, however, a different kind of regional poetry, which Federico de Onís
feels is close to that of the Modernists; by concentrating on the
popular soul and spirit in their primitive, elemental aspects

rather than on the picturesque local color or physical appearance of his region as his predecessors had done, he produced poems of a simple but human impact. This type of *costumbrismo,* regional only in a limited sense, was an original contribution of Medina and had widespread influence among local and regional Spanish and Spanish-American poets. Other collections characteristic of his manner are *Alma del pueblo* (1900) and *La canción de la huerta* (1905).

TWENTIETH-CENTURY POETRY

A. General Considerations

The twentieth century in Spain, reflecting the increased tempo of modern life, produced a series of brilliant poetic generations. The first important group of poets, searching for ideal beauty and form, the Modernists, though developing separately from the better-known Latin American form, succumbed to the poetic leadership of the Nicaraguan Rubén Darío. At the same time another important twentieth-century poetic current, the Generation of 1898, continued to emphasize the human, Existential, and metaphysical aspects of life. These writers, primarily Unamuno and Antonio Machado, stressed eternal spiritual values. They wrote in an almost colloquial manner, and their themes, beyond Modernist aestheticism, continued to influence younger generations. Between Modernism and the important poets of the Generation of 1927, a group of transition poets appeared, who in some cases anticipated the next generation, while still bordering on the Modernist manner. In any event, poets like León Felipe have a significance not clearly generational. Juan Ramón Jiménez, who like Machado was at first influenced briefly by Modernism, broke away to a purer, less ornamental, though still aesthetic poetry that strove for beauty.

The Generation of 1927 was also influenced by a number of avant-garde movements, among them the *ultraísta* movement, which around 1918 attempted to redefine poetry as metaphor in a complete rupture with Modernism and its lack of adornment. Equally important was *creacionismo,* whose principal proponents were the Chilean Vicente Huidobro and Gerardo Diego, a member of the Generation of 1927. In their initial stages, the young poets wrote, for the most part, dehumanized or depersonalized poetry, often quite hermetic. They searched for purity and the elimination of the sentimental, though from the beginning Lorca was warm, vibrant, and passionate. The intuitive Salinas, the precise and pure Guillén, and the passionate and sensual Lorca heeded, in a later phase, the call of humanity and its social and Existential needs. The dehumanized writing fused into a neo-Romantic poetry of greater intensity with the work of Aleixandre and Alberti. In their works the generation showed the influence of Surrealism or Surrealistic force. They used Freudian symbols, free association, and associative imagery of an irrational nature. They experimented with pure poetry (as defined by Valéry and Brémond), worked toward the revitalization of Luis de Góngora, and avoided the anecdotal. Later, Lorca substituted the poor black of New York for his colorful Andalusian gypsy. Guillén wrote of human preoccupations and not just the joy of life, and Salinas substituted a political and social conscience for a refined intellectualism.

In the 1930s and 1940s a Classical and religious revival took place. Poets like Luis Rosales, Germán Bleiberg, and Luis Felipe Vivanco produced graceful poetry, often with a note of religious devotion and chose Garcilaso rather than Góngora as their guide. Poets like Miguel Hernández suffered traumatic events of the Spanish Civil War that affected their creative activities. The generational date of 1935 is sometimes used, because in that year Rosales and Ridruejo produced key poetic works, the former, *Abril,* and the latter, *Plural.* Acknowledging the four hundredth anniversary of Garcilaso's death in 1536, this group is often called the Generation of 1936. Although many began as disciples of the previous generation, they rejected the intellectual emphasis for simpler, more intimate, and more human poetry. Some of the more conservative poets, because of their connection with the *Escorial* review, became known as the Escorial group. Others preferred the label "Generation of '39" for those who, like José García Nieto, wrote of God and family as well as of love in Neoclassic form. In 1943 Nieto helped start the review *Garcilaso,* and the young writers, who called themselves *la juventud creadora,* after a journal entitled *Juventud,* reflected spiritual dejection in their serene and elegant poetry. Poets opposing the Neoclassic *Garcilasistas* and what for them was escapist poetry supported the ideas of *Espadaña,* a review founded by Victoriano Crémer Alonso, which went to the other extreme and promoted *tremendista* and social poetry about the common man.

The generation had disparate voices. José Luis Hidalgo (1919—

1947) preferred a more Romantic tone. Major poets like Blas de Otero and Gabriel Celaya stressed religious, social, and political themes. Younger poets like José Hierro and Carlos Bousoño, whom some would classify as members of the first postwar generation, produced Existentialist poetry.

In 1943 the Adonais Prize did for poetry what the Nadal Prize had achieved for the novel. In 1944 Dámaso Alonso published *Hijos de la ira,* a landmark collection of protest and Existential anguish. Around 1945 Carlos Edmundo d'Ory (b. 1923), among others, experimented with *Postismo,* stressing imagination, the power of the poetic word, and a kind of Surrealism. Around 1947 the *Cántico* group, that proved influential among poets of the 1970s, appeared.

The poets of the second postwar generation, influenced by the Peruvian César Vallejo and others, is sometimes called the Generation of 1950, although some critics prefer other terms, such as the Generation of 1956–1971. José Angel Valente, Angel González, and others saw poetry as an act of discovery and stressed the poetic word beyond theme or message. They insisted on the authenticity of poetic expression, though notes of Existential anguish, religious preoccupations, and social and political elements continued. Essentially they sought to discover poetic and human authenticity, even though the poets differ in their rhetorical emphasis, humor, pessimism, or attempts to involve reader participation in the poetic expression. In seeking knowledge of ultimate mysteries, they conceived of poetry as self-revelatory.

In the 1960s and 1970s some poets experimented with poetry as reading rather than as listening experiences, conceiving of poetry as a kind of visual art with words and typographical experimentation. A new generation appeared, diversely called the third postwar generation, the Generation of 1968, or the *Generación marginada.* Major poets like Pedro Gimferrer and Guillermo Carnero together with others attempted to develop a new poetic language. They emphasized intertextuality, painting, music, and literature. Because of their fondness for cultural references and their love of certain cultural elements, terms like *culturalismo, Grecidad, neobarroquismo, Cavafianismo,* and *Cernudismo* have been used to describe their poetry. They, as had the previous generation, insisted on the value of the poetic word and the poem as an autosufficient and independent object, beyond their own reality, that is, the autonomy of art as an end in itself. They combined these elements with apparently antithetical concepts

251

involving movies, television, mass media, advertisements, and "pop" themes.

Younger poets of the group, like Luis Antonio de Villena and Luis Alberto de Cuenca, continued to reject conventional clothes, language, and life-style and to stress metapoetry. They were even more Byzantine, pagan, and Neobaroque. Some poets glorified the body and homosexual themes. Others used ironic humor, demythification, and the historical process in a new way. Still others showed traces of a new kind of Romanticism reflecting self-destructive tendencies in a world of sex and drugs.

B. Modernism

Modernism was a reaction against the prosaism of Campoamor, the effervescence of Romanticism, and what the poets called "bourgeois poetry." The Modernists wanted to reject the nineteenth century, but they discovered new beauties in Berceo, Juan Ruiz, and Santillana. In spite of their reaction against Romanticism, Modernist poets in a sense seemed Romantic in their rebelliousness and demands for absolute artistic liberty. The Modernists, trying to play all the notes of which the poetic orchestra was capable, emphasized words, acoustical elements, sensations, neologisms, and striking metaphors. The French Parnassians, interested in perfection of form, and French Symbolists like Paul Verlaine, who wanted to have music before all else, influenced the new poets. In Modernist poetry we find the rare or mysterious, the vague and the melancholy, elegance, synesthesia, various mythologies, cosmopolitanism, individualism, pessimism, and skepticism.

Modernism had a greater development in Latin America through poets like the Mexican Manuel Gutiérrez Nájera, the Cuban José Martí (perhaps the first Modernist), the Colombian José Asunción Silva, and the Nicaraguan Rubén Darío, who became the leading Modernist voice. For the first time Spanish letters were greatly affected by currents emanating from Spain's former colonies, and Spanish authors became aware of the importance of their cultural brothers across the sea. Nonetheless, Modernism existed independently in Spain, though Rubén Darío became its acknowledged leader on both sides of the Atlantic Ocean. Interpretation of Modernism went through several phases, at first stressing the new sensibility and stylistic renovation, then the aesthetic and evasive aspects, and still later, while accepting the formal renovation, recognizing also the spiritual aspects and preoccupations about life and death in Modernist works after the turn of the century.

Though Modernism and the Generation of 1898 are sometimes confused with one another, the terms are not synonymous. The former represents a revolution in technique and the latter a revolution in ideology, although for some Modernism is also an attempt at exploring the roots of Spanish spiritual life. The terms are not mutually exclusive, and one and the same writer, if affected by both, can be classified as a Modernist and also a member of the Generation of 1898. The Generation of 1898 emphasized moral and national trends; Modernism stressed aesthetic and cosmopolitan aspects. The Generation of 1898 stressed truth, Modernists beauty. Yet it is sometimes difficult to separate patriotic preoccupations and human elements from the desire to create a new style, and Modernists and the Generation of 1898 resembled each other in their love of old villages, the countryside, and the nation, the Modernists through a recall of medieval poets and the writers of the Generation of 1898 through their attempts to discover and define the Spanish soul. Thus, Machado and Unamuno, poets of this era, have little connection with Modernism, though Machado very briefly followed Darío's lead, and Juan Ramón Jiménez, the most attuned to Modernism of the three, abandoned it for a purer form of poetry.

1. *Salvador Rueda Santos* (1857–1933), a great poet who wrote too much bad poetry, was the most important name in the pre-Modernist period, and much of his poetry is purely Modernist in its poetic facility, sonority, polychromatics, versatility, and metrical renovations. He may have been the true creator of Spanish Modernism, since for a time in the last years of the nineteenth century he dominated Spanish poetry, and he introduced Darío to Madrid. Representing the Spanish version of what Darío brought to Spain, he influenced Villaespesa, Juan Ramón Jiménez, and perhaps even Darío. He published poetry as early as 1883, but his first important collection was *En tropel* (1892), with a prologue by Darío. Among his more than thirty collections are *Fuente de salud* (1906), *Lenguas de fuego* (1908), and *Cantando por ambos mundos* (1914). His *Antología Poética* appeared in 1962. Rueda experimented freely with metrical forms and musical rhythms. His boldness in this regard at times obscures his masterful use of Andalusian shadow and sunshine. He is a spontaneous poet of light, color, erotic imagery, a nature filled with plants and animals, and a special version of the Dance of Death.

Of great renown in his day because of his exuberance and lyrical passion that obscured the defects of his poetry, he was overpowered by Darío's genius, as was the Spanish poetic world of the time.

2. *Rubén Darío* (1867–1916), though he was a Nicaraguan, is included here because of his unique significance in Spanish poetry and because he gave form and definite meaning to Modernist poetry. In 1898 *La Nación,* a newspaper of Buenos Aires, sent him to Spain to report on conditions after Spain's defeat in the War of 1898. Adored by the younger poets, he influenced them all, though Machado and Jiménez only briefly. One reason some Spaniards reacted away from Darío was their feeling that although his poetry was exquisite and nearly perfect formally, it had little substance and was not concerned with life. When they first knew him, Darío created beautiful poetry, ornate and decorative. He loved elegant things and filled his poems with marble, lace, silk, gold, velvet, swans, palaces, and minuets. He was voluptuous and sensual in his poetry and to a certain extent in his private life.

His first important collection, *Azul* (1888), prose and poetry combined, was greeted by Juan Valera as "original en un sentido que nadie hasta entonces había tenido." *Prosas profanas* (1896), the peak of Modernist style, contains princesses, Parnassian imagery, and a search for beauty beyond beauty as well as a love of the exotic and refined expression. *Cantos de vida y esperanza* (1905), whose first poem, *Yo soy aquél,* rejects pyrotechnics for sincerity and profundity, abandons marble palaces, "the blue verse and profane songs." Among his many famous poems in this collection, *Canción de otoño en primavera* sings of the illusion of love and the passage of time, and *Lo fatal* of Existential anguish. Some of the other themes involve doubt and despair, Christian faith, and a love for Spain. Other works of note are *El canto errante* (1907), *Poema del otoño y otros poemas* (1910), and *Canto a la Argentina y otros poemas* (1910).

Darío's great contribution to Spanish poetry was the revolution he accomplished in meters, rhythms, and poetic techniques. He broke the bonds of traditional Spanish meters, in spite of their variety, changed the accent on the alexandrine, came very close to free verse, juggled the rhythms and stresses of his lines, varied the number of syllables, and exalted the evocative power of words. To this he added a musicality and rhythmic beats unheard up to that time in Spanish verse. Nor did he neglect the old Spanish masters as he invested the traditional Spanish meters of medieval days with his modern spirit.

Darío was a paradoxical man. He was timid and yet bold, Catholic and pagan, noble and abject. He treated of the artificial and the exotic and experimented with occult themes, but he also used themes of eternal human values and experienced an omnipresent death. He was melancholy, sensual, emotional, sentimental, passionate, musical, superstitious, hedonistic, and epicurean. Most critics viewed him only as a poet of beauty, but he also wrote, with metaphysical overtones, original and spiritually elevated poetry of the human condition.

3. *Antonio Machado y Ruiz* (1875–1939) was born in Seville. When his family moved to Madrid, he studied at the Institución Libre de Enseñanza, cradle of so many writers of the modern age. In 1907 he took a position in a secondary school in Soria, in Old Castile, where he fell in love and married. When his wife, Leonor, died in 1912, he was transferred to Baeza in Upper Andalusia, but he retained a genuine nostalgia for what had become his adopted homeland, Castile. Later, in Segovia, Pilar Valderrama, the Guiomar of his poetry, afforded him a source of happiness.

His important collections include *Soledades, galerías y otros poemas* (1907), an expansion of an earlier text, *Soledades* (1903). He deals with solitude, illusions, love, reverie, and childhood, as he searches for God through time, symbolized by the fountain or flowing water. He fuses inner and outer realities in a poetry reflecting a deep palpitation of the spirit. Though sober and unadorned, it is deeply felt, emotional poetry. His masterpiece, *Campos de Castilla* (1912), dealing lovingly but objectively with Castile, has been called "the poetic breviary of the Generation of '98." Augmented in a 1917 edition of *Poesías completas*, it sums up the spirit of the Generation of 1898 with its tragic appraisal of Castile. Machado combines historical realism with a constant idealism. On the one hand, he writes, "Castilla miserable, ayer dominadora, envuelta an sus andrajos, desprecia cuanto ignora," but, on the other, "Tras el vivir y el soñar, está lo que más importa: ¡despertar!" *Campos de Castilla* not only reflects the somber and barren landscape and Spanish lethargy but also includes a ballad, *La tierra de Alvargonzález*, inspired, Machado said, by the *pueblo*, about greed, patricide, and vengeance. The ballad is also filled with dream, mystery, and a brooding terror. *Campos de Castilla* reflects Machado's "palabra en el tiempo." Machado writes of nature and religion, and of a Spain that was great and may be again if he can rouse his countrymen from their complacency. Machado identified the states of his own soul with the sobriety, austerity, and expanse of the Castilian landscape and associated its moods with his own feelings. Everywhere one finds an air of mystery, melancholy, and solitude as he continues with an Existential preoccupation, symbolized by the road and the sea.

His third important collection, *Nuevas canciones* (1924), continues the style of *Campos de Castilla* but with added satiric notes and epigrams. This collection seems more sensual and colorful in its expansion of the series of proverbs and songs published in the 1917 edition of *Campos de Castilla*. Machado muses on popular tradition, dream and reality, as well as on the road from life to death.

Several other works should be mentioned. *Juan de Mairena, sentencias, donaires, apuntes y recuerdos de un profesor apócrifo* (1936) presents Mairena, the critic, Machado's alter ego, who, aside from irony and paradox, gives us Machado's self-description as "the poet of time." *Los complementarios,* notes and poetry written between 1912 and 1925, published in part later and then in a definitive edition in 1972, affords us insight into Machado's poetic creed, which stresses the intuitive and human over the Baroque and dehumanized. *La guerra* (1938) contains some of his last poems.

Machado, a simple and humble man, admired sincerity, honesty, and kindness. Although he mourned his wife, was traumatized by the Spanish Civil War, and longed for happier days, he maintained his solid moral values always. Mystery and clarity, gravity and irony, thought and emotion are all aspects of his sober and pure poetry. A telluric poet, whose description of the countryside was both spiritual and metaphysical to match his universal themes of God, dreams, time, and Existential despair, he explored the hidden secrets in the human soul. As he wrote of solitude, memory, time, and death, he yearned for immortality, but he could never achieve the faith for which he longed.

4. *Miguel de Unamuno y Jugo* (1864–1936) brought a very personal, highly lyrical, and poetic tone to literature. He was an essayist, dramatist, novelist, and poet. His reputation was made primarily in the field of the essay, but Unamuno the poet today ranks in stature with Antonio Machado. "Un poeta," said Unamuno, "es el que desnuda con el lenguaje rítmico su alma." His poetry cannot be classified as belonging completely to any

school. He wrote philosophical and religious poems, poetry of the Castilian landscapes, ballads, and sonnets. In many of his works he resembles Machado in his emphasis on passing time and his evocation of the countryside. The supreme poetic individual, he wrote abstract and intellectual poetry and also some that is human, warm, and personal. As with his prose works, his poetry contains many contradictions, but his basic concern is religion and the immortality of the soul.

His first collection, *Poesías de Miguel de Unamuno*, was published in 1907. It contains, together with philosophical and religious poetry, his famous *Salamanca*. Other volumes of his poetry are the pessimistic *Rosario de sonetos líricos* (1911); *Rimas de dentro* (1923); *De Fuerteventura a París* (1925), verse and prose mixed, which concentrated on the political, the island, and the sea; *Teresa* (1924), love poems; and the emotional *Romancero del destierro* (1928). Most critics consider his poetic masterpiece to be *El Cristo de Velázquez* (1920), inspired by the famous painting in the Museo del Prado. A symbolic poem in free verse, filled with mystical serenity, Baroque imagery, and with multiple Biblical citations, it offers a series of meditations on death and resurrection with Jesus as the guarantor of immortality. In depicting his own struggle to believe, Unamuno pictures an intensely personal Christ. The poem contains a series of arresting chiaroscuro elements.

In 1953 an edition of *Cancionero, diario poético,* a collection of poems written from 1928 on, was published, and an edition in a more definitive form was issued in 1984. Though he wrote on family, nature, love of the land and of country, Unamuno also focused on passing time, dreams, death, and his continuing thirst for immortality.

Unamuno, a disturbing, virile, and difficult poet, shakes the reader with his anguish. He sought answers to universal and fundamental questions about faith and human destiny. He refused to live resigned to any doctrine or dogma, and most of his poems reflect ambivalence and paradox. He rejected the refined verse of the Modernists, though he used imaginative innovations. He stressed the power of words and had much to say about definitions of poetry. Some refuse to grant him the resources of expression needed for great poetry and find his to be harsh, dry, and rough-hewn. Nonetheless, his poetry is far more musical than most critics have acknowledged, and it rarely fails to impress by its sincerity and sheer force, as a representation of the purest form of the Spanish spirit.

257

5. *Minor Modernist poets* include:

a) *Manuel Machado* (1874–1947), a poet and dramatist like his more famous brother, published his first important collection of poetry, *Alma,* in 1902. Melancholy and decadent, he provides elegant tributes to painting and experiments with various meters. He was influenced by the Parnassians, by Verlaine, and by Rubén Darío. Among his other poetic collections are *El mal poeta* (1909), perhaps his most original, which he himself labeled "detestable," though he writes of love, hope, and deception; *Ars moriendi* (1921), about the sensual pleasures of life and the equivalent seduction of death; and *Cadencia de cadencias* (1943). Manuel Machado wrote poetry that was pleasant to the ear, light, buoyant, graceful, and elegant. Touched by the Andalusian spirit, his poetry has an attractive freshness, simplicity, and popular flavor. He was the most skilled of the poets in his fusion of French Symbolism and Spanish popular forms. Beyond his Impressionism or occasional decadence, he also wrote sincere religious poetry as well as poems on art, history, Spain, love, and death.

b) *Francisco Villaespesa* (1877–1936), for some the real innovator of Spanish Modernism and the author of a hundred volumes, fifty of them poetry, was a good improviser. His is a poetry of musicality and dense adjectivization. Andalusian in origin and spirit, he wrote much on Moorish Spain, for example, *Los nocturnos del Generalife* (1915). Villaespesa, who defined literature as "exquisita enfermedad de vagos," filled his poetry with Moorish culture and the city of Granada, princesses, old castles, and Oriental melancholy. His earliest poetry was influenced by Salvador Rueda. His *La copa del Rey de Thule* (1900) was in its time more popular than the early works of Juan Ramón Jiménez. It stresses form and musicality and shows the influence of Verlaine. In later poetry Villaespesa wrote of more eternal themes such as love, time, and death. Among his other volumes of poetry are *Las canciones del camino* (1906), *El jardín de las quimeras* (1909), and *Torre de marfil* (1911). His *Poesías completas* appeared in 1955.

c) *Eduardo Marquina* (1879–1946), a dramatist like Villaespesa, wrote some declamatory odes, published as *Odas* (1900). *Eglogas* (1902) pleads for universal love for all created things. *Vendimión* (1909) reveals the poet's love of nature, and *Canciones del momento* (1910), his political and social ideas. Excessively rhetorical at times, he is sincere in his attempt to re-create the spirit of the past and to use it to form a new future.

d) *Ramón del Valle-Inclán* (1866–1936), a novelist and essayist, wrote three volumes of lyric poetry, *Aromas de leyenda* (1907), *La pipa de kif* (1919), and *El pasajero* (1920). The first volume, in song and ballads, evokes the Galician countryside and its people's dreams, religion, traditions, and legends. The second volume, his best known, has beautiful descriptions and is filled with color, though it is melodramatic, ironic, and grotesque. It reflects the author's *esperpento* period. In *El pasajero*, Valle-Inclán uses more autobiographical elements. His Baroque and symbolic imagery involves the beautiful rose but also inevitable death. This collection also reflects some of the violence of his *esperpento* phase. Only his first collection can be called Modernist, though all his poetry is musical, and he employs some Modernist techniques such as synesthesia.

C. Transitional Poets

Between Modernism and the Generation of 1927, a number of transitional poets, especially Juan Ramón Jiménez, accepted Modernism for a time but also anticipated the poetry of the succeeding generation.

1. *Enrique Diez-Canedo* (1879–1944), primarily known as a literary critic, produced numerous translations of Italian, French, English, and German works. He personified culture, good taste, and exquisite sensibility, and while he was famous as a theater critic, he was also one of the best analysts of Modernist poetry. Diez-Canedo stressed the correspondence of history and art.

Diez-Canedo's early poetry was influenced by the French Symbolists, Juan Ramón Jiménez, and especially Rubén Darío. His *Versos de las horas* (1906) contains the inevitable swans of Modernism, but even this early work reveals a sobriety and force not common to Modernist poetry. In other volumes, human and democratic, he wrote about commonplace things such as clocks, dogs, or an old chair. In *La visita del sol* (1907), *La sombra del ensueño* (1910), *Algunos versos* (1924), and other poetry, Diez-Canedo writes on a variety of themes, both stressing and rejecting the traditional. One finds in his poetry reminiscences of Machado's passing time, melancholy, and preoccupation with death. In other poetry Diez-Canedo displays the more intimate style of Juan Ramón Jiménez. His last collection of poetry, *Jardinillos de navidad y año nuevo*, was published in 1944.

2. *Ramón Pérez de Ayala* (1880–1962) was primarily famous as a novelist, though he also wrote perceptive essays. His first col-

259

lection of poetry, *La paz del sendero* (1903), deals with childhood memories, the passage of time, and a desire for inner tranquility and is filled with a sensual melancholy and a feeling for the beauty of the universe. *El sendero innumerable* (1916), which according to Salvador de Madariaga contains some of the most moving poetry of the twentieth century, concentrates on the sea, symbolic of life and death. His final volume of poetry, *El sendero andante* (1921), again concentrates on passing time and symbolizes life as a flowing river. Rubén Darío and Unamuno influenced him, and it may be said that his first poetry reflects Modernist ideas, though he differs in his intellectual emphasis and his desire to make his poetry meaningful as well as beautiful. Although his poetry is filled with taste and colors, it also stresses man's path through life.

3. *Juan Ramón Jiménez* (1881–1958), like Antonio Machado one of the major poetic voices of the twentieth century, wrote more than forty volumes of poetry. His work shows the difficulty of trying to classify poets by generations. Although his early poetry was Modernist, his later work directly influenced the poets of the following generation. During the Spanish Civil War he left Spain for America. He won the Nobel Prize for Literature in 1956.

Active in the early Modernist revolution, Jiménez fell under Rubén Darío's spell, but he soon evolved away from the sonorities of the Darian manner toward his own "interior music." Nonetheless, the evolutionary process for Jiménez was never complete, and he kept purifying his techniques and refining his poetry to achieve an absolute beauty and purity and to express his interior reality. As he said, "Un poema no se acaba, sino se abandona . . . Yo me paso la vida reviviendo, poetizando."

From the beginning the poet expressed his belief that poetic form and ideas had to be vague and intangible in an effort to discover the essence of poetry. His first works, *Almas de violeta* and *Ninfeas,* both of 1900, are filled with fleeting expressions of nature, melancholy, and lyrical beauty together with a continuing experimentation. *Rimas* (1902), whose title indicates Bécquer's influence, shared the delicacy, melancholy, and intimacy of the works of that nineteenth-century poet. This collection, aside from its search for beauty, also involves a preoccupation with death and a struggle between the flesh and the spirit. *Arias tristes* (1903), musical, subtle, and melancholy, expresses the anguish of the poet who seeks the spiritual significance of life and nature. Other early collections, such as *Jardines lejanos* (1904), are musical and mysterious, but the more Baroque productions after about 1912 emphasized also the sensual and a continuing preoccupation with death. *Platero y yo* (1914), prose poems, symbolize purity and innocence, joy and delicacy, as the poet immortalizes Moguer, his hometown—its children and landscape—in his discussion of the life and death of his little donkey, Platero.

His total break with Modernist tendencies can be seen in the free verse of *Diario de un poeta recién casado* (1917), a record of his wedding trip away from and back to Spain. Jiménez revised this volume and republished it as *Diario de poeta y mar* in 1948 and in a definitive edition in 1955. Aside from a view of the poet's soul enmeshed in love and the sea, the volume also contains daring imagery. *Eternidades* (1918) is less colorful and musical. *Piedra y cielo* (1919) treats of love, dream, memory, and reality in a new way. *Poesía* (1923) abandons the sentimental and pictorial for the pure and a conceptualization of inner soul states. *Belleza* (1923) reflects a growing subjectivity and a continuation of a more elemental, simpler, and naked poetry. These volumes from 1918 on all explore the poetic process and the attempt to verbalize the ineffable.

Various anthologies reveal the total poet from his early Symbolism to his role as "the mystic of nature" and its pantheistic evocation. Jiménez himself divided his poetry into three periods, "ecstasy of love" to 1909, "avidity for eternity" to 1921, and "search for inner consciousness" after 1921. In *La estación total,* composed between 1923 and 1936 but not published until 1946, Jiménez fuses his intimate soul states with an exterior beauty that he now possesses more fully. In 1949 he published *Animal de fondo,* about his belief in a universal consciousness, and he again sings of joy and mystical union. This collection appears later in *Tercera antología poética* (1957) as the first part of *Dios deseado y deseante,* perhaps his most profound poetry. The poet engages in a dialogue with God, a loving consciousness, and attempts symbolically to approximate the absolute. Reprinted in 1964, it marks with *Poesías últimas escogidas* (1982) the major metaphysical and moral preoccupations of the poet's last years, as he acknowledges man, nature's changing character, the passing of time, eternity, and an apprehension of God through emotion. Other collections that have appeared posthumously are *Leyenda* (1978) and *Tiempo. Espacio* (1986).

Jiménez, concerned with somehow expressing an unutterable experience, created gossamerlike poetry of delicate shades, filled with color, flowers, and representatives of the natural world. A master of chiaroscuro, in melancholy fashion he also treats of tragedy, solitude, and suffering. Beauty and purity and a zeal for perfection and a perfect love describe the poetry of this ineffable poet who longed for eternity and wrote of the transcendental connection between love and death, God and light. Since Jiménez' poetic images were often an extension of himself and not related to external circumstances, he transmitted his search for a newer, purer mode of expression and the poetic essence to the next generation. Indeed, in his later poetry he explored the creative process itself in a manner that anticipates not only the next generation but also those beyond.

4. *León Felipe Camino y Galicia* (1884–1968), a man of many professions, like Valle-Inclán led a life of legend and mystery. A restless spirit, disillusioned by the Spanish Civil War, he went abroad to continue his career, primarily in Mexico. *Versos y oraciones del caminante* (1920), his first volume of poetry, avoids the intellectual to concentrate on the moral and religious, often in mystical tones. He is more concerned with what he can say about life than the form his poem takes. His early poetry sometimes has a nostalgic and almost painful tone. At other times it is ironic. Although his poetry is almost unique, one can see overtones of Unamuno, Machado, Cervantes, and the Bible. At times his poetry resembles that of Walt Whitman, whose poems he translated. In 1929 he published *Versos y oraciones del caminante, Libro II*. Other volumes are *Drop a Star* (1933), which marked the end of acceptance and the beginning of poetic protest; *La insignia* (1937); *El payaso de las bofetadas y el pescador de caña* (1938), another tragic poem about the Spanish Civil War; *El hacha* (1939); *Español del éxodo y del llanto* (1939), about Spain and humanity; *El gran responsable* (1940), in which he stresses the poet's political, moral, and ethical responsibility to man and society and sees the poet, bishop, and politician as the symbolic figures of modern society; *Llamadme publicano* (1950), a metaphorical vision in which a symbolic wind impels Felipe to leave Spain; *El ciervo y otros poemas* (1958), about purity, innocence, and love defeated by the world's evil and a tired poet lamenting to a deaf God and waiting for death and purification by fire and wind; *Oh, este viejo y roto violín* (1965), an updated version of *Antología rota* (1947), which renews the broken poetic song and verse written by the wind as the poet comments on old age, life, time, and death; *Rocinante* (1969), about alienation from Spain, the pas-

sage of time, Guernica, and a sleepless poet; and *Puesto ya el pie en el estribo* (1983), which despairingly reflects his Existential pessimism.

León Felipe emphasizes the social and human aspects of the Christian message over salvation. He suffers for a humanity abandoned by God in a world sorely needing the idealism of don Quijote and Jesus. A human poet, he depicts human sorrows and society's evils, but he also deals with dreams, reality, time, and history. His later works are belligerent, almost declamatory, but filled with both epic and lyric force, as the poet views a dead and deserted Spain. He is a severe poet who matches his bare words with what he hopes is a naked rhythm, though some of his poetry has Surrealistic overtones. A spiritual child of the Generation of 1898, he also anticipated the Generation of 1927.

5. *José Moreno Villa* (1887–1955) in his autobiography, *Vida en claro* (1944), cites the importance of his sojourn in Germany together with his Andalusian roots. In Spain he published several studies on the history of art and Spanish painting—he himself was a painter—and he lived in exile in Mexico from 1937 on. In his early poetry Moreno Villa reflects both Modernism and the Generation of 1898. In a second phase he might well be considered a member of the Generation of 1927.

Garba (1913), a book of poetry filled with amorous tensions, recalls the poetry of Unamuno and Machado while the gypsies and Andalusian scenes foreshadow Lorca's themes. In 1914 *El pasajero*, which includes historical themes, elicited from Ortega y Gasset the opinion that Moreno Villa was one of those "que traen un nuevo estilo, que son un estilo." Although it contains elements of poetic anguish and spiritual searching, it is essentially "dehumanized" poetry. *Luchas de pena y alegría* (1915), a mixture of prose and verse, and *Evoluciones* (1918) mark the end of his first period. In 1929 he published *Jacinta, la pelirroja*, based on an affair the poet had with the lady of the title. In this volume, illustrated with his own drawings, she becomes the center of his reality. The collection, a poetry of experience and one of the best Spanish examples of erotic poetry, is also Surrealistic. *Carambas* (1931), Impressionistic and Cubist, reflects the dissolution of old literary forms. In *Salón sin muros* (1936), the poet seeks the essence of things and an internal reality and recapitulates his life and literary styles. His poetry from Mexico, *Puerta severa* (1941) and *La noche del verbo* (1942), is filled with human and religious themes and an acknowledgment of passing time.

Voz en vuelo a su cuna (1961) reveals his anguish, solitude, and nostalgia, but at the same time a stoic recognition of his life as an exile.

Moreno Villa, as a transitional poet, partakes both of Modernism and later "isms." He wrote under popular inspiration as well as artistic and cultural influences. His poetry, in part, is intellectual and Surrealistic, but it is also sad, human, and moving. In his later poetry he stressed more a metaphysical anguish and a preoccupation with the beyond.

6. *Other transitional poets* include Enrique de Mesa (1879–1929), Emilio Carrère (1880–1947), Fernando Villalón (1881–1930), Evaristo Carriego (1883–1912), Tomás Morales (1885–1921), and Ramón de Basterra (1887–1928).

D. The Generation of 1927

The poets of this generation were born between 1891 and 1905. As already noted, to a greater or lesser extent they used *ultraísmo* and *creacionismo,* Surrealism, and the Freudian world of dreams and unconscious associations. Some practiced a Neobaroque revival of Góngora to celebrate the three hundredth anniversary of his death. Nonetheless, each poet defined poetry in his own way, whatever the unusual imagery, metaphorical ambiguities, exuberant happiness, or destroyed illusions. After their intellectual, formalistic, and aesthetic poetry of exterior perfection ran its course, these poets demonstrated also a passionate concern for the passage of time and the problems of love, life, and death. Far from rebelling against previous generations, they were indebted in many ways to their poetic elders. They differed among themselves, the intuitive irregular meters of Salinas contrasting with the precise arrangements of Guillén, the primary proponent of pure poetry in the Generation of 1927. Alberti and Lorca, more instinctive and imaginative, fused popular and cultural elements and with others like Cernuda attempted Surrealistic experimentation to match Gerardo Diego's continuing interest in *ultraísmo.* Lorca's passionate human poetry, popular spirit, and unique imagery transcended the formal preoccupations of the group, which in its second phase anticipated and blended with the Neoromanticism and humanization of the next generation. As a whole, the Generation of 1927 emphasized metaphor as primary in the search for artistic perfection and beauty and promoted both the national and the cosmopolitan.

1. *Pedro Salinas* (1891–1951) was a guiding light for younger

poets like Luis Cernuda, one of his students. Salinas wrote poetry, dramas, novels, short stories, and essays and edited many classic literary works. He was one of the most perceptive literary critics of his generation. His novel, *La bomba increíble* (1951), stresses his belief in love as the hope for a grossly materialistic and destructive world. Love, as a matter of fact, is the unifying theme in his poetry, and the poet seeks its essence behind apparent reality. Salinas, influenced by Juan Ramón Jiménez, soon developed his own style. His poetry, often subtle and intellectual, was more spiritual than that of Jiménez. He chose his words very carefully to convey their conceptual values. Especially concerned with the interior reality of the poet, Salinas characterized his poetry as "una aventura hacia lo absoluto."

Presagios (1923), his first volume of poetry, meditates on nature. Although some of the poems are Baroque and intellectual, the dominant note is that of love and dominance of interior reality over reality itself. *Presagios* emphasizes the joy of youth and reflects an ongoing intellectual irony. *Seguro azar* (1929), seeking the truth behind the truth, tests the exterior reality Salinas denied in his first volume as he explores the lights, the beaches, the movies, and the Far West. He struggles for faith in the future and, as he plays with words and concepts, implies that art is a game. *Fábula y signo* (1931) contrasts the poetic reality (*fábula*) with ordinary certainty (*signo*). In his masterpiece, *La voz a ti debida* (1933), the first volume of a poetic trilogy, the poet falls in love with love itself. Reacting against the tangible world that loses its meaning, he seeks the mysterious and the ineffable. The poems muse on the genesis of love, the beloved one's reality, the search for that reality, and the struggle against the void. As he praises his beloved and wonders at her beauty, Salinas seems at times mystical, at others sensual, and at still others a platonic idealist. Salinas, existing outside time and space, sees love as both a metaphysical and a human reality. A paean to his beloved and a half-glimpsed paradise of perfect love, maintained largely through memory, *La voz a ti debida* reveals the poet's attempt, through love's power, to construct a stable inner reality. *Razón de amor* (1936), the second part, finds that the world is one of anguish and little joy and that the invisible reality the poet seeks may be only a magical dream world. Yet love is creative and offers salvation and a temporal feeling of eternity. The third volume, *Largo lamento*, published posthumously as part of Salinas' complete works in various editions from 1971 on, contains poems written before 1938 and continues his dream of love in both its carnal and spiritual aspects and implies hope in spite of a continuing repressed pain.

El contemplado (1946) is a colloquy with the sea of Puerto Rico that he loves and that fascinates him. Almost mystical in tone, it reveals the poet's fusion with nature, a recognition of nature's creativity, and a vision of the perfect sea as part of the permanent beauty of the cosmos. *Todo más claro* (1949), the most anguished of his works, concerns the horrors of twentieth-century materialism and the senseless and frenetic activity that leads only to nothingness and oblivion. The poet fears the potential of total destruction of all the works of man by the atom bomb, but at the same time he seeks the Divine Presence as a counterweight to destructive technology. Furthermore, poetry, a clarity in the darkness, may help man in a loveless world as he seeks through ruins "for the rubble of time undone." *Confianza* (1955) shows more faith in life and the world. *Vivir en los pronombres* (1974), whose title comes from *La voz a ti debida,* is an anthology of his love poems.

Although Salinas was a refined, subtle, cultured, and intelligent poet whose search for a hidden reality implied a rejection of human elements, he was sincere in his evocation of love, and his yearnings, often anguished and feverish, are those of humanity. For him poetry meant liberty and discovery, regardless of his multiple labels as Neoplatonic, Mystical, pantheistic, or metaphysical. He played with the concepts of inner and outer reality, light and darkness, pursuing the meaning of reality in a modern materialistic world.

2. *Jorge Guillén* (1893–1984) reveals many influences in his work, among them Valéry in his conceptual abstractions and Góngora in his complex intellectual metaphors. His name is also closely associated with the term *pure poetry,* although he acknowledged the impossibility of completely attaining it. Like Juan Ramón Jiménez, Guillén constantly polished, corrected, and changed his poetry in order to achieve perfect control over a variety of meters. To some his poetry seemed intellectual and impersonal, although his austerity was deceptive. From Bécquer he learned about simplicity as well as the use of dream and reverie. His Classical forms are enlivened by his tremendous mastery of words, his harmonious and beautiful imagery, his metaphors and stylistic devices. He utilized abstract imagery, but he attempted to make his abstractions concrete images that moved and lived in his conversion of reality into poetry.

The work *Cántico,* which Salinas called "unique . . . in significance and transcendence," was published in various editions between 1928 and 1950, with each new edition augmented and with later additions including colloquial language, human themes, and ethical concerns. The central theme, that life is the supreme happiness, reflects Guillén's joy in his experience of daily reality as he glorifies the light, the dawn, and the wonder of life in a harmonious universe where external and internal reality become one. Life was an affirmation of being for the poet, and existence the greatest pleasure. Guillén eternalized his momentary experiences and joy of being.

Clamor, subtitled *Tiempo de historia,* allowed the noise of the world to enter, decrying through multiple speakers its materialism, destruction, and death. *Clamor* continued to deal with life, harmony, time, and creation. The first of the collection's three volumes, *Maremagnum* (1957), confronted the noise and confusion, the insecurity and terror, of a corrosive and deforming world. The second, *Que van a dar a la mar* (1960), whose title came from Jorge Manrique, and the third, *A la altura de las circunstancias* (1963), taken from Antonio Machado, viewed life and love in a more temporal fashion. Historical events such as the Spanish Civil War and conditions involving a world of ever-present death and a future destined to succumb to time's onslaught made the poet realize that the clamor of the world could not be shut out.

In 1968 *Aire nuestro,* a trilogy including not only *Cántico* and *Clamor* but also *Homenaje* (1967), appeared. *Homenaje* explored the themes of the previous volumes but in a new way, including testimonies from and homages to fellow poets, verse portraits, imitations, and philosophical meditations. In 1973 *Y otros poemas,* published in a slightly different version in 1979, alternated between optimism and despair as it dealt with life and death. It also commented on the nature of poetry itself. *Final* (1981) became a part of the complete *Aire nuestro.* In Guillén's later poems, he includes a variety of themes—the Bible, love, death, alienation and harmony, good and evil, violence and peace, Existential hope, and the contradictions explicit in existence. In a continuing attempt to create order out of absurdity, the poet wrote on time and history, changes in nature, youth, old age, death, and eternity.

3. *Gerardo Diego* (1896–1987), like so many of his contemporaries, showed an interest in more than one art form. In his case music was a factor in his poetry. Diego was the poet of his generation most directly connected with *creacionismo* and *ultraísmo,*

and he was active in the editing and critical aspects of poetic creation of the times, becoming especially well known for his series of poetic anthologies. In his poetry one can find aspects of many poetic schools, including a duality of the cultured and the simple, pure poetry, and human poetry.

If one includes his anthologies, Diego produced approximately fifty collections of poetry. Among his works of the 1920s, *Romancero de la novia* (1920), reprinted in 1943, conveyed the impression of youthful delicacy and tenderness. *Imagen* (1922), with peculiar typographical arrangements and twisted syntax, together with *Manual de espumas* (1924) and *Limbo* (1951), represent his *ultraísta* and *creacionista* phase, though many other collections contain such elements. *Soria* (1923), augmented in 1948 and again in 1980 as *Soria sucedida,* combines the chromatic with the luminous in its treatment of memories, impressions of the Castilian countryside, real and imagined, and meditations in the later edition on old age, memories of youth, friendship, and a city that was and is. *Manual de espumas* contains musical, auditive, and visual imagery as well as daring and Cubist metaphors. It treats of love and dreams. *Versos humanos* (1925), more traditional and human, won for Diego a share of the National Prize for Literature. He combines a kind of intellectual humor with the anecdotal and autobiographical. Indeed, in most of his early poetry and to an extent even in later works, Diego combines the illogical with the permanent, the irrational with the traditional and popular.

In the following decades Diego wrote many kinds of poetry. *Vía crucis* (1931) is his first serious attempt at religious poetry. *Fábula de Equis y Zeda* (1932) uses Neobaroque games and tricks. *Angeles de Compostela* (1940), republished in more complete form in 1960 and again, together with *Vuelta del peregrino,* in 1976, may be his most ambitious collection of religious poetry. It involves dogma and theological concepts such as the resurrection of the flesh but also exhibits an occasional magical quality. His most popular collection may well be *Alondra de verdad* (1941), containing sonnets filled with emotion and musicality that deal with love, religion, a trip to the Philippine Islands, and a series of musicians. Still other collections are *Biografía incompleta* (1953 and 1967); *Paisaje con figuras* (1956), which won the National Prize for Literature; *La suerte o la muerte* (1963), containing aesthetic evocations of bullfighting, one of the poet's favorite topics; *Versos divinos* (1971), announced as early as 1925, recalling passing time and Biblical themes; *Cementerio civil* (1972), about dreams, old age, religion, and death; and *Carmen jubilar* (1975), about bullfighting, passing time, and the poet's life.

Gerardo Diego was one of the most versatile poets of his generation. There was an apparent dichotomy in his works. Some were complicated and filled with irrational imagery. Others revealed his continuing love for the traditional as well as the new, though he never abandoned the idea of art as a unifying principle. He deals with cities like Santander and Soria, the countryside, Spain, bullfighting, love, longevity, friendship, death, and, as an orthodox Catholic, religion. To the end his poetry revealed an enormous thematic and stylistic variety.

4. *Federico García Lorca* (1898–1936), probably the purest Spanish lyrical voice since Lope de Vega, was also a painter and musician, and one finds influences of both arts in his writings. In Lorca's poetry we are never sure of reality. He presents us with a double view of two realities, for example, the moon in the sky and its reflection in the water. In his poetry we find melancholy, silence, earth, and lonely cities full of old coaches lost in the night or towers from which Death watches the approach of a lonely horseman. Aside from a religious note and the eternal themes of sex, life, blood, and death, his work contains real human beings, but they are humans with dark stains—the gypsy, the Arab, peasants and noblemen, religious and pagan—driven by love, sex, frustration, violence, and beauty. His poetic world is full of subtle shades, presentiments, and melancholy at the passing of the human hour. Lorca used the ballad and traditional poetry of Spain, but he also wrote odes and elegies and used many other meters and new stylistic devices. Harmony and counterpoint and the folk rhythm of his native Andalusia, too, were notes in his poetry.

Libro de poemas (1921), filled with tenderness and youthfulness, treats of nature symbols, dream, frustrated love, innocence lost, and death, as well as Lorca's religious doubts. At times he uses the dialogue form in the style of the Middle Ages. The poet can be both sentimental and metaphysical as he contrasts youthful innocence with an adult imagination. *Canciones* (1927) contains songs for children, sensual poetry, and popular, musical, and naïve verses, as he evokes his native city, thinks of death and sex in both ironically playful and profound tones, and unveils the dramatic note so obvious in his masterpiece, *Romancero gitano* (1928), one of the most influential texts in the development of Spanish poetry. Lorca used the gypsy as a symbol of Spanish life in *Romancero gitano,* but as with his other poetry the principal preoccupations are death, sex, blood, pride, and religion. We see sequined saints and brutal Civil Guards. We suffer "black pain" along with Soledad Montoya, feel Preciosa's terror, and sympathize with the gypsy nun's solitude. Each little poem seems almost a dramatic scene with dialogue, characterization, conflict, and tension. This collection is full of beautiful images, colors, folklore, and varied symbolism. Among Lorca's striking images are "The picks of the roosters dig looking for dawn"; "When he bows his head on his chest of jasper, the night looks for a plain to kneel and worship"; "When all the roof-tops are nothing but furrows on the earth, dawn shrugs her shoulders in a vast profile of stone." Lorca used Arabic-Andalusian folklore material, other historical Spanish cultural concepts, fantasy, mystery, rhythm, color, and an intense personal emotion that makes this poetry the highest of its type. Also in 1928 two of his odes appeared. *Oda a Salvador Dalí* reveals Lorca's understanding of an intellectual consciousness and new dehumanized art forms in its examination of a world in crisis. *Oda al Santísimo Sacramento* invokes God and hopes for the poet's troubled soul.

In 1929 Lorca, who had been undergoing a deep emotional, spiritual, and mental crisis, spent some time in New York and in Vermont. From his experience there came the *Poeta en Nueva York,* not published until 1940 though written in 1929 and 1930. Polemics have arisen over the authenticity of different editions. Adapting certain aspects of Surrealism, Lorca used new metaphors and symbols reflecting his personal anguish, emptiness, and pain as he wrote of abandoned children, sleepless men, and unhappy black people, victims and yet projecting a primitive innocence of original man. Lorca spent some time with farmers and other ordinary people and knew them on their peaceful earth. On the other hand, he found New York to be that "babilónica, cruel y violenta ciudad." Lorca attempted to recover the original love and truth of his poetic voice temporarily lost in the horrors of civilization. As he viewed the mysterious forces driving human beings, he attempted to find a spiritual tranquility that the dehumanized city dweller lacked. This struggle between civilization and nature is a central thesis of this collection. Although an occasional lyrical note of peaceful, sleeping clouds intrudes over his earth populated with all manner of plants and animals who suffer and die, all too often the "saliva swords" of the grass reflect the death that awaits. Lorca understood and sympathized with the miseries of the *pueblo,* prisoners in the "river of oil," but the social message seems incidental to his work.

In 1931 Lorca published *Poema del cante jondo,* poem of the deep song, full of graceful rhythms and the essence of Andalusian folklore. Although he continued an ancient tradition, he expressed his own poetic and telluric themes as a reflection of his Andalusian soul. Inexorable death waits while the gypsies sing to guitar accompaniment, and the image of the Virgin and Christ pass by in the Holy Week celebration.

Llanto por Ignacio Sánchez Mejías (1935), the greatest elegy in modern Spanish literature, laments the death of Lorca's friend, a famous bullfighter killed in the bull ring in 1934. In the four parts Lorca goes from the specific death of his friend to its meaning and fatality in general. Death, as usual, is accompanied by blood that the poet does not wish to see as it flows upon the sand.

Other Lorca poetry includes *Seis poemas galegos* (1935), and *Diván del Tamarit* (1940), published in a partial edition in 1936, imitating Arabic *qasidas* and *gacelas,* short rhymed fixed verses focusing on death and sensual love. Posthumous publications continue to appear, among them eleven sonnets in 1984, reflecting sacrifice, life, death, and a loving mysticism and resembling the Classical notes of the Generation of 1936. The latest edition of his *Obras completas* appeared in 1986.

García Lorca wrote complex poetry involving solitude, tenderness, and agonies of the spirit. His primitive and childlike directness contrasts with a strange sophistication, and the poet also manages to create a delicate balance between the traditional and the modern. His popular rhythms, his rich metaphors, his strong emotions, his Arabic-Andalusian heritage, and his unique magical use of words have earned him a place as one of the truly great Spanish poets of all time.

5. *Vicente Aleixandre* (1898–1984) won the Nobel Prize for Literature in 1977. A long illness and his discovery of Freud and to a degree Surrealistic poetry influenced some of his work, although it may be argued that his poetry is more irrational than Surrealistic, a label Aleixandre himself did not always accept. His is a poetry of many labels, among them Existential, Mystical, pantheistic, and Neoromantic. *Eros* and *thanatos,* in opposition and fusion, serve as one of his major leitmotivs together with human and cosmic love. In earlier works man took a subordinate role to the mineral and vegetable kingdoms, but later works stress the spiritual heritage of mankind. Even so, Aleixandre always had a unitary vision of the universe.

Ambito (1928), almost Classical re-creations filled with transitions between night and day and a continuous chiaroscuro involving the archetypal sea, love, and nature, sets the stage for the battle between *eros* and *thanatos*. Aleixandre attempts to overcome exterior and self-imposed limits and a repressed sexuality and despair to achieve an affirmation of light, love, and life. The prose poems of *Pasión de la tierra*, written in 1928–1929 but not published until 1946, portray light and shadow, the conscious and subconscious, as the poet discovers that love cannot ensure his escape from destiny. This collection is Aleixandre's closest approach to Surrealism in its subconscious associations, dream sequences, incoherence, and Freudian implications involving death and sexuality. *Espadas como labios* (1932), again about life, death, and love, contrasts erotic lips and deadly swords as the poet struggles against Existential limitations and, in an erotic interplay with death, strives for light over darkness and the possibility of cosmic fusion.

Aleixandre's masterpiece, *La destrucción o el amor* (1935), which won the National Prize for Literature, concentrates, in a continuing ambiguity, on the relationship between man and the elemental forces of nature, a world of mystery and darkness, constantly evolving, a universe of unchained telluric forces in which death and love are synonymous. The poetry, filled with an almost mystical pantheism, portrays a cosmos of nature destroyed and reborn. The poet, seeking an eternal communion, longs for a final, total love, as death becomes transfigured into love itself.

Other works continue his cosmic, personal, and human themes. *Mundo a solas,* written in 1934 but not published until 1950, portrays a virginal world of light and purity (yet erotic and physical), in opposition to one of darkness and destruction. *Sombra del paraíso* (1944), for some critics his finest collection, reveals contemporary man's view of cosmic harmony and destruction. Aleixandre portrays a prehuman world of dawn, light, innocence, and serenity, though purity implies also a less-innocent reality, and personal loss. Paradise, seen by the poet only in shadowy outline, is a world from which man, expelled, can experience impending death but also the hope of a possible spiritual redemption. *Nacimiento último* (1953) is again a contrast between life and death and human fatality as a final birth. *Historia del corazón* (1954), temporal and Existential, shows us history reflected in the individual and the importance of human solidarity. *En un vasto dominio* (1962) recalls youth and the passage of time in a universe where man and nature join as parts of a larger integrated totality.

Aleixandre's final two collections, a summation of previous works and dealing with time, death, and memory, are *Poemas de la consumación* (1968) and *Diálogos del conocimiento* (1974). In the first volume the poet acknowledges the ravages of time and examines the interrelationship of wisdom and knowledge, life and death, youth and old age, as old men wait for death but dream of life and love. In the second volume we have a confrontational series of dialogues contrasting the reflective and sensual, the old and the young. One speaks always of hope and struggle, the other of fatality and renunciation. Here the poet combines Existential awareness, transcendental intuition, and the eternity of the moment to create a unity of perception that, nonetheless, shows the multiplicity of the universe. In 1987 *Nuevos poemas varios* completed the publication of Aleixandre's works. His latest poems concentrate on a metaphysical preoccupation with life and destiny, what one critic calls a trajectory of "communion, communication, and knowledge."

Throughout his poetry one sees confrontation between light and darkness, life and death. It is a biological poetry of breasts and lips, of a nature of sea, sun, and moon, of cosmic forces and cosmic love. In the final instance the poet shows us a universe of devastating beauty and human illumination, a universe of light and hope. The Apollonian and Dionysian, good and evil, light and darkness, life and death, become part of man's metaphysical union with nature. Although love serves as a metaphor for self-destruction, Aleixandre writes also of the moral and psychological aspects of humanity in a unitary universe.

6. *Rafael Alberti* (b. 1902) has been publishing poetry for over sixty years. Born near Cádiz, he has incorporated the sea as an important part of his poetry. He left Spain in 1939 and did not return until 1977. Alberti wrote, in addition to his poetry, a number of dramas. He has at one time or another utilized all the twentieth-century movements—Surrealism, *ultraísmo*, Neogongorism, pure poetry, and popular poetry, which often depends on *culto* sources. His poetry can be cold, polished, frothy, emotional, fiery, or passionate.

His first famous work, *Marinero en tierra* (1925), shared the National Prize for Literature with Gerardo Diego's *Versos humanos*. These appealing poems, musical, tender, and poignant, reveal a poet who yearns for the far-off adventure of the imagi-

273

nation. The pictorial imagery recalls the sea and the poet's nostalgia for it as a prisoner of the land. The sea, symbolizing past innocence, freedom, and a magical world, helps the poet rediscover the boy who wanted to be a sailor, though he soon realizes that the sailor suit has been locked away forever. Written mainly in *canción* form, the collection portrays a paradise lost and yet paradoxically conveys the land as a projection of the sea.

Among other works of the 1920s, aside from his masterpiece, *Sobre los ángeles* (1929), one should mention *El alba del alhelí* (1927), short poems on a variety of themes, including the bullfight, usually light and playful in tone but also with a suggestion of melancholy and dark shadows; and *Cal y canto* (1929), a Neobaroque exercise filled with erotic vocabulary of unreal beauty, whose hermetic form cannot hide the anguished poet's search for love and order.

Sobre los ángeles, more abstract and profound, provides us with a Surrealistic treatment of angels, bad, vengeful, ugly, angry, and cruel, exiled from their heavenly abode, much as the poet had lost his paradise and innocence, leading an anguished existence amid the ruins of his life, desiring salvation but finding only desolation and despair that ultimately give way to a determination to make the most of his life. Deeply personal, the poem, through the angels, represents his emotions and passions, and the work, in spite of its incoherence, conveys mystical feelings as well as an almost apocalyptic vision of Existential mortality. In the conflict between light and darkness one can see the contrast between the natural world and a dehumanized society.

In the 1930s Alberti wrote a great number of works, including political and revolutionary poetry, some of it quite agitated and doctrinaire. Representative of his half-dozen volumes of such poetry is *El poeta en la calle,* originally written between 1931 and 1936 but expanded in a series of editions, the last of which appeared in 1978. Alberti also published *Verte y no verte* (1935), an elegy to Ignacio Sánchez Mejías, which lacks the immediacy of Lorca's poem but echoes its anguished theme.

In America after 1939 he was unable to forget Spain. In *Entre el clavel y la espada* (1941), the sword represents death and struggle in Spain through the mythical bull and bloody soldier, while the carnation, the poetic imagination of love, represents liberty, life, and hope for the future. Other collections in America include *Pleamar* (1944), a song of Argentina and the sea and a comparison of the actual landscape with a remembered one of his youth; *A la pintura* (1945), expanded in later editions, which speaks of elements of painting, praises many painters, including Picasso, and their exaltation of form; and *Retornos de lo vivo lejano* (1952), involving a recollection of a personal past and nostalgia for Spain, as the poet recalls childhood, music, love, and friendships and expresses the longing of an exile for his homeland.

Other volumes of his poetry include *Roma, peligro para caminantes* (1968), which contrasts ancient grandeur and modern debris, the past and the present, and reaffirms a bitter exile; *Canciones del alto valle del Aniene* (1972), about passing time, Picasso and fellow artists, and a reprise of previous poetry along with some prose meditations; *Fustigada luz* (1980), an affirmation of hope in a world of violence and darkness; *Versos sueltos de cada día* (1982), a kind of poetic diary expressing sadness and solitude; *Todo el mar* (1985), a compendium of poems on the sea, symbolic both of a joyous youth and an approaching death; and *Los hijos del drago y otros poemas* (1986). Alberti's *Obras completas* appeared in 1988.

Alberti, a master of poetic technique and form, has written poems of great verbal beauty and striking imagery. He represents a combination of intellect and emotion, the lyrical and the contemplative, reality and illusion, in a complex world of innocence and Existential longing.

7. *Luis Cernuda* (1902–1963), expatriated in 1938 as a result of the Spanish Civil War, died in Mexico. He wrote a number of works of criticism and *Ocnos* (1942), whose latest edition appeared in 1977, a semilyrical commentary on contemporary poetry together with autobiographical reminiscences. In his early poetry one notices the structured grace of Jorge Guillén and a great attention to form. *Perfil del aire* (1927), stylized, melancholy, and Impressionistic, deals with love and nature and a world of happiness beyond the poet's reach. *Un río, un amor* (1929), Surrealistic poetry, begins his recognition of the conflict between reality and desire. In addition to contrasts between light and shadow and the sea as a cosmic elemental force, this volume shows us a poet who flees from the reality of love, viewed as a kind of death.

In the 1930s Cernuda wrote many of his most important collections of poetry. *Los placeres prohibidos* (1931) is a continuing reaction against the inhibitions imposed by society and an intensification of the erotic as part of his disillusioned attack. The poems are in part Surrealistic and oneiric visions. *Donde habite el olvido* (1934) resembles the poetry of Aleixandre in its sensual

275

identification with the cosmos. Cernuda laments the failure of a potential heterosexual love and the wounding and painful experience, the cold despair over that missed love that might have given meaning to his life. Both the elemental forces of nature and death provide a possible escape. *Egloga, elegía, oda* (1936), almost ecstatic and tinged with neo-*Garcilasismo,* nonetheless emphasizes the poet's growing sense of sadness in view of the fleeting present and the uncertain future. The title of his masterpiece, *La realidad y el deseo* (1936), ultimately became the generic title for eleven volumes of his poetry. His complete poetry was published in 1977. The work is both an affirmation of his homosexual solitude and a spiritual autobiography. Cernuda explores the relationship of reality and the poetic consciousness as well as the difference between reality, governed by rules, and desire, almost without limits. The artist's interior world involves an erotic drive as part of his opposition to reality. Even though in the struggle between soul and body he combines the sensual and the religious, he cannot resolve his torment completely.

Later volumes include *Las nubes* (1943), published as part of another work in 1940, harmonious poetry in spite of the subject matter of war, destruction, and death. The poet also recalls his adolescence and views man's relationship with God somewhat pessimistically, although in some of his religious poems he bridges the gap between an earlier paganism and Christianity. Another work of this period, *Como quien espera el alba* (1944), again stresses the dichotomy between man and society. Aside from some exotic geography, these poems treat of dreams and desire, the inspiration of love, and poetry as self-affirmation, a theme Cernuda was to continue in later volumes. *Díptico español* (1961) and *Desolación de la quimera* (1962), about homosexual passion, literature, music, and the problems of Spain, show other facets of his publications.

Cernuda wrote intellectual poetry that involved other arts. He wrote with lightness and grace, and his nature, often a mythical pagan setting of beauty and harmony, symbolized a half-glimpsed paradise he could never visit. He suffered greatly as he contrasted dream and reality and sought refuge in the memory of his Andalusian childhood. In his poetry he always included the perpetual struggle between self and the world, at times with strange combinations of dream, Platonism, and Existential reality. His later poetry became more and more bitter, and his poetic and sexual desires unassuaged, he thought in nihilistic terms of the solution as an Existential nothingness.

8. *Other poets* of the Generation of 1927 include the following:

a) *Dámaso Alonso* (1898–1990), the author of numerous volumes on Spanish philology and literature, in his early poetry about Madrid city life and spiritual and erotic frustrations contrasted beauty with a stark reality. *Oscura noticia* (1944), containing poems written over a period of twenty years, stressed the pain, sorrow, and anguish of being human in a world of love, time, and death. The poet, as in much of his later poetry, here searched for God to give meaning to his life. His masterpiece, *Hijos de la ira* (1944), rejected the current intellectual poetry, stressing social aspects of injustice and the violence to be found in a barbaric world in spite of the ever-present tenderness of maternal love. Alonso wrote about anguish, pain, cruelty, and ugliness; he wrote of Existential preoccupation with death along with sincere religious and metaphysical poems. *Gozos de la vista* (1981), a collection of his previously published poetry, and *Duda y amor del Ser Supremo* (1985), including an anthology of his poetry, deal with a variety of themes, the latter primarily with the relationship of God and man and the struggle between cynicism and belief from the perspective of old age.

b) *Emilio Prados* (1899–1962), who died in exile in Mexico, wrote more than twenty volumes of poetry. In *Tiempo* (1925), he concentrates on sea imagery. *Vuelta* (1927), more hermetic, replaces some of the Andalusian joy of life with introspection about more weighty and profound themes. *Destino fiel* (1937) contained much of his prize-winning war poetry. Among volumes written in Mexico, *Mínima muerte* (1944) stresses the paradoxical quality of life, as the poet analyzes his spiritual crisis and solitude; *Jardín cerrado* (1946), later republished as *El dormido en la yerba* (1953), deals again with solitude, dream, and a spiritual evocation of God and country as well as death; *La piedra escrita* (1961) reveals the creative poetic process; and *Signos del ser* (1962) and *Poesías completas* (1975) represent his later poetry.

Almost all Prados' poetry involves the union of opposites and the victory over limits. He views nature as pure in contrast with man's anguish and destruction. He utilizes myth in his poetry as he deals with birth, life, death, and the conflict between inner and outer reality of which his poetry itself is so much a part.

c) *Manuel Altolaguirre* (1905–1959) wrote prize-winning drama and a biography of Garcilaso that gave more insight into Altolaguirre than into Garcilaso. *Las islas invitadas* (1936), combining the melancholy and the joyous, emphasized what was to be for him a lifelong love of water and the sea. The book with some variations and in expanded form appeared as *Nuevos poemas de las islas invitadas* (1946) and in an edition in 1972. Among other titles are *Fin de un amor* (1949), about nature and the struggle between spiritual and passionate love, and *Poemas en América* (1955), which exudes mystical pantheism and at the same time deals with religious experience. Altolaguirre wrote about solitude, forgetfulness, the passage of time, and the pleasures of the flesh. Some of his poetry was idealistic, some Romantic in tone. He could write popular poetry and also in the Surrealist, *ultraísta*, or Neobaroque manner. He emphasized the world of nature, often with delicate and strange imagery, but he also concerned himself with solitude, love, life, and death. His *Obras completas* appeared in 1986.

d) Other poets, among the many belonging to this generation, include Juan Larrea (1895–1980), Mauricio Bacarisse (1895–1931), Juan José Domenchina (1898–1959), Juan Chabás (1900–1954), and several women poets, among them Angela Figuera Aymerich (1902–1984), usually included in the following generation because of her themes, and Ernestina de Champourcín (b. 1895).

E. The Generation of 1936 and the First Postwar Generation

In addition to their early light and joyful poetry, some of these poets became interested in social and then Existential problems. As part of their reaction to their reality they emphasized formal beauty, contemplation of nature, tranquility, harmony, and religious faith. Highly personal, their poetry gives intimate and nostalgic memories of their infancy, their friends, and love as well as their yearning for God. After the end of the Civil War, whose beginning together with the celebration of the four hundredth anniversary of Garcilaso de la Vega's death gave rise to the generation's name, a rehumanizing influence, a part of which may be seen in the important journal *Cruz y Raya* (1933–1936), appeared more and more in the poetry. Though the journals *Garcilaso* and *Escorial* had emphasized the Renaissance lyrical classic tradition, *Espadaña* concentrated on the social and Existential. These poets, more and more Existential, contrasted the idealized past with the miserable present, stressing the inextricable relationship between the temporal and poetry, and also acknowledging their own mortality. Each poet, however, emphasized different elements. Celaya could never forget the Civil War and its political consequences. Panero stressed the Catholic religious point of view. Hernández, perhaps the most gifted poet of the group, was the poet of the Spanish Civil War. Blas de Otero stressed sociopolitical commitment as well as religious themes, and Carlos Bousoño and José Hierro emphasized passing time and the ensuing Existential anguish. Many would limit the generation under discussion to those born before 1917, although no easy classification is possible. We have expanded the Generation of 1936 to include poets, though not strictly of 1936, who belong to the first post–Civil War generation.

1. *Leopoldo Panero* (1909–1962) wrote some early Surrealistic poetry, but his first important book publication was *La estancia vacía* (1944), an intimate view of nature, a recall of his native hearth and his mother's arms, but primarily a discussion of man, for whom only God provides a refuge and an existence as part of Him. Man alone in his "estancia vacía" must face his daily living, the reality of things, but he searches always for his God and as part of that search returns to childhood to recover Him.

Panero suffered deeply the loss of his brother Juan Panero (1908–1937), also a poet, who the year before his death had published *Cantos del ofrecimiento*, filled with human love, especially as a reflection of divine love and immortality. This same deeply religious note is characteristic of almost all of Leopoldo Panero's poetry. His *Escrito a cada instante* (1949) shows how God's name is revealed and yet removed from him "a cada instante." Indeed, the creation of poetry reflects this ebbing and flowing in the life of the poet as he receives or fails to receive his inspiration from the divine vision. Here too the poet stresses his love for the earth, especially that of Astorga, his birthplace. He suffers a sorrowful nostalgia as he thinks of his native hearth and sings to his wife, children, and God. In tones both passionate and tender he evokes God's presence in the countryside and his faith to help carry him through a family loss and his fear of the beyond.

In 1953 Panero wrote *Canto personal; Carta perdida a Pablo Neruda.* Neruda had known Panero and had collaborated with him in a review. In 1950 Neruda wrote *Canto general,* protesting, among other things, certain aspects of the Spanish Civil War, in a strong leftist political statement. Panero's reply, while defending the Nationalist position, interprets Lorca's death as the accidental result of a popular uprising. But even here, in addition to the social emphasis, Panero deals with family, a search for love, and his relationship with God.

A volume dealing in nostalgic, serene, and pure tones with a youthful love, the earth, and the countryside, *Versos del Guada-rrama,* written in the thirties but not published in book form until 1963, also reveals a continuing religious fervor as well as Existential preoccupations. The poet contrasts the transitory quality of human passion with the eternal aspects of nature. *Romances y canciones* (1960) is another title. Panero's collected poetry appeared in 1963 and his *Obra completa* in 1973.

Panero was highly praised by his contemporaries as one of the most skilled poetic voices of his time. In his emphasis on the land he extols the beautiful elements of nature in lyrical and meditative tones. Although the countryside with its light and color meant a great deal to the poet, his feeling for the earth and his political convictions were secondary to his religious beliefs. Although he represents a new kind of Humanism, associating with the anxiety of the individual, he acknowledges the mystical and sublime and sees man as a religious animal whose sorrowful life can be alleviated only through the search and love for an omnipresent God. Other elements in his poetry involve solitude, family, memory, time, and his country.

2. *Luis Rosales Camacho* (b. 1910) wrote some literary criticism but is famous as a poet. His first collection, *Abril* (1935), written in clean, harmonious, and classic lines, marked an important step toward Garcilaso and away from Góngora. April, lost, may be reborn in a loving fusion with the cosmic. His love poems, though directed to a loved one, see human love as an aspect of divine love, and God's love as a substitute for sensual yearnings. In 1972 Rosales wrote *Segundo abril,* poems composed between 1938 and 1940. It is a sad and beautiful history of the pain and disillusion involved in love lost. *Retablo sacro del nacimiento del Señor* (1940) stresses simple faith in God as a refuge. Augmented in a 1964 edition, this volume combines Existential and religious preoccupations and an examination of the beauty of the cosmos ruled by God.

One of Rosales' major works, *La casa encendida* (1949), published in amplified form in 1967 and again in 1979, explores the transmutation of time and contains the usual autobiographical emphasis. The poet recalls a loved woman, his mother, his father, and Juan Panero, all united in his memory in the lighted house that offers a key to his hopes and dreams and to his daily simple existence. The major thrust of his interplay of dream and reality and poems of the human heart is that memory serves as the enemy of forgetfulness and death and that in spite of loneliness one may yet achieve salvation through love.

Another major collection, *Rimas* (1951), with augmented editions in 1971 and 1979, emphasizes once more memories, human emotion, and religious convictions. In a variety of verse forms Rosales recalls once more in intimate fashion friends like Panero and gives us a view of poetry as introspective, spiritual, and religious, something that can provide order in a time of chaos.

Although Rosales has many other volumes of poetry, among his later publications probably *Diario de una resurrección* (1979) and *La carta entera*, in three volumes, are his best known. The first named, dealing with a personal death, stresses the usual themes of dream and life, lost time, and memory as a bridge between life and death and man's struggle to live up to an ideal. Rebirth through love and resurrection provides joy and escape from a vacuous existence. *La almadraba* (1980), the first part of *La carta entera*, uses a colloquial tone to convey a mixture of the oneiric and the real and an autobiographical search for identity in life's labyrinth. The second volume, *Un rostro en cada ola* (1982), in sometimes grotesque tones, evokes infancy and adolescence; and the third volume, *Oigo el silencio universal del miedo* (1984), examines the poetic process itself but also again deals with memory, hope, and death. One finds violence, degradation, and disillusion in his latest poetry, but man, lost in the contemporary world, strives for light and memories of youth. In essence Rosales confronts the shadows of experience with his poetic life and painfully seeks a personal salvation through a loving God.

3. *Miguel Hernández* (1910–1942), born into a poor peasant family, worked as a goatherd in his youth and experienced nature in all its reality. Having fought for the Republican side in the Spanish Civil War, he was imprisoned and died in jail. Although he wrote dramatic works he is primarily famous for his poetry.

His first collection, *Perito en lunas* (1933), written in *octavas reales*, at times appears hermetic, artificial, and Neobaroque, but as he treats of ordinary, everyday objects of nature and the moon that governs them, whatever the metaphorical transformations involved, he is talking of a concrete reality. The poet acknowledges nature's ambivalent role as both engendering and destructive. This first volume also contains some religious overtones.

Between this volume and *El rayo que no cesa* (1936), Hernández wrote *El silbo vulnerado,* sad, rustic, and pastoral, published

281

as part of *El rayo que no cesa,* and *Imagen de tu huella,* included in his complete works. His 1936 collection of poetry, filled with anger and rebellion, reveals the poet's self-discovery, erotic needs, love as pain, and ensuing despair. In addition to being sensual, however, it is autochthonous, and part of the poet's Existential despair stems from his lost contact with the earth and telluric forces symbolized by the mythic bull.

His next two volumes spoke to a world of hard realities. *Viento del pueblo* (1937), which shared the National Prize for Literature, stresses fraternity and solidarity, often in tones tormented, tender, angry, and patriotic in turn as it tells of the Spanish Civil War. Poverty and sorrow, says the poet, may clear the path for a future freedom, and he insists that it is the little man who offers the hope for that possibility. Along with the patriotic struggles and descriptions of the sober Castilian landscape are depictions of the exuberant fertility of beautiful Alicante. *El hombre acecha,* written in 1939, could not be published in Spain until after Franco's death, and it appears as part of Hernández' *Obra poética completa* (1977). The volume deals with the desolation and carnage caused by the Spanish Civil War, and the poet worries over Spain's tragic destiny.

Cancionero y romancero de ausencias, written between 1938 and 1941 and published in various editions of his *Obras completas,* is Hernández' most personally moving poetry in its love for his family, his belief in the brotherhood of man, and his denunciation of war. He muses also on temporal existence and as always emphasizes nature and the telluric in symbols such as sun, wheat, and earth. His archetypal symbols reflect a real world of light and shadow, wind and trees, but in terms of the earth he knew and had cultivated, the physical and the real.

Hernández fused the two eternal currents of Spanish literature, the *culto* and the popular. Although one finds Andalusian elegance as well as Baroque spontaneity in his poetry, it exploded with overwhelming power, passion, and tragedy. Some of his poetry deals with the Existential and the temporal. A deep and tragic poet of liberty, spiritual and sexual love, he knew all too well the unstable quality of life in a cruel and violent world, and he sang about humanity in many tones, passionate, tender, angry, and compassionate. His was a poetry of tragic beauty, and as Aleixandre said of him: "No se le apagó nunca, no, esa luz que por encima de todo trágicamente le hizo morir con los ojos abiertos."

4. *Gabriel Celaya* (b. 1911), whose real name is Rafael Múgica

but who also has written under the pseudonym Juan de Leceta, in addition to critical works has published some sixty collections of poetry. Celaya is best known for his use of poetry as an instrument of social protest. He eschews what he calls aesthetic adornments in favor of a colloquial language as part of his belief that a poet cannot isolate himself from the world and has to participate personally in social and ethical matters. Celaya has divided his poetry into several periods: up to 1944, he wrote Surrealistic, symbolic, and irrational poetry; from 1945 to 1954, Existential poetry; from 1954 to 1962, social poetry; and after 1962, poetry on a variety of themes including the absurd. But these categories do not exclude other themes. In his early poetry he evokes sexual happiness and a communion with nature, and in most of his poetry he writes of love, joy, anguish, and doubt.

In his first book of poetry, *Marea de silencio* (1935), he uses dreams and irrational imagery, but his first major success came with *Tranquilamente hablando* (1947), which in both intellectual and emotive tones deals with the work, pain, exploitation, and death of human beings and, he claimed, things as they really are. The pain and anguish continue in an expanded version of the work in 1961. *Las cartas boca abajo* (1954) treats of the Civil War, hunger, and human rather than poetic affirmation. *Lo demás es silencio* (1954) again rejects introspective for public poetry about suffering humanity and social injustice. *Cantos iberos* (1955) again is about Spain and its *pueblo*, social commitment, solidarity with the proletariat, and the possibility of a brighter tomorrow. Later collections include *Función de uno, equis, ene* (1973), *ene* being the collective, *uno* the individual, and *equis* unknown fate or God; *Buenos días, buenas noches* (1976); *Poemas órficos* (1978), in which Celaya tries to discover the essence of things and his own reality; *Penúltimos poemas* (1982), which seeks again to define poetry, this time as trying to pierce the ego's limits, and depicts the confrontation of youth and old age, erotic passion, and Existential anguish; and *El mundo abierto* (1986).

Much of Celaya's poetry has an ironic tone, although he thinks of himself as the voice of the people. He uses nature often as a background for his meditations and as a contrast with the reality of life. He tries always to communicate with his readers, and though he acknowledges the power of human love, in general he stresses that the here and now is all we have.

5. *Blas de Otero* (1916–1979) published his first important collection, *Angel fieramente humano*, in 1950. In occasionally militant tones he searches for God but believes that He has abandoned

man to solitude and death. This leads the poet to accentuate human love over the divine and, given the world's danger, the brotherhood of man. *Redoble de conciencia* (1951) portrays a suffering Spain in search of liberty. The poet is again willing to abandon his dreams for human solidarity. His most famous work, *Pido la paz y la palabra* (1955), exalts peace over even the poetry that supports it in a suffering Spain without justice or freedom. As he searches still for God and love, he hopes that his country will have a future. In *Ancia* (1958), whose title is an anagram of *Angel fieramente humano* and *Redoble de conciencia*, although he continues historical, political, and social themes, he seems more compassionate in his hunger for justice.

Among his many other collections are *En castellano* (1960), the second part of *Pido la paz y la palabra; Que trata de España* (1964), the third part, whose title also served as a general title for his collected works; *Esto no es un libro* (1963), whose affirmation and denial form the material of both life and literature; and *Expresión y reunión: A modo de antología*, whose latest version appeared in 1981.

Blas de Otero believed in the nobility of man, and he wrote always about his concern for humanity as well as of his feelings toward God. In his poetry, a combination of the clear and the hermetic, the passionate and tender, he tried to express humanity's and his own feelings about nature, the cosmos, sexuality, love, social justice, patriotism, religion, and death. As he contemplated a world of chaos and anguish, ruins and solitude, attacked by dark forces, he sought always for order, light, and peace. Whatever his Existential suffering, he wrote for the "immense majority" and felt a commitment to human beings, men of flesh and blood whose oppression and suffering he shared.

6. *Gloria Fuertes* (b. 1918), often included by critics as a member of the Generation of 1950 because of her themes and techniques, flirted briefly with *postismo*. She herself claimed that she could not define her poetry as social, mystical, or anything else, and she has called herself an *anti-poeta*.

All her poetry is autobiographical. In *Isla ignorada* (1950), feeling isolated and ignored, she writes of objects, history, dreams, fantasy, and love. *Cancionero para niños* (1952), as the title indicates, is about the world of children. Her first collection to receive critical acclaim was *Que estás en la tierra* (1962). Other works include *Ni tiro, ni veneno, ni navaja* (1965), about love, death, God, and the sterility of modern life; *Poeta de guardia* (1968), filled with colloquial plays on words, jokes, and neologisms but also showing Fuertes' pain and rage at human suffering and her criticism of a Church that ignores human problems; *Como atar los bigotes al tigre* (1969), about the old whom even death ignores and yet, despite the serious theme, filled with playful verses about a lady termite and her literary tastes; *Historia de Gloria* (1980), about fleeting love, solitude, solidarity with her people and her city, and a plea for justice for the workers and the poor; and *Obras incompletas* (1983). In the 1980s Fuertes concentrated largely on children's literature and published a number of volumes.

Fuertes is original, spontaneous, and popular. She has an affection for beggars, cats, and buildings and writes of objects and simple things. One has the impression at times that her poetry provides her with a disguise or shield against the world. She also writes of love and its absence, communication, and the foolishness of war. She chastises the rich who take advantage of the workers and rails against God's indifference, but her social and religious themes serve as part of a complex, creative process. Her language, although colloquial, is ingenious, and she handles jokes, puns, slang, and advertisements ironically. Her humor makes us laugh at ourselves, but behind her self-mockery lies a maternal tenderness. Her poetry is also filled with intertextual references.

7. *José Hierro* (b. 1922) deals in *Tierra sin nosotros* (1947) with the sea and youth, time and memory, especially of imprisonment as a living death. In spite of alienation and pain, he learns to accept what fate has in store. *Alegría* (1947), which won the Adonais Prize, views life as a struggle and a search for authenticity in a world where man is destined to die. The poet strives to create an identity through his poetry, to seek the truth behind apparent truth, and to sustain happiness in the face of an Existential reality. This Existential anguish continues in *Con las piedras, con el viento* (1950), though he places more emphasis on love as an unattainable ideal and memory as a destroyer of dreams. *Quinta del 42* (1953) again is about love, dreams, memory, human solidarity, and passing time, but he also writes about music and poetry. More colloquial in his poetry of documentation, he recalls family and views sadly his Spain and her cities and emphasizes the difficulty of communicating through rational means when faced with encroaching time and spiritual death. *Cuanto sé de mí* (1957), whose title he later used for his complete poetic works published in 1974, is another restatement of his Existential anguish and desolate confrontation with death, but he also

engages in self-colloquy about the meaning of his poetry and the poetic art. Spain and its problems still preoccupy him. Finally, *Libro de las alucinaciones* (1964) joins rational clarity with mysterious shadow. In a world of absurd fate and anticipated death, the poet has illusion and reality exchange roles, and time surrenders and present and future fuse. It is a collection of fire, wind, and sea, as well as time and experience, but the poet still denounces human injustice. Dreaming of what might have been, after a self-analysis as man and poet, he decides to write no more. He also foreshadows in this volume some of the ideas of Valente on poetry as experience and self-revelation.

Hierro defined his poetry as sincere, precise, dry, and opposed to formal beauty in the exploration of ephemeral, Existential man. Yet his language, conventional but imaginative, has a potent emotional charge. He seeks fixed values in a universe without them. He talks of the ravages of time, of love, sadness, and despair at the thought of death, man's fate, but he also shows his love for his country. Although he seeks justice for humanity, Hierro also reveals his own soul in his poetry, and in spite of his own definition of his poetic dryness, he writes with color, light, and exquisite sensibility.

8. *Carlos Bousoño* (b. 1923) began to write at a very early age. He wrote what to date is the best critical study on Vicente Aleixandre as well as a number of other well known critical texts. In his early works the poet suffered from religious doubts and sought salvation, a human God, and continuing innocence, though Spain and death were also preoccupations. Many of the poems in *Subida al amor* (1945) and *Primavera de la muerte* (1946) seem almost desperate, in spite of Bousoño's attempt to define poetry as an objective contemplation of form. Yet from time to time Bousoño includes a note of happiness, even though he knows that spring gives way to inevitable winter and death. In *Subida al amor,* Bousoño sees nature as a pantheistic experience. In *Primavera de la muerte,* he contrasts joy and beauty with a world of deceptions and the absence of God. He reveals an almost frantic love of life because of his knowledge of impending nothingness. *Hacia otra luz* (1952), containing the first two collections plus *En vez de sueño,* is a continuing expression of his Existential doubt.

In *Noche del sentido* (1957), the poet struggles to believe in spite of his skepticism. As the title suggests, the poet has to rely on untrustworthy emotions in his involvement with the world. His poetry, nonetheless, is a reaffirmation of tenderness and love. *Invasión de la realidad* (1962) suggests that in the absence of God the poet must cling to the concrete world. In attempting a metaphysical penetration of reality, all that man has to guide him, whatever the injustice and disorder of the world, Bousoño decides that reality, aside from irrational aspects of the poetic word, matters.

Bousoño started a new and more complex style in *Oda en la ceniza* (1967). He fuses the rational and irrational as he peruses personal and human suffering and seeks love and self-under-standing in the face of death. In spite of his Existential anguish, he sees life as a search for truth and love as a possible salvation. Still other poetry collections are *La búsqueda* (1971), an eternali-zation of each moment; *Al mismo tiempo que la noche* (1971); and *Las monedas contra la losa* (1973), in which the poet spends his coin (the days of his life) on the way to death. In 1980 he pub-lished *Selección de mis versos*. *Metáfora del desafuero,* which ap-peared in 1988, continues Bousoño's idea of the antithetical na-ture of man's being: life is change but also existence.

Bousoño often contrasts the ethereal, beauty, and youth with nature and the eternal. His religious security, assuaged at first, soon ceded to a disbelieving anguish at the prospect of death. Yet Bousoño's poetry seems always an affirmation of life. The poet, then, is many things, erotic, religious, Mystical, Romantic, and Existential. He debates constantly with life and death, hope and despair, seeing behind each shadow the possibility of light. In his later, more aesthetic poetry, he stresses form and intellec-tual content over sentiment, but he continues to believe that life, however transitory, is a gift to be cherished.

9. *Other poets* of the Generation of 1936 include the following:

a) *Juan Gil-Albert* (b. 1906) earned his greatest success after his return from exile. He is especially influential on the young poets of the 1970s and 1980s. Some critics place him in the Gen-eration of 1927. He has written more than twenty volumes of prose and a dozen or so of verse. Some of his poetry has Ba-roque elements, and his themes include Spain, homosexuality, art, time, life, love, nature, and death. Like the younger poets, he emphasizes cultural references and intertextuality. Among his works are *Las ilusiones* (1945), reprinted as *Las ilusiones con los poemas del convaleciente* (1975); *Concertar es amor* (1951); *Varia-ciones sobre un tema inextinguible* (1981); and *Obra poética completa* (1981).

b) *Carmen Conde* (b. 1907), who in 1979 became the first woman ever elected to the Spanish Royal Academy, has written more than thirty volumes of poetry. In much of her early poetry, the constant notes were of personification, the harmony of the forces of nature, revelation, and transfiguration. Among her many works, *Ansia de la gracia* (1945) reveals her sensuality, love of life, a mysterious and solitary countryside, and in spite of the erotic themes the constant presence of God. *Mujer sin Edén* (1947), her most famous collection, rejects the traditional culpability assigned to woman as a descendant of Eve and a sinful sexuality, as the poet explores the Biblical role of women and their ambivalent relationship to God and man and identifies with love, maternity, and faith. *Iluminada tierra* (1951) combines paganism, passion, and God, as Conde emphasizes purification through suffering. Among later volumes one can cite *El tiempo es un río lentísimo de fuego* (1978).

Carmen Conde longs for youth, despairs at old age, loves life, and seeks perfection, although for her light always triumphs over darkness. She has a positive view of nature, as she consistently rejects the negative aspects of life. She emphasizes both the erotic and metaphysical as she searches for the absolute, and her poetry, she says, is what gives meaning to her life. She has been called "la mujer-poeta más importante del siglo veinte."

c) *Luis Felipe Vivanco* (1907–1975) always affirmed God and love in his poetry and said that he wrote "como hombre, como cristiano, y como enamorado." Aside from critical works, his poetry collections include *Cantos de primavera* (1936), a contemplation of the countryside with religious devotion; *Tiempo de dolor* (1940); and *Los caminos* (1974), a compilation of light, idealism, and deeply religious poetry that extols the virtue of life, family, and countryside. Vivanco's many themes include love of nature, the hearth, the family, the role of memory, and above all religious warmth.

d) *Victoriano Crémer* (b. 1908) has written more than twenty volumes of poetry. Opposed from the beginning to the Neoclassic vein and pure poetry, he started the review *Espadaña*. His is a poetry of despair, sadness, and rebellion. Some have called his poetry *tremendista*, but essentially he stresses the warm and human over the cold and beautiful. Other themes in his poetry are love, country, justice, liberty, God, and death. From time to time his poetry has an ironic, almost sarcastic tone. His collections include *Tacto sonoro* (1944), *Las horas perdidas* (1949), *Nuevos cantos de vida y esperanza* (1952), *Lejos de esta lluvia tan amarga* (1971), and *Poesía* (1984).

e) *Dionisio Ridruejo* (1912–1975), although he fought for the Franco forces, later broke his ties with the Falangists to fight for democracy. He published his first work, *Plural,* in 1935. In his complete poetic works, published in 1976, some of his collections have titles somewhat different from those of the original publications. Among his many works are *Primer libro de amor* (1935–1949), sonnets about love and its eventual consummation, nostalgic recall, vanished youth, and identification with the universe; *Sonetos a la piedra* (1934–1942), a vision of existence through the contemplation of inanimate objects with an intellectual perception and controlled emotion; *Cuadernos de Rusia* (1941–1942), about the Blue Division on the Russian front and a reality of desolation, cold, and the wounded and the dead; and *Poesía* (1976). Ridruejo's early poetry was to some extent Baroque, but his later works, recalling those of Antonio Machado, reject Formalist poetry for more Existential themes and show Ridruejo's mastery at combining, with perfect technique, modern and Classical trends.

f) *José García Nieto* (b. 1914), founder of the review *Garcilaso,* has written, aside from prose works, approximately thirty collections of poetry. He began as the most representative *garcilasista,* and much of his later poetry is a reaffirmation of that poetry of the 1940s. In his poetry he stresses clarity, harmony, love, family, landscape, and God. Among his titles are *Víspera hacia ti* (1940); *La red* (1947), about a mystical search for God; *Tregua* (1951), which exalts the human over the beautiful; *Los cristales fingidos* (1978); and *Piedra y cielo de Roma* (1984).

g) *Germán Bleiberg* (b. 1915), writes light and graceful verse in the Garcilaso manner. *Sonetos amorosos* (1936) was reprinted in 1947 as *Más allá de ruinas.* Other collections are *El poeta ausente* (1948) and *Selección de poemas* (1974). Love, Arcadian landscapes, solitude, the world of childhood, and an affirmation of existence, in spite of Existential anguish intensified by a jail experience, are his principal themes. Bleiberg expresses love through a spiritual fusion of his soul with nature and continues to believe that after the shadows of the night comes a new dawn for the heart.

h) *Vicente Gaos* (1919–1980) fills his poetry with a spiritual experience of nature, the meaning of existence, and a search for God. Though tormented, he attempted to remain true to his Catholic orthodoxy and his belief in eternal life but in his later poetry alternated between doubt and faith. His volumes include

289

Arcángel de mi noche (1944); *Luz desde el sueño* (1947); *Concierto en mí y en vosotros* (1965), part of his complete poetry published in 1982; and *Un montón de sombras y otros poemas* (1971).

i) Other well known poets of this generation are José Antonio Muñoz Rojas (b. 1909), Ildefonso Manuel Gil (b. 1912), José Luis Cano (b. 1912), Ramón de Garciasol (b. 1913), Concha Zardoya (b. 1914), Concha Lagos (b. 1916), Susana March (b. 1918), Leopoldo Luis (b. 1918), José Luis Hidalgo (1919–1947), Rafael Montesinos (b. 1920), and Eugenio García González de Nora (b. 1923).

F. The Generation of 1950

This group of poets, sometimes alluded to as the group of the 1960s or *promoción desheredada,* added to the social themes promoted by Otero and Celaya and the Existential and poetic testimony of Hierro the idea of self-revelation through poetry. Instead of following Aleixandre's idea of poetry as communication, poets like Valente and González used it as a vehicle for self-knowledge and sensations beyond immediate experience. Metapoetry, they hoped, would provide an honest reflection of their perception of experience. Valente thought of poetry as an ontological search for its own meaning, and González believed that only the writing of the poem revealed the poet but that words alone might not be able to convey the poetic experience. Although they did not deny, as would later poets, the ability of poetry to convey to some extent a knowledge of reality, they showed a special concern for the nature of language and linguistic truth. Nonetheless, for the most part they used a colloquial language.

These poets, nevertheless, could not forget Spain and humanity, whatever their feelings about poetry as message or self-revelation and self-definition. They sing of historical man and his circumstances and see him as victimized by time in the face of death, although Valente once stated: "Pasado no tuvimos, aun lo hemos de hacer."

1. *Angel González* (b. 1925), more than others of his generation seems to support and exploit social themes, although in an ironic and parodic rather than popular fashion. In *Aspero mundo* (1956), Existential, metaphysical, and religious, the poems are both sentimental and beautiful as they alternate between positive values of love and illusion as a harsh reality. *Sin esperanza, con convencimiento* (1961) denounces injustices and recalls the

Spanish Civil War symbolically, allegorically, and ironically. For the most part bitter and pessimistic, González is occasionally joyful in his view of nature. *Grado elemental* (1962) is an attempt by González to demythify society's established values, and he experiments with caricature and irony in seeking a new vocabulary for a new reality. *Palabra sobre palabra* (1965), whose title he used later for his complete works and ever-expanding editions in 1968, 1972, and 1977, still ironic, seems more positive about nature, man, and country. The poet searches for identity and for an understanding of a deceptive reality. Finally, *Tratado de urbanismo* (1967) ends what some have called González' first poetic stage. Again he satirizes the values of the middle class, trivializes man's pursuits, recalls his infancy, and demythifies death. As he focuses on man's present, he is frustrated with a social order that inhibits the human spirit, but he uses a colloquial language to reflect experiences apparently shared in common with other members of society.

Breves acotaciones para una biografía (1969) starts the poet's second state of poetic creation, a kind of antipoetry involving the repetition of words that the poet rejects as essentially useless. *Procedimientos narrativos* (1972), a self-parody, again concerns the failure of words and metaphorical associations. *Muestra corregida y aumentada de algunos procedimientos narrativos y de las actitudes sentimentales que habitualmente comportan* (1977), filled with historical, literary, and musical allusions, comments on the nature of poetry itself and metapoetry. *Prosemas o menos* (1985) reiterates the poet's belief in the failure of the poetic word to transform reality, but he feels that poetry, nevertheless, in its precision and beauty, provides a personally rewarding aesthetic experience.

Although González writes what might be considered social poetry, at times with a humor that obfuscates an underlying grief, he is more interested in the meaning than the subject matter involved. He uses a variety of themes in his poetry—nostalgia, solidarity, the passage of time, and hopelessness of absolute truth. His apparent disarming candor makes his poetry deceptive. He employs everyday language to create a complex experience and literature about literature, as well as poetry on several semiotic levels, as he comments on the art of poetry itself and through his intellectuality and metapoetry often misdirects the reader.

2. *José Angel Valente* (b. 1929), an intellectual, almost austere poet, can be devastatingly sarcastic in his analysis of daily living

and modern politics. Yet at the same time Valente has been interested in the poetic experience as self-sustaining. He became more and more conceptual in his poetry after 1967, as he interrelated life and the poetic act and defined poetry in its continuing contrast between affirmation and negation.

A modo de esperanza (1955), winner of the Adonais Prize and a human testament of a poetized reality, treats, in Existential fashion, man's life and death, solitude, and desolation. *Poemas a Lázaro* (1960) deals with man reborn, mother love, earth, and the mystery of creation and resurrection. The poet examines the creative process as a search for self and as a knowledge of existence, love of life, and fear of death. In *Sobre el lugar del canto* (1963), Valente despairs at the injustice he sees but postulates also the possibility of hope and God.

One of Valente's greatest works, *La memoria y los signos* (1966), about deceptive memory, suffering, and love, evokes adolescence and childhood innocence as a contrast with adult knowledge. The present, something we should cherish because it is all we have, represents a metaphysical hope if one loves and believes. Yet Valente cannot forget the Spanish Civil War and other historical and political realities, but he includes historical, Existential, metaphysical, and poetic elements as part of the exploration of the difference between present human collective memory and a metaphysical one. In this process he is able to use only the language of poetry and not the language of the experience that motivates it, and the result is a constant interplay of clarity, mystery, world, and symbol.

Siete representaciones (1967), replete with Biblical references and man's destructive response to injustice, deals with the seven deadly sins. The poems of *Breve son* (1968) are more hermetic, ironic, and experimental. Valente tries to penetrate semantic values to find linguistic liberty, but at the same time he writes about misery and injustice. *El inocente* (1970), a discovery of the poetic word, expresses his solitude and his disillusion with humanity and the hypocrisy of the world. He seeks consolation in happier memories and meaningful literature.

Valente's later works include *Material memoria* (1979), about love's recognition of the material world, memory, a search for reality, and poetry as silence; *Tres lecciones de tinieblas* (1980), concerning the Kabbalah and involving a metaphor of thought as light produced in twilight; *Mandorla* (1982), which deals with time and history but especially the poetic world that involves the erotic as an ontological investigation; and *El fulgor* (1984), a poetry of knowledge and writing as a form of thinking, including self-containing hermetic poems, conceptual, paradoxical, and philosophical, and symbols of day, night, life, and death. Other titles are *Punto cero* (1972 and 1980), a collection of Valente's complete works; *Interior con figuras* (1976); *Estancia* (1980); and *99 poemas* (1981).

Valente has concerned himself constantly with poetry and the meaning of the poetic word. He believes poetry to be an adventure of self-discovery, a complex of memories, including erotic ones. Time for Valente is a psychological phenomenon produced by relationships rather than linear progression. The mind, aware of being finite, transforms experiences into poetic symbols. Valente seeks light in a world of darkness, tied in part to an evocation of infancy, adolescence, and a knowledge of a future death. Yet the present may be more meaningful than deceptive memory. Poetry for Valente means purification, struggle, exploration of his inner being, and a view of exterior reality as secondary to that search for self-understanding.

3. *Jaime Gil de Biedma* (1929–1990), critic, translator, and poet, anticipated many of the poets of the next generation in his *culturalista* tendencies and emphasis of literature on literature. Nonetheless, his poetry is quite autobiographical and social, though with ironic undertones and commentary on apparently real experiences. After what the poet called a "poetic apprenticeship" in *Según sentencia del tiempo* (1953), he published *Compañeros de viaje* (1959), about nature, a confrontation with daily life, the sweetness of love, passing time, and a nostalgic view of childhood, past realities converted into present illusions. *En favor de Venus* (1965) is an anthology of love poems, at times frankly erotic and sensual but also Romantic, idealistic, and tender. *Moralidades* (1966), autobiographical but yet deliberately imitative and intertextual, is an almost cynical poetry that objectifies his personal feelings about illusion in our lives. Gil de Biedma, a caring human being with a social conscience in spite of his critical cynicism, evokes the past and the Spanish Civil War, but as a disillusioned child with an adult perception. The poet finally realizes that existence is a bitter experience involving pathetic failure and that love and life itself may have little value. *Poemas póstumos* (1969), a debate between the young and the old, conscience and sexual pleasure, is skeptical, pessimistic, and self-critical. An adult poet confronts his younger persona in a series of dialogues contrasting a conventional reality and a poetic subconscious, the latter of which in the end seems more real. He

combines themes such as passing time with life as art, artistic creativity, reality and illusion. *Las personas del verbo* (1975 and 1982) contains his complete poetic works.

In his earlier poetry Gil de Biedma treated nature, at times with a joyous affirmation of life. He also wrote about the moral and political rejection of power. He wrote of passing time, the self, man's desire for liberty, and the subjective and illusory. At times it is difficult to penetrate his ambivalence about the amorous and the temporal, to penetrate his ironic view of reality and dream, although his autobiographical and melancholy evocation of childhood helps define his view of the tragic present. Essentially he is an erotic poet who plays with illusion and reality and his own moral and intellectual positions regarding life and death. Concerned with ethical and social issues, he also stresses the relationship of reality to the illusory and oneiric. The poet uses direct language and colloquial style, often ironic and self-mocking but occasionally confessional. He thinks of poetry more as conversation than communion and of the poem, always, as its own reality.

4. *Francisco Brines* (b. 1932) in *Las brasas* (1960), which won the Adonais Prize, deals with abandoned gardens and mysterious stars, the light of day, and nature exalted over man. In spite of his resigned contemplation, he is keenly aware of the passing of time. After some narrative poems, published in *El santo inocente y la muerte de Sócrates* (1965), he wrote *Palabras a la oscuridad* (1966), again about nature and the beauty of the world menaced by time. The poet exalts desire and human life in spite of his generally negative view regarding the human condition and time's ravages.

Aún no (1971), his first collection of the 1970s, acknowledges the loss of innocence, and the poet parodies the age in which he lives, historical events, and human vanity. He emphasizes philosophy and literature and his perpetual themes of love, solitude, and old age. Brines also attempts to include his reader here in the poetic process, for him more than an individual experience. *Insistencias en Luzbel* (1977) is Brines' most Existential work. The poet believes that the immortality afforded by youth must cede before the forces of nothingness, and his communication of human experience now includes questions about the nature of being and human destiny. Lucifer compares himself with modern man and rebels against an absurd reality of which death is a part, but man, in his anguish, can only seek to affirm his authenticity through love, sex, and poetry, in this case both

Baroque and colloquial, in which the poet seeks his own poetic purpose.

Brines' poetry of the 1980s includes *Poemas excluídos* (1985), *Antología poética* (1986), and *El otoño de las rosas* (1986). The last volume stresses his joy at having existed, the affirmation of a future existence in spite of his acceptance of personal mortality, and his ability to delay time in its passage to the nothingness that awaits only through a creative art that does not include personal salvation.

In his poetry Brines looks at youth from an adult perspective. He believes that reviewing the past gives knowledge and perhaps solace for the solitude of old age. He writes philosophical and metaphysical poetry that includes his anguished Existential concept of time, desolation, and nothingness. Nonetheless the poet feels the material world as a sensuous present he wants to possess before time robs him of youth and physical existence. He hopes that through the poetic process he can discover the meaning of a concrete personal experience. As a temporal poet, inexorably tied to a historical present, he faces a paradoxical world of love and life in spite of an awaiting death.

5. *Claudio Rodríguez* (b. 1934) intensifies the poetry of intuition and the process of textual creation. He often uses contradictory syntax and negation as assertion, combining metaphorical innovation with simple colloquial language to create ambiguities and an open text for the reader to complete. Yet for Rodríguez poetry reveals that which is human in man, both his joy of existence and religious anguish. Poetry implies a participation in life and at the same time the poetic experience thereof, a mysterious gift from heaven.

In *Don de ebriedad* (1953), which won the Adonais Prize, he dwells on both concrete and abstract surroundings and his enjoyment of nature, involving an active participation and not simply contemplation. Rodríguez wants to experience reality in soul and spirit, to seize the ineffable moment, to amplify and eternalize it. He thus discovers his path in life through the creative act. *Alianza y condena* (1965) again sings of life's beauty, but more and more the poet encounters the pain and sadness of the world. Allied to life and with a love for humanity, he nevertheless rejects materialism, condemning the hypocrisy he finds in his daily search for the truth. In spite of life's unpleasant aspects, he continues to find joy in both erotic and spiritual exaltation, an identification with nature, and the simple and beautiful aspects of life, which for him include a recalled adolescence and

295

the play of light and shadows. *El vuelo de la celebración* (1976) again praises life and seeks knowledge about human destiny, metaphysical truth, and salvation. Rodríguez writes about the magical qualities of a tear or a glance as he engages in an emotional rather than intellectual communion with the world. Man may, indeed, have lost his innocence through separation from the natural world, but the carnal experience enables him to appreciate the elemental aspects of the universe and through love to escape the corrupting influences of time. Other titles are *Calle sin nombre* (1983) and *Desde mis poemas* (1983), the latter of which is a compilation of his poetry that helped him win the National Prize for Poetry.

Rodríguez tries always to synthesize being and existence in relationship to the vegetable, mineral, and animal world. As part of his desire for communion, poetry, a kind of controlled adventure, symbolizes a possible salvation as well as the possession of the moment. Although he recognizes the disorder of the world, he speaks of joy, existence, human solidarity, faith in humanity, religion, and existence.

6. *Other poets* of the Generation of 1950 include the following:

a) *José María Valverde* (b. 1926) temperamentally belongs to the previous generation. In his poetry he uses memory to recall a pleasant past. In *Hombre de Dios* (1945), this Catholic poet searches for God in a well-ordered and beautiful world. He feels occasional terror and anguish at future nothingness but relies on the Divine Will to save him. *La espera* (1949) won the National Prize for Poetry. Here the poet still looks at the world with child-like eyes. Other collections are *Enseñanzas de la edad* (1961), *Ser de palabra* (1976), and *Antología de sus versos* (1980).

b) *Eladio Cabañero* (b. 1930) is a popular singer of love, youth, and his *pueblo*, although he also treats rebellion and social issues. Almost all his poetry is autobiographical. His collections include *Desde el sol y la anchura* (1956), an emotional reaction to the land, personified nature, and dehumanized man; *Una señal de amor* (1958), about love, solitude, and injustice but also family and countryside; *Marisa Sabia y otros poemas* (1963), which won the National Prize for Literature and deals lovingly with La Mancha and its people; and *Poesía* (1971).

c) *Félix Grande* (b. 1937), whom some would place in the following generation, is a prize-winning novelist, essayist, and short story writer. His second book of poetry, *Las piedras* (1964), won the Adonais Prize. It discusses immortality, life, and death in somewhat melancholy fashion. *Música amenazada* (1966) is about

Grande's love for music. *Blanca Spirituals* (1967), autobiographical in part and also filled with intertextuality, contains denunciatory poems about deception, sorrow, hate, and love and the poet's view of the misery and injustice of the world. *Taranto* (1971), an *homenaje* to César Vallejo; and *Las rubáiyatas de Horacio Martín* (1978), which won the National Prize for Poetry, are other collections. Horacio Martín, the poet's alter ego, expresses himself on language, love, and death and glorifies the female body. The poet himself then becomes the translator and reader of the text about love, friendship, sadness, and memory.

d) *Carlos Sahagún* (b. 1938) evokes past experience and commentary as part of the poetic process. He has published a number of poetry collections, including *Hombre naciente* (1955); *Profecías del agua* (1958), an Adonais prize-winner involving time as a flowing river, youth, water as a symbol of purity and liberty, and the ruinous effects of the Spanish Civil War; *Como si hubiera muerto un niño* (1961), about youth and love but also about a hungry and sordid childhood; *Estar contigo* (1973), a contrast between youth and old age and a substitute through poetry for the poet's loss of faith in God; and *Primer y último oficio* (1979). Sahagún, in turn sad, satiric, and biting, dwells on infancy as part of the process of confronting one's own existence in a society without liberty.

e) Alfonso Costafrida (1926–1974), Angel Crespo (b. 1926), José Manuel Caballero Bonald (b. 1926), Carlos Barral (b. 1928), José Agustín Goytisolo (b. 1928), Manuel Mantero (b. 1930), and Aqulino Duque (b. 1931) are also poets of the Generation of 1950.

G. The Generation of 1968 and Beyond

This group of poets, born between 1939 and 1953, belong, according to Carlos Bousoño, to a *generación marginada*. They assign an absolute and independent value to their poetry. Many overload their poetry with cultural references to music, painting, geography—especially that of Greece, Italy, and the Nordic countries—and literature. Neobaroque and, depending on the poet, stressing *Cernudismo, Cavafianismo, Grecidad,* or intertextuality, they show also the influence of mass media, especially newspapers and television, rock and roll, and "pop" culture. They also create their own myths and mythology and a specially syncopated language, quite often artificial, exotic, and extrarational. Still others try collage, a Freudian emphasis on the neurotic, the decadent, and the glorification of the body. These poets, for the most part, rebel against their own culture in an effort to underline their artistic autonomy, which in some cases gives their poetry an elitist cast. Many have their own special version of poetry as poetic text and a reflection of itself.

In the 1980s many of the poets continued the previously mentioned techniques and elements such as *culturalismo*. Some added a new kind of Orientalism. Some poets used the poem as a biographical reconstruction related to a mythical and epic recreation. The emphasis on linguistics and the metapoetic critique of the poetic act in the process of creation continued to be emphasized. Yet at the same time, the eighties have seen, beyond dextrous combinations of imagery and expression, a more personal poetry, and some of the poets have attempted to reintroduce themes of time, memory, and even the quotidian in reaction to the Neobaroque mentality. Some have returned to a more tender, emotional, Romantic poetry. Whatever their techniques, these poets seem comfortable with the older but eternal themes of love, time, and death.

1. *Manuel Vázquez Montalbán* (b. 1939), even better known as a novelist and short story writer, writes amorous, erotic, autobiographical poetry. In *Una educación sentimental* (1967), he uses mass culture and many cultural references. His hermetic poetry seems deceptively prosaic, as he paints a Neoromantic picture of his family, his disillusion and frustration, and a nostalgia for youth and love, which he also views cynically. *Movimientos sin éxito* (1969) utilizes slogans, free association, humor, irony, and commercials to show the impossibility of joy in a repugnant world. *A la sombra de las muchachas sin flor* (1973) contains poems of terror and erotic love. *Coplas a la muerte de mi tía Daniela* (1973) tries to condition the reader to an irrational interpretation of such timeless poetic subjects as death. *Praga* (1982) deals with different cities, politics, and a daily reality lived emotionally. *Memoria y deseo* (1986) is an anthology of Vázquez' poetic work. Vázquez attacks consumerism by using its own language and warns against a complacent reality, but he also cautions readers about the deceitfulness of myth.

2. *Père (Pedro) Gimferrer* (b. 1945) has written several poetry collections in Catalan as well as some in Spanish. *El mensaje del tetrarca* (1963) reveals a Baroque fascination with ancient myths and views of reality as but a figment of the imagination. *Arde el mar* (1966), dedicated to Vicente Aleixandre, is one of the most important collections of the Generation of 1968. Almost auto-

matic writing according to the author and definitely within the *culturalista* camp, *Arde el mar* recalls tragic times, through imagination, to create a life where dream and imagination combine to forge a present and a future with an imaginary past. Thus the author writes about a pleasant, though fictitious, infancy. *La muerte en Beverly Hills* (1968) again brings into being a special ironic reality of masks, mirrors, and movies. The poet sees youth as a poetic configuration confronting the shadows of eternity but sadly also longs for love. *De extraña fruta y otros poemas* (1968) deals with the relationship between television commercials and a lifelike reality made of love, time, and fear of the unknown. Concerned with its own reality, the poetry is filled with literary and exotic references and irrational associations. Other works include *Fuego ciego* (1972–1973), included in *Poesía* (1978); and *Apariciones y otros poemas* (1982).

In general Gimferrer, though he provides us with fragmentary visions of reality such as Barcelona and the sea, for the most part writes Baroque, metaphysical poetry in which the exotic is set within the framework of the ordinary.

3. *Antonio Colinas* (b. 1946), novelist, essayist, and translator as well as poet, won the National Prize for Literature in 1982 for his *Obra poética completa*. Colinas, a strong proponent of metapoetry, combines Classical themes with Neoromantic connotations, linguistics, graphics, and concrete visual aspects of poetry. He is one of the more elite *culturalista* poets, and he writes about music, Venice, Greece, Ezra Pound, and German Romantics like Hölderlin. *Preludios a una noche total* (1969) deals with nature, love, and the night, in somewhat Romantic terms, and invokes Hölderlin's spirit. Filled with an amorous pantheism, the poems concern love, its birth, death, and cosmic symbolism from a joyful autumn to a solitary winter. *Truenos y flautas en un templo* (1972) is filled with cultural references and what some call *poesía del lenguaje*. *Sepulcro en Tarquinia* (1975) is based in part on the four years Colinas lived in Italy. Colinas deals with the world of art, beauty, and medieval themes in a search for origins. He continues his linguistic experimentation and his cultural obsessions but also talks of time and love. *Astrolabio* (1979) creates a poetic space where sentiments and experience of real authenticity can be lived, a space that recalls mythological dreams. Through literature the poet examines the problems of human love, fatality, and death and a world represented by nature through signs and symbols that also reveal man's inferiority before the infinite. *Noche más allá de la noche* (1983) contemplates the starry night

299

and nature's open spaces and sings to Venice and the Greek Parthenon. Ruins, earth, and nature serve as Colinas' fount of inspiration. *Jardín de Orfeo* (1988) again concentrates on the poet's interior reality.

Despite the hermetic nature of most of his poetry, Colinas draws the reader into his antinomies and dichotomies of light/shadow, life/death, dream/reality. He seeks the reality beneath the reality, and he is aware of love, pain, and death, regardless of the verbal beauty of his poetry or the experimental nature of his language. He acknowledges the possibility of an integration of man and nature. More than almost any other poet he insists on overloading his work with cultural references, but he is also sincere and authentic in rejecting those members of his generation who, in relying on the cultural, turn their backs on the experience of life.

4. *Guillermo Carnero* (b. 1947), also an excellent literary critic, like so many of his generation rejects traditional language and views poetry as a symbol of experience and reality rather than an expression thereof. He chooses the reality of language over reality itself, the construction rather than the experience, and thus creates his own brand of metapoetry.

Carnero's *Dibujo de la muerte* (1967) and Gimferrer's *Arde el mar* are the two most important works of the generation. Carnero deals with the impossibility of existence in a codified manner, because love is a reminder of death, and power can be confronted only through masks. In Baroque poetry he contends that reality or its experience remains only as a projection of a literary aesthetic. The world, then, is an absurd place, false and temporary, and beauty and death are only a part of that tragic vision. His is a disconsolate and cheerless poetry of passing time and desolation.

In the 1970s Carnero continued to write about the relationship of language and experience. In *El sueño de Escipión* (1971), he is unable to apprehend concrete reality through reason or conventional language, but he can discuss the art of writing the poems being written. Frustrated by what people call reality, he turns to the literary experience and in the process constructs a reality that is the result of the poetic process itself. *Variaciones y figuras sobre un tema de la Bruyère* (1974) treats of time and poetry and a method for reading it. The poet continues a self-mocking analysis of the futility and inability of language to define an evanescent reality. *El azar objetivo* (1975) uses deliberately prosaic terminology to attack the rational. A Surrealistic creation, it confronts the irrational nature of poetic language in the creative process. Carnero's collected poetry appeared in 1977 as *Ensayo de una teoría de la visión.*

Carnero replaces real objects with their poetic representations because a poem, he says, cannot speak of any reality but its own, which is more interesting than objective reality. In spite of misgivings about the nature of language, he writes in exotic, decorative, colorful imagery about literature, art, and music rather than life, because reality is unknowable and experience inexpressible. Yet in writing about the world of art, literature, painting, and music and by insisting on the difficulty of using ordinary language, he employs that very language to criticize the normal linguistic codes.

5. *Luis Antonio de Villena* (b. 1951), a novelist and essayist and a heavy user of cultural citations, writes about hedonism, paganism, the body, and homosexual love. In addition to his cultural references and lavish situations, he uses more autobiographical elements than most members of his generation.

Sublime solarium (1971) presents culture as a mask in a poetry of decadent and Surrealistic tones. *El viaje a Bizancio* (1978), filled with Baroque sensuality, tells of a city symbolizing for the poet eternal youth, the joy of love and carnal pleasure, and perfect beauty. *Hymnica* (1979) involves a biographical but yet poetic reconstruction and exaltation of beauty and its temporary possession. *Huir del invierno* (1981) combines the mystical, sensual, and pagan with cultural and geographical references to Greece and Islam. *La muerte únicamente* (1984), whose title is based on a line from Cernuda, again concentrates on absolute beauty, self-affirmation, carnality, and death. The poet utilizes platonic tradition in elevating homosexual love to a metaphysical plane.

6. *Other poets.* Luis Alberto de Cuenca (b. 1950), one of the culturally fixated poets, has written, among several collections, *Schola* (1975). Jaime Siles (b. 1951), religious, mystical, and metaphysical, writes conceptual poetry filled with linguistic paradox. *Alegoría* (1977) and *Columnae* (1986), the latter of which explores life as a support against a collapse into meaninglessness, are among his works. Still other poets are Félix de Azúa (b. 1944), José Gutiérrez (b. 1955), and Blanca Andreu (b. 1959).

Part 6   NONFICTION PROSE

ORIGIN: THE MIDDLE AGES

The appearance of prose in Spain lagged about a century behind that of poetry. In its earliest manifestations, Spanish prose
was erudite and international in spirit. It recorded the learning
of scholars and bore a marked didactic tendency.

A.   Early Chronicles

Spaniards recorded important events as far back as the fifth century in Latin chronicles (pejoratively labeled *cronicones*), which
were largely inexact, arid, and tasteless. Spanish was not used
for recording history until the early thirteenth century.

B.   Lucas de Tuy and Rodrigo Jiménez de Rada

Lucas de Tuy (d. 1249?), known also as *el Tudense,* was born
in the second half of the twelfth century and wrote several
works, the most important of which is *Chronicon mundi,* produced in 1236 and translated into Spanish near the end of the
thirteenth century with the title *Corónica de Spaña por Lucas de
Tui.* Rodrigo Jiménez de Rada (1170?–1247), Archbishop of
Toledo, wrote several histories in Latin, the best of which was
Historia gothica o De Rebus hispaniae, produced in the first half of
the thirteenth century and translated into Spanish under the title *Estoria de los godos.* These two authors advanced the writing
of history and pointed the way to the great historical works of
Alfonso *el Sabio.*

C.   The Toledan School of Translators

During the reign of Alfonso VII, the fame of a school of translators in Toledo spread over the civilized world. When the Arabs

conquered Spain in the early eighth century, they brought with them the Oriental apologue, plus knowledge about science, mathematics, astronomy, and medicine, and had incorporated into their own culture much of what they had learned through contacts with Hellenic centers that they had captured, particularly Alexandria. Little of this knowledge was available elsewhere in Europe. The Arabs translated their manuscripts from Arabic to Latin, and scholars from all over Europe flooded Toledo in quest of learning. Oriental-Greek knowledge and scholarship were thus transmitted to Europe, and Toledo became a renowned center of culture and learning.

D. Earliest Nonfiction Prose Works: First Half of the Thirteenth Century

This period produced a number of nonfiction works. Among the most notable are *Diez mandamientos,* a dry guide for confessors; *Anales toledanos,* an arid collection of historical facts covering twelve centuries; the *Fuero juzgo,* a legal code; *El libro de los doze sabios,* an early treatise on the education of princes; *Diálogo o disputa del cristiano y el judío,* a discussion of religious faiths; *Flores de filosofía,* an anthology of philosophical maxims; *Poridat de poridades,* a collection of wise sayings; and *Bocados de oro,* a discourse on men of letters and arms, and philosophical maxims from the Orient, Greece, and Rome.

THE SECOND HALF OF THE THIRTEENTH CENTURY

A. Alfonso X, *el Sabio* (1221–1284)

Alfonso's leadership ignited a veritable renaissance of learning. Under his guidance and example, Spanish prose came of age, and Spanish replaced Latin for writing history. He was a learned man himself and directed the translation of literary, scientific, and technical works from the Arabic. He might be called the first of the encyclopedists. He gathered scholars from all corners of Spain and set them to work on the most important nonfiction works of the Middle Ages. He played the role of editor in chief but often took an active part in the preparation of his monumental books.

Among these works is *La primera crónica general,* begun about 1270, as significant as any history written in Europe in the Middle Ages. Although it covers the history of mankind from the population of the world by Noah's sons, it concentrates chiefly on Spain and brings the country's history down to the reign of Fernando III. Its authors relied on a variety of sources, but of special interest to students of Spanish literature are the prose renderings of epic poems embedded in its pages. The language of this venerable history is varied, rich, picturesque, reasonably artistic, and *castizo.* Alfonso established Spanish as an independent, literary tongue in this and other works; he himself corrected the manuscripts of his scholars. No greater service was rendered to the language until Cervantes wrote his *Quijote.* Alfonso completed the first two parts, and the third and fourth parts were finished in 1289 during the reign of Sancho IV, Alfonso's son (r. 1284–1295). Alfonso also started a history of even vaster proportions, the *General estoria,* a history of the world, but it remained uncompleted.

A second major work compiled by Alfonso's scholars is the *Siete partidas* (1256–1265), a codification of all the laws of Castile, which remains today one of the world's great legislative documents. The legal aspects of this monumental work are of slight interest to literary students, but the nearly complete documentation of the life, manners, customs, dress, and entertainments of thirteenth-century Spain that the book contains are most valuable. The book is a guide to good manners and good conduct and stipulates the responsibilities, obligations, and rights of each of the social classes from the king to the peasant, thus providing a picturesque panorama of medieval life. It also is a gold mine of philological and semantic information, for it refers to hundreds of things by name and explains and defines various terms.

Alfonso's scientific and technical works include *Lapidario* (1279), about the curative and magical properties ascribed to precious stones; *Libros del saber de astronomía,* a study of astronomy based on the Ptolemaic system; *Tablas astronómicas Alfonsíes* (1271), another work on astronomy concerned with the measurement of time and the occurrence of eclipses; *Septenario,* a treatise on the seven arts; and *Libros de ajedrez, dados, y tablas* (1280), the most important medieval work on these games.

Alfonso's genius lay in organization and synthesis. He inspired his collaborators with the enthusiasm to conclude the

305

grand cultural projects he conceived. Through his leadership, Greek, Roman, Islamic, Jewish, German, and Spanish cultures spread from his workshop to the rest of the world. He was renowned for his tolerance and his interest in both politics and religion, and he gathered scholars to his court regardless of their racial or religious identity. By continuing the important work of the Toledan school of translators, by elevating the legal and historical work of his predecessors to heights not attained elsewhere in the Middle Ages, and by guiding his important works from conception to completion, this cultural giant of the Middle Ages rendered all of Europe significant services.

THE FOURTEENTH CENTURY

A. General Considerations

Two great figures stand out in the field of didactic prose in the fourteenth century, Juan Manuel and Pero López de Ayala, famed also for their work in other literary genres.

B. Juan Manuel (1282–1347)

Juan Manuel, of noble descent, was one of the most tempestuous and dangerous barons of his time. He loved power and became embroiled in wars, rebellions, intrigues, betrayals, and assassinations and fought against his own king, Alfonso XI. After a turbulent career, he became reconciled with the king and joined him in campaigns against the Moors.

The life of this medieval firebrand does not correspond to his writings, for in them he was preoccupied with the improvement and education of his fellow man and the salvation of men's souls. His writings are serious and sober, full of stern advice, severe judgments, and reminders of moral obligations. The serenity of his writings does not reflect the passions and violence of his life.

Juan Manuel's three most important books are *El Conde Lucanor* (1323–1335); *El libro del caballero y del escudero* (1326), a didactic work containing moral disquisitions and instructions on the most varied subjects; and *El libro de los estados* (1330), an encyclopedic work based on the Buddha legend in which the Buddha is converted to Christianity, plus treatises on a variety of other topics. Of lesser significance are *El libro de la caza, Libro de los castigos, Crónica abreviada, Libro de las armas,* and *Tractado de la asunción de la Virgen María.* His lost works are *De las reglas como se debe trobar, Libro de los cantares,* and *Los engeños,* a treatise on the machines of war. Juan Manuel sought the truth and has gone down in history as one of Spain's most remarkable figures of the Middle Ages.

C. Pero López de Ayala (1332–1407)

Histories of the reigns of kings continued to appear in the first half of the fourteenth century, but none compared with those of Alfonso *el Sabio.* It was not until the latter part of the century that a historian of first magnitude appeared, Pero López de Ayala, one of the great spirits of the time and perhaps the outstanding Spaniard of his age. As a soldier, diplomat, writer, and adviser to kings, he lived in a time of turmoil and treachery and judged his world harshly. He lived through the troubled reigns of five kings. No one was better qualified to record their history.

López de Ayala was a medieval man standing on the threshold of the Renaissance. The relaxation of morals, civil strife, fratricidal wars, changes in politics and society, the crumbling of the old castes, the emergence of a middle class, growing cities, the schism in the Church, the trampling of Christian guidelines underfoot, and many other changes taking place troubled him deeply. He adopted the role of judge and censor and expressed himself with severity and bitterness. Yet despite his pessimism, he believed in the great virtues of justice and charity and in the possibility of peace and good government. He saw a basic equality in all men and believed that even the humblest human life was important.

As a historian, López de Ayala relied only on accurate sources, tried to be fair and impartial, was more interested in men's motives than their actions, and remained impassive before the sometimes violent acts he recorded. His histories, which he entitled *Crónicas,* embrace the reigns of Pedro I, *el Cruel;* Enrique II de Trastamara; and Juan I; and part of the reign of Enrique III, covering the years 1350 to 1396. His objectivity, impartiality, factual accuracy, critical approach, and psychological insight taught lessons to future historians.

THE FIFTEENTH CENTURY

A. General Considerations

Life changed radically in late fifteenth-century Spain as Ferdinand and Isabel tamed the rebellious barons and established their absolute monarchy. Noblemen drifted to the court and took to writing poetry, polishing their manners, and studying Latin. Swarms of historians recorded all events of consequence. Humanists produced their grammars and dictionaries, and moral philosophers tried to ennoble the spirit of the time. The introduction of printing in 1474 marked a new era. Verbal portraits were attempted for the first time. The Renaissance had dawned.

B. Historiography of the Fifteenth Century

Kings continued the custom of appointing an official chronicler of their reigns, but their ambition was much narrower than that of their predecessors, as they had recorded only the history of the reign of a single monarch, or even just a few years of a given reign. Also, lives of important personages other than kings and queens were recorded, and history became so specialized that some chronicles recorded single events. Two new types of writing appeared: the character sketch and descriptions of travel to exotic places. The histories are interesting not for their excellence but for the tumultuous events they record. No first-rank historian appeared, but those who chronicled the events of the time did preserve the record of the nation's approach to national unity and empire. Special mention should be made of several histories and historians.

1. *La crónica de don Juan II,* the first part ascribed to Alvar García de Santa María (1390–1460), covers the politically troubled but artistically active reign of Juan II. Its most interesting portion concerns the execution of don Alvaro de Luna and the king's reaction after his death.

2. *Pedro del Corral* produced around 1443 the *Crónica sarracina o Crónica del rey don Rodrigo con la destrucción de España,* a curious book that is a mixture of fact and fantasy. Some call it Spain's first historical novel, since the author freely substituted his own inventions for historical facts. It was very popular when it was

published in 1511 because it recalled a national tradition and reflected the glamor of chivalry. Pérez de Guzmán labeled the book "lies and manifest untruths," but it prospered nonetheless. Later, ballad writers used it as a source.

3. *Mosén Diego de Valera* (1412–1487) wrote one of the more ambitious chronicles of his day at the request, he claimed, of Queen Isabel. A prolific writer, he produced in addition to his *Crónica abreviada* a number of epistles and other histories.

4. *Alfonso Fernández de Palencia* (1432–1492), one of the abler nonfiction prose writers of the fifteenth century, was a leading Humanist of the time and produced a variety of works ranging from histories to translations of Plutarch, a dictionary of the language, and social and political satire. His greatest contribution, however, was his history of the reign of Enrique IV, first written in Latin and translated under the title *Décadas* or *Crónicas de Enrique IV*. Here he painted an appalling picture of the depravity and corruption of this sad era.

5. *Diego Enríquez del Castillo* (1433–1504) also wrote a history of the reign of Enrique IV, which in contrast with that of Fernández de Palencia represents the king as benevolent and just, his kingdom as well administered, and the people as satisfied with the government. He was in the service of the king, and his work has largely been discredited as a reliable record.

6. *Andrés Bernáldez* (d. 1513) is remembered for his *Historia de los Reyes Católicos, don Fernando y doña Isabel*. This account is prized especially for the information it contains on Columbus' voyages; Bernáldez gathered reports from the admiral's diary and from personal interviews with him.

C. Character Sketches of the Fifteenth Century

1. *Fernán Pérez de Guzmán* (1376–1460) was the first to join together a series of moral and physical verbal portraits of eminent persons. The third part of his *Mar de historias* is entitled *Generaciones y semblanzas*, and it is here that he portrays verbally thirty-five men and one woman from the reigns of Enrique III and Juan II, leaving us a splendid record of the notables of his day.

2. *Hernando del Pulgar* (1436–1493) was a happy imitator of Pérez de Guzmán and wrote the *Libro de los claros varones de Castilla*, a book of short biographies in which he traced in precise strokes the verbal portraits of twenty-four of his contemporaries.

309

D. Private Chronicles of the Fifteenth Century

Historians did not confine themselves to kings but wrote entire chronicles on the lives of prominent men. Two worthy of mention are the *Crónica de don Alvaro de Luna,* a favorable account of this famous man's life and execution, possibly written by Gonzalo de Chacón; and the *Crónica de don Pedro Niño, conde de Buelna,* by Gutierre Diez Games (1379–1450), a history that reads almost like a novel of chivalry.

E. Chronicles of Single Events

A few historians devoted a book to a single historical event. The best known of these is the *Libro del paso honroso de Suero de Quiñones* by Pedro Rodríguez de Lena. Its lasting appeal is manifested by the fact that the Duque de Rivas used it in writing *El paso honroso* in 1812.

F. Descriptions of Travels

Ruy González de Clavijo (d. 1412) wrote the best of these, *Vida del gran Tamerlán.* Enrique III sent expeditions to the Middle East in search of emperors and kings. One of them found Tamerlane, the Tartar king, who sent rich gifts back to Enrique. Out of gratitude, Enrique sent a mission to Tamerlane's court, a member of which was the author of this travelogue.

G. Humanists of the Fifteenth Century

The Renaissance gained a strong foothold in Spain in the waning years of the fifteenth century as medieval Scholasticism crumbled before the onslaught of the modern spirit emanating from new centers of thought, chiefly Italy. The study of Latin and Greek became fashionable, and philology replaced theology as the most important of studies. The philologists' interests were encyclopedic and embraced all fields of inquiry known at the time. New universities were founded, and the introduction of printing brought books within the reach of many. Though the new freedoms led some into the occult, Humanists solidly advanced their cause and opened the gates of the Renaissance.

310   1. *The Marqués de Villena* (1384–1434), a puzzling man, was

accused of being a dealer in black magic, a wizard, and a nec-
romancer and of making a pact with the devil. The works he
left are of ordinary merit. His library was burned, however,
after his death, and perhaps his better efforts were thus destroyed. His *Arte cisoria* is Spain's first cookbook. His *Libro del
aojamiento o fascinología* discusses the ways of removing the spell
of the "evil eye." He also left a treatise on the plague. His most
important work is his *Arte de trobar,* Spain's earliest work on
poetic criticism, but unfortunately only a portion of it has been
saved.

2. *Elio Antonio de Nebrija* (1441–1522) studied at Salamanca
but went to Italy at the age of nineteen and studied there for ten
years. Upon returning to Spain he taught at the University of
Salamanca, to which he hoped to bring the light of the new
learning. Later he was called to the University of Alcalá to help
produce the Complutensian Bible. He was a typical Humanist, a
walking encyclopedia, and he enjoyed the protection of highly
placed persons, including Queen Isabel. His work embraced all
fields of knowledge, and he waged a singlehanded war against
ignorance.

His works were written mostly in Latin. Among them is his
Latin grammar, *Introductiones latinae* (1481). Two particularly
important works by Nebrija appeared in 1492, *Gramática sobre la
lengua castellana,* commissioned by the queen, the first grammar
of a modern language, and the Latin-Spanish portion of Nebrija's dictionary. He finished the Spanish-Latin part in 1495.
His *Reglas de ortografía castellana* (1517) speaks for itself. Named
official historian by Fernando, Nebrija translated Pulgar's chronicles of Fernando's reign into Latin, hoping thus to achieve
greater universality.

3. *Minor figures* of the fifteenth century include Cardinal
Francisco Jiménez de Cisneros (1437–1517), who founded the
University of Alcalá and published the first critical edition of the
Bible anywhere, the Complutensian Bible; Don Alvaro de Luna
(d. 1453), who, though not a Humanist, was a central figure of
the age and made his contribution to letters in the book *Libro de
las claras y virtuosas mujeres,* a study of outstanding women from
Biblical days to his own; Alfonso de la Torre (1421–1461), who
left an encyclopedic work entitled *Visión deleitable de la filosofía y
artes liberales* (*ca.* 1440); and Juan de Lucena (d. 1506), whose
fictional *Libro de vida beata* (1463) reports on discussions between
the Marqués de Santillana, Alonso de Cartagena, Juan de Mena,
and the author.

311

THE SIXTEENTH CENTURY

Politically, this was the glorious age for Spaniards as the empire, begun by the Catholic Sovereigns, reached its peak under Carlos V. To this day it remains the largest domain ever organized under one scepter. Though Carlos tried honestly and valiantly for reconciliation with the Protestants, ultimately he decided to make Spain the champion and principal defender of Roman Catholicism in Europe in order to preserve Church unity in the face of the religious wars that he could not win. This was more than the empire could bear, coupled with all its other troubles at home and in America, where colonization was proceeding rapidly. Carlos abdicated in favor of his son, Felipe II, who despaired of controlling the strong Protestant movements and closed Spain's doors to the world.

Culturally, Spaniards enjoyed free inquiry for a time, and a liberal spirit in the realm of ideas and philosophy prevailed as Spain seemed to be headed down the rationalistic road the rest of Europe was taking. Erasmus was known and admired; but after the Council of Trent, Carlos V and later Felipe II stilled the paganistic spirit of the Renaissance and any deviation from approved dogma. Though Spain prospered for a number of years, Felipe's isolationist policies spelled eventual weakness in all areas, political, cultural, and economic.

Didactic prose reflected the political, cultural, and religious conditions outlined above. Erasmists, such as the Valdés brothers, wrote in the early years, as did philosophers. After the controls were invoked, the great Mystic literature of Spain flourished. Historians continued to produce volumes, and eyewitness history from the New World became fashionable. Prose style took two directions, namely toward simple, direct, unfettered expression on one hand and toward the rhetorical, artificial style that pointed to Gongorism on the other. This diverse and unsettled era heralded the Golden Age.

A. Moralists, Humanists, Philosophers

1. *Antonio de Guevara* (1480?–1545) wrote three books. His *Reloj de príncipes* (1529), also known by the title *Libro áureo del emperador Marco Aurelio*, is a largely apocryphal didactic novel, a politico-moralistic treatise designed to give the emperor a model of the perfect ruler. It was very popular, probably for the great diver-

sity of themes that Guevara treated, including war, religion, marriage, the family, misogynist propaganda, death, humor, anecdotes, and fables. Guevara is acknowledged as one of the leading prose stylists before Cervantes, and though his style smacks of Gongorism, he is eloquent and reveals a quick mind, a ready wit, and clever ingenuity.

Menosprecio de corte y alabanza de aldea (1539) treats the traditional theme of the perils, corruptions, and sins of city life and the simplicity and purity of rural life. Guevara testified that it was his most carefully and painstakingly written work, in which he polished his language, strove for elegance, and exercised his judgment to the utmost. Like Fray Luis de León some years later, the harassed courtier longs for the peace of the country and laments the virtues he lost in the city. Between 1539 and 1545 Guevara wrote eighty-three *Epístolas familiares* to many different people on the widest range of subjects, and his *Décadas de los Césares* is his rendering of the lives of ten Roman emperors. Though he took many liberties with facts, tampering with them or inventing them carelessly at times, he was undoubtedly in tune with his times, was an important man in his day, and had a strong influence on the development of prose writing in Europe.

2. *Juan Luis Vives* (1492–1540) personified the Renaissance in Spain and is considered by some as Spain's greatest philosopher. His chief claim to originality rests upon his use of the inductive method for philosophical and psychological discovery. He reacted away from Scholasticism toward the new Humanism, along with Erasmus and others. He eventually went to England at the invitation of Henry VIII. There he became the friend of Thomas More and served as royal tutor and lecturer at Oxford.

Preceding modern philosophers in the use of the empirical method, he insisted upon the importance of observation, introspection, and the removal of *a priori* judgments in reasoning. He will always be known as one of the stalwarts of Christian Humanism. His seventy-three works, all in Latin, are models of purity and style. Unfortunately, his contributions are not widely known, and he has yet to be acknowledged as one of the great thinkers of his time.

3. *Alfonso de Valdés* (1490?–1532) was converted to Erasmism and corresponded with Erasmus until his death. In his *Diálogo de Lactancio y un arcediano* he defended Carlos V against criticism following the sacking of Rome in 1527 and laid blame on the pope. His *Diálogo de Mercurio y Carón*, whose real intent was to defend the emperor again, mercilessly flayed various social classes, espe-

cially the clergy, scoffed at certain practices of the Church, such as bulls and indulgences, and poked fun at high Church officials for their costumes and jewelry. Along with other Erasmists, Valdés was forced to flee Spain by the Inquisition's campaign against them. He died in Vienna, having escaped the Inquisition's *procesos* instituted against him and his brother.

4. *Juan de Valdés* (1501?–1541), brother of Alfonso, absorbed the Humanistic spirit and was an enthusiastic disciple of Erasmus'. He too had to flee Spain because of his heterodoxy. His *Ciento diez consideraciones divinas* (1550) outlines his theological system, which was somewhat at variance with orthodoxy. His *Diálogo de la lengua* (*ca.* 1535), styled as the first important linguistic treatise on the Spanish language, is of much greater interest today. In it he suggested many innovations, but since it was not published until 1737, it had little effect on the development of the language. It is, nevertheless, an important statement on sixteenth-century Spanish.

5. *Pedro Mexía* (1499?–1551) compiled an interesting tome, *Silva de varia lección* (1542), a grand mixture of information and misinformation of all kinds that embodies much from Greek and Roman antiquity and from the sciences. This catchall was very popular in its day and was translated into various languages.

6. *Cristóbal de Villalón* (1510?–1562?), whose identity has never been clarified to everyone's satisfaction, was formerly credited with an interesting work, *El viaje de Turquía,* an account of his trip to Constantinople. Bataillon credits a Doctor Andrés Laguna with the authorship of this book. Villalón's *El Crotalón* is a satire on contemporary life that points up the corruption and depravities of the human race that he had observed.

7. *Fernán Pérez de Oliva* (1494?–1533), a highly educated man, wrote treatises, dialogues, and discourses of a didactic nature. His best-known work is *Diálogo de la dignidad del hombre* (1546), in which he perceives the greatness of man and sees in him the image of God.

B. Historians of the Sixteenth Century

Sixteenth-century history can be divided into two groups: that which deals with Spain and that which describes the marvels, hardships, and heroism of the conquest of the New World. A new trend toward scientific documentation of facts indicated that the age of modern historical writing had begun. Two writers of real merit stand out in this period, namely Diego Hurtado de Mendoza and Juan de Mariana.

1. *Diego Hurtado de Mendoza* (1503–1575) was an important political figure and virtual viceroy of Italy under Carlos V. His *Guerra de Granada* chronicles Felipe II's war with the *moriscos* of Granada and is rigorously accurate eyewitness history. Like López de Ayala, he felt it his right to make moral judgments and to analyze motives and actions. His unusual gift of narrative, plastic imagination, and dramatic visions, with which he visualized a scene as a stage setting, made history come alive. His style was not impeccable, but his honesty, integrity, fairness, strength, and lucidity have earned him a rank among his contemporaries second only to Juan de Mariana.

2. *Juan de Mariana* (1536–1624) wrote a thirty-volume *Historia General de España* that fixed his reputation as the best historian of his day. He began with the arrival of Japheth's fifth son in Spain and continued to the year 1516, the date of the death of Fernando, *el católico*. His purpose was to eulogize Spain, and for the sake of universality he wrote it first in Latin with the title *Historiae de Rebus Hispaniae*. The first twenty volumes appeared in 1592, five more in 1595, and the final five in 1605. He himself translated his history into Spanish in 1601 and then published a definitive version in 1606. In doing so, he enlarged it considerably. An ardent patriot, he wanted Spain's greatness known to the world and to the Spaniards themselves. Though he used legendary material, he also used something of the scientific historian's procedure. He too believed it his duty to praise right and condemn evil, and he told the truth even if it hurt. His fearlessness got him penalties on occasion, but nothing of a serious nature. His history is still regarded as one of the high marks of Spanish historiography.

3. *Lesser historians of the sixteenth century.* Jerónimo de Zurita (1512–1580) approached his task in a scientific manner and ushered in the modern age of history in Spain. Gonzalo Fernández de Oviedo (1478–1557), who spent his life in the New World, lumped a heterogeneous mass of information about the new lands into a fifty-volume work, *Historia natural y general de las Indias*, a vast repository of facts about the colonies. Hernán Cortés (1485–1547), the great *conquistador*, reported his adventures in *Cartas de relación*, written between 1519 and 1526. Francisco López de Gómara (1512–1557?), Cortes' secretary and fervent admirer, wrote his *Historia general de las Indias*, which exhibits a strong bias in his captain's favor. Bernal Díaz

del Castillo (*ca.* 1495–1584), a soldier in Cortés' army, corrected López de Gómara's account to tell what he called the "true story of the conquest" in his *Historia verdadera de la conquista de la Nueva España,* not published until 1632. Bartolomé de las Casas (1474–1566), a Dominican, wrote *Brevísima relación de la destrucción de las Indias* (1552), in which he harshly criticized Spanish colonial policy, thus fueling the propaganda of Spain's colonial competitors and igniting the fire that led to the Black Legend. Alvar Núñez Cabeza de Vaca (1490?–1564?) wrote *Naufragios,* which narrates his incredible adventures along the Gulf of Mexico and the Gulf of California.

C. Ascetics and Mystics of the Sixteenth Century

From the beginnings up to the sixteenth century, Spanish literature was in one way or another related to religion. Renaissance Humanism began to change that, but Felipe II's Counter Reformation brought religion back to a position of prominence, paving the way for the vast ascetic and Mystic writings of the second half of the sixteenth century.

1. *Juan de Avila* (1500–1569) was a leading figure in the initial phases of the luxuriant flowering of religious writings of his era. His *Audi, filia et vide* (1560) was an important contribution to the genre. More important, however, is his *Epistolario espiritual para todos los estados* (1578), consisting of 150 letters to men and women of all states and conditions, in which he offers advice, consolation, comfort, and warnings as well as speculations on the religious life in general.

2. *Fray Luis de Granada* (1504–1588) devoted himself to sacred oratory and became the preacher of greatest authority in his day. *Guía de pecadores* (1567) is his best-known prose work. It exhorts man to follow the road to salvation and includes a detailed discussion of sins and ways of combatting vices. His *Introducción al símbolo de la fe* (1582) is an encyclopedia of the Christian religion, and his *Libro de la oración y meditación* (1554) deals with the circumstances that favor or hinder true prayer.

3. *Santa Teresa de Jesús* (1515–1582) was the outstanding woman of her day and still holds the respect and admiration of the Christian world. She joined the Carmelite Order at the age of seventeen and later formed the *descalzas* branch, which expanded greatly under her custody. Teresa had no literary ambitions and wrote her books only at the request of her superiors or her nuns. Her most important work is entitled *El castillo inte-*

rior o las moradas (1577). It is a treatise on the relationship of the soul with God and the prayer stages through which one must pass to reach that Mystic state where the soul is one with Him. Her intent was to teach one how to reach this stage of perfection. Other works of Santa Teresa are *El libro de su vida* (1562–1565), *El libro de las fundaciones* (1573), and *Camino de perfección* (1565; and in a definitive edition in 1570). Fray Luis de León published these works with a prologue in 1588.

4. *San Juan de la Cruz* (1542–1591), essentially a poet, was intimately associated with Santa Teresa and joined the male branch of the Carmelites. He was the most metaphysical of the Mystics, was fond of abstractions, and acknowledged the difficulties of expressing the ineffable. Some of his prose consists of extensions of and commentaries on his poetry and explains it in great detail. Both his poetry and prose are subtle, complicated, and difficult to understand, and though he is recognized as one of the great Mystics of all time, he does not have the popular appeal of Santa Teresa or Fray Luis de León. His prose works are *Cántico espiritual, Avisos y sentencias,* and *Cartas.* His writings represent the fullest development of Mysticism in Spain. The intensity of his being and the fervor of his devotion made him unique and brought Mysticism to the heights of its expression.

5. *Fray Luis de León* (1527–1591), better known as a poet, wrote good prose works that have been underrated because of the excellence of his poetry. Stylistically he ranks among the great prosists of all time. Believing in the power and beauty of the Spanish language, with his careful craftsmanship and unerring feel for his native tongue he elevated prose style as Garcilaso had enhanced poetry. He left three major prose works: *De los nombres de Cristo, La perfecta casada,* and *Exposición del libro de Job,* all republished over the years in many editions, some in the twentieth century. Fray Luis and San Juan died in the same year, and with them the blossom of Mystic literature withered and died. No great Mystic writers appeared after their time.

THE SEVENTEENTH CENTURY

A. General Considerations

The Golden Age was in full bloom when the seventeenth century dawned, but sensitive writers were beginning to foresee the unmistakable signs of degeneration that would continue its inexorable course to and beyond the end of the century. The most striking development of the period was the emphasis on the Baroque style that had long been ripening in Spain. The two authors in the field of nonfiction prose who best represent the Baroque period and who most clearly saw Spain's true condition are Francisco de Quevedo and Baltasar Gracián. Both are *conceptistas,* both are critical of their fellow man, and both are pessimistic. Diego de Saavedra Fajardo holds third place behind these two. Historians continued to write, but none of first category appeared. Religious writing had passed its peak and now entered a period of degeneracy.

B. Francisco Gómez de Quevedo y Villegas (1580–1645)

Francisco de Quevedo was one of the few men of his time to recognize and admit the truth of Spain's creeping political, moral, and economic degeneration. Consequently at an early age he lashed out against the corruption, weaknesses, and sagging morality that were leading his country downward. His onerous warnings and unsparing criticisms earned him enmities that eventually led to his imprisonment and death; but he left a superior legacy that is extraordinarily rich and diversified and has earned him the reputation as Spain's foremost satirist and wit. He wrote poetry, political treatises, novels, ascetic works, lives of saints, literary criticism, dramas, philosophy, moral and theological treatises, history, satiric works, and fantasies. He stands as a giant in Spanish letters, and his work has left an indelible impression on succeeding generations. The one great unifying thread that runs through his work is satire, for he fearlessly attacked faults and pleaded for reform.

Quevedo's work can be classified into several categories. Those known as the humorous or festive type number twenty-two and include *Premáticas y aranceles generales* (1600), *Origen y definiciones de la necedad* (1598), *El caballero de Tenaza* (1606), and *Libro de todas las cosas y otras muchas más* (1627). His satire is not benevolent, and although it amuses, it often changes to mockery and caricature. Life was grotesque to Quevedo, and the smile on his face often changed to a grimace. A note of bitterness and even loathing invades his satire, for finding little to admire in society, he became deeply pessimistic and disillusioned. Yet he had many admirers and some friends, and foreigners felt their visit to Spain was not complete until they had seen and talked to the great man.

Outstanding among his political writings is *Política de Dios, gobierno de Cristo* (1617–1626), which sets forth his convictions concerning government, based on the Bible. A second part, published in 1634–1635, adds *y tiranía de Satanás* to the title. Again he strikes out against the decay of morals and the indifference of kings to their responsibilities. Justice, virtue, and the rights of the people were the basis of good government, and the good king was vigilant, solicitous of the people's good, tolerant, generous, and not too severe. Other political works are *Vida de Marco Bruto* (1631–1644) and *España defendida y los tiempos de ahora de las calumnias de noveleros y sediciosos* (1609). Quevedo clearly saw his own bitter, satiric spirit and said of himself in a poem: "soy / un escorpión maldiciente, / hijo al fin de las arenas, / engendradoras de sierpes."

Quevedo's philosophical doctrines are disclosed chiefly in three works: *De los remedios de cualquier fortuna* (1633), *Nombre y origen, intento, recomendación y decencia de la doctrina estoica* (1633–1634), and *Sentencias*. The stoicism of Seneca dominated Quevedo's philosophical thinking, guided him in doubts, consoled him in trouble, and defended him against persecutions. It is seen in his *La cuna y la sepultura* (1612, 1630, 1633), an ascetic work, in which the author guides man through the sorrows and misfortunes of life from the cradle to the grave, pointing out the futility of placing one's hope in worldly things and proclaiming the true values.

The prose works that brought Quevedo the greatest renown, however, are the satiricomoral pieces entitled *Sueños y discursos de verdades descubridoras de abusos, vicios, y engaños en todos los oficios y estados*. There are five (some critics add a sixth) of these *Sueños* written at different periods of the author's life, dating from 1606 to 1622. Here Quevedo directs devastating attacks at all the professions, and nearly every human type is the target of his satire and contempt, except the soldier and the poor. He sees corruption, dishonesty, deceit, injustice, and vice of every sort around him, and before he is through he paints humanity in a pitiful state. He saw little in man that could redeem him, and his *Sueños* predicted the ruin awaiting Spain. Stylistically the *Sueños* were a triumph. The language in which Quevedo expressed his tortured visions is forceful and vivid, and the uniqueness of his imagination is unsurpassed. His sardonic laughter is frighten-

319

ing. His interpretation of life is depressing to read, but we must admire his honesty, his courage, and his patriotism in composing this scathing indictment of his times. Quevedo clearly saw what was wrong with Spain, but he had no solutions to offer. Yet the cures seem to be implicit in his incisive criticisms of existing evils. He only hoped that by demonstrating the ugliness of evil and corruption, man might correct himself.

C. Baltasar Gracián y Morales (1601–1658)

Baltasar Gracián was a kindred spirit to Quevedo. Pessimistic, he viewed life as a constant struggle in which there was little hope for progress and happiness for mankind, but he did believe that two or three in every generation could rise to greatness. Gracián, too, hated fools, who in his view far outnumbered the wise. With Quevedo, Gracián represents the culmination of *conceptista* prose. All his works except two are moralistic, and his moral philosophy has earned him the reputation of being the successor of Luis Vives.

Gracián wrote six important works. The first three provide a composite portrait of the ideal figure. *El héroe* (1637) reveals Gracián's concept of the hero of the seventeenth century. The hero is first of all a man of great intellect and understanding, of good judgment and great individuality, who wins eternal fame through his writings, his virtue, his actions, or his politics. He shows interest only in those who can absorb his teachings, and he loathes the masses. If he makes a mistake he must know how to cover it up. Ability is no assurance of success, for luck plays an important part. Gracián's cynicism is also evident in his beliefs that one should not keep company with the poor or unfortunate lest he make a bad impression on the people and that he should exhibit some weakness, even if feigned, in order to counteract envy.

El político don Fernando el Católico (1640) deals with good government and proposes Fernando, who had founded an empire and brought order out of chaos, as the perfect ruler. The prince must be courageous and prudent, must choose his ministers wisely, and must not reveal his plans or motives, especially when he is preparing for war.

El discreto (1646) completes the portrait of the ideal figure. Gracián lists twenty-five excellent qualities of the *discreto* and devotes a chapter to the discussion of each attribute.

The only nonmoralistic works Gracián left were *El comulga-*

tario (1655), a guidebook to prayer; and *Agudeza y arte de ingenio* (1648), a revision of *El arte de ingenio, tratado de agudeza* (1642). The *Agudeza* is the handbook and anthology of the literary craze of the day, *conceptismo*. Gracián, both *culterano* and *conceptista*, desired to set down in writing the doctrine of *conceptismo* and provide rules and examples for future writers. He believed that obscurity was necessary and that a writer should attempt to conceal part of his meaning in order to dazzle and impress the reader. The conceit, he believed, is to the intellect what beauty is to the eyes and harmony to the ears. He avoided the obvious words, made puns, used antitheses, inversions, obscure metaphors, and all the other tricks of Gongorism. He also developed a highly condensed style, a kind of literary shorthand, for he strove ceaselessly for concision. His contempt for clarity was probably related to his contempt for the ignorant masses, and he believed the essence of good art was obscurity.

The *Oráculo manual y arte de prudencia* (1647) is a collection of three hundred maxims in which Gracián gives pungent, satiric advice on the problems of this life and seems little concerned with life after death. He has been accused of cold cynicism, hypocrisy, and anti-Christian sentiments. This is borne out to some extent in his maxims. After stating the kernel of his thought, he explains it in a short paragraph. The *Oráculo* probably influenced La Rochefoucauld and La Bruyère and certainly affected Schopenhauer, who translated it and stated that Gracián was his favorite author.

El criticón (1651–1657), Gracián's last and most ambitious work, is the product of a lifetime of reading and reflection and is his judgment of the folly and stupidity of man. It is a philosophical novel in which mankind's faults are mercilessly and bitterly condemned; but Gracián does not abandon man to hopelessness. He must struggle against the adversities and wickedness of the world and perfect himself for immortality through virtue. *El criticón* deeply influenced nineteenth-century philosophy. Schopenhauer considered it one of the best books ever written. Stylistically it represents the culmination of the Baroque manner, and ideologically, the pessimism of the age.

Gracián ranks as one of Spain's greatest writers and savants, one of few who looked beneath the surface and boldly exposed the decadence of his era. Cejador y Frauca, along with many others, saw in him an intelligent and distinguished author, philosopher, political critic, and censor of human conduct, one of Spain's deepest thinkers of all time, the equal of Quevedo and

Seneca. Like the former, he offered no solutions but apparently hoped that his indictment of society would produce reforms.

D. Diego de Saavedra Fajardo (1584–1648)

Saavedra stood in the middle of European politics for thirty years. He was saddened by what he saw happening to Spain, for he was in a position, as a diplomat engaged in international negotiations, to witness her decline and failing prestige. His experience equipped him to produce the best political treatise of the seventeenth century, *Idea de un príncipe político-cristiano representada en cien empresas* (1640). Here he gives much prudent advice to the king, expressing Spain's weaknesses and decadent state. Saavedra reveals his deep political feeling, his immense sympathy for the people, and his uncompromising qualifications for the perfect prince. How different Spain's history would be had it found a prince who had followed Saavedra's advice!

Saavedra's second most important work, the *República literaria,* begun about 1612 and published in 1655, is one of the most significant works of literary criticism of the seventeenth century. He reviews poets, historians, philosophers, and other Spanish and foreign writers. His literary judgments are well grounded, and many are still valid today.

THE EIGHTEENTH CENTURY

A. General Considerations

The Bourbons replaced the Hapsburgs on the Spanish throne, but no immediate artistic renewal occurred. The cultural level rose, however, as ideas came in from abroad and Spaniards worked from within. It was the age of the founding of academies, including the Academia de la Lengua Española, which was organized in 1714. Resistance to the Baroque period focused attention on language, and serious scientific studies tried to simplify it. The Academia de Historia was founded in 1738, the Academia de Bellas Artes in 1744, the Academia de Medicina y Cirugía in 1732, and the Academia de Derecho Español in 1763.

The academic and Neoclassic mood of the century produced countless artistic, political, literary, and religious *tertulias,* out of which came sustained literary polemics that sometimes degenerated into personal attacks. In the long run, though, serious literary discussions of the era helped to clarify uncertainties concerning the worth of both writers and works of past ages.

B. Didactic-Erudite Writers

1. *Benito Jerónimo Feijóo y Montenegro* (1676–1764), one of the most important writers of the century, was the first to introduce modern European culture to his country. He wrote eight volumes of essays between 1726 and 1739 under the general title *Teatro crítico universal.* His *Cartas eruditas y curiosas* (1742–1760) is a kind of supplement. He comments on an astonishing number of topics, but in general his works can be divided into three categories: articles on science, those on superstition, and those on philosophy. He fearlessly attacked cherished institutions and superstitions, felt that literature needed rules, believed firmly in education, and directed his most consistent attacks against medical doctors. Though he was guilty of inconsistencies and outright errors, Feijóo was a man who strove to separate truth from error and to combat ignorance. He also saw the intellectual decay of his country and cared enough to do something about it.

2. *Gaspar Melchor de Jovellanos y Ramírez* (1744–1811) studied for the priesthood but gave this up for a legal career, and in his lifetime he became an economist, historian, educator, poet, philologist, philosopher, politician, dramatist, and statesman. His experiences with the penal system led him to write his lachrymose drama, *El delincuente honrado,* a plea for prison reform. He frequented many academies, held exalted posts in the government, and was a member of the Royal Academy. He also was imprisoned, possibly for his indignation at the queen's relationship with Godoy, and, as a vehement defender of nationalism, refused a position offered to him by Joseph Bonaparte.

His prose masterpiece is *Informe en el expediente de ley agraria* (1795), which showed a broad knowledge of the practical problems of each province and promoted local autonomy; but his *Memoria en defensa de la Junta Central* (1810), in which he pleads for understanding of himself and others, is more moving. His *Memoria para el arreglo de la policía de los espectáculos y diversiones públicas y sobre su origen en España* (1790) is a treatise on the theater in which he proclaims that "la reforma de nuestro teatro debe empezar por el destierro de casi todos los dramas que están sobre la escena." He liked Luzán, was ambivalent about Calderón, but was uncharitable toward Lope. He was a reformer in-

spired by the French Enlightenment, but he was fervently nationalistic. He was Neoclassic by conviction but showed traces of
Romanticism.

In his many letters and historical studies, Jovellanos exempli-
fies the dichotomy between the old and the new. Del Río sees in
him a Romantic or at least a pre-Romantic. He was a man of the
justo medio who tried to unite old traditions to the new spirit
sweeping Europe. His character and ardent patriotism led Menéndez y Pelayo to characterize him as "el más glorioso" of all
eighteenth-century writers.

3. *José Cadalso y Vázquez de Andrade* (1741–1782), a poet and
dramatist, is better known for his prose works. Following the
death of an actress whom he loved, he refused to leave the
church where she was buried. In a state of shock, he was forcibly
dissuaded from attempting to disinter her corpse. Exiled from
Madrid following this macabre incident, he went to Salamanca,
where he produced his own account of his strange activities in a
prose piece entitled *Noches lúgubres* (1789–1790), which he desired to have printed on black paper with yellow ink. In this
work he also complained that mankind is wicked, selfish, evil,
and hypocritical and that life is a grim jest.

Eruditos a la violeta (1772), his didactic masterpiece published
under the pseudonym José Vázquez, is a prose satire directed
against poetasters and others. Here Cadalso set himself the following task: "reducir a un sistema de siete días toda la erudición
moderna." He takes up science, poetry, philosophy, natural law,
theology, mathematics, and, on the seventh day, many things.
He pokes fun at false wisdom and defends Spanish literature
from its detractors, often with a pleasant irony.

His *Cartas marruecas* (1789), supposedly inspired by Montes-
quieu's *Lettres persanes,* are composed of a correspondence between three persons, two Moors and a Spaniard. The ninety
letters disclose the deterioration of Spain but contain many comments on various other matters, such as the variety in the character of the Spanish provinces, bullfighting, lack of peace, building and scientific progress, and the dress, language, and social
conventions of the day. Cadalso characterizes Spain as a land of
underpaid teachers, false nobility, vanity, laziness, and ignorance, preceding in a sense the social satire of Larra. And like
the latter, he lived Romanticism but wrote in Classical style.
Though he harshly criticized Spain and what he called the "in-
feliz y cuitado animal llamado hombre," his criticism was born
out of a disappointed love of country and ardent patriotism.

4. *Other didactic-erudite writers* of the eighteenth century include Lorenzo Hervás y Panduro (1735–1809), Fray Martín Sarmiento (1694–1771), Padre Esteban Arteaga (1747–1799), Juan de Iriarte (1702–1771), and Padre Juan Andrés (1740–1817).

C. Critics and Literary Solons

1. *Ignacio de Luzán* (1702–1754) was the focal point about whom revolved the struggle between the nationalistic and Neoclassic schools of his time. His *Poética* (1737), which espoused chiefly Neoclassicism, consists of four main books. The first deals with the origins and essence of poetry, the second with the delight and utility of poetry, the third with the drama, and the fourth with epic poetry.

Luzán abhorred the excesses of Góngora but praised his simpler poetry. He defined poetry as that beauty of light and truth that lights up our soul and frees it from ignorance. Nevertheless, it should serve a useful purpose. He divided writing into three categories: intellectual, a combination of understanding and fantasy, and fantasy. The *Poética* had a tremendously favorable impact on a small group of people and aroused the ire of others. For the majority of critics it is the most important literary document of the eighteenth century, though the works of Feijóo and Mayáns run a close second. Luzán's objective of subordinating Spanish poetry to the rules that "cultured nations follow" was partially achieved; but the great debate over his *Poética* may have given it undue importance in the total picture of the eighteenth century.

2. *Gregorio Mayáns y Siscar* (1699–1781) was one of the most erudite men of his time, respected both at home and abroad. In addition to criticizing literary works, he edited many classics, including the works of Fray Luis de León, Juan de Valdés, Cervantes, and Saavedra Fajardo.

In *Oración sobre la elocuencia española* (1727), he lamented the low opinion Europeans had of Spanish writers. His *Orígenes de la lengua española* (1737) treated the origins of the Spanish language and a reprint of *Diálogo de la lengua,* which he attributed to Juan de Valdés. His *Vida de Cervantes* (1737) was the first biography of that writer. Like Jovellanos, he tried to reform the Spanish educational system but lacked the former's sincerity, patriotism, and warmth. He wrote on many subjects, and though he made errors, his judgments were usually sound, and he must be remembered as one who resurrected many Spanish classics.

3. *Other critics* of the eighteenth century are Blas Antonio Nasarre y Férriz (1689–1751), an extremist disciple of Luzán's; Agustín Gabriel de Montiano y Luyando (1697–1764), a Neoclassic dramatist and drama critic; Tomás Antonio Sánchez (1725–1802), the first to publish the *Cantar de Mio Cid* and the earliest editor of Berceo's complete works; and Nicolás Fernández de Moratín (1737–1780), a failure as a Neoclassic dramatist, but a passable poet and a leading proponent of Neoclassicism who wrote devastating remarks about Calderón and Lope. Leandro Fernández de Moratín (1760–1828), a better critic than his father, is best known for his *Orígenes del teatro español* (1830) and *Discurso preliminar,* also entitled *Reseña histórica sobre el teatro español y la literatura dramática en el siglo XVIII.* Juan José López de Sedano (1729–1801), Antonio de Capmany y Surís de Montpalau (1742–1813), Padre Francisco Javier Lampillas (1731–1800), Juan Pablo Forner (1756–1797), Manuel José Quintana (1772–1857), and Alberto Lista y Aragón (1775–1848) round out the list of important literary critics of the eighteenth century.

D. Historians

1. *Padre Enrique Flórez de Setién y Huidobro* (1702–1773) is probably the best ecclesiastical historian Spain has ever produced. His one major work was *España sagrada* in fifty-one volumes; he composed twenty-nine and helped in varying degrees on the others. If one wishes to know anything about churches, convents, bishops, or saints, he will find the answers here.

2. *Padre Juan Francisco Masdeu* (1744–1817) wrote several works, among them *Historia crítica de España y de la cultura española* (1783–1805), in twenty volumes. He was the first historian to treat the Cid and others like him with a scholarly approach. Although many of his findings have been refuted, his work on Roman influence in Spain is still considered a classic standard.

COSTUMBRISMO

A. General Considerations

Costumbrismo, a kind of fiction that stresses realistic description of characters, manners, and customs, consists mostly of sketches or essays that concentrate on social background rather than plot. Many, however, have a short story framework or a dialogue involving a cousin, a nephew, or a friend of the author's who reveals society's weaknesses. Of the two basic types, the *cuadro* adopts a picturesque outlook and stresses local color for its own sake, while the *artículo* is concerned more with reality from a satiric and critical point of view. It can be argued that *costumbrismo* in the nineteenth century was simply a restoration of elements found in works of sixteenth-century Spanish writers or in eighteenth-century journals. Others view it as an imitation of Addison and Steele's *Spectator Papers* or of Victor Joseph Etienne Jouy, who signed himself de Jouy. In the nineteenth century Santos López Pellegrín (1801–1846) and Sebastián de Miñano (1779–1845) wrote in the *costumbrista* manner. Whatever its origin, it was fantastically successful, and almost every writer of the day produced an *artículo* or *cuadro*. *Los españoles pintados por sí mismos* (1843–1844) contains forty-nine articles that portray Spanish life at its picturesque best and represents the zenith of the movement. Novelists such as Fernán Caballero and Alarcón used the *cuadro de costumbres* effectively. Some critical opinion feels that *costumbrismo* was necessary for the development of the Realistic novel, while other opinion finds that the lack of fiction in the early nineteenth century in Spain was caused by the journals and the *artículos*, which took up the load, satisfied the readers, and thus delayed the novel's development.

B. Mariano José de Larra y Sánchez de Castro (1809–1837)

Larra represented the conflict between the Romantic and the Neoclassic and summed up in his life the ferment of his time. Indeed, few men have been so faithful a product and a portrait of their era. Larra grew up amid the liberal-conservative quarrels and the hectic political turmoil of the first third of the century. He studied both law and medicine, but in 1826 he was forced to give up his studies and a government position because of the absolutist terror. In 1828 he started the journal *El Duende Satírico del Día,* and in 1832, *El Pobrecito Hablador,* neither of which lasted long. In the latter he described the Parnasillo, the Café Príncipe *tertulia* that he joined.

Though Larra married Josefa Wetoret y Velasco in 1829, he fell in love with Dolores Armijo in the early 1830s. If his article *Casarse pronto y mal* is autobiographical, then his passion for another married woman is easily understood. In 1837 Dolores broke off the affair, and Larra committed suicide a few minutes after she left his house. Some feel he would have killed himself in any event because of his unhappiness over the political situation and his growing neuroses.

Larra, a Romantic and yet anti-Romantic, exemplified the clash between eighteenth-century rationalism and nineteenth-century individualism. His enduring work is represented by his *artículos de costumbres,* which can be divided into three different groups: general sketches on Madrid society and current events, such as *Casarse pronto y mal;* anti-Carlist ones, such as *Nadie pase sin hablar al portero;* and those dealing with national foibles, such as *Vuelva Vd. mañana.* Another division is: *artículos de costumbres,* theatrical criticism, and political articles. One might term these sketches appearing in newspapers "novelistic essays." Larra used a variety of styles, the rhetorical-logical, mock-pompous, satirico-rhetorical, and dramatic; and he criticized nearly every aspect of Spanish life: actors, jails, lazy people, bureaucracy, censorship, mail service, coaches, inns, and so on.

In 1835 his collected articles were published under a very long title that we shall abbreviate to *Colección de artículos dramáticos, literarios, políticos y de costumbres.* These articles had appeared in a variety of journals under the pseudonyms Andrés Niporesas, El Duende Satírico, El Pobrecito Hablador, and Fígaro. His best work, however, appears in *El Pobrecito Hablador;* it was published at irregular intervals under the pseudonym Bachiller don Juan Pérez de Munguía with the object "de reírnos de ridiculeces—ésta es nuestra divisa; ser leídos—éste es nuestro objeto; decir la verdad—éste nuestro medio." Among his many famous articles are *Casarse pronto y mal; El castellano viejo,* an attack on exaggerated belief in Spanish tradition and a defense of good breeding; *Vuelva Vd. mañana,* a depiction of Spanish laziness, chauvinism, and economic decay; and *Empeños y desempeños,* an examination of the false and exaggerated concept of honor, superficial education, and spendthrift habits of Spanish gentlemen. In January 1833 Larra started writing for the *Revista Española* and adopted his famous pseudonym, Fígaro. He wrote for this review until August 1835, when government censorship closed it down. Later he joined several other journals in Madrid, among them *El Correo de las Damas, El Español,* and *Redactor General.*

Among Larra's typical political articles we find *Día de difuntos de 1836, o Fígaro en el cementerio,* a bitter attack on the corruption overwhelming Spain, a country without justice, integrity, or hope; *La nochebuena de 1836,* lacking the hilarity of some earlier articles, a symbolic discussion between master and servant over Larra's inability to promote Spanish progress; and *Los viajeros en Vitoria,* a denunciation of Church support of the Carlists and their inordinate greed.

Among his best theatrical articles is one on Hartzenbusch's *Los amantes de Teruel,* in which Larra praises the dramatist's work and takes issue with those who said that the ending was artificial in its insistence on death because of frustrated love.

Larra was a man of contradictions. He believed that literature is the expression of the progress of a people and that it has truths to contribute. In this he was Neoclassic like his model, Moratín. He wanted Spain to progress and copy France, but at the same time he wanted his country to maintain its worthwhile old traditions. He represents a special kind of Eclecticism. Some claim that his work belongs neither to the eighteenth nor the nineteenth century, yet most feel that in him the paradoxical spirit of his era and its literature found perfect fusion. Some insist that his disillusion and pessimism were not a Romantic pose but innately his own. Certain students of his writings charge that he lacks sentiment; others charge him with too much. Some feel that his criticism is unjust in its extravagance; others say his articles offer the truest picture possible of the Spain of his day.

Almost every critic has had something to say about Larra. The analysis of Lomba y Pedraja's seems representative: "De la pluma de nuestro escritor salió la prosa española de más quilates . . . en la primera mitad del siglo XIX." The Generation of 1898 treated him well, and on February 13, 1901, a group of young men marched in solemn procession to pay their respects at Larra's grave. They saw in him, according to Baroja, a "maestro de la presente juventud" who believed in freedom, tolerance, and a new Spain.

C. Ramón de Mesonero Romanos (1803–1882)

Mesonero Romanos was a product of Madrid, where he was born and died. In his earliest work, *Mis ratos perdidos, o ligero bosquejo de Madrid en 1820 y 1821* (1822), he deals with *tertulias,* dances, and bullfighting and uses a different Madrid custom to set off each month of the year. He became interested in the restoration of Golden Age drama and helped produce some between 1826 and 1830. He worked on studies of the dramatists contemporary to Lope de Vega in several volumes of the *BAE*. His *Manual de Madrid* (1831) went through several editions, and in an appendix he discussed almost every aspect of city planning.

In 1832 he began publishing his *Escenas matritenses* in *Cartas Españolas*. His first article was *El retrato,* signed with his pseudonym, El Curioso Parlante. All these articles were later published in several volumes under the title *Panorama matritense*. His *Recuerdos de viaje por Francia y Bélgica en 1840 y 1841* record his travels in Europe, and in 1836 he founded the first illustrated newspaper, *Semanario pintoresco español,* in which he published a second series of *Escenas matritenses* between 1836 and 1842. He also published *Tipos y caracteres* (1862), *El antiguo Madrid* (1861), and *Memorias de un setentón* (1880). Mesonero merited the title "Cronista de Madrid." He founded the Ateneo de Madrid, of which he was the first secretary, and became a member of the Royal Academy.

Mesonero's *Escenas* trace the social history of Spain in the 1830s and early 1840s. His earlier articles, such as *La calle de Toledo, La romería de San Isidro,* and others, are quite merry and full of local color. His later articles contain less story but are more skillfully done. He starts some with a historical background. For others he uses a dialogue form. Occasionally he uses archaic language for flavor, but he seldom exaggerates. Critics have divided his articles into groups: historical, satiric, and philosophical. Mesonero, an unemotional man of the middle class, was a benevolent observer of society. He painted the best pictures we have today of Madrid life of his time, and as the city's historian, he described it with great warmth. Sometimes a nostalgic note rings through his work, for although he accepts the new, one senses that he is a traditionalist who would like to keep the "good old days."

His clarity of style is attractive, and his little short stories are gems. Piñeyro said that some of his articles "recall the comedies of Aristophanes in the vigor and energy with which they penetrate to the very heart of the pretensions they set out to ridicule, destroying appearances and tearing into shreds false pretenses of legitimacy and piety invented to cover sordid passions." Mesonero, however, allows his smug self-satisfaction to shine in his memoirs, where he speaks disparagingly of Larra's temperament that led him to suicide, while he, "Dios sea loado," had been permitted to write the memoirs of a septuagenarian. Larra was kinder, for he said that Mesonero had come to know Spain perfectly and that he was an "imitador felicísimo de Jouy hasta en su mesura, si menos erudito, más pensador y menos superficial." Unlike Larra, Mesonero was never eager to engage in political wrangles, although he treated a few political problems in articles such as *Grandeza y miseria.* Larra was excitable, impulsive, generous, and Romantic. Mesonero was methodical and practical.

Although Mesonero wrote several critical articles on Romantic dramas and accepted Romanticism, he satirized it delightfully in *El romanticismo y los románticos,* in which he pokes fun at the exaggerations of the Romanticists.

D. Serafín Estébanez Calderón (1799–1867)

Estébanez Calderón was born in Málaga. He wrote for many newspapers and carried on a polemic with Gallardo over the authenticity of *El Buscapié.* Among his works are *Poesías* (1831), *Manual del oficial de Marruecos* (1844), *De la conquista y pérdida de Portugal* (1835), several short stories such as *Los tesoros de la Alhambra,* and a historical novel, *Cristianos y moriscos* (1838). His most famous work is *Escenas andaluzas* (1847).

Estébanez Calderón began publishing his *Escenas* in 1831 in *Cartas Españolas* under the pseudonym El Solitario. These *Escenas* are to Andalusia what those of Mesonero are to Madrid. El Solitario, however, deliberately seeks local color and archaic effect. He is more traditional than the others, and his works contain much folklore. Indeed, his language is too full of the local idiom, and the very abundance of dialect detracts from the Andalusian flavor he is trying to promote, making some of his articles seem scholarly productions, a feeling emphasized by erudite footnotes. He uses many themes, Andalusian, Moorish, and historical.

Nevertheless, he was what he professed to be, a painter of scenes, and he portrayed popular types, authentic characters, and background, often with vitality and charm. His articles contain many remarks to his readers, not with the light touch of Larra or Mesonero, but in the somewhat ponderous vein of *benévolos lectores.* His article *Un baile de Triana* discourses on various dances and Andalusian songs, as he describes the fire, pleasure, color, joy, and madness involved. *Pulpete y Balbeja* contains a bit more action, as two men fight over a young lady who turns them both down. But as Estébanez himself says here, "No hay más que decir sino que Andalucía es el mapa de los hombres regulares y

Sevilla el ojito negro de tierra de donde salen al mundo los buenos mozos, los bien plantados, los lindos cantadores."

ROMANTIC THEORISTS

A. General Considerations

It may be, as I. L. McLelland says, that national instinct in the 1750s and 1760s reawoke Spain's passive Romanticism and that "the battle against Neoclassicism was fought and won without any help from outside." E. A. Peers and others feel that the development occurred along two lines, the continuing one from the eighteenth century about the Golden Age drama, medieval themes, and the like, and the other that attempted to acclimatize foreign genres to Spain. Foreign influences were felt in Spain, thanks to Herder, the Schlegel brothers, Victor Hugo, Scott, Manzoni, and others. The real Romantic quarrel developed in Spain in poetry and drama, and the nation had its manifestos to equal Hugo's *Préface de Cromwell* and those of Manzoni and Schlegel.

Some knowledge of important theorists is imperative to understand the background against which Romanticism developed. Neoclassic writers like Feijóo questioned the overemphasis of rules. Jovellanos, Cadalso, García de la Huerta, and even Nicolás Fernández de Moratín showed Romantic urges. Juan José López de Sedano stressed the importance of ancient Spanish poetry. Much nineteenth-century theorizing, therefore, was simply a continuation of the Revival, as Peers terms it. But whether out of a conviction of the need for new literary forms or because of a patriotic defense of Spanish spirit, a series of polemics, soul-searchings, and self-examination dominated the scene.

Martínez de la Rosa, in his *Apuntes sobre el drama histórico*, appended to his *La conjuración de Venecia*, defended his Romantic work in subdued fashion and apologized for breaking the rules. In an Eclectic spirit, Larra and others attempted to make Scribe popular in Spain as a kind of compromise between popular and Neoclassic taste, although Larra endorsed Durán's view for the most part. According to Peers, the Duque de Rivas was the culminating figure, both in the Revival with *El moro expósito* and the Revolt with *Don Alvaro*. Alcalá Galiano's "anonymous" prologue to *El moro expósito* reversed his earlier criticism of Böhl von

Faber, who, though not a native Spaniard, played a vital role in the developing quarrel among Romantic theorizers.

B. Johann Nicholas Böhl von Faber (1770–1863)

Böhl von Faber was born in Hamburg, Germany. As a folklorist he was astonished at the lack of knowledge in Spain of ancient Spanish works and felt that Spaniards should seek inspiration in their seventeenth-century drama and medieval poetry. His opening shot in the battle was his 1814 translation of Schlegel's series of lectures delivered in 1808 and later published under the title *Über dramatische Kunst und Literatur* (1809–1811), in which he praised Spanish literature highly, stressing that Shakespeare and Calderón were the greatest of poets. This precipitated a debate between Böhl von Faber and José Joaquín de Mora and Alcalá Galiano on the relative merits of the Golden Age drama.

Böhl von Faber held *tertulias* in Cádiz at which Calderón's plays were performed. In addition to his newspaper polemics and the Schlegel translation, he published several other works, including the important *Teatro español anterior a Lope de Vega* (1832), which includes works by Encina, Gil Vicente, Torres Naharro, and Lope de Rueda. His literary views must have directly influenced his daughter, Fernán Caballero, and, indirectly, future Spanish literature.

C. Agustín Durán (1793–1862)

Agustín Durán, best remembered as a theorist of the Romantic movement, supported Böhl von Faber's view on the Spanish theater. He wrote extensively on the Spanish ballads and in 1821 produced *Colección de romances antiguos*. Between 1828 and 1832 he published various volumes of ballads divided according to types, *moriscos, doctrinales, amatorios, jocosos, satíricos, burlescos, festivos, históricos, caballerescos*, etc. These now form Volumes X and XVI of the *BAE* and are known as the *Romancero de Durán*. His *Discurso sobre el influjo que ha tenido la crítica moderna en la decadencia del teatro antiguo español* (1828) is one of the most important critical documents of the Spanish Romantic movement. He produced other works on the Golden Age drama, Ramón de la Cruz, Tirso de Molina, and Lope de Vega, and he wrote some original *leyendas*. He was the first really to reveal fully the quality and spirit of Spanish epic poetry, although some of his theories have been disputed by later critics. He felt the *romance* was more indigenous than the *canción,* was of broader origin, displayed Spanish character better, and in essence was the true and original Castilian poetry.

Durán loved literature that was genuinely Spanish and was not the only one to object to eighteenth-century scorn of Spanish literature or who tried to restore Golden Age drama and arouse an interest in medievalism. Martínez de la Rosa, Bartolomé Gallardo y Blanco, and Eugenio de Ochoa did their share; but Durán was the most effective defender of Golden Age drama. Whereas most quarreling centered around Lope and Calderón, Durán also studied Tirso, whose work he praised highly.

Undoubtedly his discourse of 1828 was his most important work. Piñeyro claims that when it appeared it had a great influence but was quickly forgotten until its reprinting by the Spanish Academy in its *Memorias* in 1870. Durán, however, was the critic who labeled Calderón's drama Romantic and made it stick, and his attacks on the unities and praise of Golden Age drama appear to have been the most influential of all. In the 1828 discourse Durán strongly defends his country as having once been the center of world learning and literature. He maintained that one could find the "sublime and beautiful creations of the Romantics" in the medieval age. The theater should reflect the needs and aspirations of the Spanish people and not something imposed from abroad, and the Golden Age drama exemplified these qualities. He called the native drama Romantic and felt that medieval literature served as a prelude to the works of Lope and Calderón.

He agreed that Classicism and Romanticism had a justified existence but that Golden Age drama should not be measured according to rules that were intended for Classical drama. Classical drama lacks individuality, he said, while Romantic drama concentrates on the individual. The Classicist stresses form and rules. The Romanticist chooses freedom from them and uses plot, style, and character as he wishes. Classical plays inspire order and symmetry; Romantic ones are untrammeled and unconfined. Durán also emphasized the place of Christianity in Romantic literature as part of the background of Romantic writing.

D. Antonio Alcalá Galiano (1789–1865)

In 1814 Alcalá Galiano criticized the theories of Böhl von Faber in the *Crónica Científica y Literaria de Madrid.* He lectured at the

Ateneo, wrote on history and law, and, in *Recuerdos de un anciano* (1878), commented on the contemporaries he had known. Although he wrote extensively on literary matters and was known as a violent and impassioned orator, he merits attention primarily for his "anonymous" prologue to *El moro expósito,* a somewhat lukewarm apology for Romanticism.

He admitted that a definition of the schools of Classicism and Romanticism is difficult, for many works that are Classical can be classified as Romantic. There are times and nations in which Romanticism rather than Classicism should hold sway. Nevertheless, he praises the Classical theater and maintains that French Classical literature is not really classic in the Greek sense of the word, as it copies the exterior form of a composition and alters it as circumstances dictate. Eighteenth-century Spanish poets shared the same defects, and though Meléndez made some progress, the Classical school, a French copy disguised in the style of ancient Spanish writers, held sway. Spanish poets have not freely expressed their spirit because it was fettered by the shackles of French Classicism and by limits imposed by eighteenth-century foreign critics. Luzán, says Alcalá, helped in establishing good taste, but in so doing he imprisoned Spanish literature.

Alcalá traces Romanticism in various countries, but he insists that Rivas is neither Classical nor Romantic. He analyzes the mixture of the real and the ideal in *El moro expósito* and cites the "rules" that Rivas followed. The latter tried to arouse the curiosity of his readers, to suit the style to the argument, to give real settings, to versify well, and to obey his spontaneous inspirations.

E.   José Joaquín de Mora (1783–1864)

José Joaquín de Mora, enthusiastic about the cause of the Latin American colonies, went to Chile in 1828, where he founded the *Mercurio Chileno* and engaged in a series of polemics with Andrés Bello about educational, philological, political, and literary matters. In 1843 he returned to Spain and succeeded Lista and Alcalá Galiano as the director of the Colegio de San Felipe.

Much of Mora's work consisted of critical writings in various periodicals. In 1814 and again between 1817 and 1820 he championed Neoclassicism against Böhl von Faber and others and termed Romanticism detestable because of its irregularity and its lack of good taste. He commented on its over-use of horror and felt it was overloaded with bandits, witches, and magicians. Undoubtedly, his best work is *Leyendas españolas* (1840), though he wrote a number of collections of poetry. Despite his defense of Neoclassicism, he was essentially an Eclectic, but it has been argued that he later became a Romantic convert.

F. Francisco de Paula Martínez de la Rosa (1787–1862)

Martínez de la Rosa was an active participant in most of the political events of his day. Though he sympathized with liberal principles, he scorned the *pueblo*. Rejected by both conservatives and liberals, he was unjustly termed "Rosita la Pastelera" for his refusal to adopt extremist views.

In his *Arte poética,* published as part of his *Obras literarias* (1827–1830), he reveals his Neoclassicism, finds inspiration in Boileau, and attacks the Golden Age drama. Elsewhere he is less severe, for though he speaks of the "gravísimos defectos de ese poeta [Calderón]," he adds: "queda que admirar en ellas la urbanidad amena, la dicción purísima y la versificación agradable." He blames Calderonian defects on the "age of contagion" in which he lives. He claims that Tirso is not "tan ingenioso o urbano como Calderón," but that he is superior to everyone in "malicia y sal cómica, aquella gracia inimitable que no solo encubre los defectos, sino que seduce y cautiva." He disliked the *Poema del Cid* but favored *El libro de buen amor,* though he objected to its exuberance.

His *Apuntes sobre el drama histórico* stresses the need for the *justo medio* but allows the breaking of unities of time and place. He states that he wrote the work because of the decadent state of the Spanish theater in the hope of stimulating young writers. Since historical drama unites the essential characteristics of utility and pleasure, Martínez thought it acceptable within the rules of good taste. Spanish Classical authors who had "más genio que cordura, y más talento que instrucción," were easily capable of painting a current scene but lacked ability to disinter Classical plots or treat of foreign people and cultures.

Good taste, then, was the watchword of this critic and faithful public servant. Despite his natural leanings toward Neoclassicism and away from Romanticism, the two opposing forces fused in him into a surprising moderation. He was, indeed, a man of the *justo medio.*

G. Other Didactic Writers

1. *Ramón López Soler* (1806–1836), a young Barcelonian critic who might have become one of the great names of the nineteenth century had he lived to fulfill his early promise, wrote for *El Constitucional* and *El Europeo* in the 1820s and edited *El Vapor* and the *Revista Española* in the 1830s. He also wrote several historical novels, among which the most famous is *Los bandos de Castilla: o, El caballero del cisne* (1830), an imitation of Sir Walter Scott's *Ivanhoe* that Mesonero Romanos called "Ivanhoe in disguise." López Soler admitted that he translated part of Scott's novel and imitated it in other parts, though he added a Mediterranean vehemence absent in the northerner's work. He published several novels under the pseudonym Gregorio Pérez de Miranda.

In *El Europeo* he discussed such matters as the philosophical history of Spanish poetry and the pre-Romantic symptoms in the work of Meléndez and others. Romanticism, he thought, originated in Christianity as represented by the Crusades and in the ideas of knighthood, symbols of medieval virtue, but neither his admiration of the picturesque in the Middle Ages nor the sentimental in religion contains originality.

His greatest critical fame stems from his short prologue to *Los bandos de Castilla,* which several critics considered an important Romantic manifesto. More important is his definition of Romanticism: "libre, impetuosa, salvaje, la literatura romántica es el intérprete de aquellas pasiones vagas e indefinibles . . . En medio de horrorosos huracanes, de noches en las que apenas se trasluce una luna amarillenta, reclinada al pie de los sepulcros . . . suele elevar su peregrino canto." López Soler saw excellent qualities in both Classicism and Romanticism and felt they could exist side by side.

2. *Eugenio de Ochoa* (1815–1872), one of the younger members of the Parnasillo Café, wrote a historical novel, two dramas, lyric poetry, translations of Hugo and Scott, and a series of important critical works on Spanish writers and literature. His many titles include *Apuntes para una biblioteca de escritores españoles contemporáneos en prosa y verso* (1840) and a series of "Treasures," including *Tesoro del teatro español* (1835–1838), on the origins of Spanish theater, Lope, Calderón, and eighteenth- and nineteenth-century drama; and *Tesoro de escritores místicos españoles* (1847).

Ochoa is important also as the founder of the most important

337

Romantic journal, *El Artista* (1835–1836). Although he later regretted somewhat his ardent defense of Romanticism, he conceived of the movement as a revolution to sweep away Neoclassic debris. He saw Calderón as the true apostle of Romanticism and the Romanticist as a youth with a soul full of brilliant illusions, as a reflection of the age of knighthood, and as a patriot more interested in the virtues of the Middle Ages than in Greek heroism.

3. *Leopoldo Augusto de Cueto* (1815–1901), the Marqués de Valmar, was Rivas' brother-in-law and his most fervent admirer. Cueto wrote poetry and drama but was primarily a critic. He contributed to countless periodicals and wrote many excellent studies, including works on Zorrilla, Quintana, and the *Cantigas* of Alfonso *el Sabio*. He delivered a famous eulogy in memory of Rivas at a session of the Spanish Academy. His most famous work is *Historia crítica de la poesía castellana en el siglo XVIII* (1893), an elaboration of an earlier work, *Bosquejo histórico-crítico de la poesía castellana en el siglo XVIII*, begun in 1869.

Cueto uttered penetrating comments on all the eighteenth-century writers. He discussed Feijóo's moral conviction, Jovellanos' clarity, Gallardo's lack of good taste, Cienfuegos' sentiment and feeling, and Quintana's energetic and manly sentiments. Although he denies Meléndez Valdés emotion and energy of expression, he praises his flexibility, grace, and delicacy and considers him to have been the best poet of his time.

4. *Jaime Luciano Balmes Urpiá* (1810–1848), a Catalan priest, represents with Donoso Cortés the conservative Catholic aspect of critical writing during the first half of the nineteenth century. He directed various reviews, such as *La Civilización, La Sociedad,* and *El Pensamiento de la Nación*. He was the leading writer of the latter. He wrote constantly on social, political, philosophical, and religious matters, and for many is the greatest Spanish philosopher of the nineteenth century.

His complete works fill thirty-three volumes. Of these the important ones are *El protestantismo comparado con el catolicismo en sus relaciones con la civilización europea* (1844), *El criterio* (1845), *Filosofía fundamental* (1846), *Filosofía elemental* (1847), and *Escritos políticos* (1847).

5. *Juan Donoso Cortés* (1809–1853), aside from his masterpiece, *Ensayo sobre el catolicismo, el liberalismo y el socialismo* (1851), wrote a variety of articles and discourses. In 1829 at the opening of the course in the Division of Humanities at Cáceres, he delivered a Romantic eulogy on Byron, Walter Scott, Madame de

Staël, and Schiller. He stressed his belief that the moderns instead of the ancients should be followed in the development of new literary pathways. After his early Romantic enthusiasm he became more of an Eclectic, as can be seen in *El clasicismo y el romanticismo* (1838). One of the most brilliant orators of his time, he was, according to Piñeyro, next to Larra "the most original and brilliant prose writer among all those who were born or flourished in the so-called Romantic period."

6. *Manuel Milá y Fontanals* (1818–1884) acquired a solid Classical culture, although Romanticism was his early passion. He was influenced by Chateaubriand, Schiller, Schlegel, and especially Manzoni and Scott. As a young man he contributed to *El Vapor,* and Peers felt he "stood for a historical form of Romanticism." Although he was a romance philologist, folklorist, and historian, his principal fame lies in the realm of literary criticism. He was one of the first in Spain to study comparative literature on a scientific basis. Menéndez y Pelayo, his best student, published his complete works and insisted that Milá y Fontanals was essentially a poetic man and without doubt the foremost Spanish critic of his time.

Among Milá y Fontanals' many literary studies are *Arte poética* (1844); *Observaciones sobre la poesía popular* (1853); *De los trovadores de España* (1861), a study of the influence of Provençal poetry in Spain and Portugal; *De la poesía heroico-popular* (1874); *Principios de literatura general y española* (1874); and *Romancero catalán* (1884), a study of the relationship between popular Catalan poetry and the Castilian epic. He belonged to a group that was trying to renovate Catalonian literature, and he fought for it throughout his life.

7. *José Amador de los Ríos* (1818–1878) is known primarily as a medievalist and historian. He taught literature at the University of Madrid and produced many works on a variety of subjects, such as *El Marqués de Santillana* (1853), *El arte mudéjar* (1859), and *El arte latino-bizantino en España* (1861). His two most famous works are *Historia crítica de la literatura española* (seven volumes, 1861–1865), which stops with the reign of Ferdinand and Isabel; and *Historia social, política y religiosa de los judíos en España y Portugal* (three volumes, 1875–1876).

Countless names could be added to the list of scholars, critics, and essayists of this period of the nineteenth century. Pedro Felipe Monlau y Roca (1808–1871) produced *Diccionario etimológico de la lengua castellana.* Pascual Gayangos (1809–1897) taught Oriental languages, translated Ticknor's *History of Spanish*

Literature, and contributed studies to the *BAE.* Cayetano Rosell (1817–1883) wrote history and criticism, edited works of many famous authors, and contributed to the *BAE.* Pablo Piferrer (1818–1848) helped Milá y Fontanals in his bid for Catalonian literary renovation, edited a collection of Spanish classics, and wrote on art and archeology. José M. Quadrado (1819–1896), Francisco Pi y Margall (1824–1901), and Manuel Cañete (1822–1891) produced well-known works in history, archeology, and literary criticism.

CRITICS, SCHOLARS, AND HISTORIANS OF THE SECOND HALF OF THE NINETEENTH CENTURY

A. Juan Valera y Alcalá Galiano (1824–1905)

Although Valera won greater fame as a novelist, he is just as important as a critic. His critical prose contains the same classic serenity found in his novels, a serenity and calm that lead him into the error of exaggerating his praise and saying something good about everybody whenever possible. He wrote countless newspaper and magazine articles on an amazing variety of philosophical, religious, aesthetic, and literary subjects. He signed many of these with pseudonyms such as Eleuterio Filogyno and Currita Albornoz, after the heroine of Coloma's *Pequeñeces.* He introduced Leopardi's works to Spain; translated parts of Heine, Goethe, and several North American poets; and wrote on Espronceda, the character of the novel, Spanish lyric and epic poetry, Donoso Cortés, Spanish philosophy, religious freedom, and the Portugal of his day. Among his more important works are *Estudios críticos sobre la literatura, política y costumbres de nuestros días* (1864), *Disertaciones y juicios literarios* (1878), *Apuntes sobre el nuevo arte de escribir novelas* (1887), *Cartas americanas* (1889), *Nuevas cartas americanas* (1890), *La metafísica y la poesía* (1891), and *Florilegio de poesías castellanas del siglo diecinueve* (five volumes, 1902–1903).

Valera had many polemics with several famous writers. His famous clash with Pardo Bazán was one of the principal literary fights of the time. Valera felt that a novel should not be a prosaic and vulgar reflection of human life. A good novel, he said, was poetry, not history, and things should be painted not even as they are, but more beautiful than they are. He opposed trends toward French Realism and resented especially the sociological implications. He was repelled by the Naturalistic emphasis on the base as an affectation and accused French authors of confusing life with literature, which for him were two different things. The most important aspect of any work was that it not be ugly. In answer to Pardo Bazán's *La cuestión palpitante,* he charged that a Naturalistic novel was not a novel. He took the Naturalists to task for their mania in supposing they were preparing the way for a great social change by their work and for their emphasis on the depraved, not as the ancients had done with humorous intent, but in deadly seriousness. Valera wondered how Pardo Bazán could be a true Naturalist and yet be a good Catholic. Since Valera was a Humanist and interested in the entire man and since he felt that man helped direct his own destiny, he was especially upset by the deterministic factors inherent in Naturalism.

Cartas americanas shows that he knew both Latin American and North American literature. It was he who supported Longfellow as a corresponding member of the Spanish Academy, and he liked Poe, Emerson, and especially Whittier. His best-known article on American subjects is his letter to Rubén Darío about *Azul.* Although at first he felt it might be an imitation of Hugo, he soon came to realize that Darío had "gran fondo de originalidad muy extraña." He was surprised at how well Darío was able to assimilate French elements while maintaining his Spanish form. The "afrancesamiento" of *Azul,* he said, was only a "galicismo de la mente," and he was struck by the strong personality of the poet and the "rara quintaesencia" of the work.

Valera's letters from Saint Petersburg to Leopoldo Augusto de Cueto and others in 1856 and 1857 reveal not only the society of the time but also certain characteristics of the Russian people that exist to this day. He treats of the museums, churches, funerals, trains, soldiers, the luxury of the rich, the many banquets, and the difficulty of finding one's way around in Russia without a knowledge of Russian. He discusses the curiosity of the Russians, their potential for great power, their self-love, their nationalism, and their love of exaggeration. He feels that the Russian is more sensual than abstruse and is vain, presumptuous at times, and scornful of most European nations. Yet he found the society of Saint Petersburg "tan amable y tan aristocrática y estas mujeres tan elegantes y tan hermosas."

Valera wrote about almost all the writers of Spain at one time or another in his articles. He denied that his friend Estébanez Calderón used an archaic language and an artificial style. He considered the poetry of Campoamor the most delicate poetry of the age and praised Espronceda, Rivas, and especially Quintana.

B. Emilia Pardo Bazán (1852–1921)

Pardo Bazán wrote studies on a great many authors that are still quoted today. Her first work was *Examen crítico de las obras del Padre Feijóo* (1877). She wrote also on Pereda, Galdós, Alarcón, and many other Spanish authors. She wrote on Darwinism and the Christian epic. She produced travel books, plays, verses, biographies, and, of course, novels and short stories. Among her many titles are *Literatura y otras hierbas* (1887); *La revolución y la novela en Rusia* (1887); *Nuevo Teatro Crítico*, a monthly periodical that began in 1891 and lasted until December 1893, in which she discussed books, theater, history, psychology, Campoamor, Pereda, Alarcón, and culture in general; *Polémicas y estudios literarios* (1892); *Lecciones de literatura* (1906); *Por Francia y por Alemania* (1890); *Por la España pintoresca* (1895); and *Por la Europa católica* (1902). She also started *Biblioteca de la mujer* in 1892 and published many works on and by women authors.

Pardo Bazán gave her criticism honestly. She said Pereda's writing was like a "huerto hermoso, bien regado, bien cultivado, pero de limitados horizontes." Criticisms of this nature and certain lectures she gave aroused the enmities of many conservatives, especially since she seemed convinced that the emptiness, corruption, and decadence of Spain had led to its political downfall. She also aroused a great furor with her most famous critical work, *La cuestión palpitante,* attacked by Alarcón, Valera, and Pereda.

This work began to appear in 1883 in *La Epoca* as a series of articles, later published in book form. She saw two aspects of Naturalism, the repulsive dealing with the miserable and disgusting instincts of man, which she consciously rejected, and the idea that all things belong to nature. She wanted to adopt certain ideas of the new movement but give them a Spanish meaning. The French novel was good in its realistic orientation, but it was, nonetheless, "errada y torcida en bastantes respectos." She condemned the deterministic aspects of Zola's philosophy but defended his artistic excellence. She regarded Zola as the leading "explainer" of the new theory, but she pointed out that he failed to prove Darwinism scientifically, and she would not accept it.

She also rejected his "bestia humana" and insisted on a realism that offered a "teoría más ancha, completa y perfecta que el naturalismo." In her prologues she accepted more of Zola, even "algo de su pesimismo . . . de la miseria humana." She condemned the overabundance of pathological cases in the Naturalistic work and found that the experimental novel might not be experimental since the experiment often existed only in the mind of the author.

Her other well known critical work is on Russia. She comments on the sudden revelation of Russia's national literature and geography, the Jewish problem, the Oriental aspects of the national culture, Russian history, Russian autocracy, the agrarian communes, and the various social classes. She traces the development of Russian literature from its origins through the Realistic period. Turgenev, she says, "stood in the gulf that separated the two halves of Russia yet maintained a contemplative and thoughtful attitude." He was a true thinker and poet, a classic writer and a visionary with an unsullied heart. She felt that Dostoyevski's heroes were incomprehensible. He was an apostle, a philosopher, and a fanatic, full of mystical Realism. Tolstoy, a nihilist and mystic, unfortunately became a "heretic and rationalist." In comparing French and Russian Realism, she explains that Russia is still an enigma, and she offers no conclusive judgments. Indeed, in summing up her criticism, it would not be unfair to say that she rarely offered it, except in an occasional defense of her own inconsistent positions with regard to Naturalism.

C. Leopoldo Alas (Clarín) (1852–1901)

Clarín, for many years the most popular critic in Spain, was often considered the most penetrating and intellectual one. He lived in a decaying age, a period of conflict between the traditional and Catholic, and the Europeanized liberals. In this quarrel, in spite of his reputation as the most feared critic of his day and as an aggressive, passionate, and wild revolutionary, he was essentially a conservative and religious man. If he was cutting in his remarks, if he took sides and fought valiantly for what he thought was right, if he was on occasion blind to the merits of those who disagreed with him, then he proved, simply, that he was human. But the critic who inspired actual terror in his victims was not the critic of the five volumes of *Solos de Clarín*, who was kindly and resembled Valera, his literary opponent. He showed *Krausista* affinities in his tolerance and comprehension and opposed the purely mechanical and materialistic approach.

Among his many works are *El derecho y la moralidad* (1878), *Solos de Clarín* (1881), *Sermón perdido* (1885), *Benito Pérez Galdós, estudio crítico-biográfico* (1889), *Ensayos y revistas* (1892), and *Palique* (1893). Between 1879 and 1898 he wrote numerous critical articles in various periodicals, some of which he signed with the pseudonym Zoilito.

Clarín anticipated the religious tension of Unamuno and the technique of Azorín and other members of the Generation of 1898. He opposed the Modernists, with the notable exception of Azorín. He accused Darío of "galicismo interior" to which he objected. He played a large part in the discussion of Naturalism in Spain. He was considered a follower of Zola's and possibly was the real leader of the movement instead of Pardo Bazán. Although at one point in his career he saw Naturalism everywhere, even in lyric poetry, he had grave reservations about the movement. Clarín accepted *Krausista* influence, which he later abandoned for an Eclectic position, but he never accepted Positivism or science. He felt that science might destroy the intangible values of society, and he accused Zola of indulging in superficial Positivism and writing "muchas vulgaridades de adocenado experimentalista." In his introduction to *La cuestión palpitante,* he refused to accept the experimental techniques of the French Naturalists. He believed that Spanish Naturalism might imitate the French in subject matter and certain techniques but that it should always have a moral goal. He even felt that free will could overcome the defects imposed by heredity, an obvious contradiction to the tenets of Naturalism. He stated, however, that Naturalism was not a description of the ugly, seamy side of life, that Pardo Bazán was not an imitator of things repugnant to the senses, and also that she was not one of those women writers who tried to substitute tenderness and sentimentality for lack of talent. As did most Spanish Realists, including Pardo Bazán and Galdós, Clarín encouraged the writing of novels on transcendental problems. He was, in fact, one of the first representatives of the neospiritual or neoidealistic school.

Clarín's pupil, Pérez de Ayala, saw that "por ser Clarín tan gran maestro fué tan gran escritor . . . es que todas sus obras contienen una enseñanza permanente." This is probably the true picture of Clarín, not the narrow defender of a specialized doctrine, not the feared critic, but the man who offered teaching of permanent value.

D. Francisco Giner de los Ríos (1839–1915)

In 1876 this philosopher and educator founded the all-important Institución Libre de Enseñanza. The idea of the Institución's founder was to create a school with an environment based on mutual love, respect, and tolerance and remove it from any partisan political or religious influence. Among the first teachers were Nicolás Salmerón and Joaquín Costa. A student came there not to learn from books exclusively but to observe nature and learn truth based on personal investigation. Giner concentrated a great deal on the study of the history of fine arts, for he believed that beauty should be a guiding principle in life. Physical education, too, was part of the program, as were industrial arts, job training, and field trips of various kinds.

Giner's works are not confined to philosophy and education. He wrote on literature, art, law, religion, sociology, and especially the philosophy of law, but he became more and more convinced that Spain's primary problem was one of education. His collected works run to some twenty-two volumes, including *Estudios literarios* (1866), *Estudios jurídicos y políticos* (1875), *Estudios filosóficos y religiosos* (1876), *Institución Libre de Enseñanza* (1882), and *Estudios sobre educación* (1886). Giner also wrote articles and essays for various journals and made many translations.

He accepted the philosophical standard of his teacher, Sanz del Río, that one must through means available arrive at harmony with the world. The way this was to be done was not predetermined, but education contained a key. Since he was Sanz del Río's outstanding student, Giner, with prophetic zeal, sought to create new men at his Institución Libre de Enseñanza. He had a profound effect upon his students, and a whole generation of intellectual leaders depended on him for their early guidance. He was an idealist, but a pragmatic one who believed in testing theories and in applying idealism to practical problems of life. He agreed, in the *Krausista* tradition, that as society becomes more closely equated with the image of God, man approaches the heights. He sought to reform Spanish education, worked for penal reform, and became intensely interested in and concerned about the problem of juvenile delinquency. He sought to impart a kind of religious idealism to many who later lived by it in their social struggles. He was the most important precursor of the Generation of 1898. Among his pupils and friends were Cossío, Unamuno, Altamira, Juan Ramón Jiménez, and the Machado brothers. Antonio Machado dedicated a loving poem to Giner's memory, and Unamuno called him the Spanish Socrates, the great "agitador de espíritus." Giner engendered this kind of feeling and spirit in all his students, many of whom looked upon him as a father or even with almost religious devotion.

Undoubtedly Giner deserved that love and respect. He was distressed by the misunderstandings of the world, and he worked for tolerance, peace, and harmony among men. He based his life on love, humility in the sight of God, and the cultivation of the religious ideal of God as the model by which to live.

E. Marcelino Menéndez y Pelayo (1856–1912)

This Spanish critic and philosopher occupies in Spanish literature a place greater than that which Sainte-Beuve holds in French letters. From 1875 on he produced an astounding amount of literary and cultural material. Indeed, one admirer said that if some worldwide catastrophe were to destroy the whole planet, a good part of the world's culture could be resurrected if only the works of Menéndez y Pelayo were saved. Menéndez y Pelayo knew all the major European languages and literatures. An insight into his background can be obtained by examining his polemic against Azcárate and Manuel de la Revilla, begun in 1876 and continuing for many years thereafter, about whether Spanish science and philosophy existed. Menéndez wrote a violent defense of Spanish philosophy, attacking *Krausistas* and liberals. For the conservatives this was an ardent defense of patriotism and orthodoxy. For the liberals it was an example of fanaticism and intransigence. The twenty-year-old Menéndez had not yet matured, of course, as a critic, but he never changed his basic position.

The major works of Menéndez y Pelayo are *Historia de los heterodoxos españoles* (1880), *Historia de las ideas estéticas en España* (1883–1891), *Obras de Lope de Vega* (1890–1902), *Historia de la poesía hispanoamericana* (1911–1912), *Orígines de la novela* (1905–1910), *Antología de poetas líricos castellanos* (1890–1908), and *Calderón y su teatro* (1881). Among his lesser works, if anything Menéndez did can be called lesser, are *Antología de poetas hispanoamericanos* (1893–1895), *Ensayos de crítica filosófica* (1892), *La ciencia española* (1880), *Horacio en España* (1877), *Historia de la poesía castellana en la edad media* (1911), *Estudio de crítica literaria* (1884–1908), and *Las cien mejores poesías líricas castellanas* (1908).

His *Historia de los heterodoxos* was less objective than later works. He himself later admitted his "excesiva acrimonia o in-temperencia de expresión con que califican ciertas tendencias o se juzga de algunos hombres." This acrimony that led the "rightists" to consider him their champion aroused the antipathy of others who never forgave him, even when they admired his scholarship. He tried to prove, among other things, that at heart every Spanish writer, whatever his professed beliefs, was unable to escape his religious heritage. In his *Historia de las ideas estéticas* he considered a field almost untouched in Spain up to that time. He studied not only Spanish ideas but the cultural and literary history of all Europe, including Christianity, the Middle Ages, and the Renaissance as world movements. In *Calderón y su teatro* he admits that Calderón is inferior to Lope in variety and spon-taneity and to Tirso in character creation and comic grace, but he insists that nobody excels him in grandeur of concept as a great Catholic and symbolic poet. Menéndez y Pelayo ranked Calderón, in spite of his defects, after Sophocles and Shake-speare as the greatest dramatist of all time.

Every critic of note has had something to say about Menéndez y Pelayo. Valera, who did not think much of him when he en-tered the Royal Academy, later admitted that he was "el mejor y más celebrado" of all Spanish authors who wrote works other than those of mere entertainment. Américo Castro did not think highly of his individual works, but he felt that Menéndez led the way for those who wished to see with modern eyes and judge with a modern viewpoint the artistic creation of the past.

F. Rafael Altamira y Crevea (1866–1951)

Altamira, a disciple of Giner de los Ríos', taught at the Institu-ción Libre de Enseñanza. He wrote on a variety of subjects and even tried fiction, but his best work lies in the fields of history, education, and law. He was active in teaching reform, to be ex-pected from an Institución man. His *La enseñanza de la historia* (1891) became the guide for a generation of history teachers.

Of his some sixty volumes, many of them amplified rewritings of earlier works on history, politics, teaching, and international law, his *Historia de España y la civilización española* (1900–1911) is the most famous. He traces here the development of institu-tions, customs, and laws from their remote origins to modern times. He describes the causes active in Spanish cultural history, how they work, and what effect they had. He analyzes contro-versial subjects with a logical and impassive objectivity. For his

347

scrupulous adherence to historical facts and historical concepts, he has been considered the outstanding interpreter of the history of Spain. Altamira presents an organic picture of Spanish life, its meaning, psychological backgrounds, and individual and collective historical events. Even though he has strong feelings on certain subjects such as war and Spanish cultural values, he tries to tell the whole truth. He presents not only Spanish history but also a kind of universal history, not to justify Spanish actions but to "indicate the universality of certain human acts or ideas to show how difficult it is to avoid them and how imperative is the duty incumbent on us to help correct them, instead of confining ourselves to disclosing the errors or cruelties of others."

Beneath Altamira's objectivity and cold spirit, however, one senses a controlled passion as he focuses attention on Iberian and Hispanic considerations, the people and their psychology, as he seeks to promulgate a new international spirit of approximation.

G. Joaquín Costa (1844–1911)

Another immediate forerunner of the Generation of 1898 and an honorary member thereof, along with men like Cossío and Ramón y Cajal, was Joaquín Costa. He was a brilliant student, but although he taught at various institutions, including the Institución Libre de Enseñanza, he did not obtain in his lifetime the professional rewards his talent merited.

Costa was especially interested in the philosophy of history and historical investigation. He was a jurist, historian, Republican politician, sociologist, and agrarian reformer. His many works include *La vida del derecho* (1876), on political economy and jurisprudence; *Poesía popular española* (1881); *Reconstitución y europeización de España* (1900); *Oligarquía y caciquismo* (1901–1902), his most famous work, based on the series of lectures he gave at the Ateneo; *Tutela de pueblos en la historia* (1917); and *La religión de los celtíberos* (1917).

Costa was not interested in the spiritual and aesthetic values of the times but rather in political and agricultural reform. He was the leader of the school that fought for Europeanization of Spain, and one critic called him the "Apostle of Europeanization." He was, indeed, a vehement defender of *regeneracionismo*. He wished to regenerate the spirit of Spain, affected as it was by the loss of its colonies and its ruined agriculture and economy, and he insisted that Spain had to jump several centuries to catch up with Europe and the rest of the world. His most famous dictum in this regard was "echar doble llave al sepulcro del Cid." Some of his enemies felt he was negating rather than extolling the value of the Spanish spirit. He supported the truly popular in Spain, rather than outworn tradition or the artificial overgrowths of nineteenth-century society, and he hoped to cure part of what ailed Spain through refreshing breezes of modern Europe.

His *Krausista* background manifested itself in most of his works. He felt Spain's destiny was tied in with that of Africa and sought a colonial policy of peace and education. He was opposed to what he termed the "centralismo de España," and in some of his essays he anticipated Ortega y Gasset's ideas on government.

H. Other Didactic Writers

Of necessity we have omitted many worthy authors such as Antonio Cánovas del Castillo (1828–1897) and Emilio Castelar (1832–1899), the greatest political orator of the century. Important as precursors of the Generation of 1898 are authors such as Ricardo Macías Picavea (1847–1899), a *revisionista* professor at the Instituto de Valladolid. He wrote on educational reform, but his most famous work is *El problema nacional: Hechos, causas y remedios* (1891), in which he studies Spanish life and seeks remedies for its decadence. Even more important are Santiago Ramón y Cajal (1852–1934) and Manuel Bartolomé Cossío (1858–1935). The former, a physician and histologist who won the Nobel Prize, belonged in spirit to the Generation of 1898. He wrote scientific and literary essays about Spain's problems, its need for psychological and moral regeneration, its lack of scientific progress, and its intellectual segregation, but he refrained from the pessimism of many of the younger writers of the day. His most influential work was *Reglas y consejos sobre investigación biológica: Los tónicos de la voluntad* (1897), which went through many editions. He examined in detail the causes often given for the decadence of Spain, such as climate, lack of rainfall, provincialism, and religious fanaticism. He emphasized that Spain was backward but not decadent, uneducated but not degenerate. Manuel Bartolomé Cossío, the most intimate colleague of Giner de los Ríos in the Institución Libre de Enseñanza, had great influence on the following generations, especially in his chosen field of art. His most important work is *El Greco*, a biographical and artistic study that offered a new interpretation of the

349

sixteenth-century artist. The Generation of 1898 and the Modernists were fascinated by El Greco, and Cossío's book, while not published until 1908, helped focus their spiritual commitments, for Cossío interpreted El Greco as the maximum spiritual symbol of the Spanish Renaissance.

THE GENERATION OF 1898

A. General Considerations

Angel del Río has pointed out the great debt owed by the Generation of 1898 to the eighteenth century, to many nineteenth-century writers, and to the Institución Libre de Enseñanza, especially in the field of aesthetic and objective scientific education. Almost all the members of the Generation of 1898 felt the direct influence of the *Krausistas,* from whom derived part of their anguish, religious restlessness, and pessimism. From Giner they inherited love of countryside and moral perspective, and through Costa they realized the need for Europeanization. Other nineteenth-century writers such as Galdós and Clarín, through their liberal ideas and tolerance, and Menéndez y Pelayo, through his historical sense, helped create the intellectual framework within which the Generation of 1898 worked.

These young writers, drawing upon native sources, upon the new European cultural emphasis, and upon their new concepts of history, sought some historical constant in Spain's heritage. A new nationalism, individualism, and introspection filled the air. Some writers emphasized more the Spanish tradition; others sought salvation in Europeanization and more pragmatic approaches. In many, a dichotomy appeared as they sought both. A strong measure of European influence was omnipresent, and the new generation concentrated on the work of Schopenhauer, Carlyle, and Nietzsche. Most critics agree on this European influence but on little else about the Generation of 1898.

Writers on the Generation of 1898 cannot agree on its composition, its tenets, or its right to the label "Generation." Jeschke sees a unity in the Generation of 1898's skepticism and pessimism. Melchor Fernández Almagro views its concern as the "problema de España," as differentiated from the Modernists who were interested in aesthetics. Laín Entralgo seeks to divide them into two groups, one whose work "está muy directamente afectada por la situación histórica de España de que el desastre es símbolo," and another that he calls "literatos puros y más influídos por el modernismo." Some critics have made much of the well-known anagram of Corpus Barga, VABUMB, composed of the first letters of the names of Valle-Inclán, Azorín, Benavente, Unamuno, Maeztu, and Baroja. In 1910 Azorín included Benavente, Valle-Inclán, Baroja, Unamuno, and Maeztu in what he called the Generation of 1896. In 1913 he changed the name to Generation of 1898, not because of the effect of the war between Spain and the United States but because of the symbolic significance of that date as a turning point in Spanish life. In his 1913 article Azorín listed the characteristics of the Generation of 1898 as consisting of love of old towns and the countryside, a revival of primitive poets, and a love of El Greco, Góngora, and Larra. Guillermo Díaz Plaja refused to admit the Modernists as members of the Generation of 1898 and viewed them as antithetical to it in concept, subject matter, interpretation, and emphasis. Baroja denied the existence of any generation. He called the Generation of 1898 a "ghost generation" because it had no spiritual solidarity and lacked common aspirations or even common age groups. Maeztu recognized his group as a generation, with some reservations, and compared it with the German "Sturm und Drang" movement.

Nevertheless, most of the writers, despite their disparate backgrounds and viewpoints, seemed united in a protest against the immediate past and in a demand for the need of a new interpretation of history and tradition for the future. Although most of them were from the provinces, they sought inspiration in Castile and in the spiritual qualities of the Cid and don Quijote. Some sought a fusion of the Spanish tradition with the modern European one, while others wanted a completely new deal. In a sense the atmosphere was very much like that of the early days of Franklin Delano Roosevelt's New Deal, with its excitement, experimentation, and insistence on economic and social reforms. In their artistic, literary, political, and economic rejuvenation, the Generation of 1898 sought to create not only a new vision of Spain but also a new Spain.

Certain writers, who placed emphasis on aesthetics, offered erudition and philosophical and idealistic preoccupations as well. Others who appeared to have a cultural, intellectual, and critical orientation, or a historical and political one, also wrote on aesthetic considerations. If one says that Maeztu is more interested in politics than art, Menéndez Pidal in scholarship and

351

history than in aesthetics, and Azorín more in aesthetics than in history, the difference is simply one of degree. Whether the essays were erudite treatises on science, history, literature, or art, interpretative essays of a poetic nature on the countryside and the people, or philosophical essays seeking the meaning of Spain and its cultural heritage, all the authors, in one way or another, out of their doubts and negativism evolved an interpretation of the Spanish soul. They sought to resolve the problems of man in the modern world, to create a new style, and thus, as Laín Entralgo points out, left a threefold impact on future generations, that of language, aesthetic sensibility, and patriotic aspirations. Whether they were a generation may never be fully determined, but they all worried about progress and a new future. These writers, demonstrating great literary ability, outlined, at times through a somewhat instinctive philosophy, most of the central issues of twentieth-century Spanish thought.

B. Angel Ganivet (1865–1898)

Ganivet, also a novelist, wrote works that, according to Fernández Almagro, one of his biographers, fall into three groups: those of an aesthetic nature, those of a political preoccupation for Spain, and those about moral considerations of man.

A variety of judgments exists about Ganivet, but his ideas do not differ from those of other members of the Generation of 1898. Insisting on the importance of being a man, he believed in engaging in life rather than contemplating it. He reflected on the tragedy of life, the value of Spanish culture to itself as a unique one, and yet at the same time on European and cosmopolitan factors. A complete individualist, Ganivet dreamed of the possibility of a new Spain, an amalgam of Greek culture and Christianity.

In *Granada la bella* (1896), Ganivet examines the aesthetic impact of the city as he contrasts the old and the new, light and shadows. In *Cartas finlandesas* (1898), he contrasts Finland with Spain through the description of customs, domestic life, and holidays. *Hombres del norte* (1905) deals with Scandinavian and northern culture, Schopenhauer, Nietzsche, and Ibsen. *El porvenir de España* (1905) is a collection of his correspondence with Unamuno, whom he met in 1891.

Ganivet's most important and best-known work is *Idearium español* (1897), which is divided into three parts. In the first part Ganivet seeks to define Spanish spirit in the *pueblo* and the Spaniard. In the second part he discusses Spanish politics after the Renaissance. In the third part he attempts to determine the future of Spain in view of the defeats of the past and present. For Ganivet the chief Spanish defect consists of abulia, a paralysis of the will, which can be counteracted only by a strong exertion of the *voluntad*. Through its contacts with the Arabs in the Middle Ages, Spain had a culture superior to all others in the Western world, but it lost that superiority at the beginning of the sixteenth century, as it lost the synthesis of the East and West. Spaniards lacked organizational ability because of their individualism; yet they were the first to create a real organized army. Spain was a warrior nation, dispersing its energies in action instead of concentrating on spirit, and this led to decadence. Yet Spain's expression should be sought in action and not in ideas. Spain needs Segismundo, not Hamlet, and salvation will come from action. Spain must reorganize its spiritual forces to create a new Spain and renounce the use of force that its tradition created for it. Spain can cultivate a spirit that other countries cannot have because they have not won and lost an empire. Furthermore, Spain does not need science, for its spiritual qualities are the most important. In this work, Ganivet attempts, in an allegorical representation of the dogma, to define Spain as the country of the Immaculate Conception. He makes other statements about virginity, art, religion, and other topics in this evocative yet inconclusive work.

Ganivet was a literary writer who entered the world of ideas and was at the same time an artist and a thinker. Like others of his generation he worried about Spain, was disturbed about the national destiny, and sought in himself, through introspective and subjective analysis, to determine the peculiarly Spanish in the Spanish spirit.

C. Miguel de Unamuno y Jugo (1864–1936)

Unamuno, an essayist, social critic, philologist, philosopher, poet, playwright, and novelist, wrote approximately sixty volumes, excluding his letters. Although he had many disciples and friends, Barea said, "He was the founder of no school, the center of no movement. . . . And yet the trace of his work and personality exists in the writing and in the minds of almost all younger Spaniards concerned with the problems of their country."

Although Julián Marías found Unamuno's work somewhat irrational and although Unamuno's works seem unsystematic,

353

contradictory, and even inconsistent, language for him, keenly aware as he was of the power of words, meant communication in a practical and utilitarian way and also as a poetic and aesthetic action. He felt it was necessary to renovate the Spanish language, and he was prepared to accept innovations. Although he knew that language had psychological revelations to offer, he insisted on the necessity of a true scientific study of the language. Essentially, Unamuno believed that reason and rationalism tend to disturb true communication, which is a poetic act. A poet in an act of personal creation may destroy the logic inherent in words in order to convey the true reality, which is an intimate and irrational thing. Life cannot be shut in by words, and the writer, to maintain communication and his individuality, must avoid the danger of becoming enclosed within any system.

As many critics have noticed, it is very difficult to try to define the ideas of Unamuno exactly, for his method of writing and his dynamic and constant battle with life led to many contradictions. José Ferrater Mora, in commenting on these contradictions, says that Unamuno insisted as much on reason as on the irrational and that his conflict—and his originality—consisted precisely "en el incesante vaivén que caracteriza en este respecto—y en otros muchos—su pensamiento." Unamuno himself said he had but one aim, to seek the truth in life, a truth that he hoped to find in his constant spiritual struggle to affirm his faith and to survive. Thus, one can say that basically Unamuno was an idealist and humanitarian, that he fought against materialism, and that his many essays on education, politics, religion, and literature, while often apparently paradoxical, form a consistent pattern.

Unamuno's culture was probably the greatest of his generation. Among his titles, the more important ones are a seven-volume collection, *Ensayos* (1917–1918); *Mi religión y otros ensayos* (1910); *Soliloquios y conversaciones* (1911); *Por tierras de Portugal y España* (1911); *Contra esto y aquello* (1912); and *La agonía del cristianismo*, first published in French in 1925. His three masterworks, however, are usually considered to be *En torno al casticismo*, written in 1895 and published in 1902; *Vida de don Quijote y Sancho, según Miguel de Cervantes Saavedra* (1905); and *Del sentimiento trágico de la vida en los hombres y en los pueblos* (1913).

En torno al casticismo first appeared in *La España Moderna*. These five essays, which should be considered as a whole although they have individual titles such as *La tradición eterna, La casta histórica de Castilla,* and *El espíritu castellano,* seek to interpret

Spanish history and the meaning of culture. Unamuno is concerned about live ideas and not the scientific method. Science is universal, but culture is national. As with most of his generation, Castile was for him the great symbol of Spanish spirit. In determining this essence of Spain, language is important, and wherever one speaks Spanish, there one can find a part of Spain. The concept *castizo* is a false one of superficial nationalism, for underneath lies the true character of people and individuals. The worth of others can be recognized without giving up one's own national characteristics. In this connection Unamuno discusses a new and as yet unborn Spain, one of an eternal tradition that can be vitalized by foreign ideas. This tradition, however, must be sought in the present and not in the past, although the present too is depressed by the old reactionary Inquisition in attenuated form. Unamuno resolves his apparent paradox by describing what he terms "intrahistory," a search for the eternal in the temporal. The present consists of two strata, one of the immediate historical moment and the other the intrahistorical present, a sedimentation and eternalization of the successive historical presents already met. Thus, passing history occurs always on what Unamuno calls a permanent intrahistorical base, and consequently in "el alma de España viven y obran, además de nuestras almas, las almas de todos nuestros antepasados." Unamuno sees a revitalization of these traditions through a new current from Europe, something he rejected later for a greater concentration on the spiritual and religious struggle.

Vida de don Quijote y Sancho, a running commentary on Cervantes' work, interprets Quijote and Sancho as spiritual symbols of hope and redemption for the Spanish soul. Unamuno urges the acceptance of the concept of *hacer bien*—glory, action, and longing for immortality. Action conquers faith. Faith is born from fear of the unknown. A crusade is necessary to rescue don Quijote as a symbol of life and to reassert his great moral value. In keeping with Unamuno's central philosophical tenet about personal immortality, he sees quixotic madness as the fear of death and an attempt to continue to exist in another spatial-temporal context. Don Quijote must be saved both from the rationalists and from those who pretend to be faithful to his ideals while they reduce their dimensions by selfish actions. Sancho is perhaps even more admirable than his master, for his faith is more beset by doubts.

Del sentimiento trágico de la vida, which as Orringer has shown owes much to Albrecht Ritsch, concerns the omnipresent anguish of Unamuno in the confrontation between faith and reason faced by the man of flesh and blood. Man wishes to know whence he came and where he is going because he does not want to die. This man of flesh and blood is a real man, not a philosopher's construct. He wants to live and be immortal, a problem whose real heart theologians and philosophers cannot reach. Knowledge prepares for spiritual life, but man has need of faith to sustain him in his greatest problem, that of existence. There is a conflict in men between faith and knowledge, eternity and time, the spiritual and the secular, and this conflict is impossible of rational solution. The attempt to rationalize faith has landed man in the abyss of despair. Only faith will help sustain man in his essential tragedy of knowing his destiny. Thus man—and Unamuno—exhibit an anguished longing for an irrational faith that will bring self-perpetuation. The knowledge that this faith is apparently irrational helps cause the tragic sense of life. Man is a product of love and hunger, and his concern is to save both his soul and his flesh. Man's self-love broadens to include all mankind, and from this love comes God, not a God of reason, but a human God who can be reached only through faith and love.

In *La agonía del cristianismo*, Unamuno seeks to define Christianity "agónicamente," for it is a constant struggle and agony that is yet necessary for its survival.

In his works Unamuno analyzed the psychological and social aspects of the Spaniards and their character, but personally he accepted the quixotic world of faith over reason and science. Obviously Existential, Unamuno's work reveals his struggle between Christian faith and rational thought, his anguish, and the themes of immortality, life through action, life as a drama to be lived, and life in which each person creates himself through deeds and works. In his negation, doubt, desperation, and agony, Unamuno concerns himself with the deepest level of conscience and consciousness. He believes that life must make itself and that man must live from within himself. Man is an end and not a means. Unamuno appears in all his essays as he seeks to establish his own authenticity and his relationship to God and man. Often he finds meaning in the search itself. Some of these metaphysical relationships are not easy to follow, as he discusses the immortality of the soul, the agony of the final boundary of death, and the central desire for a personal immortality. Unamuno, perhaps Spain's first contemporary writer together with Ortega y Gasset, looms as one of the intellectual giants of twentieth-century Spain.

D. José Martínez Ruiz (Azorín) (1873–1967)

José Martínez Ruiz, also a novelist and dramatist, known to Spanish literature as Azorín, traveled incessantly around Spain, which in part accounts for his intimate knowledge of types, villages, and countryside. His descriptions of Spanish landscapes reflect melancholy, resignation, and stoicism. Azorín felt that the excellence of a writer depended on his treatment of nature and the countryside.

Azorín first used the pseudonym Cándido and then Ahrimán. In his first years as an author he wrote many articles on social and literary themes. In these he resembled Larra in his satiric and iconoclastic outbursts on life and literature. In 1900 he published his first complete work on a subject that was to be dear to his heart thenceforth, *El alma castellana*. In 1902 he used his pseudonym, Azorín, for the first time with the publication of *La voluntad*, whose title was related to the abulia postulated by Ganivet.

Among Azorín's many works are *La ruta de don Quijote* (1905), *Los pueblos* (1905), *España* (1909), *Lecturas españolas* (1912), *Castilla* (1912), *Clásicos y modernos* (1913), *Al margen de los clásicos* (1915), *Rivas y Larra* (1916), and *El paisaje de España visto por los españoles* (1917). Later essays include *Una hora de España* (1924), *Tiempos y cosas* (1944), *Ante Baroja* (1946), *Memorias inmemorables* (1946), and *El oasis de los clásicos* (1952).

In most of his essays or short sketches, Azorín is interested in the small, humble, daily happenings of life. He was, as he said, "un pequeño filósofo." Nothing much happens in these essays or vignettes, as life goes on day after day in the same way. In *Los pueblos* and *La ruta de don Quijote*, for example, he offers us dramatic pictures of what Madariaga called "little albums of Spanish life." His poetic vision of Spain concentrated on the details, the small and the unchanging, which for him had an almost universal and eternal significance. He sought the essence of Spain in its books and in the daily lives of its citizens, which he built up in layers by constant repetition of small things. For him the great events of life and history pass by, and the vulgarities and the commonplaces of life are unending. Ortega called him "un sensitivo de la historia," not a philosopher. In the Spain of today is

357

the Spain of yesterday. Azorín reacted against technology in favor of the ordinary people of a real and traditional Spain, though he viewed reality and interpreted Spanish life in an original and new way.

His intimate and Impressionistic re-creations concentrate in large measure on the countryside. Even though Alicante gave him birth, Castile became for him the symbol of Spanish spirit as it did for Antonio Machado and Unamuno. His lyrical and pictorial descriptions build enduring images out of the hour, lights, shadows, a glance, and countless other fugitive details. Castile with its ruins of past greatness conveys an eternal and positive spirit. Its beauty evokes a profound tenderness without the anguish of Unamuno or the rebellion and ugliness of Baroja. Azorín's vision is calm, almost impassive, full of nostalgia and melancholy. He builds from the ruins of Castile—the old cities, the wonderful cathedrals, the homes, and the people. His humble and almost monotonous, though picturesque, portrayals convey at times a greater sense of tragedy than that of flamboyant writers. He tells us about Spanish books and paintings, but in a deeper sense he depicts an eternal Castile that will never die because it exists in a time zone that was yesterday, is today, and will be tomorrow.

The domination of time, therefore, becomes of great concern to Azorín, as does Spanish sensibility involved in its passage. He seeks continuity in Spanish history and seems to say that everything changes but everything returns, too, in a kind of reincarnation, even though it may not be physically identical. This preoccupation with the past dwells not only on the landscape and history of Spain but on its authors and literature. Azorín practices a special kind of creative literary criticism as he tries to relive an author's work and life. He often creates a feeling of immediacy as though the author were with us and had just left the room for a moment. Azorín gives new life to Classical Spanish authors in his spiritual re-creations. He demonstrates the eternal qualities of the changing and yet unchanging literary works and in the process reveals the same conflict between time and eternity that exists in Unamuno's work.

E. Ramiro de Maeztu (1875–1936)

Maeztu, a journalist and conservative political theorist interested also in economics, sociology, and literature, wrote his first important work, *Hacia otra España* (1899), during a youthful Socialist phase. In this work, influenced by Nietzsche and Joaquín Costa, he stressed the need for material progress and lamented the hypocrisy of those in power. He believed in the necessity of Europeanization. Later, however, he rejected what he had written in his first work. His experiences as a correspondent during World War I and the influence of the religious and ultra-patriotic T. E. Hulme changed him completely, and he became an ultraconservative. *La crisis del humanismo* (1919), which had appeared first in English as *Authority, Liberty, and Function in the Light of War* (1916), stressed the idea that God is stability, goodness, and truth. He recognized the role of original sin and that of the Catholic Church in man's salvation. He clearly preferred the authoritarian state over the individual.

In 1926 Maeztu published *Don Quijote, Don Juan y La Celestina.* Although don Quijote represented for Maeztu the symbol of life, he felt that Quijote was a parody of the spirit of chivalry and had destroyed the *pueblo.* Don Juan, on the other hand, the symbol of power, was correct in imposing his will, for love without force has no value. Celestina represents wisdom, and man should strive for a synthesis of the three entities. *Defensa de la hispanidad* (1934), which Maeztu called "libro de amor y combate," concerns his search for a new Spanish empire built on Catholic ideals and the ideas of the state in the sixteenth century. He prefers the word *hispanidad* as a replacement for race and uses it to signify brotherhood of all Hispanic countries. A posthumous collection of his articles, *El nuevo tradicionalismo y la revolución social,* appeared in 1959.

Maeztu organized Acción Española in 1931 and edited the group's periodical of the same name. Through it he exercised a profound influence on the youth of the day. Aside from his major works, Maeztu wrote countless articles in which Spain continued to be his obsession. An essentially religious man, he wanted to awaken his country to a consciousness of its sleeping spiritual soul.

F. Ramón del Valle-Inclán (1866–1936)

Valle-Inclán, novelist, dramatist, and poet, was interested mainly in the world of the imagination and the words necessary to describe that world. An extraordinary prose artist whose works are filled with musicality and beauty, he shows always, whether he is writing about Galdós, Baroja, Modernism, or painting, an aesthetic and intellectual appreciation of literature. Aside from

La media noche (1917), about the war, his major effort at the essay was his collection *La lámpara maravillosa* (1916), an exotic discourse on his personal aesthetics, the contemplation of pure beauty, old cities, religious and erotic love, and a preoccupation with eternity. He subtitled this collection "spiritual exercises," and in it seeks knowledge. More important than his philosophy is his discourse on the power of words and the need for a new literary language. Although he has a pagan orientation at times, he stresses here the magical element on which primitive Christian miracles are based. He evokes the past through cities like Toledo and immortalizes Santiago de Compostela as a dream of granite, unchanging and eternal. Although Juan Ramón Jiménez said of this collection that Valle-Inclán's lamp had no oil but only smoke, it reveals his poetic and artistic creativity as well as an aesthetic appreciation of literature.

G. Pío Baroja y Nessi (1872–1956)

Baroja, primarily a novelist, shows in his essays the same opposition one finds in his fiction to established institutions and a disillusionment with Western countries and culture, although Nietzsche and other ideological interests tempted him for brief periods. In his essays on almost every conceivable subject, he usually includes autobiographical details and recalls friends and enemies. He wrote hundreds of articles on literary criticism and on political and social topics. His memoirs and travel books overflow with his comments on life and culture. Among his many collections of essays are *El tablado de Arlequín* (1903), *Juventud, egolatría* (1917), *Nuevo tablado de Arlequín* (1917), *Momentum catastrophicum* (1919), *La caverna del humorismo* (1919), *Divagaciones apasionadas* (1924), *Ayer y hoy* (1939), *Pequeños ensayos* (1943), and *Desde la última vuelta del camino: Memorias* (seven volumes, 1944–1947).

His literary, artistic, political, and social relationships with his country differ little from volume to volume. In *Juventud, egolatría,* he discusses war, writing, history, biography, politics, and religion. The ongoing skepticism in this collection, perhaps his best known, represents the leitmotiv of Baroja's works. His *Memorias* reflect the essential Baroja and include his comments on style and language. Anti-Semitic and xenophobic, Baroja nevertheless prided himself on his sincerity in his denunciations of the evils of Spanish life. Although he stressed constantly the need for action as a possible solution for problems, he was essentially pessimistic about human progress. Yet, though he found little good in humanity, he claimed that he hoped for truth, justice, and goodness in this world.

H. Ramón Menéndez Pidal (1869–1968)

Menéndez Pidal, the greatest Spanish scholar of the twentieth century, wrote on the most varied aspects of Spanish language, literature, and history. His first important work, *La leyenda de los Infantes de Lara* (1896), won a Royal Academy of History prize. Founder of the Centro de Estudios Históricos, where he trained an entire generation of philologists and teachers from 1910 on, he also began the *Revista de Filología Española* in 1914.

In addition to hundreds of articles in various fields, the more important of his works are *Manual elemental de gramática histórica española* (1914)—in later editions he omitted *elemental*—perhaps the best morphological and phonetic treatment in Spanish; *Cantar de Mio Cid* (1911), a masterpiece of paleographic and linguistic analysis that made him the acknowledged expert on matters pertaining to the Middle Ages (he changed and augmented it several times); *Poesía juglaresca y juglares* (1924), which went through many editions; *Orígenes del español* (1926), an exhaustive treatment of factors influencing the development of the Spanish language up to the eleventh century; *Flor nueva de romances viejos* (1928); *La España del Cid* (1929), containing information on the entire framework of the European Middle Ages as well as on the Cid; *Romancero hispánico* (1953); and continuous studies on the Spanish language, the epic, and the *romancero*. He also edited the monumental *Historia de España* (1952–1962).

In his many studies on the Spanish epic, the ballad, and poetry in general, he maintained that the *cantares* and primitive poetry enclosed the heart and soul of the Spanish people. He tried to determine the relationship between that poetry and the chronicles and history. He continually stressed the value of popular poetry, and in addition to introducing the scientific method into linguistic, philological, and historical research in Spain, he sought to create a new vision of Spanish culture. Although in works like *El Padre Las Casas: Su doble personalidad* (1963) he shows his conservative and nationalistic bias, it may be said that in his publications he interpreted the Spanish soul and spirit as well as any member of the Generation of 1898.

I. Other Literary Critics and Scholars

Lack of space has forced the exclusion of many writers of high caliber from previous generations, among them Emilio Cotarelo y Mori (1857–1936), literary historian and authority on the history of the Spanish drama; Francisco Rodríguez Marín (1855–1943), a Cervantine scholar; and Julián Ribera (1858–1934), a well-known Arabist. In the Generation of 1898, other writers include Adolfo Bonilla y San Martín (1875–1926), literary scholar and philosopher who wrote primarily on Cervantes; Eduardo Gómez de Baquero (1866–1929), better known by his pseudonym, Andrenio; Miguel Asín Palacios (1871–1944), philologist and expert on Islamic philosophy and religions and interpreter of Arabic culture and Arabic Spanish literature; Victor Said Armesto (1874–1914); and José María Salaverría (1873–1940), a representative of the ultrapatriotic and reactionary in his native country.

THE GENERATION OF 1914

A. General Considerations

Some critics believe that the generation following the Generation of 1898 should bear the name *novecentismo,* a term first used by the Italian Massimo Bontempelli and popularized in Spain by Eugenio d'Ors. For some this term implies the urge toward aesthetic and intellectual renewal in the post-1898 generation. Others use *novecentismo* to describe the entire literary output of the twentieth century through the 1930s. Still others prefer the designation Generation of 1914. Ortega y Gasset, the intellectual leader of this generation, unlike Unamuno, who gave "pedazos de su corazón," was more coldly critical and cosmopolitan. To Unamuno's man of flesh and blood with his desire for immortality, Ortega opposed the thinker who views life as a problem. The passion and emotion, good or bad, of the Generation of 1898 gave way to unemotional, historical analysis, not only of Spain but of culture in general. The present became more important than the past, and though these writers were interested in aesthetics, they did not consider landscape, art, or literature as a reflection of the Spanish soul. More scientific in their philosophy, the Generation of 1914 sought to put Spanish problems into a universal and theoretical format and through discipline and clarity to understand a country in transition.

B. José Ortega y Gasset (1883–1955)

Ortega, philosopher, literary critic, and essayist, wrote brilliantly and originally also on other subjects such as sociology and history. Although he went through various contradictory stages, he liked German culture but was also torn by the need to affirm his own country's values. He admonished Spaniards to reorganize their thought along German scientific and objective lines, but he also wanted Spain to form a civilization that while continuing to be Spanish would at the same time be European. He may have underestimated the value of the culture of his own country, but his intimate knowledge of the general cultural currents in Europe qualified him better than most of his contemporaries to make such comparisons. In 1923 Ortega founded the *Revista de Occidente,* one of the most important journals of modern Spain, in which he introduced Spain, in a systematic way, to foreign cultures.

José Ferrater Mora divides Ortega's work into three periods: Objectivism, stressing ideas over the human; Perspectivism, about absolute relationships; and *racio-vitalismo* or *razón vital,* his Existential viewpoint. Nonetheless, Ortega usually insisted throughout his work that living preceded theorizing and saw life as a continual risk-filled adventure.

Ortega's first great work was *Meditaciones del Quijote* (1914), a synthesis of reality and fantasy. The maximum creation of Spain was *Don Quijote,* and no other book has the same power of symbolic allusions to universal feelings about life. Ortega investigates the *quijotismo* of the novel and of the man, but he stresses that the quixotic elements are those, not so much of don Quijote, but of Cervantes himself, even though Quijote is an essential circumstance of Spain and part of Spanish destiny. Julián Marías sees the somewhat unconnected essays of *Meditaciones del Quijote* as a complete unit and as perhaps the first approximation to a metaphysical theory of human life as well as to a Spanish reality.

The Existential implications of Ortega's theories are quite apparent both in the *Meditaciones* and in later works. He himself claims: "Apenas hay uno o dos conceptos importantes de Heidegger que no preexistían a veces con anterioridad de trece años, en mis libros. Por ejemplo: la idea de la vida como inquietud, preocupación por la seguridad, se halla literalmente en mi

363

primera obra, *Meditaciones del Quijote.*" Ortega says that man cannot avoid his present or past circumstances or escape the future, but the essence of human life is to determine the future, and even a decision not to act affects it. As man lives and acts in a hostile universe, the central reality involves consciousness of self, for only man can exercise a unique freedom of choice. In his essay *En torno a Galileo* (1933), he expresses the idea that man, unlike objects, through present action to construct a future, creates a future that permits understanding and changing the present, and things teach him that he is in the world anything but a thing. The difference between a man and a stone is not that man has understanding but that the essence of the stone once fixed is immutable. Man, on the contrary, has to decide at each moment what he is going to do and what he is going to be.

Ortega wrote eight volumes of *El espectador* (1916–1934), but his next important work was *España invertebrada* (1921). Ortega disdains the popular element and says that a select minority will act as a nerve ganglion for the body or public. He seeks to analyze the decadence of Spain, maintaining that there was never a glorious period in Spain and that the present decadence is simply a prolongation of original defects from the Middle Ages on. Part of Spain's illness may be attributed to the absence of a select minority, and since there are things that only a select minority is capable of doing, the masses should be willing to obey the directives of these superior men.

El tema de nuestro tiempo (1923) emphasizes his theory of vitalism, that life is more important than thought and that it embodies a tension between the spiritual and the biological. Ortega repeats that he is himself plus his circumstances. Reason is important, but it must be a vital or historical reason and not a pure or mathematical one. Life is not a being but rather a coming to be, something to be achieved, a value to be realized, and vital reason is a function of that life and is at its service. Thought is a biological function, and emotion also belongs in this category. The cultural imperative assumes several forms. For thought it is truth. For will it is kindness. For the emotions it is beauty.

La deshumanización del arte (1925) concerns the new art that tries to avoid life forms, to be a game and nothing more. Art is ironic, and art is truth, but the human qualities must be eliminated and reality deformed, for to stylize is to deform and depersonalize reality. Artistic creation is artistic only to the degree that it is not real, and it must not have any social function whatsoever. The same year Ortega wrote his notes on the novel in which he describes the impossibility of finding new themes. Even though he is utterly pessimistic about the future of the novel, he feels that in its decline it may yield some of the greatest products, for the works of highest rank are likely to be products of the last hour, when accumulated experience has completely refined the artistic sensitivity.

In 1930 Ortega wrote one of his best-known works, *La rebelión de las masas*. His theme here is that "mass man" has triumphed, that protagonists no longer exist, and that we are left only with the chorus. Vulgarity runs rampant, and "mass man" crushes everything different or outstanding and seeks to bring it down to a level of mediocrity. Seeking to be like everyone else, he does not recogize that he has any superiors. Indeed, to be different is almost indecent. The masses have been given instruments of modern living, but because of lack of education "mass man" lives in civilization like a primitive, showing no gratitude for any of the wonderful inventions or progress of the modern world that he accepts as his right. The process started in the eighteenth century with the affirmation of the rights of man, accelerating with the economic well-being of the nineteenth century and the scientific progress of the twentieth. The solution is to return to a system of power for the select minority. Europe is becoming decadent, likely to fall into the extreme of either Communism or Fascism. A kind of United States of Europe is necessary to form a continental country that will be able to compete in a modern world.

Among Ortega's other works are *Goethe desde dentro* (1932), *Estudios sobre el amor* (1939), *Ensimismamiento y alteración* (1939), *Historia como sistema* (1941), and *El hombre y la gente* (1957). Many important posthumous publications, among them *La idea de principio en Leibniz* (1958), appear in Ortega's *Obras completas* (twelve volumes, 1962–1983). Goethe intrigued Ortega because of his concept of reality, his *Faust,* his Naturalistic concepts, his Existential feelings, his ideas on real and effective fate and ideal or superior fate. In *Estudios sobre el amor,* Ortega explores woman's duality and the difference in human terms between the sexes. Although sexuality is an important part of love, love is not sexuality. In *Ensimismamiento y alteración,* Ortega stresses the need for meditation and withdrawing into oneself as a project for future action, just as any action is a result of previous contemplation. Without drawing into himself and alert thought, man would not be capable of living. In his work on Leibniz, Ortega reexamines via his own philosophy the work of that philosopher whom he views as a crucial figure in the discovery of ultimate principles. In *El hombre y la gente*, Ortega explores society and its relationship to the individual. He sees the former as a threat to individual authenticity and sees the individual rather than society as the irreducible reality.

Ortega was interested in all branches of criticism, music, painting, sculpture, poetry, and drama. For him culture was constantly evolving, and he sought a new way of looking at the interrelationships of Spanish culture with that of other nations, among them the countries of Latin America. He had to use the circumstances of life to reason, and only in living could there be meaning and understanding. Thus, it is important to contemplate and learn about life, which is biographical as well as biological, and every life needs to justify itself in its own eyes. Life, however, is not determined either by one's thought or by one's environment but by the interplay of the two and between man and his culture. In human life, while we cannot think outside time, we know that it represents a task to be done and that reason is but one function of that task. In any event, each individual has the potential for achieving his own authenticity. Ortega's view of history as a matter of unique but interrelated generations also proved to be provocative and influential on younger writers.

C. Eugenio d'Ors y Rovira (1882–1954)

Until about 1916 Eugenio d'Ors wrote in Catalan under the pen name of Xenius, but after that date he wrote largely in Spanish. The author of almost one hundred works, including fiction and drama, d'Ors was interested in politics (after the Civil War he became a devotee of *hispanidad* and a Franco supporter), literature, philosophy, science, and especially art. It was he who popularized the word *novecentismo* for his generation, and he shared the vitalistic philosophy of Ortega. He was a perfectionist in all he attempted. His prose reflects his artistic aspirations in its cold, artificial, and symmetrical balance. Some critics see in him a return to a kind of *conceptismo* or Baroque style. He advocated a Classical sense of life, harmonious, ordered, and within limits.

D'Ors wrote a series of *glosas* over a period of almost fifty years to reflect his thoughts on philosophy and culture. Various collections appeared, *Glosas* (1906–1917), *Nuevo glosario* (1921), and *Novísimo glosario* (1946). He tried to establish principles and to look beyond the anecdotal to reach the transcendental. He evinced a personal concern for the unity of Europe. The *glosa* is a kind of expanded epigram, sometimes contained in a larger work. Many of d'Ors's glosses are casual, and he included some of them in his novels, especially in his best-known one, *La ben plantada* (1911). D'Ors's other major works are *El secreto de la filosofía* (1947) and the posthumous *La ciencia de la cultura* (1964). In his work on philosophy he discusses reason, intelligence (as an instrument of philosophical knowledge), and life as transcending the limits of individual existence. He also attempts to reconcile Thomist thought with experimental science. In his work on culture and science he tries to systematize history in accordance with unchanging cultural values and to formulate immutable principles of culture through the ages. Among his other essays are *Grandeza y servidumbre de la inteligencia* (1919), *Tres horas en el Museo del Prado* (1922), *El arte de Goya* (1924), and *El estilo de pensar* (1945).

D'Ors thought of man as comprising a body, soul, and what he termed "angel" or superconscious aspects of mental life. He always preferred the rational and the intelligent over the poetic, as he tried to find permanent values in the welter of modern artistic and intellectual movements, but with an ever-increasing defense of authority and an ardent Catholicism.

D. Salvador de Madariaga (1886–1978)

Madariaga, a citizen of the world, was a politician, poet, essayist, historian, novelist, and dramatist, as well as a diplomat and professor. He also wrote travel literature. His first book of essays was *Shelley and Calderón* (1920). Others are *Ensayos angloespañoles* (1922); *The Genius of Spain* (1923); *Guía del lector del Quijote* (1926); *Ingleses, franceses, españoles* (1929), written in English the year before; *España, ensayo de historia contemporánea* (1931), a coherent account of Spain, its problems, spirit, and history; *Hernán Cortés* (1940); and *Bolívar* (1951). Important among his later works are *Presente y porvenir de Hispanoamérica* (1974); *Españoles de mi tiempo* (1974); *Dios y los españoles* (1975); and *Cosas y gentes* (1979), a collection of essays on a variety of topics and figures like Baroja, Bolívar, and Las Casas.

Madariaga's passion and idealism differentiate him from his contemporaries in their cold intellectualism. He believed with Unamuno in humanity, but he was not tortured as was Unamuno. He is undoubtedly a clearer and more logical writer. Ma-

367

dariaga resembles the writers of the Generation of 1898 in his passion for the exposure to European culture. He also devoted much of his research to the field of Spanish-American history, but he believed that Cervantine themes would give one the key to an understanding of Spanish history. He also followed Unamuno in his ideas on the interrelationship between Quijote and Sancho and the process of *quijotización*.

E. Ramón Pérez de Ayala (1880–1962)

Pérez de Ayala, a philosopher and essayist as well as a poet and novelist, wrote most of his essays for newspapers. Some of his best-known ones are to be found in his novels, for all his work shows a critical attitude of a kind better suited to essay than to fiction. Aside from his newspaper articles and a description of a visit to the Italian front during World War I, his early important collections consist of two works, *Política y toros* (1918) and *Las máscaras* (two volumes, 1917 and 1919). The former collection concerns bullfighting as the fanatical preoccupation of the Spanish people. For action the Spaniard substitutes words, not only in bullfighting but in all areas of national life. Essentially, Pérez de Ayala viewed the bullfight as a sensual, aesthetic, and tragic experience. *Las máscaras*, although it reveals an intellectual author, is more passionate than usual. Pérez de Ayala offers us essays on a variety of literary figures, Lope de Vega, Ibsen, Shakespeare, and Benavente, among others. He was especially critical of Benavente for excessive wordiness, a sterile imagination, and a lack of originality. Later works include *Divagaciones literarias* (1958); *Más divagaciones literarias* (1960); *Principios y finales de la novela* (1958); *Amistades y recuerdos* (1961); *Tabla rasa* (1963); *Tributo a Inglaterra* (1963); *Pequeños ensayos* (1963), newspaper articles on a variety of subjects from war to literary criticism; *Nuestro Séneca* (1966); and *Escritos políticos* (1967).

F. Américo Castro (1885–1972)

Castro, a philologist, historian, and critic, contributed major interpretations involving Spanish language, literature, and culture in addition to editing a number of texts. In *El pensamiento de Cervantes* (1925), he views *Don Quijote* as a complete reflection of all the themes and preoccupations of the Renaissance. Castro studies Cervantes' intellectual background, the ideological influences on his world, his sources, and especially the Humanistic and Erasmian aspects of his work. In this work and in others Castro tried to analyze the great figures of the Golden Age, not only as Spaniards but also in their relationship to other European movements of the time and as founders of the modern world. In 1948 he wrote *España en su historia: Cristianos, moros y judíos,* later republished as *La realidad histórica de España* (1954), a major work of Spanish historiography and one that evoked a continuing series of polemics. He explains in this work the universal significance of Spanish history, examines cultural structures he termed "moradas vitales," and states that to know the past one has to live intensely and meaningfully in the present. For him, in historical terms, Spain began around A.D. 1000 as an amalgam of Christians, Arabs, and Jews who lived together in a kind of productive tension. Spain's tragedy was the destruction of this unity in 1492 with the expulsion of the Jews. Some critics accused Castro of denigrating Spain, but he succeeded in destroying the myth of Spanish exclusivity in the Iberian peninsula, stressing over and over the importance of the Jews and Moors. Other works include *De la edad conflictiva* (1961); *Apuntes de vivir hispánico* (1970); *De la España que aún no conocía* (1972); *Sobre el nombre y el quién de los españoles* (1973); and *Españoles al margen* (1973), a collection of articles from different periods.

G. Gregorio Marañón (1887–1960)

Marañón, a scientist, historian, sociologist, cultural theorist, and literary critic, was primarily known for his biological studies, though he wrote on women, love, painting, and a host of other topics. He stated often that Galdós had exerted a great influence on his life. Marañón specialized in endocrinology but revealed an extraordinarily broad medical knowledge. He wrote psychological interpretations of historical figures, and his individual analyses also involve an examination of the entire period. Among his many works are *Tres ensayos sobre la vida sexual* (1926), *Ensayo biológico sobre Enrique IV de Castilla y su tiempo* (1930), *Raíz y decoro de España* (1933), *Las ideas biológicas del Padre Feijóo* (1934), *El Conde-Duque de Olivares* (1936), and *El Greco y Toledo* (1956). Although he was a scientist, religion for him was an integral ingredient of life, and he was interested in the human aspects of man. He sought, he said, man in illness rather than illness in man.

369

H. Others

1. *Manuel Azaña* (1880–1940), president of the Spanish Republic for a time, published an important autobiographical novel, *El jardín de los frailes* (1927). He believed in the modernization of Spain and wrote extensively on what he called "la materia española," which involved critical essays on Ganivet, Valera, and others. Among his works is *La invención del Quijote* (1934).

2. *Federico de Onís* (1885–1966), essayist and literary critic, wrote on a variety of subjects. Among his many works are *Disciplina y rebeldía* (1915) and the well-known *Antología de la poesía española e hispanoamericana* (1934).

3. *Tomás Navarro Tomás* (1884–1979) was a world authority on phonetics, dialects, and meter. His many works include *Manual de pronunciación española* (1918), *Métrica española* (1956), and *Capítulos de geografía lingüística de la península ibérica* (1975).

4. *Manuel García Morente* (1886–1942) wrote on philosophy and history and promoted the introduction of European philosophical thought to Spain. His works include *Idea de la hispanidad* (1938) and *Ideas para una filosofía de la historia de España* (1943).

Enrique Diez-Canedo (1879–1944), especially known as a theatrical critic; Julio Camba (1882–1962), humorist and caricaturist of Spanish foibles; Juan Zaragüeta (1883–1974); Fernando de los Ríos (1879–1949); Eugenio Noel (1885–1936), whose real name was Eugenio Muñoz; Luis Araquistáin (1886–1959); and Angel Sánchez Rivero (1888–1930) are also worthy of note.

THE GENERATION OF 1927

A. General Considerations

Some call this generation that of "la Dictadura." Others prefer to label it the generation of the *Revista de Occidente*. In this post–World War I group we find experimentation with a host of new "isms," not only Cubism, Ultraism, and Creationism but also Communism and Socialism. Among other things these authors reevaluated the Baroque writers. Two of the well-known reviews of the time were the *Revista de Occidente*, founded by Ortega y Gasset, and *La Gaceta Literaria*, directed by Giménez Caballero.

B. José Bergamín (1895–1983)

Bergamín, a staunch defender of the Spanish Republic, founded the influential review *Cruz y Raya*. When he emigrated to Mexico in 1939, he started Editorial Séneca, which published a number of important Spanish works including Lorca's first edition of *Poeta en Nueva York*.

An essayist (with twenty-nine volumes of prose), literary critic, journalist, poet, and dramatist, he was one of the most attractive and unappreciated writers of twentieth-century Spain. His style was, for the most part, hermetic and Neobaroque, and he made good use of paradox and irony. He wrote perceptively about Cervantes, Lope, Quevedo, and Unamuno as well as on the bullfight, the theory of poetry, painting, and music. In 1923 he wrote what was to generate other collections of aphorisms, *El cohete y la estrella*. His last volume was *Aforismos de la cabeza parlante* (1983). He wrote many collections of poetry, a number of which appeared the year he died. One of his most interesting volumes of essays, *El pozo de la angustia* (1941), reprinted in 1985, deals with theological problems. He attempts to combine Marx, an anguished Christianity, and the idea of personal salvation. As with much of his work, it also expresses a continuing Existentialism. He had a passion for bullfighting, about which he wrote many works, including *El arte de birlibirloque* (1930), *La música callada del toreo* (1981), and *La claridad del toreo* (1985). Among his other titles are *Terrorismo y persecución religiosa en España* (1941), reprinted in 1977 as *El pensamiento perdido; La voz apagada* (1943), republished in 1964; *Fronteras infernales de la poesía* (1958), reprinted in 1980; *Lázaro, don Juan y Segismundo* (1959); *Al volver* (1962), reissued in 1974 as *Antes de ayer y pasado mañana;* and *La importancia del demonio y otras cosas sin importancia* (1974).

Bergamín greatly resembled Unamuno in his contradictions, anguished struggles, and spiritual agony. He was at different times intellectual, passionate, lyrical, and yet ascetic. Liberal in politics and a devout Catholic, he was first of all a Spaniard who never forgot the past and potential greatness of his native land.

C. Xavier Zubiri (1898–1983)

A student of Ortega y Gasset's, Zubiri studied also with Heidegger, whose Existentialist views he did not entirely share. Zubiri championed a rigorous philosophy, employing precision and sci-

371

entific objectivity; yet he affirmed religion and God as the indispensable ingredients in man's life.

Zubiri's masterpiece is *Naturaleza, historia, Dios* (1944), which went through many editions, including one in 1977. He reveals here his own inner conflicts and deals with different kinds of knowledge, intellectual intuition, and religious passion. The central problem of philosophy involved the process of its own maturation. Another important work, *Sobre la esencia* (1962), a treatise on general metaphysics, served as a foundation for his anthropological work. He discusses here the problem of the radical structure of reality. *Inteligencia sentiente* (1980), *Inteligencia y lógica* (1982), and *Inteligencia y razón* (1983) expand Kant's transcendental aesthetics, logic, and dialectic. These texts complement Zubiri's *Sobre la esencia* as a metaphysical expression of experience and its relationship to reality, the role of being, feeling, thinking, and human intelligence. In the final months of his life Zubiri worked on *El hombre y Dios*, about humanity and God, the formal projection of divine reality, and God as a finite reproduction. Another of his important works is *Siete ensayos de antropología filosófica* (1982), about man, his personal reality, and theological problems.

Zubiri was the most important philosopher of his generation, and his philosophy could not be separated from his religious faith and devotion to truth. Called the last of the pure metaphysicians, he treated every conceivable subject, but especially the relationship of physical reality, essence, and existence. Man's task is the search for truth of things, and man is the radical reality open to things that culminates in what Zubiri called "religación," or a fundamental relationship with God, the final reality. He stated that Spaniards had to face reality just as man in general, as part of philosophical truth, had to awaken to the facts of his existence.

D. Juan Rof Carballo (b. 1905)

Rof Carballo, best known for his medical studies, has written also on anthropology, social psychology, psychobiology, and myth. He was greatly influenced by both Heidegger and Zubiri but rejected orthodox Freudian theory about sexuality. In his psychoanalytic texts he promotes the role of tenderness and love in achieving full human authenticity and in man's quest for his own identity. He has written extensively on the reciprocal influences between parents and children, affective relationships, lifestyles, and the stages involved in the growth process.

After the Spanish Civil War he sided with those who sought more liberty and against the neotraditionalists, though he himself lamented the loss of traditional values. Rof Carballo rejects Humanism and pure reason as answers to life's problems in favor of faith and the basic findings of the Judeo-Christian tradition. His works include *Patología psicosomática* (1949), *El hombre a prueba* (1951), *Entre el silencio y la palabra* (1960), *Urdimbre afectiva y enfermedad* (1964), *El hombre como encuentro* (1968), *Biología y psicoanálisis* (1972), and *Historia universal de la medicina* (1975).

E. Francisco Ayala (b. 1906)

Ayala, better known as a short story writer and novelist, is an excellent sociologist and has also written extensively on a variety of subjects including culture and literary criticism. He has studied Spanish Classical literary figures like Cervantes and Quevedo, more modern writers like Galdós and Unamuno, and, from his own generation, Aub and Chacel. His essays and fiction are strongly related and fuse in some of his works. Among his many publications are *Los derechos individuales como garantía de la libertad* (1935), *El problema del liberalismo* (1941), about freedom, independence and humanity; *Razón del mundo* (1944), generally about Spanish history and culture and more specifically about the intellectual's responsibility for Spain's retreat from the Western world in the sixteenth century (an enlarged version appeared in 1962); *Tratado de sociología* (1947), an important sociological work that, though conceived as a textbook, deals with free will in society, man's evolving state, and the futility of attempting to apply traditional scientific methods to the social sciences; *El escritor en la sociedad de las masas* (1956), about the isolation of men of letters and their ability to arouse the readers' social conscience; *La crisis actual de la enseñanza* (1958), about deteriorating academic standards in the United States and Argentina; *Reflexiones sobre la estructura narrativa* (1960), dealing with the relationship of an author to his work and the essential ambiguity and impurity of a literary work because of the inexact nature of words; *Realidad y ensueño* (1963); *De este mundo y el otro* (1963); *Los ensayos: Teoría y crítica literaria* (1972), concerning, among other subjects, man's victimization by the chaos of a modern, impersonal world; *El escritor y su imagen* (1975), on Ortega y

Gasset, Azorín, and other writers; *Palabras y letras* (1983); *La estructura narrativa y otras experiencias literarias* (1984), containing previously published as well as new essays; *La imagen de España* (1986); and *Las plumas del fénix* (1989), which deals with a number of authors and various aspects of literature. In general, Ayala's essays reveal a continuing ambivalence between spirituality and pragmatism, the individual and society, existence and death.

F. Other Writers

1. *Ramón Gómez de la Serna* (1888–1963), whose special intergenerational position we have already explored, was a writer of sensation and fragmentary impressions. In his collection of essays *Lo cursi y otros ensayos* (1943), he viewed what he termed "post-Romantic sentimentalism" as in bad taste. He wrote extensively on art and twentieth-century literature, and he also wrote biographies: *Goya* (1928), *Azorín* (1930), *El Greco* (1935), and *Valle-Inclán* (1944).

2. *Claudio Sánchez Albornoz* (1893–1984), historian, archeologist, and the head of the Spanish Republican government in exile, returned to Spain in 1976. One of the best scholars on the Middle Ages, he wrote also on politics, economics, religion, and history. He thought of Spain as a historical enigma, as his work *España, un enigma histórico* (1956) testifies. He worked with Menéndez Pidal on the monumental *Historia de España*. Among his many other works are *Estampas de la vida en León durante el siglo X* (1926); *La edad media y la empresa de América* (1933); *España y el Islam* (1943); *La España musulmana* (1947); *Españoles ante la historia* (1958), an attack on Américo Castro's theories; *Estudios críticos sobre la historia del reino de Asturias* (1972); and *Aún del pasado y del presente* (1984).

3. *Ernesto Giménez Caballero* (b. 1899), who wrote fiction, worked as a journalist, and was a prolific essayist, together with Guillermo de Torre in 1927 founded the important journal *La Gaceta Literaria*, which promoted a series of "isms." Giménez Caballero first came to the public's attention with *Notas marruecas de un soldado* (1923). His early leftist politics ceded to an ardent belief in the Falangist cause, and he became the political, religious, and elitist spokesman for the Falangist regime. His many works include *Genio de España* (1932), about Unamuno and the "nietos del '98"; *Arte y estado* (1935), about architecture at the service of the state; *España nuestra* (1943); *Norteamérica sonríe a*

España (1952); *Don Quijote ante el mundo (y ante mí)* (1975); *Memorias de un dictador* (1979); and *Retratos españoles* (1985), containing studies on *Don Quijote* and Quevedo, Ganivet, and many other writers.

4. *Guillermo de Torre* (b. 1900), who has edited numerous texts and literary anthologies, started as a very important *ultraísta* critic. His *Literaturas europeas de vanguardia* (1925), a panoramic synthesis of the new tendencies, included an amazing documentation of all the "isms" between 1910 and 1925. Through the years he continued to study avant-garde movements and to publish authoritative commentaries on modern literature. He became a citizen of Argentina and has lived there for many years. His works include *La aventura y el orden* (1943), *Menéndez y Pelayo y las dos Españas* (1943), *Ortega, teórico de la literatura* (1957), *Del 98 al barroco* (1963), *La difícil universalidad española* (1965), and *El espejo y el camino* (1968).

Among the many other prolific and important writers of this generation, one should include Samuel Gili Gaya (1892–1976), César Barja (1892–1952), Antonio Solalinde (1892–1937), Juan Larrea (1895–1980); Melchor Fernández Almagro (1895–1966); Joaquín Xirau (1895–1946), Amado Alonso (1896–1952), José Fernández Montesinos (1897–1972), Eugenio Montes (1897–1982), Angel del Río (1900–1962), Juan Chabás (1900–1954), José Gaos (1900–1969), David García Bacca (b. 1901), Luis Recasens Siches (b. 1903), Joaquín Casalduero (1903–1990), and Joaquín Entrambasaguas (b. 1904).

THE GENERATION OF 1936

A. General Considerations

The Generation of 1936 suffered through the traumatic events of the Spanish Civil War, over which its writers constantly agonized. Many of the famous poets, Luis Rosales, Dionisio Ridruejo, Gabriel Celaya, and others, also contributed to the essay as did the playwright Antonio Buero Vallejo and the novelists Camilo José Cela and Gonzalo Torrente Ballester. These writers, because of the Civil War, have been described as belonging to a destroyed, burnt, or shattered generation. The essayists, after the previous generation's fling with aesthetics, returned once more to the daily and historical problems of Spain but also to

375

man and society in general. According to Laín Entralgo, his generation had to strive for the universal in order to understand its
own country. Marías, Aranguren, and others debated the role
of Spain in Europe, Europe in Spain, and that of the exiled
Spanish intellectuals. During the 1940s there were many polemics between conservative Catholics and the more liberal (but still
Falangist) intellectuals. Ortega and Zubiri still dominated philosophical life, though Marías, Ferrater Mora, and others were
contributing important works. In the 1950s censorship had been
relaxed sufficiently so that writers could admit the influence of
Krausismo and the Institución Libre de Enseñanza and examine
the intellectual inheritance they left to twentieth-century Spain.
No general agreement exists about who belongs to the generation. Marías, for example, declared that those born before 1910
did not belong.

B. Pedro Laín Entralgo (b. 1908)

Laín Entralgo, one of the leading Catholic intellectuals of twentieth-century Spain, shows the influence of Zubiri in his writing,
though he once declared that his was a "generación sin maes-
tros." He helped found the influential *Escorial* review. Laín is
well known for his many medical works, and he has also written extensively on psychosomatic medicine in its relationship to
man's role as a healthy or sick member of society. In many of
his writings he combines metaphysical, philosophical, scientific,
and theological knowledge. He views medicine and its practice as
both technical and social and as reflective of the cultural and historical situation. One of his favorite themes involves the need for
the anthropological synthesis and implementation of important
discoveries made by Freud, Adler, and Jung. Laín has also written very important Humanistic and cultural works and works on
Spanish political, social, and historical problems. Throughout his
life the problems of Spain have been at the center of his works.
Laín believes firmly in *hispanidad,* that America is an extension of
Europe, and that Spain has a special task in fulfilling its European mission and saving a threatened European culture, in error for many centuries, by opposing Christianity to Communism. After Franco's death Laín wrote *Descargo de conciencia,
1930–1960* (1976), apologizing for some of his positions, though
he also contends that nobody was completely innocent or guilty
because of social or political judgments during the Franco years.
In spite of his Catholic beliefs (he invented the word *prereligioso*

to convey the lack of a meaningful religious experience) and his condemnation of atheism, he accepts the Existential function of belief as part of an authentic mode of being and a theory of human reality philosophically and scientifically intelligible. Nonetheless, he prefers the religious to the secular, which has the capability of deforming the spiritual possibilities of man.

His works include *Medicina e historia* (1941); *Las generaciones en la historia* (1945); *La generación del noventa y ocho* (1945), in which he proposes the need for an integration of Catholic belief with social, political, and spiritual contemporary knowledge; *España como problema* (1948), about modern Spain's inability to create a satisfactory political and social structure, based on Laín's synthesis of nineteenth-century Spanish thought and attempt to define the essence of Spain and its Catholic existence; *Palabras menores* (1952), which discusses the role of the Catholic intellectual in the modern world; *Sobre la universidad hispánica* (1953), a discussion of the university system, its role and mission, which should be the transmission of knowledge, teaching, research, and incitement and formation of men; *Las cuerdas de la lira* (1955), concerning Spain's diversity and regionalism; *La aventura de leer* (1956); *La espera y la esperanza* (1957), involving a theory of hope based on a concept of human expectation and the Existential precondition to action; *La empresa de ser hombre* (1958), about belief, intellectual life, and the search for ultimate reality; *A qué llamamos España* (1971); *Antropología médica para clínicos* (1984); *En este país* (1986); and *Ciencia, técnica y medicina* (1986).

C. José Luis Aranguren (b. 1909)

Aranguren, a leader among liberal Catholic thinkers and a proponent of advanced European thought, has written extensively on ethics, philosophy, morals, and theology. Thoroughly grounded in Classical ethics from Aristotle to Zubiri, he is independent and original in his writings on ethics and morals. Though he has written about the relationship of religion and Existentialism, he conceived of his own task as a wakening, through his work, of the social conscience of others in opposing injustice. He was greatly influenced by British Empiricism and by Neopositivistic thought. In the 1960s social and political problems preoccupied him more than religious ones. He had a great influence on the thought and activity of university students.

Aranguren's works include *La filosofía de Eugenio d'Ors* (1945); *Catolicismo y protestantismo como formas de existencia* (1952), reprinted in its latest form in 1980, a comparison of the two religions, their elements in Unamuno's works, and commentary on the teachings of religion and Zubiri and other writers; *El protestantismo y la moral* (1954); *Crítica y meditación* (1955), which views the poet as a prophet who seeks to reconcile daily life with the idealistic world of God and discusses other aspects of politics, literature, and religion; *Catolicismo día tras día* (1955), which rejects the intellectual sterility of a rigid Spanish Catholicism; *Ética* (1958), in which Aranguren shows that man is moral because he needs to interact with others and outlines the duty of the intellectuals to aid in forming a better society; *La ética de Ortega* (1958); *La juventud europea y otros ensayos* (1961), an accusation against the Church for living in fear rather than with hope and for its lack of social action, as well as a plea for honesty in human communication; *La comunicación humana* (1967); *El marxismo como moral* (1968); *La cultura española y la cultura establecida* (1975); *Estudios literarios* (1976); *Propuestos morales* (1983); and *La guerra civil española: una reflexión moral 50 años después* (1986).

D. José Antonio Maravall (1911–1986)

Maravall, the author of more than thirty books on the Middle Ages, the Renaissance, the Baroque period, the Enlightenment, and contemporary culture, was a liberal historian who wished to interpret Spanish history in a new way. He saw history as an antidote for tradition, and he believed his country to be an integral part of European history. He wrote also on sociology, political science, economics, and literature. He covered the entire history of Spain from the hegemonic aspirations of Castile, through the interrelationship of the Baroque and the politics of an absolute monarchy, to the modern state and what he called "social mentality." His works include *La teoría española del estado en el siglo XVII* (1944); *El humanismo de las armas en "Don Quijote"* (1948); *El concepto de España en la edad media* (1954); *Velázquez y el espíritu de la modernidad* (1960); *El mundo social de la "Celestina"* (1964); *Antiguos y modernos* (1966), about social progress; *Estudios de historia del pensamiento español* (1967); *Estado moderno y mentalidad social* (1972); *Teatro y literatura en la sociedad barroca* (1972); *La cultura del barroco* (1975), about Spanish drama and a culture undergoing a social crisis of major proportions; *Utopía y contra-utopía en el Quijote* (1976), a global interpretation from a sociohistorical point of view; *Utopía y reformismo en la España de las Austrias* (1982); and *La literatura picaresca desde la historia social, siglos XVI y XVII* (1986), again about the Baroque crisis.

E. Julián Marías (b. 1914)

Marías, a pupil and disciple of Ortega y Gasset's, has written mostly on philosophical themes but also on the theory of language, the disjunctive reciprocity of the sexes, history, politics, travel, a theory of generations, anthropology, literary criticism, and many other topics. He has written essays on Plato, Aristotle, and Scholastic philosophy. He sees the primary task of the Christian today to absorb the philosophical past for perspective, since the past, an integral part of us, determines our lives. In expanding his mentor's *razón vital*, Marías looks on life as a task. In the process of creating a personal metaphysics, man finds the radical reality of individual life. Marías stresses truth as a component of human life. He sees philosophy as something in the process of becoming but later describes it as a responsible vision in an attempt to find truth. He views philosophy in biographical terms as a necessity for an understanding of the empirical structures of human life. Although he believes in certainty, Marías sees philosophy as a dramatic action rooted in uncertainty. In his literary criticism he has combined intuition with a systematic analysis, seeing literature in its relationship to the meaning and happiness in human life.

Among Marías' many publications are *Historia de la filosofía* (1941); *El tema del hombre* (1943), a philosophical anthology; *Miguel de Unamuno* (1943); *Introducción a la filosofía* (1947), describing the real situation of Western man, the philosophical activities necessary for our circumstances, the vital function of truth, the relationship of being and things, and the problem of God; *El método histórico de las generaciones* (1949); *Ortega y tres antípodas* (1950); *La filosofía en sus textos* (1950), one of the most authoritative philosophical anthologies; *El existencialismo en España* (1953), about the long-term existence of Existentialist thinking in Spain; *Los Estados Unidos en escorzo* (1956); *Ortega I: Circunstancia y vocación* (1960); *Los españoles* (1962); *Antropología metafísica: la estructura empírica de la vida humana* (1970), stressing one of his most important contributions to the field of philosophy; *La España real* (1976), the first volume of what was to be a trilogy but later expanded; *La devolución de España* (1977), the second part about the return of Spain to the Spaniards with the death of

Franco; *España en nuestras manos* (1978), the third part; and *Cinco años de España* (1981), the fourth part about a new democracy in Spain; *La mujer en el siglo XX* (1980), which Marías described as promoting the mutual equality of the sexes but that some find to be sexist; *Ortega: Las trayectorias* (1983–1984); *La felicidad humana* (1987); *La mujer y su sombra* (1987); and *Una vida presente: Memorias* (1988).

F. Enrique Tierno Galván (1918–1986)

Tierno Galván, a proponent of Neopositivism, the rational, and realism, rejected the seductive role of literature together with Existentialism and metaphysics as promoting an understanding of the real world. Interested in the immediate and concrete, he preferred practice over theory, utility to beauty, and insisted on the need for Spain to appreciate and adapt to the material world, to abandon its mythical view of itself, and to enter the modern world. Tierno Galván recognized in Marx the origins of modern sociology. He engaged in a moral criticism of Spanish society, but though he promoted technology, science, and efficiency, he separated bureaucracy from Spanish vitality. Tierno Galván did not believe in a philosophy to enhance the individual and, rejecting traditional Humanism, believed rather in man's importance as a social being.

Among his many works are *La realidad como resultado* (1957), aphorisms on social epistemology and scientific development; *Desde el espectáculo a la trivialización* (1961), concerning a host of topics from bullfighting to the movies and the social adaptability of intelligence as the *sine qua non* of understanding one's period; *Tradición y modernismo* (1962); *Acotaciones a la historia de la cultura occidental en la edad moderna desde el fin de la Edad Media hasta la actualidad* (1964); *Diderot como pretexto* (1965); *Conocimiento y ciencias sociales* (1966); *Razón mecánica y razón dialéctica* (1969), claiming that beyond an empirical applied sociology, one needs what Tierno Galván called "dialectical intelligence"; *La humanidad reducida* (1970); *Sobre la novela picaresca y otros escritos* (1974); and *Cabos sueltos* (1981), about the cultural and political life of Spain.

G. Others

Members of this generation are extremely important in the intellectual development of modern Spain through their writings on literary criticism, philosophy, history, culture, and almost all fields of endeavor. Others include María Zambrano (b. 1907); Ricardo Gullón (b. 1908); Guillermo Díaz Plaja (b. 1909); Rafael Lapesa (b. 1909); Carlos Clavería (b. 1909); Antonio Rodríguez Moñino (1910–1970); Jaime Vicens Vives (1910–1940); Luis Diez del Corral (b. 1911); Antonio Tovar (1911–1985); José Ferrater Mora (b. 1912); Dionisio Ridruejo (1912–1975), better known as a poet; José Manuel Blecua (b. 1913); Martín de Riquer (b. 1914); Rafael Calvo Serer (b. 1916); and Paulino Garagorri (b. 1916).

THE GENERATION OF 1956

A. General Considerations

In the 1950s a series of works on the essence of Spain generated a continuing debate between liberal Catholics and traditionalists. A rebirth of Marxist theory (unpublished until the 1960s) and an effort to reintegrate Spanish philosophy into world currents and to stop viewing it as theology's handmaiden occurred. Manuel Sacristán, a Marxist and an expert on logic and mathematics, engaged in a polemic with Gustavo Bueno about the role of philosophy, and writers like Aranguren and Tierno Galván sought to demythify Spanish life, all of which spurred interest in newly awakening social sciences. The increasing importance given to Anglo-Saxon philosophy by liberal Falangists, the February 1956 student revolt against the Franco regime, and the publication, in the face of government censorship, of manifestos by Dionisio Ridruejo and others, helped promote Humanistic, liberal, and scientific philosophy. In addition to analytic thinking, Zubiri, Marías, and Aranguren inspired the younger generation with a new kind of Christian spirituality. The recognition of Spain by the United Nations in 1950 had helped to accelerate the liberalizing influence, especially in Spanish universities between 1951 and 1956. With the admission of Spain into the United Nations in 1955, the incompatibility between Falangist thought and liberalism became more marked. The death of Ortega y Gasset in 1955 was also symbolically important. The Generation of 1956, then, was more rational, critical, and scientific than its predecessor. It was receptive to Structuralism, semiology, and Marxism, rejecting official ideology and contrasting European freedom with Spanish intransigence.

381

B. Carlos Castilla del Pino (b. 1922)

A psychiatrist, philosopher, and anthropologist, Castilla, like Tierno, views man as a social being prone to act in the real world and subject to analysis rather than ethical and moral considerations. Differing from Ortega, he believes that a personal project depends on circumstances as much as on personal performance, for the personal is only a small part of the radical reality called life. Nonetheless, he accepts the idea of the uniqueness of man as an individual and the importance of ethics and morality under certain circumstances. In many of his works he studies the interrelationship between anthropology and psychiatry. His works include *Un estudio sobre la depresión: Fundamentos de antropología dialéctica* (1966), in which he attempts to transcend a personal concept of medicine by emphasizing the social relationship of neurotic behavior; *La culpa* (1968), which supports the concept of dialectical materialism; *Dialéctica de la persona, dialéctica de la situación* (1968); *Psicoanálisis y marxismo* (1969); *La incomunicación* (1970); *Cuatro ensayos sobre la mujer* (1971); *Introducción a la hermenéutica del lenguaje* (1972); *Sexualidad, represión y lenguaje* (1975); *La cultura bajo el franquismo* (1977); *Teoría de la alucinación* (1984); and *Cincuenta años de psiquiatría* (1987).

C. Fernando Lázaro Carreter (b. 1923)

The author of a number of linguistic and philological studies, he has also edited a number of texts, composed dramatic works, and written many literary studies. Among his editions is his revised version of the Rennert-Castro study on Lope de Vega (1968). In 1953 he wrote *Diccionario de términos filológicos,* an unusual work that went through several editions. He has written on the medieval theater, Lazarillo de Tormes, Lope de Vega, Góngora, and Vicente Aleixandre, among others. His works include *Las ideas lingüísticas en España durante el siglo XVIII* (1949), *Menéndez Pelayo: Su época y su obra literaria* (1962), *Estilo barroco y personalidad creadora* (1966), *Lengua española: Historia, teoría y práctica* (1971), *Estudios de poética: La obra en sí* (1976), and *Estudios de lingüística* (1980).

D. Manuel Sacristán (1925–1985)

A Marxist who wrote extensively on Lenin, Marxism, science, philosophy, and Neopositivism, Sacristán was especially interested in relating the philosophy of science to Marxism as a legitimate philosophy in its dialectical understanding of what Sacristán called "totalidades concretas." A specialist in contemporary logic, he attempted to provide a cultural philosophical basis for the political tradition of Marxism. Although he accepted morality as part of the dialogue between Christianity and Marxism, he refuted Heidegger's antirationalism. He sought always a scientific basis for philosophy and viewed criticism as a rational process. He thought of his role as a Socratic one and influenced university students and the next generation of writers. His works include *Las ideas gnoseológicas de Heidegger* (1959), *Introducción a la lógica y el análisis formal* (1964), *Sobre el lugar de la filosofía en los estudios superiores* (1968), *Teoría sociológica contemporánea* (1978), and *Panfletos y materiales* (1983), an anthology. His *Obras completas* includes *Marx y el marxismo* (1983) and *Papeles de filosofía* (1984).

Sacristán, Tierno Galván, and Castilla del Pino thought of themselves as *dialécticos* as opposed to *analíticos*. They attempted to demythify the traditional image of Spain and its philosophy, but often the dichotomy was more imagined than real.

E. Others

Other members of this generation include Gustavo Bueno (b. 1924), who wrote on political economy and metaphysics and engaged Sacristán in a polemic on philosophy's role in the world; Francisco Candel (b. 1925); Agustín García Calvo (b. 1926), a student of anarchism, politics, and linguistics; José María Castellet (b. 1926), who wrote on culture and published well-known literary anthologies; Manuel Ballestero (b. 1927), who wrote on didactic philosophy and its relationship to Existentialism; Emilio Lledó (b. 1929), a philosopher, linguist, and historian; Luis Jiménez Moreno (b. 1929), an expert on Nietzsche's philosophy; José Luis Abellán (b. 1933), whose works include studies on Unamuno and Ortega and a monumental *Historia crítica del pensamiento español* (three volumes, 1979; Volume IV, 1984); Pedro Cerezo Galán (b. 1935), who wrote on Machado, Seneca, and critical reason; and Elías Díaz (b. 1935), a philosopher, an expert on the sociology of law, and the author of one of the best intellectual histories of twentieth-century Spain, *Notas para una historia del pensamiento español actual, 1939–1972* (1974), an updated version of which was published in 1978.

383

THE GENERATION OF 1968

A. General Considerations

In the early 1960s a relative cultural and economic liberalization occurred as Spain received more and more exposure to publications from the outside world. Vatican II also had a liberalizing influence. The 1968 French uprising and the concomitant Spanish student unrest also served as a rallying point. Some of the writers practiced a kind of neo-Nietzschean philosophy. Neo-scholastic philosophy was soundly criticized, and more and more Marxist studies were published. Scientific development of sociology continued, as did a kind of democratization, but some of the writers' individualism took on a hedonistic note. As in the case of Spanish fiction, many essays now emphasized the role of the erotic in human life. In general the writers incorporated into their works Marxism, psychoanalysis, Existentialism, and Structuralism. After Franco's death essayists showed an even greater independence in discussing power and the state, and there was an acceleration of the return to forbidden ideas. The writers had a new freedom to follow their own logic rather than Catholic or Fascist dogmas.

B. Xavier Rubert de Ventós (b. 1939)

Theoretically an anarchist, Rubert de Ventós rejects both the political right and left. As do most members of his generation, he stresses the role of the individual in a bureaucratic society. He has written on philosophy, culture, history, ethics, and morality but is probably best known for his work on aesthetics. His works include *El arte ensimismada* (1963); *Teoría de la sensibilidad* (1969); *Moral y nueva cultura* (1971), about history, ethics, moral criteria and inconsistencies, and the burden of surplus possessions; *Utopías de la sensualidad y métodos del sentido* (1973); *La estética y sus herejías* (1974), which combines philosophy and literary and artistic analysis with social criticism, discusses systems theory and Wittgenstein's philosophy, and underlines the artist's duty to tell the truth about the reality he represents and to refuse to act as society's conscience; *Ensayos sobre el desorden* (1976), about power and imperialism and the city as a consumer-oriented entity that destroys individual initiative; *De la modernidad: Ensayo de filosofía crítica* (1980); and *El laberinto de la hispanidad* (1987), a historical analysis of Spanish policy toward Latin America, the unique in Spanish culture, and Spain's Catholic Baroque inheritance as contrasted with the Protestant materialistic legacy of the United States.

C. Eugenio Trías (b. 1942)

A philosopher and essayist, Trías has written on Structuralism, psychology, and metaphysics as well as on Plato, Goethe, Nietzsche, Thomas Mann, and Hegel. Nelson Orringer has divided his work into two periods, 1969–1971 and 1974–1981. In the first he discussed the issues of the 1960s and Structuralist methodology. In the second he concentrates on European culture and advocates a return to European roots to save Western culture, which he analyzes in relationship to others. He also analyzes philosophy from an ethnological and, especially, anthropological point of view and views man's status as an "unconditional condition."

Trías' works include *La filosofía y su sombra* (1969, reprinted in 1983), concerning metaphysics and its role in reality; *Teoría de las ideologías* (1970); *Filosofía y carnaval* (1970); *Metodología del pensamiento mágico* (1970); *La dispersión* (1971), a collection of aphorisms that views society as a theater and human personality as a mask; *Drama e identidad* (1974); *El artista y la ciudad* (1976), which discusses a variety of topics such as the meaning of love and desire and their connection with the objective world, the unfortunate dichotomy between art and productivity, the liberation of human creativity, the artist's alienation from European culture, and a hoped-for revitalization of Europe's Classical philosophy; *Meditación sobre el poder* (1977); *Conocer Thomas Mann y su obra* (1978); *La memoria perdida de las cosas* (1978); *Tratado de la pasión* (1980); *Filosofía del futuro* (1981), concerning the interplay between being and nothingness, the role of power, and true power as creation; *Lo bello y lo siniestro* (1982), on aesthetics as well as the individual's ability to progress; and *Los límites del mundo* (1985).

D. Eduardo Subirats (b. 1947)

Subirats writes about the deficiency of critical reason in Spain, the perversion of rational thought through the years, the effect of avant-garde dehumanization on man's interior dimension, and a concomitant petrification and empty and totalitarian

385

forms. He sees architecture as a metaphor for the creation of cultural values. His works include *Utopía y subversión* (1975); *Figuras de la conciencia desdichada* (1979); *La ilustración insuficiente* (1979); *Contra la razón destructiva* (1979); *El alma y la muerte* (1983), which treats the relationship between Mysticism and the rational tradition, the soul purified by an ecstatic vision of God as opposed to the soul purified by the discourse of reason; *La crisis de las vanguardias y la cultura moderna* (1985); *La flor y el cristal: Ensayos sobre arte y arquitectura* (1986); and *La cultura como espectáculo* (1988).

E. Fernando Fernández Savater (b. 1947)

A novelist, short story writer, and dramatist as well as a leading philosopher of his generation, Savater attempts to deal with scientific truth in an age of crisis. He has attempted to identify the religious through the rational, but he rejects abstract reason as the only instrument of thought, recognizing as he does the influence of literature and myth. A skeptic whom some find nihilistic, he writes with suave irony about ethics and human love, particularly their rejection of cruelty and violence, and sees them, in spite of his skepticism, as an affirmation of the possible in the face of the irremediable. Among his many other themes are the opposition of society and the state, the meaning of the will, liberty, the interrelationship of reason and the imagination, drugs, horse racing, movies, and history as a nonneutral art.

His works include *Nihilismo y acción* (1970); *La filosofía tachada* (1972), a demythification of society's standard values; *Apología del sofista, y otros sofismos* (1973); *Ensayo sobre Cioran* (1974); *Escritos politeístas* (1975); *La infancia recuperada* (1976); *Para la anarquía* (1977); *La piedad apasionada* (1977); *Panfleto contra el Todo* (1978), one of his most important works, which reproaches the leftists for their support of power in disregard of the individual, for the state tends to level and decrease human rights and suppress liberty; *El estado y sus criaturas* (1979); *La tarea del héroe* (1982), which won the National Prize for Essay, discussing independence, magnanimity, nobility, ethics, moral pretensions, tragedy, political repression, and democracy; *Las razones del antimilitarismo* (1984); *Instrucciones para olvidar al "Quijote" y otros ensayos generales* (1985); *El contenido de la felicidad* (1986), concerning the universal desire for happiness, its translation as "what we want," religious imagination, and other themes; and *Filosofía y sexualidad* (1988).

F. Others

Many other writers of this generation would deserve study in a more comprehensive work on the essay. Typical are Javier Ciordia Muguerza (b. 1939), who writes on ethics, sociology, and rationalism; Helio Carpintero (b. 1939), the author of a well-known study on twentieth-century philosophers, who has also written on Freud in Spain and contemporary psychology; Andrés Amorós (b. 1941), who has written extensively on Spanish literature, especially the novel; Carlos García Gual (b. 1943), who has explored Arthurian legends, Greek poetry, and the European novel; Alfredo Deaño (b. 1944), a logician; Miguel Angel Quintanilla (b. 1945), who writes on the philosophy of science and contemporary Spanish philosophy; and José E. Rodríguez Ibáñez (b. 1948), a sociologist of note. Still other names are Jacobo Muñoz, Fernando Sánchez Dragó, Jesús Mosterín, and, among younger writers, Helena Béjar (b. 1956).

INDEX

Index

Index

Index

Index

Index

Index

Index

Index

Index

Index

Index

Index

Index

Index

Index

Index

Index

426

Index

Index

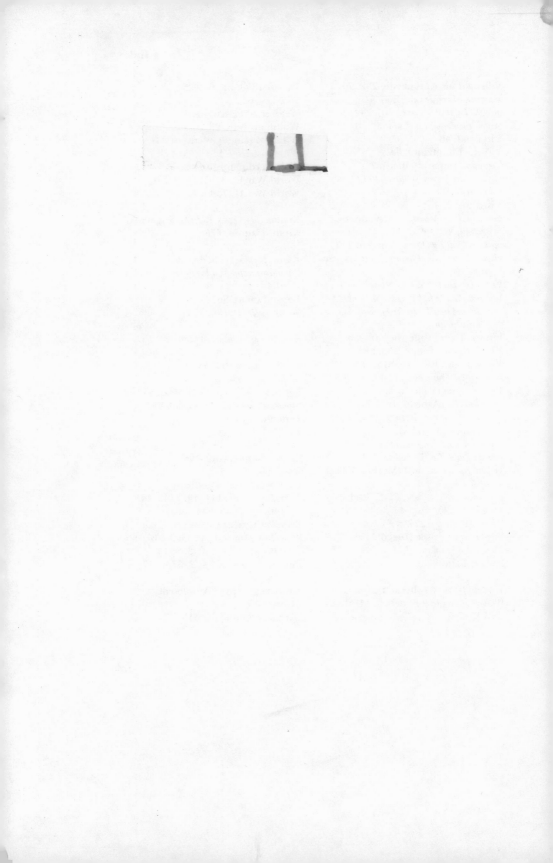